Marxist perspec-
tives in archae-
ology

DATE DUE

MARXIST PERSPECTIVES IN ARCHAEOLOGY

MARXIST PERSPECTIVES IN ARCHAEOLOGY

EDITED BY MATTHEW SPRIGGS

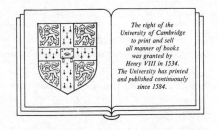

The right of the
University of Cambridge
to print and sell
all manner of books
was granted by
Henry VIII in 1534.
The University has printed
and published continuously
since 1584.

CAMBRIDGE UNIVERSITY PRESS

CAMBRIDGE

LONDON   NEW YORK   NEW ROCHELLE

MELBOURNE   SYDNEY

Published by the Press Syndicate of the University of Cambridge
The Pitt Building, Trumpington Street, Cambridge CB2 1RP
32 East 57th Street, New York, NY 10022, USA
296 Beaconsfield Parade, Middle Park, Melbourne 3206, Australia

© Cambridge University Press 1984

First published 1984

Printed in Great Britain at the University Press, Cambridge

Library of Congress catalogue card number: 83-7739

British Library Cataloguing in Publication Data
Marxist perspectives in archaeology. (New directions
in archaeology)
1. Archaeology
I. Spriggs, Matthew II. Series
930.1   CC165
ISBN 0 521 25544 9

WD

CONTENTS

To Vaneigem, Debord, Garvey: precursors

CONTRIBUTORS

Luis F. Bate, National School of Anthropology and History, Mexico.

Peter Gathercole, Darwin College, University of Cambridge.

Antonio Gilman, Department of Anthropology, California State
   University.

John Gledhill, Department of Anthropology, University College
   London.

C.A. Gregory, Clare Hall, University of Cambridge.

Phil Kohl, Department of Anthropology, Wellesley College.

Kristian Kristiansen, Ministry of the Environment, Copenhagen.

Susan Kus, Detroit, Michigan.

Michael Parker Pearson, Department of Archaeology, University of
   Cambridge.

Mike Rowlands, Department of Anthropology, University College
   London.

Matthew Spriggs, Department of Anthropology, University of Hawaii
   at Manoa.

Maurizio Tosi, National Museum of Oriental Arts, Rome.

ACKNOWLEDGEMENTS

This book has been a long time in the making. I first mooted the idea in 1976 and Cambridge University Press became interested early in 1978. My own interest in Marxist theory and archaeology began in 1974: whoever it was who left a copy of Terray's 'Marxism and "Primitive" Societies' lying on a table in the Haddon Library deserves my thanks. Pete Wright and Sid Walker were early allies and spurred on my continued interest. Jack Goody's seminar on Marxist anthropology was an early forum for discussion of many of the issues raised here. Ian Hodder asked me to prepare this volume for CUP. During its genesis various people at CUP have been most helpful and patient: Claire Davies-Jones, Robin Derricourt, Katharine Owen and Geraldine Stoneham. I would like to thank the Department of Prehistory, Research School of Pacific Studies, Australian National University and the Department of Anthropology, University of Hawaii at Manoa for facilities during manuscript preparation. Many people offered advice and suggestions during production of the volume. As well as the contributors I would like to thank Harry Allen, Jim Allen, Celia Barlow, Teresa Brennan, Mick Eaton, Stephanie Fahey, Roland Fletcher, Richard Ford, Quentin Given, Klim Gollan, Jack Golson, Clare Hartwell and Malcolm, Colin and Suzanne Haselgrove, Emma Henrion, Stephen Hugh-Jones, Nic Modjeska, Jonathan Jones, Chloe Munro, Daphne Nash, Bruno Pajackowski, John Pickles, Colin Renfrew, Ivan Ward, and Doug Yen.

PART 1

Introduction

Chapter 1

**Another way of telling:
Marxist perspectives in
archaeology**
Matthew Spriggs

Photographs so placed are restored to a living context: not of
course to the original temporal context from which they were
taken – this is impossible – but to a context of experience. And
there, their ambiguity at last becomes true. It allows what they
show to be appropriated by reflection. The world they reveal,
frozen, becomes tractable. The information they contain
becomes permeated by feeling. Appearances become the
language of a lived life.

John Berger (1982: 289)

Where from?

Marxism is a rich tradition, having been an element in
Western social science since the late nineteenth century. Now
that this partially hidden tradition has come into prominence
it is time to examine its strengths and weaknesses, if only to
transcend its limitations. The increasing interest in Marxist
theories in the social sciences in the 1960s and 1970s has had a
profound effect on history, sociology and anthropology but
has only more recently come to influence archaeological thinking. This interest is the result of a general crisis in the social
sciences, the widespread recognition of the inadequacies
(theoretical, political and practical) of established approaches
in the wake of major world-wide economic and political
changes from the mid-1950s onwards (Copans and Seddon
1978: 1–2). In anthropology more specific influences have
come from theoretical developments in France, from the
radical critics of anthropology as a child of colonialism, and

from the so-called Hegelian and phenomenological Marxist theorists (Kahn and Llobera 1981: 264). The history of the recent interest in Marxism and anthropology in France, Britain and the USA has been discussed in general terms by Copans and Seddon (1978), and its early strong focus in France in more detail by Kahn and Llobera (1981: 264–300). There has been a growing feeling in the social sciences (expressed well by Godelier) that there is:

> the need to carry out a theoretical revolution in the humane sciences, a revolution that becomes daily more urgent if we are to rescue these sciences from the dead-ends of functionalist empiricism or the helplessness of structuralism in the face of history. It seems to me that such a revolution must today proceed by way of the reconstruction of these sciences on the basis of a marxism that has been radically purged of all traces of vulgar materialism and dogmatism.
> (Godelier 1972: xii–xiii.)

Archaeology too was not unaffected by the crisis, but both in the USA and Britain the 'new archaeology' took the form of a positivist and functionalist vision reflecting more the tenets of the 1950s 'orthodox consensus' in American sociology (cf. Giddens 1979: 234–59) than the new directions developing elsewhere in the social sciences. This is all the more surprising since archaeology had already produced in V. Gordon Childe an early discussant (from a Marxist perspective) of many of the themes that came to the fore in social science in the 1960s and 1970s, particularly concerning the 'sociology of knowledge' (for instance Childe 1947; 1949a; 1949b; 1956; cf. Gathercole, Kus, Rowlands, this volume). While Childe doubtless influenced students, it is interesting that no significant Childeian theoretical 'school' developed in the 1940s and 1950s.[1]

One of the more positive aspects of the 'new archaeology' was its insistence that, 'Archaeology is anthropology, or it is nothing' (Phillips 1955: 246–7; cf. Binford 1962). There was a concern among archaeologists to break down the barriers between their discipline and sociocultural anthropology (a concern at that time only very rarely reciprocated by the anthropologists). The question was inevitably raised of the kind of anthropology archaeology should become, bringing the latter at one remove into wider social science debates. As one commentator put it, 'if archaeology is pre-Marxian (British) anthropology it *would* be nothing' (Groube 1977: 79). The recent renewed interest in Marxist theory among Western archaeologists thus largely developed via the influence of trends in sociocultural anthropology (Spriggs 1977: 3–5),[2] and Childe was only later discovered as a revered ancestor. As Klejn has written (1977: 20), 'A quarter century ago, Childe was a white crow among Western archaeologists. We are now witnessing a certain "Childeization" of Western archaeology.'

For many years, of course, there has been an interest in Marxist ideas among archaeologists in the socialist countries; and Soviet archaeology had a formative influence on Childe's Marxism. Since Childe, however, Soviet archaeological theory has had little influence on Western archaeologists except perhaps on those working in Western Asia (Kohl 1981a; this volume). Summaries of recent Soviet theoretical perspectives are given by Klejn (1977), Bulkin *et al.* (1982) and in a volume edited by Gellner (1981). Chang has summarized developments in Chinese archaeology since 1949 (1977; 1981: 166–8).

Where?

Marxism means many things to many people and today it is by no means the monolithic system of thought it is often represented to be. As Kahn and Llobera point out (1981: 301–6) there can be no 'pure' Marxism in a contemporary context. Giddens notes (1979: 234) that recent Marxist theorizing has tended to replicate the theoretical divisions and conceptions of previous social science approaches, producing functionalist Marxism, structuralist Marxism, and so on. Following Giddens (1979: 150–3) we can distinguish at least seven views of Marx's materialism which various commentators (pro and con) have adhered to, a diversity of views reflecting the often ambiguous and contradictory descriptions of the 'materialist interpretation of history' in Marx's own writing. These views are:

1 A methodology for historical analysis developed in opposition to Hegel's idealist philosophy.

2 A conception of human *praxis* 'emphasizing that human beings are neither to be treated as passive objects, nor as wholly free subjects' (1979: 150–1), a view opposed both to idealism and Feuerbach's 'mechanical materialism'. The objects of study are definite social practices geared into human needs.

3 An associated viewpoint emphasizing the significance of *labour* in the development of human society, where labour is understood either as 'the interplay of human activity and material nature' (1979: 151) (a concept of labour shading into that of *praxis*), or alternatively as having the more limited meaning of work process, economic activity. Very different kinds of history are produced using these two different conceptions.

4 A theory of social change stressing determination by economic factors. Precise definitions are again crucial here, particularly of 'economic' (cf. Gregory, this volume) and of 'determination'. Ambiguities in Marx's own formulation have allowed economic and technological determinist interpretations of Marxism to be developed, such as the cultural materialism of Harris (1968; 1979).

5 A functional theory of the relations between infrastructure ('base') and superstructure stressing the need (in opposition to idealist perspectives) to connect political and ideological institutions to economic institutions as parts of a totality. As Giddens notes this viewpoint is explicit or implicit in much Althusserian and structural-Marxist anthropology.

6 A reductionist theory of consciousness treating the content of human consciousness as determined by 'material factors', ideas being considered as reflecting the material conditions of social life and having little or no autonomy.

7 A theory of the central importance of class divisions, where 'the history of all hitherto existing societies is the history of class struggles' (Marx and Engels 1968: 35).

These various interpretations of Marx's materialism are not all mutually exclusive and current Marxist perspectives may stress one or a range of them. Giddens himself accepts the validity of 1, 2 and in part 3, 4 and 7 (1979: 153). The discerning reader can perhaps find all seven views represented in this book. Several current perspectives in Marxist anthropology can be loosely delineated: the Althusserian Marxists (Meillassoux, Rey and Terray), the structural Marxists (early Friedman, Godelier) and the World Systems Approach (Ekholm, later Friedman) being most easy to pinpoint. In addition there are the Critical Theorists, the so-called Hegelian Marxists and the phenomenological Marxists (Diamond, Habermas, Krader, Scholte). Many individual anthropologists (and archaeologists) cannot be so neatly typed, however, and use approaches drawn from aspects of the above and other traditions such as Weberian theory. Eric Wolf (1981) and Peter Worsley (1981) are examples, offering influential viewpoints which are not closely associated with any of the previously mentioned perspectives. This is not the place for a detailed summary of the different Marxist perspectives in anthropology. Several recent publications in archaeology and anthropology have presented and discussed these viewpoints in detail.[3]

While it is necessary to stress the divergence of viewpoints that a phrase such as 'Marxist anthropology' hides, there are a series of positions which unite the views of many Marxist anthropologists and archaeologists. These are summarized below:

1 All view Marx as an important intellectual ancestor and their analyses as being ultimately inspired by ideas he first developed. All however would also accept that there is much 'dead wood' in Marx's work as well as ambiguities and underdeveloped theory which need to be critically examined. As Kahn and Llobera put it (1981: xi–xii): 'A unified human and social science cannot exist without being inspired by the theoretical insights and theoretical contributions of Marx; Marxism cannot survive as a creative endeavour without constantly borrowing from new developments in the social sciences.'

2 Following from this many would accept the need to break down current disciplinary boundaries and aim to produce a unified human and social science in history. In this sense 'Marxist anthropology' or 'Marxist archaeology' are self-contradictory terms and the idea of a 'Marxist economic anthropology' even more so (cf. Copans and Seddon 1978: 40; Gledhill 1981;

Kahn and Llobera 1981: ix–x). So far this acceptance is more honoured in the breach.

3 There is a general dissatisfaction, as mentioned in the beginning of this paper, with previous approaches in the social sciences such as functionalism, structuralism and phenomenology. There is wide divergence, however, on the question of the contribution other approaches can make to developing Marxist theory, particularly in regard to structuralism. While Marxists have developed often devastating critiques of other approaches, particularly of functionalism, they are often prone to employ functionalist arguments in practice.

4 There is a concern to reject the ideal/material and subject/object dichotomies traditional to much of Western thought. 'The chief defect of all existing materialism (that of Feuerbach included) is that the thing, reality, sensuousness, is conceived only in the form of the *object or of contemplation*, but not as *sensuous human activity, practice*, not subjectively' (Marx and Engels 1970: 121). O'Laughlin puts the point well: 'thought can appropriate the concrete; material structure is knowable' (1975: 343; cf. Kus, this volume).

5 Social reality is seen as a contradictory reality, following from 'the conception of social structure as a unity of opposites and from differences of interests between individual agents and groups. Contradiction and conflict of interest provide an initial basis for an understanding of change, domination and legitimation of the social order' (Tilley 1982: 37).

6 Social structures are viewed as dialectical, dynamic processes, relations between being and becoming, and so cannot be known positively through their surface form. As in structuralist thinking reality cannot be understood on the surface of things (O'Laughlin 1975: 343). 'All science would be superfluous if the outward appearance and the essence of things directly coincided' (Marx 1894: 817).

7 There is a recognition of the social basis of knowledge. Knowledge is historically dependent and so the positivist goal of absolute certainty is unobtainable (see the works of Childe previously referred to, Gathercole, Kus, Pearson, Rowlands, this volume). As recognized by Merleau-Ponty: 'We can never be the past: it is only a spectacle before us, which is there for us to question. The questions come from us, and thus the responses in principle do not exhaust historical reality, since historical reality does not depend upon them for its existence' (1964: 194).

This book is not an attempt to develop a Marxist 'school' of archaeology. For reasons I hope have become clear such a project is both impossible and undesirable. The selection of papers presented here has been deliberately eclectic, designed to represent a *range* of Marxist perspectives on questions of

interest to archaeologists. Several major themes are examined
by the authors, sometimes from widely divergent positions.
These are discussed below.

It has been stressed already that Marxism is not a dogma,
and that a critical stance is general among those developing
Marxist perspectives in the social sciences. One of the important themes of this book is to examine a range of Marxist concepts in order to separate living ideas in Marx's work from
'dead wood', a theme taken up in detail by Gathercole,
Gilman, Gledhill, Gregory, Kus and Pearson. One central concern is the dynamic of history. All would probably agree that
contradiction and *conflict* provide an initial basis for an understanding of domination, legitimation and change. Giddens,
contrasting functionalism and Marxism, has put the point well:
'Don't look for the functions social practices fulfil, look for
the contradictions they embody!' (1979: 131). The levels at
which contradictions and conflicts operate in any particular
historical situation, however, are open to debate.

The most classic formulation is that of the contradiction
between forces and relations of production, many contributors
following Marx's classic statements from the 1859 *Preface*.
Gilman (this volume) sees this contradiction as the key to the
Upper Palaeolithic Revolution and as long as the tendency
(found in many earlier Marxist writers) of reducing this to
technological determinism rather than dialectic relation is
avoided, it remains a useful concept (cf. Pearson, this volume).
Giddens (1979: 154; 1981: 88−9) is surely mistaken, as
Pearson points out, to suggest that this contradiction is *only* of
importance within capitalism. There are many cases in prehistory where this dialectic can be examined (cf. Spriggs 1981).
As Bate points out in Part 2 on 'Situating the economic', if
we are to gain a clear appreciation of this dialectic a more
quantified approach to the consideration of productive forces
is necessary. This point is further taken up by Tosi in relation
to craft specialization and the division of labour in emerging
class systems.

A second contradiction (also discussed by Pearson) is
between the appropriation and consumption of surplus and
the social organization of its production, a theme handled
sensitively by Gledhill in his contribution. This of course links
to the idea of the central importance of class struggle in Marxist thought, raising the question of how Marxism can understand the pre-class societies of history and prehistory (Gilman,
Gledhill, Pearson, this volume). Both Gilman and Pearson
stress the tensions and divisions underlying the corporate
solidarity of the social group in pre-class societies. Gilman
points out that distinct 'interest groups' do occur — males
versus females, elders versus cadets, and so on (cf. Terray
1972). Looked at in this way the tiresome debate among
Marxist anthropologists about whether women or cadets form
a 'class' in the classic sense of the term might be resolved.

When we discuss class interests and power, we have to
consider the questions of ideology and the legitimation of
power. These topics are covered in Part 3 on 'Representation
and ideology'. Giddens (1979; 1981) has made an important

contribution in this field, an area of theory where Marx is the
inevitable starting point but which is in need of considerable
development. In this volume Kristiansen, Kus and Pearson
consider current notions of ideology and their limitations,
criticizing the commonly held position that ideology is determined by the economy rather than co-existing in a reflexive
relationship with it (cf. Kus 1979; 1982; Leone 1982; Tilley
1982). As Tilley suggests, 'The degree, and the nature of the
legitimation of the social order, would appear to be a key
element in maintaining social reproduction rather than transformation and the strongest form of this legitimation is likely
to involve ideological forms of manipulation, which serve to
justify the social order' (1982: 36).

A reductionist view of ideology owes much to a base–
superstructure model of social totalities, with a strongly determinist notion of an economic 'base' in relation to the ideological and juridico-political 'superstructure'. As Gathercole
(this volume) notes, the usefulness of a base–superstructure
metaphor has been a subject of debate within Marxist circles
for some years. It is often discussed among Marxist anthropologists in terms of the problem posed by kinship for the idea
of a determinant economic base (cf. Gregory, this volume).
The structural-Marxist reformulation of the concept of mode
of production has satisfied some but Kus (this volume) considers that this concept has outlived its usefulness and that
rather than developing it further it should simply be dropped.
We are close to a watershed in Marxist thought on this question, one considered in detail by Giddens (1981), Gledhill
(1981) Kahn and Llobera (1981: 285−300; 306−14) and
Rowlands (1982), and the reader is referred to their discussions of the issue.

The major break with much of Marxist anthropology
that Kus is suggesting is a step most other contributors are not
at present prepared to take. Their arguments are not with the
concept of mode of production itself but about the usefulness
of particular modes of production as units of analysis. All
would, however, agree on a basic division between pre-class
and class formations. The controversy over the concept of an
'Asiatic mode of production' has raged in Marxist circles for
almost a century (Giddens 1981: Chapter 3; Godelier 1978b).
Gledhill (this volume) considers it a useful concept not
because similarities between European feudalism and other
systems do not exist but because more general classifications
such as Amin's 'tributary mode of production' do not offer a
better point of departure. Gilman (this volume) favours a
division of 'tributary' and 'kin-ordered' modes of production,
and further defends the idea of a 'primitive communist' mode
as representing the pristine form of human social organization.
Bate on the other hand uses the term primitive communism in
a more general way to represent pre-class or kin-ordered
society. As well as the original formulations of modes of production by Marx (primitive communist, ancient, slave,
germanic, asiatic, feudal and capitalist), recent years have seen
the putting forward of many others − among them the
'African' mode (Coquery-Vidrovitch 1975), the 'Lineage'

mode (Rey 1975), the 'Domestic' mode (Sahlins 1972) and more recently the 'Foraging' mode (Lee 1981), none of which has achieved any general acceptance.

Closely linked with questions about the validity of the mode of production concept is a concern among some contributors over the relevant spatial units of analysis. This is the question of global systems (cf. Wallerstein 1974; 1980) — whether the single society as usually studied by anthropologists is a sufficient unit of analysis, given the larger socioeconomic systems of which all societies are a part. The Global Systems Approach produces a critique of the mode of production concept from a different perspective than that of Kus, seeing a mode of production as only a partial system within a larger total system of reproduction (Ekholm 1980; Friedman 1976). While several of the authors represented in this volume discuss the importance of regional and even 'global' considerations in their analyses, some see problems with Ekholm's and Friedman's particular formulations (see Gledhill, Kohl, this volume; cf. Schneider 1977).

Questions of relevant units of analysis lead us to a necessary discussion of the level of generalization we seek to achieve in explanation. The new archaeology has tended to concentrate on general explanations ('laws'), as having primacy over consideration of particular details. This search for universal 'laws of human behaviour' however has yet to yield significant results. Pearson (this volume) discusses some of the inherent problems involved, noting that the general cannot usefully be given precedence over the particular. Kohl (this volume) is essentially making the same point in his critique of evolutionism: 'Clearly, the attempt to draw comparisons among different societies is a legitimate and appropriate exercise, but this effort should not obscure or gloss over fundamental differences that distinguish societies and that must be explained in terms of each society's specific historical development.' Hodder (1982b: 9–14; 1982c: Chapter 10) in formulating what he calls 'contextual archaeology' has similar concerns, even tipping the symbolic hat to Childe along the way, but the lengths to which he goes *not* to mention the links of his approach to Marxism are somewhat disconcerting. Part 4 of this volume deals with the social transformations of concrete societies in history viewed 'contextually', not as abstract ideal stages of social evolution (cf. Rowlands 1982). These case studies and the others throughout the book are intended to show that specifically Marxist accounts of non-capitalist societies are possible and can provide new explanatory frameworks for studying social change, building on but transcending past approaches.

A theme of several of the papers is the evaluation of these past theoretical approaches. There are clearly divergent opinions presented here, particularly as regards the importance of the structuralism of Lévi-Strauss. Gregory uses Lévi-Strauss to expand Marx's concept of reproduction, and vice versa: 'Marx's concept of reproduction overlooks the exchange of people necessary for biological reproduction, while Lévi-Strauss' concept of reproduction is concerned almost exclus-

ively with the exchange of people.' It is clear from his paper, however, that he does not consider himself a structural-Marxist in the usual sense of the term. While not discussing the structuralist influence on current Marxist theory in detail, Gilman refers to it as 'effete Marxism', whereas Kristiansen conceives of structural-Marxism as a starting point to develop theory in concert with Ekholm and Friedman's Global Systems Approach. A similar divergence of opinion on the value of Lévi-Strauss's structuralism to archaeology and detailed critiques of that and related approaches can be found in the papers of Hodder's (1982a) *Symbolic and Structural Archaeology*. The criticisms of functionalism raised by the contributors to that volume would also be shared by the authors represented here (cf. Friedman 1974; Giddens 1979 (especially Chapter 7); Gilman 1981; Godelier 1972: vii–xlii). Other associated approaches closely linked to the new archaeology such as cultural ecology, cultural materialism and evolutionism are discussed in detail by particular authors in their substantive contributions (Gilman, Gledhill, Kohl, Kristiansen, Pearson). Childe has already been mentioned as an early discussant of many of the themes mentioned above and several of the contributors evaluate aspects of his ideas (Gathercole, Gregory, Kus; cf. Hodder 1982b: 12–13; Spriggs 1977: 5–9; Thomas 1982). In discussing previous approaches the concern is to build on the theoretical and methodological advances they embody, while transcending their evident limitations.

Where to?

The studies in this book are in many cases tentative explorations and can be seen more as steps towards the development of Marxist perspectives in archaeology rather than as fully developed analyses. In 1976 when I last considered the question of Marxism and archaeology (Spriggs 1977) it was easier to see structural-Marxism as a potentially unifying perspective, and difficulties with the approach were less obvious than they appear today. At that time there was a slowly growing interest in Marxism among Western archaeologists but few substantive case studies. The considerable development of theory and increasingly sophisticated applications since then suggest that the next few years will see increasing consideration of the value of Marxist perspectives in archaeology. Perhaps, as Kristiansen argues: 'Marxist theory may be able to offer a long-needed theoretical and explanatory "superstructure" that can cope with the impressive methodological developments of the last two decades.' In discussing this point Gregory notes that: 'The ultimate test of the superiority of one conceptual approach over the other is whether or not it can produce theories that have greater explanatory power.' It is at this level that the usefulness of Marxist perspectives in archaeology will ultimately be judged by the uncommitted (cf. Gledhill, Kristiansen, this volume).

In this respect it is interesting to note the convergence between the views of some of the contributors represented here (see Part 3 for example), those represented at the Cambridge Seminar on Symbolic and Structural Archaeology

(Hodder 1982a), the sociology of Giddens (1979; 1981) particularly his notion of structuration, and the historical anthropology being developed by Sahlins. All of these are concerned to incorporate a notion of practice in structure, and structure in practice and so avoid a narrowly 'idealist' or 'materialist' position: 'The great challenge to an historical anthropology is not merely to know how events are ordered by culture, but how, in that process, the culture is reordered. How does the reproduction of a structure become its transformation?' (Sahlins 1981: 8).

This convergence, called by Tilley 'dialectical structuralism' (1982: 26), is in part based on a concern with questions of representation and the legitimation of the social order, concerns that we can expect to see increasingly addressed in the archaeological literature in future as the role of material culture in social processes is further explicated.

As well as enriching archaeology as a discipline, the development of Marxist perspectives in the subject are likely to lead also to a richer anthropology and sociology. Gilman (this volume) has pointed out that Marxist accounts of non-capitalist social formations have until now largely been based on ethnographic studies, whose time span is insufficient to provide evidence for examining the dynamic of social change within such formations. Add to this the traditional distrust of history by sociocultural anthropologists, associated with a functionalist emphasis on social statics, and most Marxist analyses become difficult to distinguish from cultural ecology or synchronic structuralism (Gledhill 1981). As Gilman reasons: 'The only way out of this practical and theoretical impasse is to place at the centre of our attention the archaeological record. With all its defects this provides the only (and thus the best) evidence for the long-term trajectories of kin-ordered societies.' For a long time anthropologists tended to scoff at history. Now, in part because of the influence of Marxist theory, they are coming to realize that history cannot be ignored. But the history they seek is often prehistory and, however grudgingly, they will have to seek out the archaeologists to get to it. This is equally true of sociologists such as Giddens, whose otherwise stimulating arguments are at their weakest when dealing with prehistory, dismissed as representing 'cold' societies in Lévi-Strauss's unfortunate term and categorized in a static, functionalist model using outdated secondary sources (see Giddens 1981: 69–108). It becomes increasingly clear that serious Marxist social scientists will need to become at least conversant with the work of historians and archaeologists. Certainly few would now doubt that, in Gledhill's words, it is 'difficult to see how we could become fully conscious of the nature of either the colonial object or capitalism without reworking our consciousness of history beyond the temporal boundary of these phenomena' (1981: 4).

One of the formative influences in the renewed interest in Marxism and anthropology was from the critics of anthropology as a child of colonialism, writers such as Gough (1968) and Asad (1973). Archaeology as practised in much of the world has an equally questionable history. Marxist perspectives in archaeology should help question the practice of our craft as well as its explanatory frameworks. For instance, often we are engaged in writing someone else's prehistory but the political implications of this are rarely examined and the legitimate concerns of their descendants rarely addressed (cf. Trigger 1980). A closer examination of the political implications of writing prehistory is necessary, as discussed by Kohl, Gathercole and Rowlands. Archaeological data are not neutral, they can and are being used to serve political ends and these ends need to be scrutinized (cf. Ford 1973). As usual, Childe considered this question in some detail but discussion of the sociology of knowledge has since been muted in the archaeological literature. 'It is no good demanding that history should be unbiased. The writer cannot help being influenced by the interests and prejudices of the society to which he belongs — his class, his nation, his church' (1947: 22), and, as a growing number of feminist studies show, 'his' sex. We can expect in future to see more consideration given to the implications of this.[4]

It would be unfortunate if the perspectives offered here are rejected (or blindly accepted) simply because of the political connotations of the label Marxist. That said, if Marxist perspectives offer convincing explanations of prehistory these have obvious implications in terms of modern history and, as Marx was always at pains to stress, in terms of action in history. If these perspectives in archaeology provide another way of telling, they must also suggest another way of doing. 'Marxism is still very young, almost in its infancy, it has scarcely begun to develop. It remains therefore, the philosophy of our time. We cannot go beyond it because we have not gone beyond the circumstances which have engendered it' (Sartre 1968: 30).

Notes

1 Marx and Engels were themselves dimly aware of the developing discipline of archaeology, but for reasons relating to the structure and practice of the subject they remained ill-informed of its potential contribution to their theories. Archaeology thus had no appreciable influence on them, and vice versa (Kohl, in press).

2 In making this statement I cannot speak for archaeologists outside of North America, Scandinavia, the United Kingdom and France. For instance, the strong revolutionary Marxist tradition in Central and South America has clearly had an influence on archaeologists there, as has the work of V. Gordon Childe, and there is only minimal reference to other Western Marxists (Lorenzo 1981).

3 Several edited volumes in English contain many of the major papers in Marxist anthropology, critical reviews of particular theoretical positions and extensive bibliographies. These include *Marxist Analyses and Social Anthropology* (Bloch 1975), *The Evolution of Social Systems* (Friedman and Rowlands 1978a), *Relations of Production* (Seddon 1978), *Toward a Marxist Anthropology* (Diamond 1979) and *The Anthropology of Pre-Capitalist Societies* (Kahn and Llobera 1981). The major 'schools' of thought are represented by papers in these various volumes. The collection edited by Kahn and Llobera (1981) is particularly important for its critical reviews of various approaches and extensive bibliography. Other major sources of Marxist anthropology are journals such as *Critique of Anthro-*

pology, *Dialectical Anthropology* and *Economy and Society*. For structural-Marxism essential works are Godelier's *Rationality and Irrationality in Economics* (1972 orig. 1966) and *Perspectives in Marxist Anthropology* (1977 orig. 1973) as well as more recent papers (Godelier 1978a; 1982). Recent criticisms of Althusserian and structural-Marxist approaches include O'Laughlin (1975), Goodfriend (1978), Kahn (1978), Kahn and Llobera (1980) and Gledhill (1981). Friedman, a notable structural-Marxist at one time (1974) has since, with Kajsa Ekholm, been involved in developing a Global Systems Approach (Ekholm 1978; 1980; Ekholm and Friedman 1979; 1980; Friedman 1976; 1978; 1979a: 10–15; 1979b; 1981; 1982; Friedman and Rowlands 1978b). Other relevant anthropological literature includes Amin (1976), Gregory (1980; 1982), Kelenen (1976), Lee (1981), Legros (1977), Modjeska (1977), Siskind (1978), and Wolf (1981).

Recent archaeological works in English using Marxist perspectives include the following (a by no means exhaustive list): Bender (1978; 1981), Bradley (1981), Frankenstein and Rowlands (1978), Gilman (1976; 1981), Gledhill (1978), Gledhill and Larsen (1982), Gledhill and Rowlands (1982), Götze and von Thienen (1981), Haselgrove (1977), Ingold (1981), Kohl (1975; 1978; 1979; 1981b), Kohl and Wright (1977), Kristiansen (1978; 1981; 1982), Leone (1978; 1981; 1982), Meltzer (1981), Nash (n.d.; 1978), Rowlands (1979; 1980; 1982), Rowlands and Gledhill (1977), Shanks and Tilley (1982), Thomas (1981), Tilley (1981a; 1981b; 1982) and Tosi (1973; 1976). It is only since the mid-1970s that an appreciable number of Western archaeologists have stated their interest in Marxist theory. There have of course been many other 'closet' or 'hidden' Marxists in archaeology: those using theories clearly derived from Marxism but who have chosen not to identify the source of their ideas. It is not my intention to 'expose' these authors but included among their number are several of the better-known archaeologists of the 1960s and 1970s.

While it cannot be discussed here the growing interest in Marxism among geographers should also be noted: see *Geography and Marxism* (Quaini 1982) which contains an excellent annotated bibliography by Russell King.

4 This is a point made forcefully by Leone in an important review article. He discusses in some detail the necessity of critical self-reflection in interpretation, urging that: 'The archaeologist must have an active involvement with the ideological process in order to distinguish between that knowledge of the past that is needed to understand the present accurately, and that knowledge of the past that present society would emphasize in order to reproduce itself as it is now constituted' (1982: 754). However, after discussing the issue persuasively in explicitly Marxist terms it is disappointing that he concludes by saying that, 'It is better to label such ideas materialist and leave the political involvement with Marxism behind' (1982: 757). This would appear to represent a classic example of the 'vulgar history' he was earlier criticizing!

Acknowledgements
Peter Gathercole, Antonio Gilman and Phil Kohl commented on earlier drafts of this paper. The mistakes and misconceptions are my own contribution.

Bibliography
Amin, S. 1976. *Unequal Development: An Essay on the Social Formations of Peripheral Capitalism.* Hassocks: Harvester Press.

Asad, T. (ed.) 1973. *Anthropology and the Colonial Encounter.* London: Ithaca Press.

Bender, B. 1978. Gatherer–hunter to farmer: a social perspective. *World Archaeology* 10: 205–22.

1981. Gatherer–hunter intensification. In A. Sheridan and G. Bailey (eds.), *Economic Archaeology: Towards an Integration of Ecological and Social Approaches.* BAR International Series 96: 149–57. Oxford: British Archaeological Reports.

Berger, J. 1982. Stories. In J. Berger and J. Mohr, *Another Way of Telling*, pp. 279–89. New York: Pantheon Books.

Binford, L.R. 1962. Archaeology as anthropology. *American Antiquity* 28: 217–25.

Bloch, M. (ed.) 1975. *Marxist Analyses and Social Anthropology.* London: Malaby Press.

Bradley, R. 1981. The destruction of wealth in later prehistory. *Man* (ns) 17: 108–22.

Bulkin, V.A., L.S. Klejn and G.S. Lebedev, 1982. Attainments and problems of Soviet archaeology. *World Archaeology* 13 (3): 272–95.

Chang, K.C. 1977. Chinese archaeology since 1949. *Journal of Asian Studies* 36: 623–46.

1981. Chinese archaeology and historiography. *World Archaeology* 13 (2): 156–69.

Childe, V.G. 1947. *History.* London: Cobbet.

1949a. The sociology of knowledge. *Modern Quarterly* (ns) 4: 302–9.

1949b. *Social Worlds of Knowledge.* L.T. Hobhouse Memorial Trust Lecture No. 19. London: Oxford University Press.

1956. *Society and Knowledge.* London: Allen and Unwin.

Copans, J. and D. Seddon, 1978. Marxism and anthropology: a preliminary survey. In D. Seddon (ed.), *Relations of Production: Marxist Approaches to Economic Anthropology*, pp. 1–46. London: Frank Cass.

Coquery-Vidrovitch, C. 1975. Research on an African mode of production. *Critique of Anthropology* 4/5: 38–71.

Diamond, S. (ed.) 1979. *Toward a Marxist Anthropology.* The Hague: Mouton.

Ekholm, K. 1978. External exchange and the transformation of Central African social systems. In J. Friedman and M.J. Rowlands (eds.), *The Evolution of Social Systems*, pp. 115–36. London: Duckworth.

1980. On the limits of civilization: the structure and dynamics of global systems. *Dialectical Anthropology* 5: 155–66.

Ekholm, K. and J. Friedman, 1979. 'Capital', imperialism and exploitation in ancient world systems. In M.T. Larsen (ed.), *Power and Propaganda: A Symposium on Ancient Empires*, pp. 41–58. Copenhagen: Akademisk Forlag.

1980. Towards a global anthropology. In L. Blusse, H.L. Wesseling and G.D. Winius (eds.), *History and Underdevelopment*, pp. 61–76. Leiden: Centre for the History of European Expansion.

Ford, R.I. 1973. Archaeology serving humanity. In C. Redman (ed.), *Research and Theory in Current Archaeology*, pp. 83–93. New York: John Wiley.

Frankenstein, S. and M.J. Rowlands, 1978. The internal structure and regional context of Early Iron Age society in south-western Germany. *Bulletin of the Institute of Archaeology, London* 15: 73–112.

Friedman, J. 1974. Marxism, structuralism and vulgar materialism. *Man* (ns) 9: 444–69.

1976. Marxist theory and systems of total reproduction. *Critique of Anthropology* 7: 3–16.

1978. Crises in theory and transformations of the world economy. *Review* 2: 131–48.

1979a. *System, Structure and Contradiction: The Evolution of 'Asiatic' Social Formations.* Social Studies in Oceania and South East Asia 2. Copenhagen: The National Museum of Denmark.

1979b. Hegelian ecology: between Rousseau and the world spirit.

In P. Burnham and R.F. Ellen (eds.), *Social and Ecological Systems*, pp. 253–70. London: Academic Press.

1981. Notes on structure and history in Oceania. *Folk* 23: 275–95.

1982. Catastrophe and continuity in social evolution. In C. Renfrew, M.J. Rowlands and B.A. Segraves (eds.), *Theory and Explanation in Archaeology: The Southampton Conference*, pp. 175–96. London: Academic Press.

Friedman, J. and M.J. Rowlands (eds.), 1978a. *The Evolution of Social Systems*. London: Duckworth.

1978b. Notes towards an epigenetic model of the evolution of 'civilization'. In J. Friedman and M.J. Rowlands (eds.), *The Evolution of Social Systems*, pp. 201–76. London: Duckworth.

Gellner, E. (ed.) 1981. *Soviet and Western Anthropology*. New York: Columbia University Press.

Giddens, A. 1979. *Central Problems in Social Theory: Action, Structure and Contradiction in Social Analysis*. London and Basingstoke: Macmillan.

1981. *A Contemporary Critique of Historical Materialism. Vol. 1 Power, Property and the State*. London and Basingstoke: Macmillan.

Gilman, A. 1976. Bronze Age dynamics in southeast Spain. *Dialectical Anthropology* 1: 307–19.

1981. The development of social stratification in Bronze Age Europe. *Current Anthropology* 22 (1): 1–23.

Gledhill, J. 1978. Formative development in the North American Southwest. In D. Green, C. Haselgrove and M. Spriggs (eds.), *Social Organisation and Settlement: Contributions from Anthropology, Archaeology and Geography* (2 vols.) BAR International Series 47: 241–90. Oxford: British Archaeological Reports.

1981. Time's arrow: anthropology, history, social evolution and Marxist theory. *Critique of Anthropology* 16: 3–30.

Gledhill, J. and M.T. Larsen, 1982. The Polanyi paradigm and the dynamics of archaic states: Mesopotamia and Mesoamerica. In C. Renfrew, M.J. Rowlands and B.A. Segraves (eds.), *Theory and Explanation in Archaeology: The Southampton Conference*, pp. 197–229. London: Academic Press.

Gledhill, J. and M.J. Rowlands, 1982. Materialism and socio-economic process in multilinear evolution. In C. Renfrew and S. Shennan (eds.), *Ranking, Resource and Exchange*, pp. 144–50. Cambridge: Cambridge University Press.

Godelier, M. 1972. *Rationality and Irrationality in Economics*. London: New Left Books.

1977. *Perspectives in Marxist Anthropology*. Cambridge: Cambridge University Press.

1978a. Infrastructures, society and history. *Current Anthropology* 19: 763–71.

1978b. The concept of the 'Asiatic Mode of Production' and Marxist models of social evolution. In D. Seddon (ed.), *Relations of Production: Marxist Approaches to Economic Anthropology*, pp. 209–57. London: Frank Cass.

1982. Myths, infrastructures and history in Levi-Strauss. In I. Rossi (ed.), *The Logic of Culture: Advances in Structural Theory and Methods*, pp. 232–61. New York: J.F. Bergin.

Goodfriend, D.E. 1978. Plus ça change, plus c'est la même chose: the dilemma of the French structural Marxists. *Dialectical Anthropology* 3 (2): 105–27.

Götze, B. and V. von Thienen, 1981. Archaeological remarks on a revised theory of evolution. In A. Sheridan and G. Bailey (eds.), *Economic Archaeology: Towards an Integration of Ecological and Social Approaches*. BAR International Series 96: 77–86. Oxford: British Archaeological Reports.

Gough, K. 1968. Anthropology and imperialism. *Monthly Review* 19 (1): 12–27.

Gregory, C.A. 1980. Gifts to men and gifts to god: gift exchange and capital accumulation in contemporary Papua. *Man* (ns) 15: 626–52.

1982. *Gifts and Commodities*. London: Academic Press.

Groube, L.M. 1977. The hazards of anthropology. In M. Spriggs (ed.), *Archaeology and Anthropology: Areas of Mutual Interest*. BAR Supplementary Series 19: 69–90. Oxford: British Archaeological Reports.

Harris, M. 1968. *The Rise of Anthropological Theory*. New York: T.Y. Crowell.

1979. *Cultural Materialism: The Struggle for a Science of Culture*. New York: Random House.

Haselgrove, C. 1977. After civilization: archaeology, anthropology and the study of urbanism. In M. Spriggs (ed.), *Archaeology and Anthropology: Areas of Mutual Interest*. BAR Supplementary Series 19: 91–116. Oxford: British Archaeological Reports.

Hodder, I. (ed.) 1982a. *Symbolic and Structural Archaeology*. Cambridge: Cambridge University Press.

1982b. Theoretical archaeology: a reactionary view. In I. Hodder (ed.), *Symbolic and Structural Archaeology*, pp. 1–16. Cambridge: Cambridge University Press.

1982c. *Symbols in Action: Ethnoarchaeological Studies of Material Culture*. Cambridge: Cambridge University Press.

Ingold, T. 1981. The hunter and his spear: notes on the cultural mediation of social and ecological systems. In A. Sheridan and G. Bailey (eds.), *Economic Archaeology: Towards an Integration of Ecological and Social Approaches*. BAR International Series 96: 119–30. Oxford: British Archaeological Reports.

Kahn, J.S. 1978. Perspectives in Marxist anthropology: a review article. *Journal of Peasant Studies* 5 (4): 485–96.

Kahn, J.S. and J. Llobera, 1980. French Marxist anthropology: twenty years after. *Journal of Peasant Studies* 8 (1): 81–100.

Kahn, J.S. and J. Llobera (eds.) 1981. *The Anthropology of Pre-Capitalist Societies*. London and Basingstoke: Macmillan.

Kelenen, P. 1976. Towards a Marxist critique of structuralist anthropology. *Sociological Review* 24 (4): 859–75.

Klejn, L.S. 1977. A panorama of theoretical archaeology. *Current Anthropology* 18 (1): 1–41.

Kohl, P.L. 1975. The archaeology of trade. *Dialectical Anthropology* 1 (1): 43–50.

1978. The balance of trade in southwestern Asia in the mid-third millennium B.C. *Current Anthropology* 19 (3): 463–92.

1979. The 'world economy' of west Asia in the third millennium B.C. In M. Taddei (ed.), *South Asian Archaeology 1977*, pp. 55–85. Naples: Istituto Universitario Orientale.

1981a (ed.). *The Bronze Age Civilization of Central Asia: Recent Soviet Discoveries*. New York: M.E. Sharpe.

1981b. Materialist approaches in prehistory. *Annual Review of Anthropology* 10: 89–118.

In press. Archaeology and prehistory. In T. Bottomore (ed.), *A Dictionary of Marxist Thought*. Oxford: Blackwell.

Kohl, P.L. and R.P. Wright, 1977. Stateless cities: the differentiation of societies in the Near Eastern Neolithic. *Dialectical Anthropology* 2 (4): 271–83.

Kristiansen, K. 1978. The consumption of wealth in Bronze Age Denmark: a study in the dynamics of economic processes in tribal societies. In K. Kristiansen and C. Paludan-Müller (eds.), *New Directions in Scandinavian Archaeology*. Studies in Scandinavian Prehistory and Early History 1: 158–90. Copenhagen: National Museum of Denmark.

1981. Economic models for Bronze Age Scandinavia: towards an integrated approach. In A. Sheridan and G. Bailey (eds.), *Economic Archaeology: Towards an Integration of Ecological and Social Approaches*. BAR International Series 96: 239–303. Oxford: British Archaeological Reports.

1982. The formation of tribal systems in later European prehistory:

Northern Europe: 4000–500 B.C. In C. Renfrew, M.J. Rowlands and B.A. Segraves (eds.), *Theory and Explanation in Archaeology: The Southampton Conference*, pp. 241–80. London: Academic Press.

Kus, S. 1979. *Archaeology and Ideology: The Symbolic Organization of Space*. Ph.D. Thesis, University of Michigan. Ann Arbor: University Microfilms.

1982. Matters material and ideal. In I. Hodder (ed.), *Symbolic and Structural Archaeology*, pp. 47–62. Cambridge: Cambridge University Press.

Lee, R.B. 1981. Is there a foraging mode of production? *Canadian Journal of Anthropology* 2 (1): 13–19.

Legros, D. 1977. Chance, necessity and mode of production: a Marxist critique of cultural evolutionism. *American Anthropologist* 79 (1): 26–41.

Leone, M.P. 1978. Time in American archaeology. In C. Redman *et al.* (eds.), *Social Archaeology: Beyond Subsistence and Dating*, pp. 25–36. New York: Academic Press.

1981. Archaeology's relationship to the present and the past. In R.A. Gould and M.B. Schiffer (eds.), *Modern Material Culture: The Archaeology of Us*, pp. 5–14. New York: Academic Press.

1982. Some opinions about recovering mind. *American Antiquity* 47 (4): 742–60.

Lorenzo, J.L. 1981. Archaeology south of the Rio Grande. *World Archaeology* 13 (2): 190–208.

Marx, K. 1894. *Capital: Vol. III A Critique of Political Economy*. Moscow: Progress Publishers, 1971.

Marx, K. and F. Engels, 1968. *Selected Works in One Volume*. London: Lawrence and Wishart.

1970. *The German Ideology*. London: Lawrence and Wishart.

Meltzer, D.J. 1981. Ideology and material culture. In R.A. Gould and M.B. Schiffer (eds.), *Modern Material Culture: The Archaeology of Us*, pp. 113–25. New York: Academic Press.

Merleau-Ponty, M. 1964. *The Primacy of Perception*. Evanston: Northwestern University Press.

Modjeska, N. 1977. *Production Among the Duna*. Unpublished Ph.D. Thesis. Canberra: Australian National University.

Nash, D. n.d. *Foreign Trade and the Development of the State in Pre-Roman Gaul*. Ms.

1978. Territory and state formation in Central Gaul. In D. Green, C. Haselgrove and M. Spriggs (eds.), *Social Organisation and Settlement: Contributions from Anthropology, Archaeology and Geography* (2 vols.) BAR International Series 47: 455–82. Oxford: British Archaeological Reports.

O'Laughlin, B. 1975. Marxist approaches in anthropology. *Annual Review of Anthropology* 4: 341–70.

Phillips, P. 1955. American archaeology and general anthropological theory. *Southwestern Journal of Anthropology* 11: 246–50.

Quaini, M. 1982. *Geography and Marxism*. Totowa, N.J.: Barnes and Noble.

Rey, P.-P. 1975. The lineage mode of production. *Critique of Anthropology* 3: 27–79.

Rowlands, M.J. 1979. Local and long-distance trade and incipient state formation on the Bamenda Plateau. *Paideuma* 25: 1–19.

1980. Kinship, alliance and exchange in the European Bronze Age. In J. Barrett and R. Bradley (eds.), *Settlement and Society in the British Later Bronze Age*. BAR British Series 83: 15–55. Oxford: British Archaeological Reports.

1982. Processual archaeology as historical social science. In C. Renfrew, M.J. Rowlands and B.A. Segraves (eds.), *Theory and Explanation in Archaeology: The Southampton Conference*, pp. 155–74. London: Academic Press.

Rowlands, M.J. and J. Gledhill, 1977. The relationship between archaeology and anthropology. In M. Spriggs (ed.), *Archaeology and Anthropology: Areas of Mutual Interest*. BAR Supplementary Series 19: 143–58. Oxford: British Archaeological Reports.

Sahlins, M. 1972. *Stone Age Economics*. Chicago: Aldine–Atherton.

1981. *Historical Metaphors and Mythical Realities: Structure in the Early History of the Sandwich Islands Kingdom*. ASAO Special Publications 1. Ann Arbor: University of Michigan Press.

Sartre, J.P. 1968. *Search for a Method*. New York: Vintage Books.

Schneider, J. 1977. Was there a pre-capitalist world-system? *Peasant Studies* 6 (1): 20–9.

Seddon, D. (ed.) 1978. *Relations of Production: Marxist Approaches to Economic Anthropology*. London: Frank Cass.

Shanks, M. and C. Tilley, 1982. Ideology, symbolic power and ritual communication: a reinterpretation of Neolithic mortuary practices. In I. Hodder (ed.), *Symbolic and Structural Archaeology*, pp. 129–54. Cambridge: Cambridge University Press.

Siskind, J. 1978. Kinship and mode of production. *American Anthropologist* 80 (4): 860–72.

Spriggs, M. 1977. Where the hell are we? (or a young man's quest). In M. Spriggs (ed.), *Archaeology and Anthropology: Areas of Mutual Interest*. BAR Supplementary Series 19: 3–17. Oxford: British Archaeological Reports.

1981. *Vegetable Kingdoms: Taro Irrigation and Pacific Prehistory*. Unpublished Ph.D. Thesis (2 vols.) Canberra: Australian National University.

Terray, E. 1972. *Marxism and 'Primitive' Societies*. New York: Monthly Review Press.

Thomas, N. 1981. Social theory, ecology and epistemology: theoretical issues in Australian prehistory. *Mankind* 13 (2): 165–77.

1982. Childe, Marxism and archaeology. *Dialectical Anthropology* 6: 245–52.

Tilley, C. 1981a. Conceptual frameworks for the explanation of sociocultural change. In I. Hodder, G. Isaac and N. Hammond (eds.), *Pattern of the Past*, pp. 363–86. Cambridge: Cambridge University Press.

1981b. Economy and society: what relationship? In A. Sheridan and G. Bailey (eds.), *Economic Archaeology: Towards an Integration of Ecological and Social Approaches*. BAR International Series 96: 131–48. Oxford: British Archaeological Reports.

1982. Social formation, social structures and social change. In I. Hodder (ed.), *Symbolic and Structural Archaeology*, pp. 26–38. Cambridge: Cambridge University Press.

Tosi, M. 1973. Early urban evolution and settlement patterns in the Indo-Iranian borderland. In C. Renfrew (ed.), *The Explanation of Culture Change: Models in Prehistory*, pp. 429–46. London: Duckworth.

1976. The dialectics of state formation in Mesopotamia, Iran, and Central Asia. *Dialectical Anthropology* 1 (2): 173–80.

Trigger, B. 1980. Archaeology and the image of the American Indian. *American Antiquity* 45 (4): 662–76.

Wallerstein, I. 1974. *The Modern World System: Capitalist Agriculture and the Origins of the European World-Economy in the Sixteenth Century*. New York: Academic Press.

1980. *The Modern World System II: Mercantilism and the Consolidation of the European World-Economy, 1600–1750*. New York: Academic Press.

Wolf, E. 1981. The mills of inequality: a Marxian approach. In G.D. Berreman (ed.), *Social Inequality: Comparative and Developmental Approaches*, pp. 41–57. New York: Academic Press.

Worsley, P.M. 1981. Marxism and culture: the missing concept. *Dialectical Anthropology* 6 (2): 103–21.

PART 2

Situating the economic

Chapter 2

**The economy and kinship:
a critical examination of
some of the ideas of Marx
and Lévi-Strauss**
C.A. Gregory

Introduction

The object of this paper is to examine critically Marx's historical materialism in the light of some of the theories developed by Lévi-Strauss. As the author is an economic anthropologist rather than an archaeologist it is necessary to begin by situating the discussion *vis-à-vis* archaeology.

Archaeology, according to David Clarke (1968: 14), consists of three spheres of interrelated activity: data recovery, systematic description, and thirdly, the integrating, synthesizing process of generating models, hypotheses and theories. Clarke (*ibid*.: xiii) also adds that 'Archaeology is an undisciplined empirical discipline. A discipline lacking a scheme of systematic and ordered study based upon declared and clearly defined models and rules of procedure. It further lacks a body of central theory capable of synthesizing the general regularities within its data in such a way that the unique residuals distinguishing each particular case might be quickly isolated and easily assessed.'

If this account of archaeology has any validity — a debatable point of course — then theoretical development in other social sciences, such as anthropology and economics, can assist the archaeologist in the hypothesis generating stage of the archaeological process.[1] Clarke has opted for cybernetics, a new approach to the analysis of structural wholes developed in the 1940s by Weiner. A central concept in cybernetics is 'feedback' and the method has been applied to a wide range of problems in many disciplines ranging from the programming of Cruise missiles to Australian kinship systems. Childe, on the other hand, opted for historical materialism, an old approach that was first developed by Marx, and one that is much more limited in its applicability. Historical materialism has become a stale orthodoxy in the USSR but this need not, and should not, be its destiny. The great advantage of historical materialism as a method is its 'planned obsolescence'. New data should be applied to the method to produce new methods in the same way that the method is applied to the data to produce new theories. Childe approached historical materialism in this way; he modified Marx's method in the light of new archaeological data and the new theories of Morgan and others (cf. Trigger 1980).

This paper is in the Childe tradition in that it tries to develop the method of historical materialism further by critically examining Marx and Morgan in the light of Lévi-Strauss's *The Elementary Structures of Kinship* (1949). But there is an important sense in which it is not in the Childe tradition: it makes no attempt to examine critically the method in the light of new archaeological data. The paper is essentially theoretical and it tries to make some sense of the proposition that the economic base is 'the real foundation on which arises a legal and political superstructure' (Marx 1859: 20) by (a) re-examining the notion of 'economy' in the light of the problem posed by kinship and (b) developing a number of testable propositions that give concrete meaning to the base—super-structure metaphor.

The theoretical propositions of this paper have been developed to explain the anthropological data; their relevance for explaining the archaeological data is suggested by Childe's claim that the ethnographers' picture 'can with due caution be used to supplement the archaeologists' picture' (1946: 250). I recognize that there is much contemporary debate about this point (see Gould 1980) and leave it for the archaeologist to judge.

The structure of this essay is as follows. First, Marx's concept of the economy is examined in the light of Lévi-Strauss's theory of kinship. A flaw is identified and a new definition of the economy, that deals with the general relations of production to consumption, is advanced. This is then contrasted with the orthodox economists' definition of the economy. After that, Marx's approach to the definition of particular economies is contrasted with Lévi-Strauss's approach and finally a number of classificatory frameworks are developed for analysing the different economic forms that have existed historically. It is from these classificatory frameworks that a number of propositions concerning the base—superstructure metaphor are derived.

Kinship and the economy

'A central problem for Marxist "economic anthropology",' note Copans and Seddon in their survey of neo-Marxist contributions to the subject, 'is that of the role of kinship in "primitive" society' (1978: 36). How does kinship fit into Marx's conceptual framework? Is it part of the economic base or part of the ideological superstructure? Is it dominant, determinant or both?

The attempt to answer these questions has given rise to many different tendencies within neo-Marxism. Godelier, for example, notes that in an 'archaic' society kinship relations dominate social life and that the recognition of this fact poses the problem of understanding Marx's proposition that the economy is 'ultimately' determinant. Godelier resolved the problem by arguing that kinship is 'both infrastructure and superstructure' and that 'the correspondence between productive forces and productive relations is at the same time correspondence between economy and kinship (1966: 94—5). Terray regards this formulation as inadequate. For him the situation is more complex: 'concrete kinship relations must be seen as the product of a triple determination operating on a given substratum' (1972: 143). Meillassoux (1960) has a different opinion and Rey (1971) yet another.[2]

Why is kinship a central problem for Marxist economic anthropology? How can the emergence of these different tendencies be explained? The answer, it seems to me, has its origins in a problem in Marx's concept of reproduction and the aim of this section is to highlight this by contrasting Marx's concept of reproduction with Lévi-Strauss's. My argument is that Marx's concept of reproduction overlooks the exchange of people necessary for biological reproduction, while Lévi-Strauss's concept of reproduction is concerned almost exclusively with the exchange of people.

The starting point for most neo-Marxist literature is Marx's distinction between the 'forces' and 'relations' of production. This distinction is fundamental to Marx's approach but an even more fundamental distinction, and one that has been virtually ignored by contemporary commentators, is his distinction between 'production and productive consumption' and 'consumption and consumptive production' (Marx 1859: 188—217). This distinction is one between the reproduction of things and the reproduction of people and it is here that the problem lies.

The concept 'production and productive consumption' (i.e., the reproduction of things) is the general framework within which the classical economists — Quesnay (1759), Smith (1776), Ricardo (1817), and Marx (1867) — developed their analysis of capitalist reproduction. Marx's *Preface* (1859) contains a discussion of the concept but this is couched in an 'Hegelianese' which is exceptionally difficult to comprehend, and even more difficult to summarize. Fortunately, however, a simple numerical model of the concept is given in Volume 2 of *Capital* (Marx 1893: Chapter 10) where the problem of capitalist reproduction is analysed.

Marx analyses capitalist reproduction in terms of a very simple model. The economy is divided into two major departments: I, means of production, 'commodities having a form in which they must, or at least may, pass into *productive consumption*'; II, articles of consumption, 'commodities having a form in which they pass into the individual consumption of the capitalist and the working class' (1893: 399). Iron, in the form of a machine, is an example of the former; wheat, in the form of bread, is an example of the latter. In each department the capital consists of two parts: variable capital (v), the labour-value of real wages; constant capital (c), the labour-value of raw materials used in production. The value of the entire annual product of each department consists of c + v + s, where s is the surplus-value (unpaid labour).

The condition of simple reproduction implies a relation of interdependence between the two departments and one possible quantitative relation that will bring this about is the following:

I: 4000c + 1000v + 1000s = 6000 (c + v + s)
II: 2000c + 500v + 500s = 3000 (c + v + s)

In department I £6000 worth of iron is produced. Of this, £4000 is used as raw material to produce more iron and £2000 as input into the wheat production process. In department II £3000 worth of wheat is produced. In department II £1000 is used to feed workers and capitalists and £2000 to feed the workers and capitalists in department I. Thus the iron is *productively consumed* to produce more things and the wheat is consumed by individuals.

Productive consumption is a general concept. It is a feature of all economies and not just the capitalist economy. Indeed, it could be argued that one of the defining characteristics of humankind is that things are productively consumed to produce other things. But in order to define productive consumption in general a distinction must be drawn between the general property of a thing and a particular property of a thing. In so far as capitalist reproduction is concerned a distinction must be drawn between 'use-value' and 'exchange-value'. The former refers to the natural physical property of a thing that a given society finds useful and the latter to an historically specific social property. The fact that wheat is used as food tells us nothing about the particular structure of any society but the fact it has an exchange-value does. Exchange-value, or price, is not a natural property of a thing. It presupposes certain social conditions and only when these conditions are met does production and productive consumption take the quantitative form of the reproduction schema above.[3] In order to define production and productive consumption in general, then, it must be expressed in use-value form. The use-value form of Marx's reproduction schema above is:

I: iron + labour → iron
II: iron + labour → wheat

This is a simple illustration of what Marx meant by the general relations of production and productive consumption. To produce iron as an output, iron and labour must be used as means of production; to produce wheat, iron and labour must be used as an input also, i.e. iron and labour must be productively consumed.

It is clear from this simple illustration that the concept of 'production and productive consumption' only describes part of the reproduction process. This is because labour is an input but not an output. Thus the concept 'production and

productive consumption' describes the production of things by means of things and labour. What is needed to complete the picture is a concept that describes the production of labour by means of things and labour. This is what the concept 'consumption and consumptive production' is meant to capture. As the terms used would suggest, it is a mirror image of 'production and productive consumption'. But Marx's mirror image is somewhat distorted as I will now attempt to show.

'Consumption,' Marx notes, 'is simultaneously also production, just as in nature the production of a plant involves the consumption of elemental forces and chemical materials. It is obvious that man produces his body, e.g., through feeding, one form of consumption. But the same applies to any other kind of consumption which in one way or another contributes to the production of some aspect of man. Hence this is consumptive production' (1859: 196).

The concept 'consumption and consumptive production' plays no part in Marx's analysis of capitalism, which is to say that he ignores the problem of domestic labour. This particular oversight manifests itself as a problem with the concept of domestic labour in general. 'Consumption and consumptive production' requires a discussion of the general relations between production, consumption, distribution and exchange of labour. Marx, as the above quotation illustrates, discusses the relation between the production and consumption of labour but not the exchange and distribution of it. 'Distribution,' he says, 'is a distribution of *products*' (1859: 201, emphasis added). He likewise confines the concept 'exchange' to an exchange of things.

Before developing this concept further it is useful to consider Marx's concept of reproduction as a whole. The reproduction of things and labour, Marx correctly notes, 'are links of a single whole, different aspects of one unit' (1859: 204). He also correctly notes that 'exchange is simply an intermediate phase between production and distribution, which is determined by production and consumption' (1859: 204). However while his conclusion that production and productive consumption 'is the decisive phase' (1859: 204) is valid for capitalism, there are no *a priori* grounds for its validity in general. It may be possible to assert on empirical grounds that the production of things is 'decisive' because of the evidence for technological progress over the ages. However such empirical propositions have no role to play in a discussion of the general relations of reproduction because they are 'nothing but abstract conceptions which do not define any of the actual historical stages of production' (Marx 1859: 193). Thus, at this level of conceptual analysis, the problem is a logical one and there is no reason why the sphere of the production of things should be accorded any special status on these grounds. All that can be said is that consumption determines production and production determines consumption. In so far as the definition of particular economies is concerned, distribution is the decisive phase. Distribution, as Marx notes (1859: 201), has a twofold aspect: on the one hand it is a distribution of products between people and on the other hand it is a distribution of people among the means of production. The latter is crucial because it defines a particular mode of reproduction within the general framework. This argument is developed further below.

Lévi-Strauss (1955: 70) claims that he rarely broaches a new sociological problem without first stimulating his thought by rereading Marx's *Critique of Political Economy*. However, this claim is difficult to reconcile with the concept of reproduction that is implicit in *The Elementary Structures of Kinship*. For Lévi-Strauss economics is about the exchange of things. Exchange is the supreme category for him and he treats it as if it were independent of production, consumption and distribution. Kinship too is conceptualized as a form of exchange by Lévi-Strauss and he relates it to the economy in the following way:

> The rules of kinship and marriage serve to ensure the circulation of women between groups, just as economic rules serve to ensure the circulation of goods and services, and linguistic rules the circulation of messages. These three forms of communication are also forms of exchange which are obviously interrelated (because marriage relations are associated with economic prestations, and language comes into play at all levels).
>
> (Lévi-Strauss 1963: 83)

This conception of the economy owes more to the linguist Saussure than to Marx. Furthermore, from his explicit statements on the economy in *Elementary Structures* it would seem that his concept of the economy is closer to that of the contemporary economists rather than Marx. Scarcity, and not reproduction, defines the general framework used by mainstream economists and Lévi-Strauss's statement that ' "The system of the scarce product" constitutes an extremely general model' (1949: 32) suggests an attachment to that framework. In any case it would account for his error in seeing exchange as the decisive category independent of production. Scarcity can be treated as a special case of reproduction but the opposite is not true; and therefore a framework of analysis that focuses on scarcity cannot analyse reproduction because, by definition, a scarce thing is non-reproducible. However, Lévi-Strauss's perspective has enabled him to make an important contribution: the conception of marriage as an exchange of female labour (1949: 38–9). This is the missing link in Marx's analysis of the concept 'consumption and consumptive production' and it needs to be grafted onto it.

Marriage is obviously a phase of the process of reproducing people and the concept 'consumption and consumptive production' can be developed by considering the following model of cross-cousin marriage of the type to be found in *Elementary Structures*:

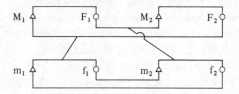

This model is based on the assumption that siblings cannot marry.[4] If the assumption that people eat wheat is added to it the model can be rearranged in the following way:

$$\text{wheat} + M_1 + F_2 \rightarrow m_1 + f_1 \quad \text{household 1}$$
$$\text{wheat} + M_2 + F_1 \rightarrow m_2 + f_2 \quad \text{household 2}$$

This is a model of the production of people by means of people and things and is the mirror of the concept 'production and productive consumption' that we have been searching for. In household 1 the adults consume wheat and engage in the domestic labour of producing children. For reproduction to continue household 1 must exchange daughters or sons with household 2. The same applies for household 2. At this general level of analysis it cannot be said *a priori* that it must be women who are exchanged. From a logical point of view either men or women can be exchanged. The proposition that women are exchanged is an empirical observation that needs to be explained. Marx's proposition that production is the decisive phase has the same status.

The conclusion that emerges from this is not that kinship is something different from the economy but that kinship is part of the economy. It is wrong to think of the economy as simply the reproduction of things. It is also the reproduction of labour and, to the extent that kinship systems are about the relations of reproduction of labour, then kinship is part of the economy.

This suggested resolution to the conceptual problem posed by kinship enables a number of interesting hypotheses to be developed at a more concrete level of analysis. However, before introducing these it is useful to contrast Marx's conception of the economy with that of the mainstream economists' conception. This conception is quite different and because of it mainstream economists perceive social reality in an altogether different way.

Political economy and economics

The concept of the economy developed above differs greatly from the mainstream economists' conception of the economy and as Lévi-Strauss displays some fondness for the orthodox conception it is useful to briefly contrast the two approaches so that the methodological assumptions may be laid bare. This digression is necessary because archaeologists and anthropologists who employ the concept of the economy are forced to adopt one approach or the other, and the theoretical consequences of this choice are far reaching. The formalist versus substantivist versus Marxist debate in economic anthropology (see Dalton 1969; Gudeman 1978) has its origins in this choice. However those debates have to some extent failed to get to the real issues because they have not arrived at the crux of the matter which is the 'paradigm shift' that occurred in economic thought around 1870.

Marx's approach to the economy belongs to a tradition of thought that can be called 'political economy'. His theory of capitalism is set within a general framework, the broad outlines of which were first sketched by Quesnay (1759) and developed by Smith (1776) and Ricardo (1817). There are important differences between the theories of these writers but these pale into insignificance when their theories are compared with the post-1870 theories of the economy. These post-1870 theories belong to a completely different paradigm in that different concepts and methods are used. These differences are reflected in a different terminology and a different name for the subject. Jevons (1871) was one of the pioneers of this new approach and he suggested that the name of the subject be changed from 'political economy' to 'economics'. This suggestion was adopted.

The basic methodological differences between the two approaches can be reduced to three points. The first difference between political economy and economics relates to the social data of the analysis. This is a difference between 'society' and the 'individual'. For political economy the social relations between groups in the sphere of production constitutes the starting point. For example, the social data for Quesnay's model of seventeenth-century France were a three-class model consisting of the landlord class, the 'productive' class of agricultural workers, and a 'sterile' class of manufacturing workers; Ricardo, who did not share Quesnay's thesis about the 'sterile' nature of manufacturing labour, distinguished between the proprietors of land, the owners of capital, and the labourers; Marx had a similar starting point to Ricardo but laid more emphasis on the capitalist–worker relation. With the rise to dominance of economics the social data of the analysis ceased to be the social relations of production and became the psychological relations of consumption. The mental relation between an individual and finished goods became the starting point. The methodology of political economy is based on the assumption that society conditions the behaviour of the individual and that society is not the simple sum of its parts, in other words, that laws independent of people's wills govern their behaviour. The methodology of economics, on the other hand, holds that the individual is dominant and that society is nothing more than the sum of its parts. As one of the founders of this new school said, 'Society is not different from its component parts, it only establishes between these parts certain relations which are additional to the powers of the isolated man, and do not supersede them' (Hearn 1863: 5). This methodological shift meant that the analysis of the economy was no longer the study of people in specific historical settings but the study of the economic behaviour of a universal economic man.

The second difference concerns the theory of explanation. With political economy the hypothetico-deductive method of analysis is employed. The starting point is the concrete historical facts from which theoretical abstractions are made. Highly simplified models, based on highly restrictive assumptions, are constructed in order to capture the dominant and determinant features of the object of investigation. These restrictive assumptions are relaxed one by one in order to approach reality by the method of 'successive approximations'. The analysis proceeds in a logico-historical way so that, for example, barter exchange is analysed before exchange involv-

ing money and hunting and gathering is analysed before agriculture. Smith, for example, begins his *Wealth of Nations* (1776) with an analysis of price formation in a 'savage nation of hunters and fishers'. Progress is made within this paradigm by discarding theories that are based on false assumptions, or that have errors in the logic of the argument, and replacing them with alternative theories which are superior on these accounts. This is not the case with economics however. In the economics paradigm explanation is synonymous with prediction. A good theory is one that predicts well and it does not matter that this theory may be based on faulty assumptions or faulty logic. The methodology of the political economy paradigm, noted by Harry Johnson – an eminent member of the economics profession – 'rested on the belief that one can dispose of a theory by finding an error in its logic or lack of realism in its assumptions . . . That belief is false: the contemporary accepted methodology of positive economics maintains that one can falsify a theory only by falsifying its predictions' (Johnson 1974: 23). The central role given to prediction does not necessarily mean that economics is concerned only with the future. The ability to predict past historical events is also seen as a test of the explanatory adequacy of a theory.

The third basic difference between political economy and economics concerns the conception of the people–land relation. For economics the central fact of human existence is scarcity and this means that the economic problem is a problem of choice: the problem of the allocation of scarce resources between competing ends. For political economy, on the other hand, abundance rather than scarcity is nature's gift and the economic problem is the problem of the organization of the relations of reproduction of things and labour. Political economy does not deny that some scarcity exists in the form of rare statues, pictures, books, coins, and old wines, it merely argues that such things form a very small part of the mass of commodities daily exchanged in the market. 'By far the greatest part of those goods which are the objects of desire,' writes Ricardo, 'are procured by labour; and they may be multiplied . . . almost without any assignable limit, if we are disposed to bestow the labour necessary to obtain them' (Ricardo 1817: 12). This particular difference is brought out in the different approaches to the theory of rent. From the perspective of economics rent is a 'gift of nature'. But from the perspective of political economy, 'The labour of nature is paid, not because she does much, but because she does little. In proportion as she becomes niggardly in her gifts, she exacts a greater price for her work' (Ricardo 1817: 76).

These three fundamental differences in the methodology of political economy and economics generate numerous other differences in the theoretical models constructed within these frameworks. The concepts developed to describe a given phenomenon are instilled with different meanings even though the same word may be used. More often than not, however, different words are used. The central concept of political economy is the words 'commodity'. This refers to the social form that things and labour assume in certain historical settings. The central concept of economics, on the other hand, is the word 'good'. This term epitomizes the subjectivist and individualist approach that economics adopts. That thing is a 'good' from my perspective if I desire it and a 'bad' from your perspective if you do not desire it. Thus the term 'good' describes the mental relation that exists between a person and an object. The term 'commodity', on the other hand, epitomizes the objectivist approach of political economy. It refers to the relation that is established between things in certain historical settings. The word embodies the concept 'price' because it comes from *com*, meaning together, and *modus*, a measure.

Economics is the dominant paradigm today and it continues to hold sway despite attacks on its epistemological basis and the logic of its theoretical constructions (see Harcourt 1972). It is tempting to explain this in terms of the ideological function economics performs but such an explanation begs a large number of questions. The reasons for the rise to dominance of economics are complex and do not lend themselves to simple summary. In any case it must be remembered that economics and political economy are two different paradigms and therefore incommensurable. There is no commonly agreed set of criteria with which they may be compared and evaluated. This problem is a familiar one to philosophers of science (Feyerabend 1970) and in the last instance the choice of a paradigm is largely a matter of taste: one has to decide which approach produces theories with the greatest explanatory power.

Classifying societies

Given the general conceptual framework outlined above, the task is now to use this framework of analysis to generate hypotheses about particular economic systems. This requires, in the first instance, a mode of classifying the existing archaeological and anthropological data on different economic systems.

Perhaps the best known classification of economic systems is the technological classification that is produced as an answer to the question 'How is food produced?'. By sifting through the anthropological evidence it is possible to develop the following classification:

1 food hunter/gatherer
2 food producer using stone tools
3 food producer using bronze tools
4 food producer using iron tools
5 food producer using machinery

This list is unique among economic classifications because it is possible to confirm it with reference to archaeological data (Childe 1942: 30–2). Indeed, it was developed by archaeologists before any reliable anthropological data became available.

But, given the concept of the economy developed above, other more interesting classifications can be developed from the anthropological data. From the perspective of historical materialism a key variable is the distribution of the means of production and a different classification can be developed by posing the question 'How are the means of production distributed?'. This gives the following classification:

I   dual-clan/elder
II   phratry/elder
III   tribe/big-man
IV   nation/chief
V   confederacy/king
VI   slave/master
VII   serf/landlord
VIII share-cropper/landlord
IX   wage-labourer/capitalist

This list is a synthesis of the ideas of Morgan and Marx, and is a classification that Engels more or less developed in his *Origin of the Family* (1884). These different categories have been exhaustively defined by Marx and Morgan but it is useful to recall them briefly and to restate the logical basis of the classification.

Categories VI to IX are class relations and describe a relation of oppressor to oppressed. Categories I to V are clan relations and describe a relation of leader to led. Clan relations are logically prior to class relations because clan relations define a 'unity' of the producer with his means of production whereas class relations define a relation of 'separation'. Strathern's map of the clan boundaries among the Mbukl of highlands Papua New Guinea illustrate the concept of 'unity' (Strathern 1971: 41). Land is a condition for a clan's existence and among the Mbukl this unity is captured by the term *pukl*. This term refers to a physical root and also a kinship link and joining a clan implies making 'roots' with it (1972: 22). In a class-based society these roots are broken either partially or completely. For example a serf has possession of the land from which he obtains his subsistence but he does not own it. It is controlled by the landlord who gives it to him in exchange for labour. A wage-labourer on the other hand has neither possession nor ownership of his means of subsistence and is forced to offer his labour-power for sale on the market in order to survive. In England the enclosure movement was the process that brought about the final separation of workers from their means of production.

But what is the logical basis for ranking the different types of clan? The possession of lands in common is not the only defining characteristic of clans. There are many others of which the obligation not to marry within a clan is perhaps the most important (see Morgan 1877: 292–3). However it is not so much these characteristics as the level of superstructural complexity that defines the ranking. A confederacy is a group of nations, a nation is a group of tribes, a tribe is a group of phratries and a phratry is a pair of clans. A pair of clans is the irreducible minimum because one clan cannot be defined independently of another. These distinctions can be illustrated diagrammatically as shown opposite. These are simplifications but they enable actual systems to be classified. For example, the Australian Kariara tribe, described by Brown (1913), had a phratry structure: A and B constituted one moiety and C and D the other. A man from A married a woman from C and their children belonged to B, a man from C married a woman from A and their children belonged to D; likewise the men of groups B and D exchanged 'sisters' and their offspring belonged to groups A and C respectively.

The association of elders with dual-clans and phratries, big-men with tribes, chiefs with nations and kings with confederacies can be established empirically from the anthropological record from Australia, Melanesia, America and Africa respectively. The logical basis of this classification is not obvious though. While it may be possible to establish a logical ordering that goes elder—chief—king (e.g., a king is a supreme chief and a chief a supreme elder) it is difficult to fit big-men into the picture. Big-men differ from elders, chiefs and kings in that their status is achieved rather than acquired as a birthright. But there is a logical basis for this classification and this will become apparent after the next classification scheme has been considered.

A third classification of economic systems can be derived by asking 'What social form does exchange take?' This gives the following classification:

  a) restricted gift exchange of female labour, G1 . . G1
  b) generalized gift exchange of female labour and things, G1 . . G2 . . G1
  c) incremental gift exchange of things, G2 . . G2$'$
  d) direct gift exchange of things, G2 . . G3 . . G2
  e) direct commodity exchange (barter), C . . C
  f) circulation of commodities, C . . M . . C
  g) merchant capital, M . . C . . M$'$
  h) usurers' capital, M . . M$'$
  i) commodity exchange of wage-labour, M . . C . . M$'$
  j) interest-bearing capital, M . . M$'$

This framework is a synthesis and development of the ideas of Marx, Mauss and Lévi-Strauss on the theory of gifts and commodities.

Consider first of all the forms of commodity exchange, categories (e) to (j). An evolutionary theory of these forms is given in Marx's *Capital* (1867: Chapters 1—3) but what concerns us here is the logical basis for the classification. Barter is the simplest form of exchange and this comes first. It is useful to follow Marx and describe it by the shorthand formula C . . C, where C stands for commodity. Exchanges of this type presuppose that the transactors are in a state of reciprocal independence and that they treat each other as the owners of *alienable* objects (Marx 1867: 91). (Gift exchanges, by way of contrast, presuppose that the transactors are in a state of reciprocal dependence and that they treat each other as the possessors of inalienable objects.) The simple circulation of commodities is the next stage and this can be described by the formula C . . M . . C, where M stands for money. An intermediate stage is C . . C . . C and the transition is effected by one commodity — e.g., gold — becoming a measure of value. This transformation achieves the separation of sale C . . M from purchase M . . C. The simple circulation of commodities can be described as 'selling-in-order-to-buy' and is the logical precursor to transactions that involve 'buying-in-order-to-sell-at-a-profit', M . . C . . M$'$. Merchant capitalists buy cheap here, M . . C, to sell dear there, C . . M$'$, in order to make a profit M$'$ minus M. Trading in commodities is a logical precursor to trading in money. Usurers borrow and lend at interest and these transactions can be described by the formula M . . M$'$. Money up to now is commodity money — e.g., gold — and the next two transactions can be understood either as a transformation from commodity-money to symbolic-money, i.e., paper money, or as a transformation from the exchange of things to the exchange of labour. The emergence of labour-power as a commodity presupposes the complete separation of the producer from his means of production, stage IX in the previous classification.

The existence of these forms can be established by examining the economic history of Europe. But they are by no means historical relics. In the rural markets of contemporary India all these types continue to exist simultaneously. The poor farmer comes to the market with rice in order to exchange it for a chicken. If he can't barter it immediately he will first sell the rice for money and use the money to buy the chicken later. Rich merchants come to the market with imported commodities to sell at a profit and money lenders come with their rupees to lend.

Consider now the different forms of gift exchange. Marx believed that commodity exchange was the *only* form of exchange and that it had its origins in the barter exchange of things on the boundaries of clan-based societies (1867: 91). He erroneously believed that exchange did not exist within a clan-based society. The ethnographic data have proved him wrong. Mauss studied this data and came to the conclusion that 'Economic evolution has not gone from barter to sale and from cash to credit. Barter arose from the system of gifts given and received on credit, simplified by drawing together the moments of time which had previously been distinct' (1925: 35). Mauss developed a three-stage theory of the evolution of commodity exchange. The first stage was' "total prestation" —

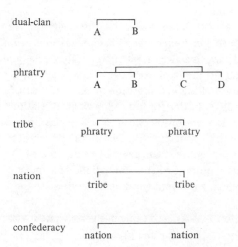

prestation between clan and clan in which individuals and groups exchange everything between them' (1925: 68). By 'everything' he means 'courtesies, entertainments, ritual, military assistance, *women*, children, dances, and feasts' (1925: 3, emphasis added). The second stage was the gift-exchange of things and total prestation was the base from which this stage arose. The third stage was the commodity economy. Lévi-Strauss developed this analysis by concentrating on stage one and by conceptualizing women as the 'supreme gift'. He drew a distinction between restricted exchange and generalized exchange. 'The term "restricted exchange" includes any system which effectively or functionally divides the group into a certain number of pairs of exchange-units so that, for any one pair X−Y there is a reciprocal exchange relationship' (1949: 146). 'Alongside and beyond exchange in its restricted sense . . . there may be imagined, and there exists, a cycle which is less immediately discernible, precisely because it involves a more complex structure. It is to this that we give the name "generalised exchange" ' (1949: 233).

Lévi-Strauss's distinction between restricted exchange and generalized exchange is nothing more than a distinction between direct exchange and circulation, and as such it is analogous to Marx's distinction between C . . C and C . . M . . C. Writing G1 as the supreme gift and G2 as a lower-level gift (e.g., pigs), the distinction between restricted and generalized exchange becomes G1 . . G1 and G1 . . G2 . . G1. In the latter form of exchange 'a woman (G1) is replaced by a symbolic equivalent' (Lévi-Strauss 1949: 470).

Given these formulae it is now possible to demonstrate the logic of Mauss's argument that total prestation is the basis from which the gift exchange of things arose. Gift exchanges of the form G1 . . G2 . . G1 give rise to exchanges of the form G2 . . G2' where the latter is the formula for incremental gift exchange. This is because gifts are inalienable and their exchange creates a debt relation between the transactors that can only be eliminated by reversing the transaction. As Marilyn Strathern notes,

> In *moka*, pigs and shells are exchanged for each other, but ideally a reversal of the initial transaction should effect an eventual transfer of pigs for pigs and shells for shells. In the same way, while at each marriage bride-wealth is given for a woman, a second woman should ultimately be given in return for the first, and thus bride-wealth for a bridewealth.   (1972: 73)

An exchange of pigs for shells can likewise be written G2 . . G3 . . G2 and this gives rise to G3 . . G3' for the same reason. It should be noted that the numbers represent the rank a gift has. Thus G1 is the supreme gift, G2 is the second ranking gift, and so on. Women are always G1, shells are usually G2, pigs G3 and food G4, but there may be many sub-rankings within these rankings.

Three classifications have been defined so far: the first based on the level of technology, the second on the mode of distribution of the means of production and the third on the mode of exchange. These will be described hereafter as the *technology*, *distribution* and *exchange* classifications respectively.

These three classifications have so far been considered as independent of one another. But they are obviously interrelated and the question of that interrelationship can now be posed. For example, is there one connection between hunter-gatherers and restricted exchange?; between tribes and incremental gift exchange?; between wage-labour and machinery? Does technology determine distribution and exchange or is it the other way around?

When attempting to answer these questions it is useful to follow Childe (1956: 15) and to distinguish between 'chronological relations' and 'chorological relations'. The former is concerned with temporal connections between events and is the basis of evolutionary theories; the latter is concerned with spatial associations.

Consider first the chorological relations between technology, distribution and exchange. What associations can be hypothesized between a given level of technology, the mode of distribution and the mode of exchange? Table 1 attempts to summarize these and is a juxtaposition of the three classifications given above. In this form the chorological relations are the 'horizontal' associations between the three classifications; for example, hunter-gatherers with dual clans and restricted exchange. This procedure, then, generates a number of hypotheses that require further examination.[5] The most interesting from an anthropological point of view are the following:

> Proposition 1: restricted exchange is associated with hunting and gathering.

Table 1 *Chorological relations between technology, distribution and exchange*

A Technology (How is food produced?)	B Distribution (How are the means of production distributed?)		C Exchange (What form does exchange take?)
1 hunter-gatherer	I	clan/elder	a) G1 . . G1
	II	phratry/elder	
2 stone	III	tribe/big-man	b) G1 . . G2 . . G1
			c) G2 . . G2'
	IV	nation/chief	d) G2 . . G3 . . G2
			e) C . . C
3 bronze	V	confederacy/ king	f) C . . M . . C
4 iron	VI	slave/master	g) M . . C . . M'
	VII	serf/landlord	h) M . . M'
	VIII	share-cropper/ landlord	
5 machinery	IX	wage-labourer/ capitalist	i) M . . C . . M'
			j) M . . M'

Proposition 2: restricted exchange is associated with dual-clan organization, the dominance of elders and the absence of incremental gift exchange.

Proposition 3: incremental gift exchange presupposes bridewealth transactions but the reverse is not necessarily true.

Proposition 4: incremental gift exchange is associated with tribal organization and big-manship.

It is beyond the scope of this article to consider the empirical evidence for and against these propositions. What follows is an attempt to suggest in general terms the probable strengths and weaknesses of each.

Proposition 1 appears to be quite strong if one takes a long view of the data. For example, the Australian aborigines were hunters and gatherers and they are used as the classic illustration of restricted exchange. Additional evidence in favour of it comes from the Sepik District of Papua New Guinea. Here restricted exchange predominates and economic activity 'bears a much closer resemblance to the life of hunters and gatherers' (Gell 1975: 18). But with a closer look at the data the proposition begins to weaken. There are many cases in Papua New Guinea and elsewhere where restricted exchange is used by shifting agriculturalists.

The other propositions seem much stronger. Data from the Sepik district (e.g., Gell 1975; Mead 1937; Thurnwald 1916; Tuzin 1976) support Proposition 2; data from the highlands of Papua New Guinea (Pospisil 1963; Salisbury 1962; Strathern 1971) support Proposition 3; and data from the Milne Bay area (Leach and Leach 1983) support Propositions 3 and 4. Proposition 3 helps us understand the elder/big-man/chief problem referred to above. Big-men acquire their status from success at playing the incremental gift exchange 'game'. A necessary (but not sufficient) condition for this to arise is bridewealth exchanges G1 . . G2 . . G1. Restricted exchange precludes this and hence precludes big-men. Another necessary condition is the absence of chiefs. Thus it is possible for bridewealth to be associated with chiefs and the absence of incremental gift exchange as is the case in many parts of Africa.

Consider now the chronological associations that can be hypothesized to exist between the technological, distribution and exchange classifications. These are generated by reading down the columns of Table 1. For example, it is possible to hypothesize that a restricted gift exchange economy evolved into a generalized gift exchange economy, which in turn evolved into a commodity economy. Engels, Morgan, Mauss and Lévi-Strauss have all shown a preference to advance propositions of this kind over the chorological kind mentioned above. In other words, they have used contemporary anthropological data to develop evolutionary theories of European prehistory.

This method has for many years been subjected to much criticism by the anthropological establishment. Fortes (1969), for example, follows Radcliffe-Brown in calling it 'conjectural history' and considers the method completely unsound. There

is indeed much merit in his argument. The societies studied by anthropologists are contemporary societies, not 'living fossils' from some mythical stage of European prehistory. The mistake made by Morgan *et al.* was to confuse the 'logical history' (Meek 1967) of socioeconomic forms with the evolutionary theories of these forms. A logical history is simply a convenient way of classifying wherein simple forms are classified as logically prior to more complex forms. For example, restricted exchange can be classified as logically prior to generalized exchange in the same way that barter can be classified as prior to more complicated forms of commodity exchange that use money. To employ this method of classification as a prelude to analysis is one thing; to say that it is then an evolutionary theory is quite another. It need not have anything to do with evolutionary theories as the chorological analysis above illustrates. The anthropological data on colonized countries such as Papua New Guinea present the analyst with a confusing array of economic forms. A 'logical history' is just one way of classifying these forms prior to an analysis that may be concerned only with a single point in time.

Notwithstanding the above, a 'logical history' classification can be used as the basis of an evolutionary theory. However, the jump from one to the other is a big one and it presupposes many conditions. For example, acceptance of Mauss's (1925: 35, 68) proposition that gift exchange economies preceded commodity economies, and that restricted exchange preceded generalized exchange presupposes (a) the empirical validity of chronological relations in the technological classification, i.e., that a stone age preceded a bronze age, which preceded an iron age etc., and (b) the empirical validity of the chorological relations between the technology, distribution and exchange. If these conditions can be shown to hold then the hypothesis that gift exchange precedes commodity exchange can be entertained. However, while the archaeological evidence seems to be able to confirm the chronological relations of (a), it has so far told us little about the chorological relations of (b). While the anthropological evidence can perhaps tell us much more about the latter, it is precisely this link between technology and other economic forms on which the anthropological evidence is weakest. Much more empirically based theoretical work is needed on the link between technology, distribution and exchange over the ages. This, of course, is the domain of the archaeologist.

Conclusion

What conclusion is the archaeologist to draw from this discussion? My aim has been to examine some of the ideas of Marx and Lévi-Strauss on kinship and the economy in the light of the anthropological evidence. I have tried to expose some of the weaknesses in their theories and also to reveal some of their strengths when compared to other conceptions of the economy, particularly that used by mainstream economists. Every society has an economy and a kinship system and every analyst, whether they be archaeologist, anthropologist or sociologist, must employ some conception of these categories. If I have done anything then it is to show that these categories are highly problematical and must be used with due caution. Both for Marx and for orthodox economists, the concept of the economy is something more than just a description of technological processes. However, these conceptions are very different and the conceptual framework used will determine to a large extent how social reality is perceived. The ultimate aim of building conceptual frameworks and classificatory systems is to develop theories that can explain human behaviour. Thus the ultimate test of the superiority of one conceptual approach over the other is whether or not it can produce theories that have greater explanatory power. The usefulness of historical materialism to archaeologists will be determined by its ability to meet this test.

Notes

1 The opposite is also true. Archaeologists have access to a time depth that anthropologists do not; this enables them to generate hypotheses which would not occur to an anthropologist or economist.

2 For an elaboration of these different positions see the excellent summary in Copans and Seddon (1978).

3 In *Capital* Volume 1 Marx devotes a lot of space to the elaboration of these social preconditions. See, in particular, the last part of his book dealing with 'primitive accumulation'.

4 Lévi-Strauss (1949) did not treat this as an assumption but as something more in the nature of a biological fact because of the apparent universality of the incest taboo. Hopkins (1980), among others, has criticized him for this on the basis of evidence of the existence of brother-sister marriage in Roman Egypt. This model is based on an additional assumption that marriage is necessary for biological reproduction. Leach (1970) has criticized Lévi-Strauss for confusing sex and marriage in this way. However, if these points are stated as assumptions rather than social facts they can be justified because they permit the clarification of certain relations without the introduction of unnecessary complexity.

5 Note that because of the logical bases for each classification these hypotheses are 'hierarchical', e.g., a barter economy precludes money lending but a money economy may include barter as a subordinate activity. See also Proposition 3 below.

Bibliography

Brown, A.R. 1913. Three tribes of Western Australia. *Journal of the Royal Anthropological Institute* 43 (January to June, 1913): 143–94.

Childe, V.G. 1942. *What Happened in History*. Harmondsworth: Pelican.

1946. Archaeology and anthropology. *Southwestern Journal of Anthropology* 2 (3): 243–51.

1956. *Piecing Together the Past*. London: Routledge and Kegan Paul.

Clarke, D.L. 1968. *Analytical Archaeology*. London: Methuen.

Copans, J. and D. Seddon, 1978. Marxism and anthropology: a preliminary survey. In D. Seddon (ed.), *Relations of Production: Marxist Approaches to Economic Anthropology*, pp. 1–46. London: Frank Cass.

Dalton, G. 1969. Theoretical issues in economic anthropology. *Current Anthropology* 10 (1): 63–102.

Engels, F. 1884. *The Origin of the Family, Private Property and the State*. Reprinted in the Selected Works of Karl Marx and Frederick Engels. Moscow: Progress Publishers, 1970.

Feyerabend, P.K. 1970. Against method: outline of an anarchistic theory of knowledge. *Minnesota Studies in the Philosophy of Science*, Vol. 4. Minneapolis: University of Minnesota Press.

Fortes, M. 1969. *Kinship and the Social Order: The Legacy of Lewis Henry Morgan*. London: Routledge and Kegan Paul.

Gell, A. 1975. *Metamorphosis of the Cassowaries: Umeda Society, Language and Ritual*. London: Athlone Press.

Godelier, M. 1966. *Rationality and Irrationality in Economics*. London: New Left Books, 1972.

Gould, R.A. 1980. *Living Archaeology*. Cambridge: Cambridge University Press.

Gudeman, S. 1978. Anthropological economics: the question of distribution. *Annual Review of Anthropology* 7: 347–79.

Harcourt, G.C. 1972. *Some Cambridge Controversies in the Theory of Capital*. Cambridge: Cambridge University Press.

Hearn, W.E. 1863. *Plutology, or the Theory of the Efforts to Satisfy Human Wants*. Melbourne: Robertson.

Hopkins, K. 1980. Brother–sister marriage in Roman Egypt. *Comparative Studies in Society and History* 22 (3): 303–54.

Jevons, W.S. 1871. *The Theory of Political Economy*. 4th ed. London: Macmillan, 1931.

Johnson, H.G. 1974. The current and prospective state of economics. *Australian Economic Papers* 13 (22): 1–27.

Leach, E.R. 1970. *Lévi-Strauss*. London: Fontana, 1974.

Leach, E.R. and J.W. Leach (eds.) 1983. *The Kula*. Cambridge: Cambridge University Press.

Lévi-Strauss, C. 1949. *The Elementary Structures of Kinship*. London: Eyre and Spottiswoode, 1969.

1955. *Tristes Tropiques*. Harmondsworth: Penguin.

1963. *Structural Anthropology*. London: Allen Lane, 1968.

Marx, K. 1859. *A Contribution to the Critique of Political Economy*. Edited with an Introduction by Maurice Dobb. Moscow: Progress Publishers, 1970.

1867. *Capital*. Vol. 1: *A Critical Analysis of Capitalist Production*. Moscow: Progress Publishers, 1971.

1893. *Capital*. Vol. 2. Moscow: Progress Publishers, 1971.

1894. *Capital*. Vol. 3: *A Critique of Political Economy*. Moscow: Progress Publishers, 1971.

Mauss, M. 1925. *The Gift*. London: Routledge and Kegan Paul, 1974.

Mead, M. 1937. *Cooperation and Competition Among Primitive Peoples*. New York: McGraw.

Meek, R.L. 1967. *Economics and Ideology and Other Essays*. London: Chapman.

Meillassoux, C. 1960. Essai d'interprétation du phénomène économique dans les sociétés traditionelles d'autosubsistence. *Cahiers d'Etudes Africaines* 4: 38–67.

Morgan, L.H. 1871. *Systems of Consanguinity and Affinity of the Human Family*. Washington: Smithsonian Institution.

1877. *Ancient Society*. London: Macmillan.

Pospisil, L. 1963. *Kapauku Papuan Economy*. New Haven: *Yale University Publications in Anthropology* 67.

Quesnay, F. 1759. The 'tableau economique'. In R. Meek (ed.), *The Economics of Physiocracy*, pp. 108–202. London: George Allen, 1962.

Rey, P.-P. 1971. *Colonialisme, néo-colonialisme et transition au capitalisme: exemple de la 'Comilog' au Congo-Brazzaville*. Paris: Maspero.

Ricardo, D. 1817. *On the Principles of Political Economy and Taxation*. Vol. 1. In *The Works and Correspondence of David Ricardo*. Edited by P. Sraffa with the collaboration of M.H. Dobb 1951–81. Cambridge: Cambridge University Press.

Salisbury, R.F. 1962. *From Stone to Steel*. Cambridge: Cambridge University Press.

Smith, A. 1776. *An Inquiry into the Nature and Causes of the Wealth of Nations*. London: Everyman's Library, 1970.

Strathern, A.J. 1971. *The Rope of Moka*. Cambridge: Cambridge University Press.

1972. *One Father One Blood: Descent and Group Structure Among the Melpa People*. Canberra: ANU Press.

Strathern, M. 1972. *Women in Between: Female Roles in a Male World, Mount Hagen, New Guinea*. London and New York: Seminar Press.

Terray, E. 1972. *Marxism and 'Primitive' Societies*. New York: Monthly Review Press.

Thurnwald, R. 1916. Banaro society. Social organisation and kinship system of a tribe in the interior of New Guinea. *Memoirs of the American Anthropological Association* 3 (4): 251–391.

Trigger, B.G. 1980. *Gordon Childe: Revolutions in Archaeology*. London: Thames and Hudson.

Tuzin, D.F. 1976. *The Ilahita Arapesh*. Los Angeles: UCLA Press.

Young, M.W. 1971. *Fighting with Food: Leadership, Values and Social Control in a Massim Society*. Cambridge: Cambridge University Press.

Chapter 3

**The notion of craft
specialization and its
representation in the
archaeological record
of early states in the
Turanian Basin**
Maurizio Tosi

Introduction

Craft specialization has long been recognized by Marxists
and non-Marxists as a factor of significant weight in the development of complex societies. As a result of their strong historical connections to the labour movement, Marxists feel in
some way emotionally tied to this particular aspect, but in the
field of archaeology their specific contributions to the question have not been particularly remarkable beyond the extent
of introductory pronouncements. Whatever their political
orientation, archaeologists have used their data more to reconstruct manufacturing techniques than forms of labour organization within the productive forces. The important contribution of Semenov (1957) to the reconstruction of early work
methods from the systematic analysis of wear traces on tools
was explicitly a Marxist-oriented study, but it has remained so
far the only contribution in this direction in the whole of
Soviet archaeology, which has otherwise been more oriented
toward culture-historical strategies of interpretation. The step
from this level of analytical taxonomy to the evaluation of the
social organization of work will require the integration of
further classes of data in a framework of definitions more in
accord with the archaeological record.

The importance of craft production to the rise of early
states in the Middle East was most explicitly stated by Childe
in many of his writings on social evolution (see in particular
Childe 1934; 1942). His main assumption was that a further

division of labour had fostered an increase in population
density and led to the birth of cities as centres of industry and
trade. The population of these centres would have been different from that of any settlement preceding them, because it
was primarily composed of specialists (1950: 5—7). In more
recent years these views have been considered by many to be
unsound because they overlook the fact that any significant
increase in population has to be based on a growth in agricultural productivity, while craft specialists and the production
of commodities in general would have accounted for a minimal
fraction of the system (Trigger 1980: 74—5). So far, archaeologists have not been able to evaluate the relationship of
these two aspects of production nor the actual role of commodity production in the development of complex societies,
since we have not made adequate use of the imposing but disparate archaeological evidence collected at an increasing rate
from all regions of the world.

In my opinion three new classes of information should
be integrated with the traditional artifactual evidence: settlement pattern, information-recording devices, and biological
and physico-chemical analysis. An attempt is made in this
paper to bring the last two of these into a conceptual framework that might allow future correlation with locational
studies of settlement hierarchy. A preliminary test is applied
to protohistoric sites in eastern Iran and southern Central Asia,
mostly excavated in recent years, in order to encourage dis-

cussion of a central aspect in Marx's analyses of the mechanisms of capital formation. Whether the reorganization of commodity production was also relevant to the emergence of primary states remains an open question, but 'Marxist archaeologists', whatever we mean by such an ambiguous term, can hardly avoid confronting it.

Formulation of categories and testing procedures

In discussing the organization of material production, degree of craft specialization is best determined as variability of output per capita for a given product within the population sampled. This variability can be spatial and/or temporal. At least five parameters are involved: (1) population; (2) kind of commodity; (3) output of commodity; (4) time range; (5) spatial distribution. Rarely are these parameters directly available from the archaeological record. For our particular example we can claim control of only two of the five. Differences in the spatial distribution of different manufacturing processes becomes the data base for ranking different archaeological contexts in either diachronic or synchronic perspective. Variability over time will remain uncontrolled unless exceptional conditions of deposition and preservation occur, or unless we are dealing with the processing of strictly seasonal resources. To conform with the archaeological evidence, our operational definition of craft specialization and our criteria for classification should be as context-free as possible.

The investigation procedure is centred on a two-part evaluation of archaeological data, first viewed in terms of their spatial distribution and then as indicators of various crafts as shown in their manufacturing stages. Our index of the scale of craft production in terms of labour allocation is derived from a presence/absence matrix of various classes of manufacturing indicators. The analysis is extended by taking into account three locational attributes:

1. Relative proportion of site covered by archaeological indicators of craft production.
2. Relative concentration of craft indicators per unit area.
3. Degree of spatial co-occurrence of different processing activities.

Per capita corrections are estimated on the assumption that a given unit of space within the settlement represents a given unit of population (cf. Kramer 1980). The assumption of uniform population density is of course questionable; nevertheless in the absence of data on its variability we attempt a preliminary analysis to be corrected eventually by more exact population data. Six main categories of increasingly complex forms of labour allocation are used in order to examine the growth of craft specialization as a mechanism of class society. The distribution of archaeological indicators, recorded from both surface and excavation data, can be evaluated against this taxonomic ordering. The same body of data (artifacts and biological remains) will then be organized to provide information on the processing of matter, according to the kind of commodities produced, in order to evaluate the other axis of

variability. Manufacturing techniques will have to be reconstructed in their historical context to determine how labour was used within the different settlement units of the territory considered. The first positive outcome of this strategy will be the organizing of the available array of physico-chemical and biological data for the purpose of testing palaeoeconomic hypotheses.

Types of labour allocation

We may rule out as purely hypothetical an economy embodied in a society without any form of labour division and so for the purpose of this paper the minimal unit of observation in the allocation of labour forces is taken to be the household (Fig. 1.1). Indicators of craft production are present in each dwelling unit or its dependent surroundings, with little variability in spatial patterning suggesting that little or no labour was allocated to craft production outside immediate control of the *household* (cf. Suckling 1976: 107).

Fig. 1. Main types of craft allocation in relation to settlement system.

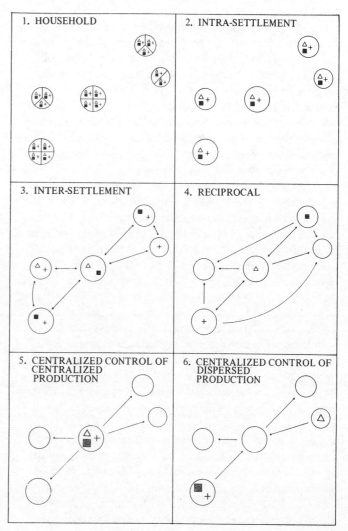

As the first level in differential allocation of labour we consider *intra-settlement* craft specialization (Fig. 1.2), characterized by the distribution of archaeological indicators for one or more crafts in a single or small number of activity areas. More complex is *inter-settlement* specialization, where degree of differentiation between settlements reflects larger volumes of local exchange and higher economic integration over a larger territory (Fig. 1.3). Further degrees of craft specialization at a subregional level might develop this inter-settlement form of allocation into an interdependent *system* with functionally centralized and physically dispersed commodity production (Fig. 1.4). In both cases the archaeological indicators will be found at only a few sites. Their restricted distribution might be correlated with sources of raw materials or good agricultural soils supporting inferences about proximity of resources and transport optimization in the development of interdependence between settlements. Our reconstruction of these patterns of labour allocation might be severely limited by our poor control over chronology. Considering that proximity of natural resources provides only a partial explanation for centralization, it can be expected that certain craft activities were shifted over a short period of time from one site to another.

Centralized craft production consists of two main forms of labour allocation: the more frequent case which shows centralized control combined with physical concentration of workshops in the hegemonic settlements (Fig. 1.5) and the other where centralized control governs the output distribution from physically dispersed production units (Fig. 1.6). Either form could be identified by the relative proportion of the site covered by archaeological indicators of craft production (locational attribute 1) and relative concentration of craft indicators per unit area (attribute 2).

Such a simplified outline of labour allocation can serve as a general scheme of classification, but for the purpose of our analysis it might present critical shortcomings. The most immediate source of sampling bias is that all crafts are treated as compact entities, although they are in fact aggregates of manufacturing operations not necessarily occurring in close proximity in time and space. For most commodities the different stages of the production process are dispersed in different places to respond to either economic or political factors of optimization. This is to be expected in every system and should be taken into account, in particular to evaluate the impact of elite control over labour organization for commodity production. Spatial dispersion of craft production processes could increase with centralized control over the production system as a whole as an aspect of economic integration. Degree of dispersion provides a further axis of variability to assess integration and centralization in emerging complex systems. One way to examine this archaeologically would be to establish the ratio of semi-finished to finished commodities among the final products found in particular activity areas. The production of each commodity can be described as a series of historically selected operations or

stages. These minimal units of observation need to be established for each craft according to the manufacturing process and the techniques adopted in a given cultural context. For this purpose we shall use manufacturing stages as basic entities in the explanation of commodity production.

Types of activity areas

An activity area is a *place where labour is allocated for performance of one or more stages of manufacture*. Organizational complexity in craft production will be evaluated in terms of the size of activity areas and the number of manufacturing stages performed in close spatial proximity.[1] This takes into account only one aspect of centralization and elite control, but one better represented in the archaeological record.

Four types of activity areas can be defined:
1 *Atelier*: small activity area with few facilities used only for a limited number of manufacturing stages of a single craft, with a low per capita output of commodities. Typical ateliers would be unlikely to exceed one or two per cent of small sites.
2 *Workshop*: small activity area, covering a significant proportion of a small site, where a broad spectrum of manufacturing stages was performed together.
3 *Factory*: large activity area, being used for only a few stages of a single commodity production, with extensive facilities.
4 *Craft quarter*: large activity area, with marked concentration of facilities around which different crafts were performed in close proximity, with high yields of presumed per capita production. Typical craft quarters would occupy a significant percentage of large sites (10–25%).

We should not expect such categories of labour allocation to be mutually exclusive, as alternative forms of craft production have clearly coexisted in certain historical periods. Growth of complexity in the organization of craft production may well be associated with increasing hierarchical control over the specialized sectors of the production system. Archaeological data should shed light on the relations between elite and craft organization which, as has been suggested, form a focal point in the emergence of early class-divided societies.

Types of archaeological indicators

As products of human activity, artifacts store information on material and processing. Determination of resource allocation and reconstruction of the technology required by their transformation into commodities have long been primary objects of archaeological research. This information can be applied systematically to the study of early labour organization provided that specific functional definitions are established for archaeological finds as indicators of craft production, to link them directly to spatial units as well as in relation to indicators of subsistence or other important activities. We propose to group these archaeological indicators for craft production in the following six classes:

1. Facilities (FCL): Fixed installations built for processing any raw material (e.g. pottery kilns, copper smelting furnaces, etc.).
2. Tools for manufacture (TFM): Movable artifacts made or adjusted to produce other commodities (e.g. potters' wheels, casting moulds, bone awls or reprocessed wasters such as potsherds rounded and pierced for yarn spinning).
3. Residues (RSD): Nonutilized remains after processing of commodities, including wasters, lithic debitage, defective products and broken sections of certain tools.
4. Semifinished products (SFP): Masses of raw material prepared in convenient form for further processing (e.g. copper ingots, flint blocks or unexhausted cores, rough-hewn timber, etc.).
5. Stocked and unworn products (SUP): Supplies of finished commodities held in reserve, awaiting distribution with no deterioration from use and transport.
6. Materials for recycling (MFR): Worn or fragmented end-products useless for further processing. These are strongly context-dependent. The available examples for our particular case are copper rolled knife blades or split lapis lazuli beads stocked in jars.

In establishing location and size of craft activity the six classes rank at different levels of reliability. While density of facilities or concentrations of tools and residues provide a direct measure of craftwork intensity, the presence of stocked or recyclable material is of low interpretive significance, especially in instances of isolated occurrence. In general, identification of activity areas based on the spatial co-occurrence of several classes of indicators would be more reliable than scatters of items from a single class.

These archaeological indicators also provide a conceptual device for classification and ranking of physical manifestations of human labour. *Facilities* and *tools* are the clearest indicators of the forces of production developed in the historical context under investigation. To increase the reliability of the archaeological record for palaeoeconomic reconstruction, and consequently its significance for any Marxist approach, further classification might consider such variables as energy cost, collective versus individual requirements for workload, social utilization, local or exotic origin of raw materials used in production, etc.

Control of commodity production

Craft activity will be evaluated by further grouping the available data in terms of two variables: classes of archaeological indicators and kinds of commodities produced. Artifactual finds represent goods that at one time were used within the site under observation. Technology is the process of making and using artifacts as material outputs of people's transformation of nature into commodities (Christensen 1977; Mitcham 1978: 251). Not all utilization results in fabrication.

In order to emphasize variability in craft allocation of an early production system, we need to concentrate on the manufacturing aspect of this phenomenological continuum. Given the expressed aim of this paper, commodities will be more loosely defined as the products of an individual manufacturing process. Whatever the morphological variability between individual artifacts may be, as long as they originate from the same production line, they will be considered as the same commodity.

Classification of commodities is context-dependent. It should be based on the grouping of all objects collected from the cultural complex under scrutiny according to attributes of use and material that determine the manufacturing stages, as well as the distances involved in the supply network (Jarrige and Tosi 1981: 127). As stated before, manufacturing stages are historically determined and may vary greatly in space and time, although end-products often turn out to be morphologically similar. Descriptive classifications of commodities based exclusively on the end-products might result in largely misleading conclusions. To evaluate differences in labour allocation and to allow correlation among sites and/or chronological phases, commodities will be primarily classified according to the following two parameters: (1) type of manufacture; (2) type of final product. The third commonly used variable, type of raw material, will be taken into account only as a secondary parameter in considering manufacturing processes.

So far the dominant tendency in archaeology has been to evaluate prehistoric exchange patterns in terms of supply-and-demand for specific raw materials, and a large proportion of archaeological studies on early trade aimed at pinpointing centres of production and consumption of a given commodity are founded on the identification of raw materials and *their sources*. Without detailing the critical problems in this approach (or more specifically the question of the reliability of the analytical procedures developed to ascertain source areas), it should be pointed out that it assumes similar value orientation to our own as regards sources and adopts our own categorization of physico-chemical or material properties in classifying the matter appropriated by these precapitalist systems. However specific the characterization of a raw material can be, it is not of great analytical use if prehistoric demand was not immediately oriented toward a particular resource, but towards a single attribute easily shared by several materials. This most directly applies to items of prestige value.

Demand for semi-precious stones might have been directed towards obtaining a colour signifying status while paying little attention to the material that provided it. Greater selectivity might arise as a later development, partly reinforcing some of the trends recognizable earlier on and partly for elite competition in monopolizing sources and workshops of higher standards. This might even apply to the rejection of certain commodities, as in the case of turquoise in Early Dynastic Mesopotamia (Tosi 1974a), a rejection which was extended to include all green stones as if they represented discredit. A relevant example of attribute selectivity for prehistoric eastern Iran is represented by indiscriminate use of two or three varieties of iron oxides from widely separated sources to produce yellow paints for polychrome vases (Reindell and Riederer 1978).

Each site can be represented by a list of commodities whose production would have required a finite number of manufacturing stages which can be established archaeologically. The relationship between the manufacturing stages reconstructed from the artifact inventory and those directly present in the archaeological record of the same site will establish the degree of dependence or control over the means of production and commodity flow at that site. This relationship can be expressed in a simple index by the following formula:

$$LCCP = \frac{X \ : Y}{X_1 : Y_1}$$

where:

LCCP = local community's control of commodity production

X = number of commodities used (= number of manufacturing processes required to produce them)

Y = number of manufacturing stages required for X commodities

X_1 = number of commodities processed according to archaeological indicators of craft

Y_1 = number of manufacturing stages documented by archaeological indicators

Centres with a broad span of control over production will exhibit index values approaching 1; sites producing commodities for external use will be identified by figures less than 1, while all indices above 1 will scale increasing dependence on external production. Modes of craft production and elite control as expressed by differences in labour allocation will be examined quantitatively, by comparing the LCCP index values to the rank-size ordering of the settlement system. The approach is interesting because it combines information on settlement organization and the dispersed body of physico-chemical and biological studies. It will require the processing of an imposing mass of data, but this is exactly what is needed to set future theory-building in palaeoeconomy on more solid ground.

Physical concentration of workshops (Fig. 1.5) will express indices approaching 1 only for the largest settlements of the system, as against high values for minor sites, representing low LCCP and marked dependence on the centre's production. The main implication will of course be the increasing control by the centre over rural surplus and the consequent fostering of further growth of commodity production in the hegemonic towns that is supposed to represent one of the most remarkable characters of 'urbanism' (Sachs 1966: 16; Johnson in press).

Physically dispersed allocations of centrally controlled craft production (Fig. 1.6) would represent a reverse ratio, exhibiting higher values for the largest settlement in the system and lower values for the small overspecialized centres. Finally, the relationship between rank-size scaling of settlement and LCCP as expressed by number of manufacturing stages can be illustrated by adapting Johnson's indices of relationship between population estimates and gross tonnage of merchant vessels (1980: 237–9, Figs. 3–4).

Outline of testing strategy

1 *Data recovery*: Basic information on labour allocation in heavily-deflated arid land environments is primarily derived from settlement surfaces (e.g. Redman and Watson 1970; Bulgarelli 1974). Residues of manufacturing processes, particularly those associated with kilns, furnaces and lithic manufacture, were discarded in great quantities over short periods of time. Since they were of no economic interest they would not have been removed for recycling and so their present distribution can be related to the total area of the site used in manufacture. Excavations not only provide supplementary evidence of low-residue manufacturing processes, but also ensure stratigraphic correlation among exposed activity areas. The two kinds of information are complementary and the lack of either one affects test reliability. Often, large-scale excavations have taken place long before research has been oriented toward surface analysis. Nevertheless data from earlier excavations can be reorganized as indicators of manufacturing stages (Table 1), while the surface pattern of residues can be chronologically seriated anew with small integrative trenches (Dyson *et al.* n.d.; Bulgarelli 1979).

2 *Identification of finds*: Archaeological remains are first treated as indicators of resources and processing techniques in order to establish what goods were produced and the stages of their manufacture.

3 *Determination of variability in spatial allocation*: Products and provenances are examined to show the distribution of manufacturing stages and the variability of labour allocation within the settlement system (Table 2). Relative area of craft production is established separately for surface evidence and excavated contexts in order to assess comparability of data. The reliability of context correlation should be related to functional similarity in the use of space (Costantini and Tosi 1975).

4 *Correlations*: Variability in craft allocation is compared to rank-size settlement patterns and related to spatial frequency of indicators of other important activities: information processing, administration, religion and ceremonial, marketing, etc. By developing indices of co-occurrence between manufacturing stages and discarded administrative devices (tablets, sealings, counters, etc.) (see Table 3, p. 47), the analysis might be extended to evaluate relations with allocation of bureaucratic control and information

processing (Fig. 12). The approach will then allow evaluation of the changing relationship between hierarchical organization and craft specialization in the growth of elite control over rural surplus.

Early craft quarters in the Turanian basin

The northern coast of the Gulf is marked by a compact series of mountain ridges, narrowing where the easternmost extensions of the Zagros merge in the Makran to link the Iranian heartland to the Indian subcontinent. Between Shiraz and the Indus plain this mountain range splits to form a northward loop, the Baluchistan highlands, carving in the Asian landmass a depression of some 1,700,000 sq. km which the mountains isolate from the influence of marine moisture. This mosaic of dry lowlands, encompassing the greater part of eastern Iran and the southern fringes of Central Asia, is the 'Turanian basin' (abbreviated to Turan) (Tosi 1977: 47–8).

In spite of proximity to the ocean the climate is an arid continental steppe where precipitation is too limited to play an important role in the vegetation cycle. Biotic systems and the material basis of human economy are ultimately governed by the snow stored over the winter months on the highest elevations draining into the basin: the Hindukush to the east, the Elburz and Kopet Dagh to the north (Fig. 2). Most of the meltwater is dispersed through countless streams intersecting the mountains in narrow valleys and breaking up into small deltaic fans a few kilometres after they enter the lowland basins. The volume of water captured by each stream is insufficient to penetrate these depressions to any great depth. The only exceptions originate in the Hindu Kush massif; the northern watershed is drained by the Tedžen and Murghab into the Karakum desert, meanwhile its eastern and southern runoff are captured around the Kuh-i Baba by the Hilmand and Arghandab. Their parallel courses merge at the end of the Arachosian plain east of Kandahar and flow 350 km further west across the Registan desert to break into Sistan, the largest land-locked deltaic basin between Mesopotamia and Sind. At the end of its 1400 km course after great losses due to evaporation, the Hilmand fills the oval-shaped depression with the finest sediments and feeds three lakes having on average a total surface of 2000 sq. km (Meder 1977).

From a hydrological point of view each of these Turanian deltaic networks acts as a closed system, either isolated at the centre of the desert depression or aligned like comb teeth along the piedmont strips. Turan can be described as an archipelago of small green islands widely scattered in a sea of silt and gravel. Settlements have to be located either along the piedmont escarpment or along watercourses, but mostly crowd like bunches of grapes in the deltaic fans. The average distance between fans alongside the southern and northern piedmonts of the Hindu Kush and the Kopet Dagh is approximately 70 km, a full two-days' journey for a loaded camel caravan, whereas in the southern basins isolation is far more extreme: about 350 km separate Sistan from the

Arachosian plain to the east, and about 300 km the Lut oasis belt to the west. Water and soil scarcity define within very narrow limits size and distribution of agriculturally based settlements, and deviations from the rule require a very high energy cost to redirect the flow of water and resources. Episodically in the history of Turan labour investments and technological innovations, no matter how massive or radical they were, have been overwhelmed by sudden and total interruptions of water supply. At the origin of this discontinuity there is a paradox: the larger the delta and thus the settlement area, the more remote and unpredictable the water sources. Moreover, the large gaps of desert wastelands separating each riverine system from the next would have hindered until late in protohistoric times any attempt to integrate these isolated ecosystems into larger political entities.

These environmental constraints could hardly have been overcome before the introduction of mount animals for reducing transport time, leading to the possibility of increasing economic complementarity. Archaeological evidence suggests that only at the beginning of the second millennium BC were camels used in Turan to draw wheeled vehicles (Altyn depe c. 2000 BC. See Masson 1981: Table 30), after a period where they probably first contributed to meat and hair supply (Compagnoni and Tosi 1977). Horses appear shortly thereafter, at least on the northern (Kuzmina 1971) and eastern limits of Turan (at Pirak c. 1700 BC. Meadow, in Jarrige 1979: 334). In earlier periods Turanian societies probably operated their production systems under conditions of economic autarky, with little or no reliance upon foreign goods to meet their subsistence requirements. Unlike the vast and largely uniform alluvial plains of the Middle East, the deltaic oases in Turan were in close proximity to a variety of mineral and other natural resources, due to the wide spectrum of their environmental settings and the intense tectonic activity of the region (Costantini and Tosi 1977: map on p. 334; Jarrige and Tosi 1981: 118–20). If we define the *economic space* of a given population as a territory externally delimited by the radius of provenance of all biological and mineral resources exploited by its production system, full operability of the Turanian centres in the third millennium BC would have been physically possible within a radius of 50 to 250 km.

The problem at hand is to attempt a reconstruction of the relations of production developed in these closed systems, from the latter part of the fourth millennium through the whole of the third millennium BC. The archaeological evidence suggests that after 3200 BC almost every Turanian territory underwent a steady economic growth that culminated around 2500 BC, when hegemonic centres in each system reached their maximum expansion and manifested forms of increasing hierarchical complexity (Masson 1968; Tosi 1977). To understand the particular economic form developed in Turan during the third millennium BC craft specialization can be examined in detail as an important aspect of elite control over the production system, directly related to the degree of centralization in a settlement system. No textual or historical data are avail-

Fig. 2. The Turanian Basin and the main centres of the fourth and third millennia BC.

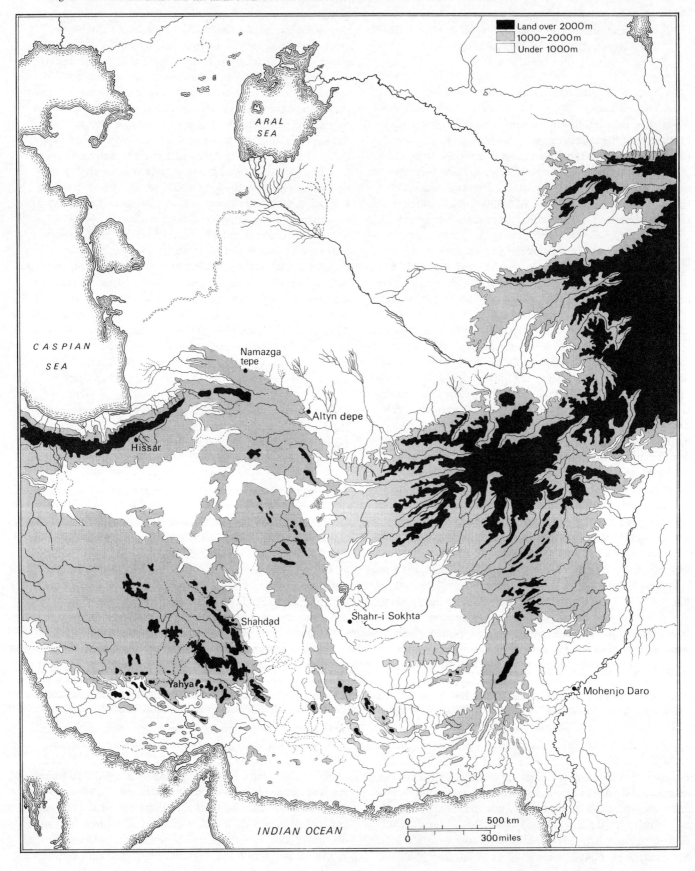

Land over 2000m
1000–2000m
Under 1000m

ARAL SEA

CASPIAN SEA

Namazga tepe

Altyn depe

Hissar

Shahdad

Shahr-i Sokhta

Yahya

Mohenjo Daro

INDIAN OCEAN

500 km
300 miles

able so far, and all the relevant information will be derived from the archaeological record.

Prehistoric research in the area was expanded at the end of the sixties, both in Soviet Central Asia (Masson and Sarianidi 1972; Gupta 1979; Kohl 1981) and in eastern Iran (Lamberg-Karlovsky and Tosi 1973). Four prehistoric sites have produced information relevant to the evaluation of variability in the spatial allocation of craft production in Turan during the third millennium BC: Tepe Hissar, Shahdad and Shahr-i Sokhta in eastern Iran and Altyn depe in southern Turkmenia (Fig. 3). The following is a brief description to serve as introduction to those unacquainted with the region:

Tepe Hissar: A group of low dissected Bronze-age mounds rising on top of a buried Chalcolithic site esti-

mated to be 12 ha. in extent, at the southern outskirts of Damghan, in northeastern Iran. Occupation extends from the mid fifth to early second millennium BC. Excavations in the early 1930s produced a rich documentation of its material culture, the first to be documented for northern Iran, mainly through extensive exposures of architectural structures and the recovery of over 1500 graves. Surface survey was initiated in 1972 for selective recovery of the lithic industry and a lapis lazuli processing area on the southeastern section of the central mound was detected (Bulgarelli 1974). In 1976 reconnaissance was completed within the scope of a broader restudy of the whole site and the most representative activity areas (lapis lazuli, copper, pottery) were

Fig. 3. Location and type of activity areas in different Turanian centres. Relative proportions are measured on standardized sizes of settlement area.

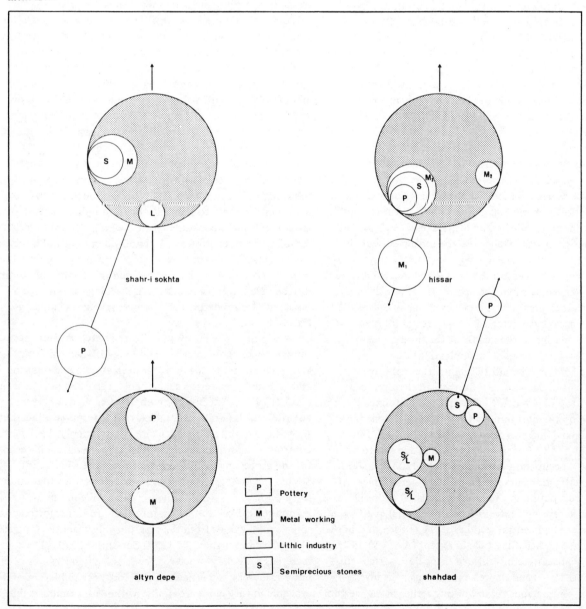

shahr-i sokhta

hissar

P   Pottery

M   Metal working

L   Lithic industry

S   Semiprecious stones

altyn depe

shahdad

chronologically seriated by small test-trenches (Dyson *et al.* n.d.; Bulgarelli 1979). In spite of its relatively small size, Hissar was extensively involved in craft production, with close to a quarter of its surface area covered by residues (Fig. 4).

Altyn depe: An even, round mound of approximately 26 ha., rising on the Meana-Caaca inter-riverine silt plain, an embayment of the northern Kopet Dagh at its eastern-most section in southern Turkmenia, with early Chalco-lithic to Middle Bronze-age continuous occupation (c. 4500–1700 BC). A long research programme directed by V.M. Masson (1965–80) has revealed the urban character of the site, at least for the latter part of the third millennium BC (period Namazga V), with monu-mental architecture, fortification walls, richly furnished elite burials and increasing allocation of space to craft activities (Masson 1981, incorporating earlier works). Pottery factories have been studied in great detail as part of an investigation of craft production (Masimov 1976; Masson 1978; 1981).

Shahdad: The most extensive protohistoric site in south-eastern Iran, lying on the eastern outskirts of the Shah-dad oasis at the edge of the Lut desert. The archae-ological area incorporates at least three different sites, because the prehistoric settlement shifted upstream between the fifth and the early second millennium BC (Meder 1979: 80–3; Fig. 27). Total area of the site is approximately 400 ha., although the third millennium BC site would not have exceeded 150 ha. Archaeological excavations began in 1969 and were first focused on the exploration of some 300 graves datable to the second half of the third millennium BC (Hakemi 1972). In later years research was extended to the settlement but the results have not yet been published. Surface survey was undertaken by Salvatori in 1977–8 and located different activity areas scattered throughout the site (Salvatori and Vidale in press). Test trenches at one of Salvatori's activity areas have detected a large area of kilns and furnaces, dating to the middle of the third millennium BC (I. Bayani personal communication).

Shahr-i Sokhta: The most prominent protohistoric settlement in Sistan. For the most part it is spread on the flat top of a dissected Plio-Pleistocene terrace located on the northern margin of a fossil deltaic fan of the Hilmand and was densely settled during the third millennium BC. In spite of its considerable size (c. 150 ha.), occupation lasted only from 3200 to 1800 BC, and investigations have so far failed to detect traces of earlier occupation in this severely deflated region. Exca-vations have been centred on two residential quarters in the eastern and central sections of the terrace, and in the large graveyard that is 21 ha. in extent (AA. VV. 1977). Activity areas were investigated using both surface sur-vey (Tosi 1976) and limited excavations. One investi-gated a semiprecious stone working atelier in the western section of the site (Tosi and Piperno 1973) and another a decentralized factory site for pottery manufacture at Tepe Rud-i Biyaban 2, 29 km south-east of Shahr-i Sokhta (Tosi 1970).

By the end of the fourth millennium BC each one of these sites, ranging between 12 and 18 ha., was the largest or the only settlement in its riverine territory. The tendency to centralized settlement distribution was accentuated during the first half of the third millennium BC by both the steady areal growth of centres and the stability in size of rural villages. This degree of centralization finds little comparison in the rest of the Middle East and has been reported, albeit rather unsystem-atically, wherever comprehensive archaeological evidence has become available (Masson 1968; Tosi 1973). Survey data suggest that expansion might be reflected in the increased number of rural settlements distributed along deltaic branches, but there is no emergence of intermediate-sized settlements. In the smallest piedmont fans like Damghan (c. 500 sq. km) this centralization reaches its ultimate stage with population concentrated in one significant settlement, Hissar, as early as the beginning of the third millennium BC (survey data by Maurer, in Dyson *et al.* n.d.). In larger riverine plains the expansion rate of the capital centre is striking: between 2700 and 2400 BC Shahr-i Sokhta grew from some 35 ha. to over 150 ha. (Tosi 1976: Fig. 5), whereas none of the contempor-ary rural settlements, spread all over the fossil Hilmand deltas in southern Sistan, exceeded 1.5 ha. (Meder 1977).

Central place tendencies of settlement systems have been attributed to articulation with a larger system or to failure of integration (Johnson 1980: 242–3). Although the first expla-nation might apply to Hissar in the third millennium BC, the latter seems more consistent with the geographical isolation of most Turanian territories in a period when they still lacked any animal suitable for long distance transport. Commodities were transferred quite intensively, and the amount of cultural interconnection recorded in the archaeological evidence is outstanding considering the distances involved (Lamberg-Karlovsky and Tosi 1973).

For the third millennium BC the only available means of shipment were human backs, and long-distance land trade across Turan and to the west has been ascertained only for highly valuable materials such as gold, carnelian or lapis lazuli (Tosi 1974b) or for finished commodities such as carved chlorite vessels (Kohl 1979). Analyses of resource allocation suggest only minimal reliance on external supply. Each system controlled the whole spectrum of natural resources necessary for the processing of the commodities in use. At Shahr-i Sokhta the only ascertained introduced materials that entered the production system during the third millennium BC were marine shells from the south, turquoise from the north and some exotic woods from the east, possibly from the Gangetic plain (Costantini and Tosi 1977; Costantini 1979). These materials were only processed for prestige items, whereas all other resources, in particular those for tool production, were available in very close proximity, within a maximum radius of

250—300 km including the Hilmand's deltaic basin and the Chagai hills in northern Baluchistan (Costantini and Tosi 1977: 334). These are extremely arid surroundings and no competing settlement systems of comparable size are to be expected at any time.

To a great extent these geographical conditions are shared by all four sites, but it is unlikely that response to the environment would have led to the exaggerated centralization of the Turanian settlement systems which occurred during the third millennium BC. Social transformation is commanded by the historical context, not by environment. By the time early state structures began to develop around 3000 BC, each territory had probably been steadily inhabited and farmed for thousands of years. The social entities that had dominated through the Chalcolithic would have had a far more powerful effect in conditioning the developing institutions of these complex societies than ecology. Proximity to natural resources and scarcity of farmland were indeed important variables, but their effect on the new order would have been mediated by the influence of the old.

Unfortunately, however, still too little is known about the fifth and fourth millennia in the region to incorporate the evidence of this earlier period in our analyses. The development of central place systems in the Turanian alluvial plains might be explained as the drive of political elites to control the rural population by allocating services to the centre, among them craft production with the resources and the labour it required. The physical centralization of specialists may in fact account for the nucleation of facilities and services, but it does not necessarily mean that the population was drained from the countryside to the centre. As long as surplus was extracted only from rural labour an effective reduction of these production forces would have resulted in stagnation of the economy. If we continue to interpret central place distribution in Turan only in terms of population density we should infer that the greatest proportion of people living in the centres was engaged in farming. However this solution fails to account for the sizeable proportion of the area of these centres which was obviously allocated to craft activities. It must be remembered that areal expansion is the only information we ultimately control and the exaggerated functional differentiation that resulted from the incorporation of more services within the urban centres might greatly increase variability in population density within the settlement system.

Craft quarters are directly related to site expansion at three of the four sites we consider here: Altyn, Shahdad and Shahr-i Sokhta. At each of them the establishment of *large* activity areas involved large sections of the periphery accounting for a third or a quarter of the total surface area of these sites (Fig. 3).

At Shahr-i Sokhta a first craft quarter was already established at the beginning of phase 6 (c. 2700 BC) in a vacant area to the west of the settlement (Fig. 5). Around 2400 BC more areas were occupied for craft activity, while the Western Workshops became a residential sector. By that time the graveyard

had expanded across the whole terrace and the new craft quarters were installed south of it, again on vacant parcels of land.

At Altyn depe in period Namazga V (2400—1800 BC) craft quarters occupy two areas to the north and south of the residential areas: pottery wasters and kilns spread over several hectares in the northern outskirts (Masimov 1976; Tosi 1976: 131, Fig. 12), and copper-smelting wasters gather over a smaller area at the southern end of the mound, west of the gate (Masson 1970: 61—3). If we consider their location in relation to the Chalcolithic occupation of the site (Masson 1977: Fig. 12), the craft quarters appear to have reoccupied abandoned sections of the Chalcolithic settlement. The same situation is found at Hissar where copper-processing activity areas were installed at the beginning of the third millennium in the southern section of the site. Once allocated to craft production an area retained its non-residential character. When copper-processing units were displaced a lapis lazuli bead-making atelier was set up directly between the heaps of residues and then this was followed, after a phase of utilization as graveyard, by the installation of pottery kilns (Bulgarelli and Tosi in Dyson *et al.* n.d.). The final use of this part of the site was again as a graveyard, while residential quarters and larger copper-processing areas extended the settlement to the north and south respectively (Fig. 4).

There are some general characteristics common to all areas of specialized commodity production in Turan. Pottery production was present from the very beginning in factories covering either entire suburban settlements, such as Tepe Dash at Shahr-i Sokhta, or large peripheral portions, as in all other sites so far surveyed. Conversely, copper production was carried out in much smaller ateliers, interspersed with other manufacturing activities. Excavations in sq. EW at the Western Workshops of Shahr-i Sokhta and in sq. DF/DG of Hissar's south hill have demonstrated a strong co-occurrence of copper working with processing of semiprecious stone jewellery items. Work was carried out in small courtyards with the bulk of residues and discarded tools disposed of on the spot. Too little has been excavated so far of these activity areas to reconstruct the detailed spatial patterning of work, but the low degree of residue displacement might allow future evaluation of per capita output. Houses and domestic facilities in general are few and scattered, both at the pottery factories and in the craft quarters. Once specialized activity areas came into being, they were formally distinguished from the residential quarters no matter how small the site remained.

Growth of commodity production would have represented an important cause of areal expansion over relatively short periods of time. Again there is no need to explain all settlement growth in terms of changes in population density, especially considering that our unit of observation is surface area, not people. Recalling our initial definition of craft specialization we can partly explain the disproportionately centralized distribution of Turanian settlement as differentiation in allocation of labour to the production of commodities. In the

Fig. 4. Main activity areas of Bronze-Age Tepe Hissar, Iran, after surface evaluation survey of October 1976. 1. areas with pottery slags; 2. calcite bead-making wasters; 3. high concentrations of metal slags (copper smelting); 4. low concentrations of metal slags; 5. high-to-low concentrations of lapis lazuli wasters and unfinished beads; 6. flint working areas; 7. pottery kilns. Note selective allocation of manufactures in southern section of site, in spite of its relative small size. Areas covered by craft indicators are almost one third of the whole site.

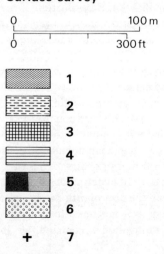

TEPE HISSAR 1976

Surface survey

0   100 m

0   300 ft

1

2

3

4

5

6

+   7

Islamic Qaleh

D   E   F   G   H   I

Red Hill

Treasure Hill

North flat

Main mound

Painted
pottery
flat

South Hill

Sasanian mound

The Twins

Fig. 5. Location of activity areas at Shahr-i Sokhta in relation to other main utilizations of the settlement space: 1. limit of the Plio-Pleistocene terrace; 2. maximum surface extension of Southern Workshops; 3. Western Workshops; 4. graveyard; 5. presumed residential areas; 6. pottery factory at Tepe Dash. Excavated areas: E. test trench in sq. EW; R. burnt building; X. phase 7–4 houses.

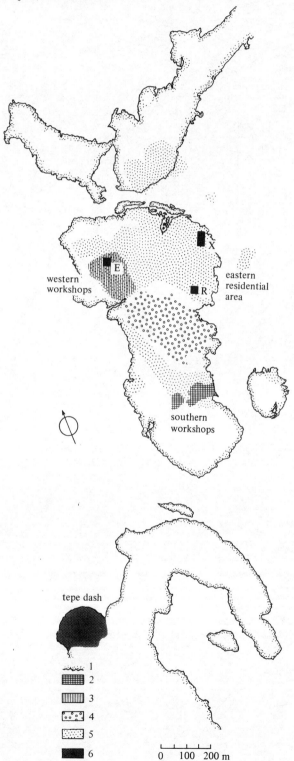

earlier phase of centre expansion, between 3000 and 2600 BC, control of craft production would not necessarily have required the alienation of farmers from rural villages which would have diminished the number of people generating surplus at the moment when economic takeoff had to be most sustained. The earliest phases of this expansion accentuated an existing trend toward the rationalization of certain manufacturing processes by accelerating the reallocation of existing specialists into craft quarters. These quarters in Turan were populated by specialists from settlements which had already developed into centres of small riverine territories hundreds of years earlier and where production of commodities had been remarkable in volume and quality all through the Chalcolithic period in the fifth and fourth millennia BC.

The change in the spatial distribution of activities took place in those territories where the majority of the population was already concentrated in the main centre, like Hissar or Altyn, and where no further demographic expansion was possible without integration into larger systems. The settlements involved in craft production remained the same or even contracted in size. Hissar is the best case at hand: almost one third of the total surface was given over to craft production, particularly copper smelting (Fig. 4). It is possible that already in the second half of the third millennium BC larger political systems were coming into being throughout Turan achieving differing degrees of economic integration among the various territories of the region (Jarrige and Tosi 1981: 139). The strong cultural connections of Hissar with the rich Gorgan plain 80 to 150 km to the north support the impression that the Damghan area might already have become integrated quite early in the third millennium, linking the large centres in the Gorgan farmlands and the copper sources around the edge of the Khevir desert. These are suggestions we are still not able to test, and the only degree of integration we can evaluate is still confined to a within-site or within-territory scale.

The Shahr-i Sokhta evidence for craft production

System integration is determined on the one hand by the reliance of villagers on central services, and on the other by the capacity of the centre to meet rural demand. Johnson has recently suggested that subsidizing large scale craft production would have been an explicit strategy of the centre administrators 'to undercut rural producers and decrease the demand for rural craft products' (in press). The case he makes refers to Early Uruk in Susiana and would correspond to an incipient stage of political complexity, but there is a concealed general question of tactics that remains essentially unanswered: how did the elite accomplish the subsidizing of craft production in the centres where it was already being carried out within a different set of social relations?

Physical centralization of craft production and increasing degree of specialization are processes we can divide into two distinct stages:

1 Control of existing specialists by their reallocation

from household workshops to new sections of the settlement.

2 Expansion of the production system to meet the requirements of the rural hinterland and growth of external demand as the degree of economic and social integration increases.

Only at the second stage would unskilled labour from the countryside be easily incorporated at the lowest levels of more complex and hierarchically organized production processes, primarily in capital-intensive industries such as copper processing or pottery production. The population of centres would grow at this point.

To what extent this model can be tested depends on our capacity to articulate it with a large corpus of diversified archaeological data. In this paper the first stage of the transformation is evaluated in the light of the archaeological record from Shahr-i Sokhta. The formulation of a detailed research design and good preservation of organic materials have allowed recovery of a mass of palaeoeconomic information which has been organized to allow examination of these specific propositions. Unfortunately the relatively short duration of occupation of the site bars us from a more in-depth examination of the conditions of craft production prevailing during the fourth millennium BC, out of which the later forms of differential allocation of productive forces emerged.

The classification of archaeological finds in Table 1 provides a vivid description of the extent and kind of craft production at Shahr-i Sokhta during the third millennium BC. In use were 25 main groups of products, produced by at least as many manufacturing processes, extracting and transforming ten main classes of natural resources. Abundant and diverse data including even such perishable materials as wood and fibres were recovered. Craft indicators are numerous, although the information they supply remains uneven and biased. Paucity of evidence in some cases is related not only to intrinsic factors of reprocessing or post-depositional destruction of residues and tools, but also to limited research on manufacturing processes. Following the discovery and excavation of specific activity areas, greatest detail has been obtained for pottery and copper production, and the working of alabaster and semiprecious stones. To evaluate spatial variability it will be necessary to reduce the field of observation and select comparably represented manufacturing processes (Table 2).

By considering six classes of archaeological indicators proposed in Table 1 for each group of commodities we could expect 210 potential information segments. The archaeological record illustrates 44: little more than one-fifth of the potential segments for 22 related products. The most frequent classes of indicators are residues (22/25) and tools for manufacturing (14/25). Fixed facilities can be expected only for some manufacturing processes, mostly those capital-intensive ones that require permanent allocation of land parcels for installations, such as ore smelting or pottery firing, whereas stocked semi-

finished or end-products seldom occur. The three unrepresented classes of products are: 2.3 gold, silver and electrum, 4.5 conical lamps of calcite and soapstone and 7.1 carpentry and furniture. Lack of indicators for lamp manufacture might simply result from their close association with stone vase manufacture. Although lamp production was quite distinctive both in technique and production distribution, we might have easily misinterpreted either residues or tools. Valuable raw materials such as gold, silver or wood in arid lands, are not discarded but constantly reprocessed.

Keeping in mind our initial aim to illustrate craft specialization by forms of allocation, such a close co-occurrence of finished products and manufacturing residues would imply minimal reliance on external supply of finished goods. Between 2800 and 2200 BC Shahr-i Sokhta probably produced all classes of commodities used by its population. This hypothesis needs to be evaluated against more accurate determinations of chronology. Since not all the 22 products are equally documented in the archaeological record, eight of the most representative ones have been selected: pottery, copper, lithics, alabaster vases, lapis and turquoise beads, chalcedony beads, leather work and woven goods (Table 2). They involve capital-intensive manufacturing processes such as those using kilns or furnaces (pottery, copper) or the processing of raw materials from distant sources (lapis lazuli, turquoise). Labour-intensive processes with no requirement for permanent installations are also included, as in the processing of organic materials (leather work and woven goods) or local mineral resources (alabaster for vases and chalcedony for beads).

Questions of sampling bias also apply to within-site provenances. Control of such bias depends on two essential preconditions: precise spatial definition of the structural repositories of craft indicators and their total excavation. Selected provenances include eight buildings and three activity areas, grouped separately in Table 2 to demonstrate presence/ absence of indicators and spatio-temporal variability. Each provenance can be assigned to one or more chronological phases, and buildings have been seriated accordingly from earliest to latest. For the purpose of this work the Shahr-i Sokhta sample is restricted to the Eastern Residential Area (Fig. 6) where entire buildings have been exposed. Five of the buildings overlap in sector X and have all been entirely excavated with the exception of the phase 7 'early houses' in sq. XC/XD where the test trench uncovered the intersection point of three contiguous buildings (Fig. 7; most updated plan in Tosi 1981a: Fig. 2).

Structural layout of buildings underwent very little change between phases 7 and 4 (c. 2800–2300 BC): rectangular mud-brick flat-roofed construction, ranging between 96 and 200 sq. m, with access to a squarish courtyard. This is the largest of all rooms (20–30 sq. m) and it served as a pivot for internal communication including access to the upper storey. The staircases were always built along a wall of the courtyard, close to the main entrance (see for example House of Stairs in

Table 1 *Archaeological craft indicators*

Type of product	1. Facilities	2. Tools for manufacture	3. Residues	4. Semifinished products	5. Stocked and unworn products	6. Materials for recycling
1. Ceramic						
1.1. Pottery	1. Kilns 2. Vitrified fragments of kiln linings	1. Lunate smoothers from bowl rims 2. Paint bowls & palette sherds 3. Wheel dishes 4. Wheel stands	1. Kiln wasters	n.r.	n.r.	n.r.
1.2. Coroplastics	n.r.	n.r.	1. Unfinished overfired specimens of figurines	n.r.	n.r.	n.r.
1.3. Bangles, Beads etc.	n.r.	n.r.	1. Unfinished overfired specimens of bangles	n.r.	n.r.	n.r.
2. Metal						
2.1. Copper & bronze alloys	1. Furnaces 2. Fragments of furnaces 3. Tap-slags	1. Crucibles 2. Casting moulds	1. slags 2. prills 3. ore-crushing debitage	1. ingots 2. rods 3. partly hammered blades	n.r.	1. rolled blades
2.2. Lead and Galena ore	n.r.	n.r.	1. slags (*litage*) 2. PbCa nodules 3. ore-crushing debitage	1. ingots	n.r.	n.r.
2.3. Gold, Silver and Electrum	n.r.	n.r.	n.r.	n.r.	n.r.	n.r.
3. Glass paste						
3.1. Beads	n.r.	n.r.	1. slags	n.r.	n.r.	n.r.
4. Stone						
4.1. Lithic Tools of Chipped Stone	n.r.	1. Hammer stones 2. Anvil stones	1. cores 2. debitage flakes	1. unretouched unworn parallel-sided blades	1. stocks of unworn blades	n.r.
4.2. Lithic Tools of Ground Stone	n.r.	1. Quern stones	1. waste flakes of ore	n.r.	n.r.	n.r.

Table 1 (*cont.*)

Type of product	1. Facilities	2. Tools for manufacture	3. Residues	4. Semifinished products	5. Stocked and unworn products	6. Materials for recycling
4.3. Stone Vases of Alabaster and Calcite	n.r.	1. Basalt abraders	1. Waste flakes or calcareous pebbles 2. Fragments of shaped unhollowed rough-hewns 3. Fragments of abraded hollowed rough-hewns	n.r.	n.r.	1. reused bases of conical bowls
4.4. Soapstone Vases	n.r.	n.r.	1. Waste flakes of chlorite with cutting marks	n.r.	n.r.	n.r.
4.5. Conical Lamps of Calcite & Soapstone	n.r.	n.r.	n.r.	n.r.	n.r.	n.r.
4.6. Stone Seals	n.r.	1. Jasper/granite drill bits	1. Heulandite splinters	1. Blanks of chlorite seals	n.r.	1. Reused chlorite seals
4.7. Beads of Lapislazuli & Turquoise	n.r.	1. Hammer stones 2. Flint bladelets 3. Flint drill bits 4. Polishers 5. Anvil stones 6. Sockets for upper end of bow-drill shafts	1. Unworked waste lumps of raw material 2. Waste beads unfinished at various stages of processing 3. waste debitage 4. waste flakes from the making of associated lithic industry	1. Prepared small blocks of raw material 2. Unperforated beads	n.r.	1. Broken beads stocked for reprocessing
4.8. Beads of Chalcedony (Chipping- & polishing techniques)	n.r.	1. Hammer stones 2. Basalt abraders 3. Drills of flaked jasper, chert or granite 4. Polishers 5. Anvil stones	1. Unworked pebbles or lumps of raw material 2. Unfinished beads at various stages of processing 3. Waste debitage	1. Prepared blocks of raw material 2. Unperforated beads	n.r.	1. Broken beads stocked for reprocessing

Table 1 (*cont.*)

Type of product	1. Facilities	2. Tools for manufacture	3. Residues	4. Semifinished products	5. Stocked and unworn products	6. Materials for recycling
4.9. Beads of softer stones (Soap- & Lime-stone)	n.r.	n.r.	1. Unworked lumps of raw material 2. Unfinished beads at various stages of processing 3. Waste debitage	1. Prepared pieces 2. Unperforated beads	n.r.	n.r.
5. Shell						
5.1. Ornaments of large gastropods (*Xancus pyrum*, *Fasciolaria trapezium*, *Murex* sp.)	n.r.	1. Hammer stones 2. Cutting blades 3. Abraders 4. Drills	1. Unworked shells 2. Large un-worked sec-tions of shell walls 3. Unfinished bangles at various stages of processing 4. Waste sec-tions of shell 5. Small waste debitage	1. Unworked pieces	n.r.	1. By-products: Columellas for polishers and hammers 2. Cosmetic containers in gastropod apexes
5.2. Beads of small gastropods (Chipping-and-rubbing techniques)	n.r.	n.r.	1. Unperforated shells 2. Waste beads during perforation 3. Waste peri-stomal lips of cowry shells	n.r.	n.r.	n.r.
6. Bone						
6.1. Tools	n.r.	1. Flint cutters 2. Polishers	1. Waste splinters 2. Unfinished products	n.r.	n.r.	n.r.
6.2. Beads, Seals etc.	n.r.	1. Flint cutters 2. Carving tools of stone 3. Carving tools of metal 4. Polishers	1. Waste debitage	n.r.	n.r.	n.r.

Table 1 (*cont.*)

Type of product	1. Facilities	2. Tools for manufacture	3. Residues	4. Semifinished products	5. Stocked and unworn products	6. Materials for recycling
7. Wood						
7.1. Carpentry and furniture	n.r.	n.r.	n.r.	n.r.	n.r.	n.r.
7.2. Vessels, Door-sockets, tools, small sculptures	n.r.	1. Metal tools 2. Stone tools	1. Waste splinters with traces of shaving and cutting	n.r.	n.r.	n.r.
8. Leather/skin	n.r.	1. Bone awls & needles 2. End-scrapers & other stone tools 3. Wood spatulae & polishers 4. Wood lasts 5. Bronze knives	n.r.	n.r.	n.r.	n.r.
9. Textiles	1. Sections of courtyards with holes for loom emplacement	1. Wood spindles 2. Wood, stone, pottery, bone whorls 3. Pegs for horizontal looms 4. Wooden shuttles 5. Wooden thread-beating combs	n.r.	1. Unwoven thread	n.r.	n.r.
10. Basketry, matting and cordage	n.r.	1. Bone netting needles	1. Waste reeds and other vegetal fibres	n.r.	n.r.	n.r.

n.r.: not represented

Manufactured commodities at Shahr-i Sokhta in periods II–IV (2700–1800 BC) and corresponding archaeological indicators of craft production. The specific bibliographic references are provided in appendix 1 under the same 4-digit coded entry.

Table 2 *Space/Time variability in distribution of craft indicators at the ten considered provenances of Shahr-i Sokhta.*

Uncertain dating is represented by strip filling; rare occurrence of a class of indicators is represented by lighter filling. Indicators are listed according to the following code:

1 FCL: Facilities   2 TLM: Tools for manufacture   3 RSD: Residues   4 SFP: Semifinished products   5 SUP: Stocked and unworn products   6 MFR: Materials for recycling

Fig. 8). Number of rooms varies between 9 and 13 according to the size of the building. Interdependence of rooms is further confirmed by the number and distribution of domestic facilities: one dome-shaped bread oven for the whole house (Tosi 1969: Fig. 94; 1981a: 109, Fig. 15) and a very limited number of grain and water storage jars often concentrated in a single room. Buildings were grouped in blocks of two or four, divided by narrow alleys, and it is thought that they were primarily houses for kin-related groups, possibly families including up to ten individuals.

In spite of its large size and the imposing thickness of its walls, similar considerations permit the 'burnt building' of phase 1 (c. 1800 BC) to be treated as a dwelling compound (Tosi 1981a: 76–92; Biscione 1979). The squatter occupation of phase 0 refers to the latest use of the site, when shortly after the building's destruction a few walls, kilns and cooking facilities were installed in the ruins.

The three activity areas are distributions of residues located near the western and southern edges of the terrace (Fig. 5). Tepe Dash is the largest pottery manufacturing centre in Sistan and lies to the south-east. Among the activity areas only the Western Workshops have been excavated, where a 200 sq. m trench has uncovered parts of a lapidary factory or atelier (Biscione *et al.* 1975: 40–4) with an occupation range

beginning as late as phase 6, i.e. almost 500 years later than the Eastern Residential Area.

Table 2 illustrates spatio-temporal variability in the distribution of craft indicators at Shahr-i Sokhta according to the ten selected provenances. Between phases 7 and 4 craft production is increasingly taken out of the households, although no noticeable changes can be detected in residential architecture or functional layout. This development is most evident around the middle of the third millennium BC, in the transfer of all capital-intensive manufacturing (copper, lapis lazuli, turquoise) from houses to larger activity areas. According to the proposed set of criteria we would classify them as either factories (Tepe Dash) or craft quarters (the Western Workshops). In the case of pottery the trend to relocation was effective already when Shahr-i Sokhta was founded in the late fourth millennium BC, and as long as it was inhabited this production took place at Tepe Dash. Quite significantly large kilns are first found in the main urban area during the short and episodic occupation that followed destruction of BB_1 before definitive abandonment. Weaving and leather working continued to be performed in houses, but the scanty remains so far found do not rule out the possibility that factories might have already been in operation. As was later the case in the Near East, these products of the countryside, derived from

Fig. 6. Aerial view from east of Shahr-i Sokhta Eastern Residential Area (bottom) and Central Quarters (top) (courtesy of G. Gerster).

agriculture and animal husbandry, could have been transformed into exchange-value commodities by further appropriation of domestic labour.

The general impression derived from Table 2 is one of steady centralization of certain sectors of craft production which become 'specialized' as a consequence of relocation. This transformation of production can be explained as an expression of the suggested elite strategy of increasing dependence of the rural population on centralized services (Johnson in press). However, pottery production was certainly not used to this end. During phases 4 and 3, as Shahr-i Sokhta grew to its maximum extension and Tepe Dash was fully functioning over a surface of 5 ha., at least three new factories were founded in rural areas to the east and south. They meausre 0.5 to 1.0 ha. in extent and bear no traces of any activity other than pottery making. At least 50 large kilns would have been operating at the same time at Tepe Rud-i Biyaban 2, 29 km from Shahr-i Sokhta (Fig. 9). Physico-chemical analyses have shown that while manufacturing techniques were similar at the two sites, clay sources were different. This implies dispersed production for one of the commodities most in demand by the rural population (Reindell and Riederer forthcoming). To what extent this situation contradicts the picture suggested by

the relocation of copper and stone manufacturing will need to be determined by future investigation, although, considering the current lack of chronological control, we can not expect a picture without some degree of internal inconsistency.

Table 2 further suggests that areal expansion of Sistan's metropolitan centre might not necessarily reflect a comparable population growth. The establishment of craft quarters, relocating facilities and activities outside residential units would not only have led to a growth in size of the centre but led to more differentiated land use patterns and tenure forms within the settlement. As at Hissar or Altyn depe, craft quarters indicate a sharp separation both from residential areas and from the places performing other central functions (Fig. 3). In both the northern sites craft quarters were placed on peripheral land parcels, reoccupying considerable sections of abandoned Chalcolithic sites (Masson 1977: Fig. 12). At Shahr-i Sokhta on the other hand settlement had a more recent history and the new location of specialized craft sectors appears in the archaeological record as a more abrupt expansion.

As long as we define craft specialization as differential allocation of per capita commodity output we can conclude that the Shahr-i Sokhta evidence, which illustrates the high degree of centralization that characterizes the Turan during

Fig. 7. Aerial view from east of residential units in sq. X at Shahr-i Sokhta. From left to right: House in XH, House of Foundations, House of Stairs with in front House of the Pit, and Earlier Houses in XC/XD (courtesy of G. Gerster).

Fig. 8. Shahr-i Sokhta: isometric view from NE of House of Stairs (from Tosi 1969).

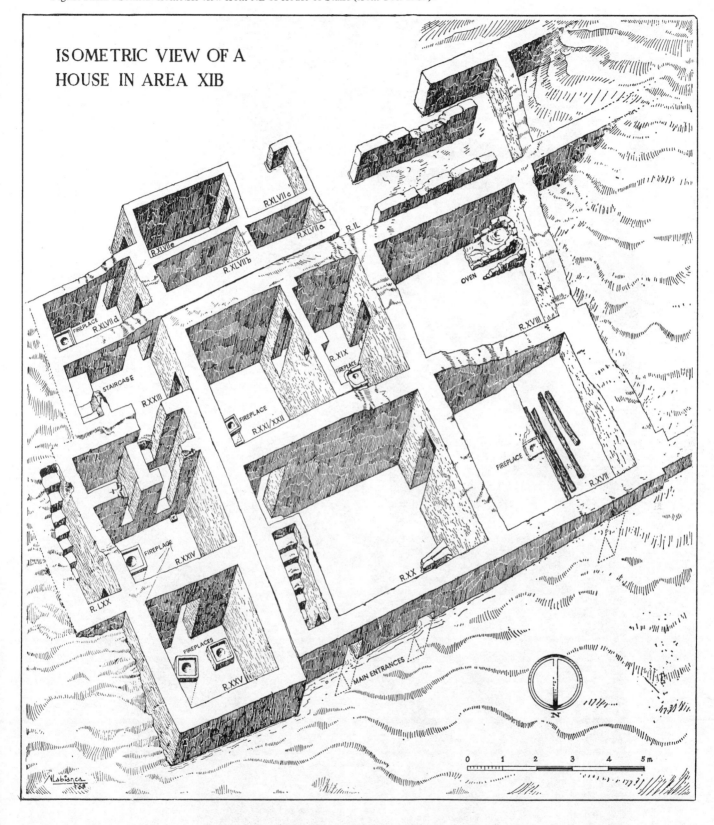

Fig. 9. Pottery kilns and factory floors at Tepe Rud-i Biyaban 2.

the third millennium BC, supports the proposition that the development of craft quarters in the region complements concentration of population and optimization of use of local resources. To consider this simply as a process of adaptation to particular environmental conditions would avoid the major question: what kind of political institutions and relations of production enabled such centralized systems to develop and survive for almost half a millennium?

Administration and craft production

Given lack of textual information and the limited amount of archaeological data we presently control for the prehistoric period in Turan, it is unlikely that in the near future we shall be able to expand our analyses to consider in detail relations between craft specialization and degree of social complexity. These are probably best represented as elaborations of new hierarchical levels in an expanding system of vertical differentiation. This was a system aimed at articulating under elite control the primary basis of wealth: the land and its agricultural output.

Relations of production remain elusive in our archaeological evidence, but one line of fruitful research on this would be in integrating craft evidence and settlement variability with the material expressions of the institutionalized processes of social control over the economic system. The size and complexity of the systems operating even in the smallest of the Turanian territories could hardly be managed without multi-level administrative organization that would articulate the different economic sectors and pursue control of material allocation for surplus extraction.

Variability in administrative specialization is best illustrated in the archaeological record by differences in the distribution of devices for record-keeping and control over storage and transfer of commodities. All the Turanian centres so far explored shared the same technique found throughout the Middle East and which developed in the Mesopotamian lowlands in the second half of the fourth millennium BC. This was based on the use of sealings on clay on door-fastening pegs, movable containers and tablets, controlling under a single sign of formal endorsement all storage and exchange transactions (Ferioli and Fiandra 1979; Fiandra 1981). Proto-Elamite writing was used at Shahr-i Sokhta as early as phase 10 (Amiet and Tosi 1978), but no tablets were found in later contexts, possibly suggesting an increasingly restricted location for record-keeping activities. In contrast, discarded clay sealings (Fig. 10) marking confinement of wares are relatively abundant, together with stone and metal seals, clay and stone counters, and 'tally disks'. These last form a class of information-recording devices restricted so far to the Hilmand valley: clay disks 3 to 4 cm across bearing an incised sign on one face and a number of tallying pecks on the other (Fig. 11). They occur at Shahr-i Sokhta in phases 7–5 and at Mundigak, beyond the Arachosian plain at about 2500 BC (Casal 1961: Fig. 131.20).

Table 3 examines their distribution in the eight exca-

vated contexts we sampled for craft specialization. The ratio of discarded administrative devices in houses declines through the first half of the third millennium BC, almost in direct relation to the number of craft indicators illustrated in Table 2.

If increased craft specialization is directly linked to growth of elite control over the production system, it would be inversely related to household capacity to control storage and transactions of goods. Information processing and control

Fig. 10. Main types of discarded administrative devices from Shahr-i Sokhta: *top*, door sealing with round stamp seal impressions; *bottom*, jar stopper with impressions from two different stamp seals. Both specimens from House of Stairs in phase 6. Scale in centimetres.

Fig. 11. Front and back views of tally disks from phases 7–5 houses in sq. X at Shahr-i Sokhta. Scale in centimetres.

Table 3 *Distribution of suggested indicators for administrative activity in the eight excavated contexts sampled at Shahr-i Sokhta for analyses of craft allocation.*

Provenance	Clay sealings	Seals			Counters		Tally disks
		Stone	Metal	Ceramic	Spheres	Others	
Earlier houses in Sq. XC/XD	82	4			2		1
House of stairs	73	9	1		19	2	6
House of the pit	44	8			16	1	1
House of foundations	3	4					1
House in Sq. XH	4	1					
Burnt building (Primary occupation)	7			2	4		
Burnt building (Squatter occupation)							
Western workshops in Sq. EW	3	1					

For dating of provenances see Table 2. Note decline of administrative devices with progressive detachment of manufacturing activities from residential units.

over distribution would tend to be monopolized by the dominant elite, and the number of discarded administrative devices in houses should gradually decrease. Fig. 12 presents a preliminary attempt to illustrate the relationship between these two orders of variability by plotting the number of discarded administrative devices on the y-axis and indices of craft occurrence (COI) on the x-axis. As indicators of administrative activity we used only clay sealings and tally disks. Seals are highly movable and tend to be reused in various ways and small counters can too easily be confused with other classes of artifacts. COI are derived for each context by multiplying the number of manufacturing stages detected by the number of classes of products they represent. An area with co-occurrence of copper slag and flint wasters will bear COI = 4 (copper smelting + blade making × 2 = 4). In terms of craft location it will be regarded as more complex than an area with copper slag and refining crucibles whose COI = 2 (copper smelting + copper refinement × 1 = 2). The procedure is still essentially a qualitative analysis of co-occurrence, since any quantitative consideration concerning the volume of each production process is far too context-dependent to be generalized at this early stage. Table 4 lists the groups of products considered with the expected manufacturing stages for each of them. Totals are listed in Table 5 together with their COI computed as percentages of the total number of expected manufacturing stages (8 × 41 = 328); these totals are plotted on the x-axis in Fig. 12 against number of discarded administrative devices.

The results are suggestive although there are too few sampled provenances to determine significant cluster distribution. They reveal a scattered pattern, which ranges from conditions of household autonomy in craft production and administrative management (House of Stairs and Early Houses in XC/CD) to craft quarters with little or no sign of administrative activity (the Western Workshops) and to contemporary households almost devoid of craft activities but important in management activities. An example of the latter is the House of the Pit, which for over a century during phase 6 (2700–2600 BC) faced the House of Stairs and the House of Foundations.

The Burnt Building marks a complete regression in both

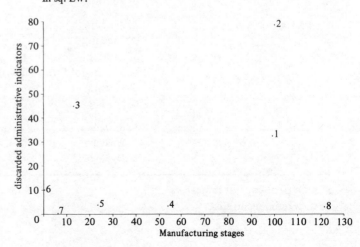

Fig. 12. Relationship between administrative and craft indicators in each of the provenances considered at Shahr-i Sokhta: 1. Early Houses in sq. XC/XD; 2. House of Stairs; 3. House of the Pit; 4. House of Foundations (earlier building); 5. House in sq. XH; 6. Burnt Building (primary occupation in phase 1); 7. Burnt Building (squatter occupation in phase 0); 8. Western Workshops in sq. EW.

Table 4 *Distribution of expected stages according to occurrence of indicators in sampled provenances.*

Groups of products	Expected manufacturing stages	Provenances							
		EH	HS	HP	HF	HX	BB$_1$	BB$_0$	WW
1 Pottery	1. Treatment of clay								
	2. Vessel construction		?						
	3. Painting (black)								
	4. Firing							x	
	5. Painting (polychrome)								
2 Copper and bronze alloys	1. Ore breaking								
	2. Smelting in furnaces	x			x	x			x
	3. Refining in crucibles	x	x		x	x			x
	4. Casting of blades and rods	x							x
	5. Hammering of objects								x
	6. Casting of seals and other objects								
3 Lithic industry	1. Production of arrowheads	x							
	2. Production of blades	x	x		x				x
	3. Production of denticulates								
	4. Production of drill bits								x
4 Alabaster and limestone vases	1. Reduction of ore								
	2. Shaping by chipping								
	3. Hollowing								
	4. Thinning/Smoothing				x	?			
	5. Polishing				x	?			
	6. Decoration by incising (rare)								
5 Lapis lazuli and turquoise beads	1. Reduction of ore								x
	2. Chipping	x	x						x
	3. Smoothing								x
	4. Drilling								x
	5. Polishing								x
	6. Decoration by incising (rare)								?
6 Chalcedony beads	1. Reduction of ore		x						x
	2. Chipping		x						x
	3. Smoothing								x
	4. Drilling								x
	5. Polishing								
7 Leather and skin	1. Scudding		x	x	x				
	2. Dressing								
	3. Cutting	x	x	x	x	x			
	4. Shaping of forms (shoes)	x							
	5. Piercing	x	x	x	x	x	x	x	
	6. Sewing	x	x	x	x				
8 Cloth	1. Spinning	x	x	x	?	x			
	2. Weaving	x	x	x					
	3. Dyeing	?	?	?					

x: high frequency of indicators

?: uncertain occurrence

Table 5 *Shahr-i Sokhta. Distribution of discarded administrative devices compared with indices of craft occurrence (COI) in the individual provenances.*

Provenances	No. of discarded administrative devices	%	No. of detected manufacturing stages	No. of crafts	Index of craft occurrence
Early houses in sq. XC/XD	33	18.53	13	5	65 % 328 = 19.81
Houses of stairs	79	44.38	11	6	66 % 328 = 20.12
House of the pit	45	25.28	6	2	12 % 328 = 3.25
House of foundations	4	2.24	9	4	36 % 328 = 10.97
House in sq. XH	4	2.24	5	3	15 % 328 = 4.57
Burnt building 1	10	5.61	1	1	1 % 328 = 0.30
Burnt building 0	0	0.00	2	2	4 % 328 = 1.21
Western workshops	3	1.68	16	5	80 % 328 = 24.39

axes of variability. By the beginning of the second millennium BC the society governing the economic system had undergone a radical transformation. Neither cities nor large craft centres survived the change, in spite of their long previous dominance in all territories of Turan. The earliest forms of urbanism in this part of Asia exhibited a steady climb that ended in a rapid collapse. Although part of the explanation might rest in the dependence of these closed ecosystems on distant highland rainfall, the primary causes must be sought in the social conditions that preceded the fall of cities all over Turan. The marked centralization that was a feature of these societies during the second half of the third millennium BC could have been in part a response to environmental constraints, but in the long run the efficiency of the system deteriorated and its degree of integration diminished.

Concluding remarks

Our interpretations are still so provisional that there should perhaps be no concluding remarks, but a note of caution needs to be added to avoid overestimation of the role of craft specialization in the emergence of class society. Craft specialization can be seen as a powerful means to promote economic inequality, by differentiating forms of labour and relative income or by developing dependence of rural populations on central services. This hypothesis however can as yet hardly go beyond the level of a statement of political faith. We have so far been largely unsuccessful in making use of the archaeological data in illustrating the processes involved in the emergence of class societies. The main point to be made in this paper is that further development will require the handling of much larger and more diverse bodies of data than has so far been attempted.

There is no firm evidence that the hierarchical complexity we look for is dependent on selective allocation of the productive forces. Craft production would have comprised only a part of the whole system, bound almost exclusively to elite strategy and over-represented in our data by the peculiarities of the archaeological record. The majority of the

population remained tied to agricultural production and control of *this* was the ultimate target of any elaboration of hierarchical control of craft allocation.

The reorganization of craft production which occurred almost everywhere in the Middle East between the late fourth and early third millennium BC did not represent an 'industrial revolution': surplus continued to be extracted from the land which was not invested in capital-intensive production but was either stockpiled or dispersed exclusively for the perpetuation of the system. It is curious to notice that for almost the entire third millennium BC no significant technological innovations were introduced in any craft. Most manufacturing processes and construction works were purposely labour-intensive, and the quality of craftsmanship was generally poor compared to the products of the previous millennium and the one following. Our 'answer will find a question' only in the organization of agricultural production, but the rural population has so far remained substantially invisible to us.

Appendix 1: Bibliographical references to archaeological indicators of craft production listed in Table 1 as recorded at Shahr-i Sokhta

1 Ceramics

    1.1 *Pottery* Lamberg-Karlovsky and Tosi 1973: Figs. 20, 142; Tosi 1969: Fig. 30b; Tosi 1970: 189; Tosi 1976: Fig. 14; Tosi 1981a: 91, Figs. 84−5; Tosi 1981b: 134, Fig. 23; Unpublished materials.

    1.2 *Coroplastics* Unpublished materials.

    1.3 *Bangles, Beads, etc.* Unpublished materials.

2 Metal

    2.1 *Copper and Bronze Alloys* Hauptmann 1980: Figs. 1−3; Tosi 1981b: 165, Figs. 97, 98; Unpublished materials.

    2.2 *Lead and Galena Ore* Unpublished materials.

    2.3 *Gold, Silver and Electrum* Not represented.

3 Glass paste

    3.1 *Beads* Unpublished materials.

4 Stone
- 4.1 *Chipped Stone Tools* Bulgarelli 1977: 273–6; Tosi 1968: Figs. 26, 109; Tosi 1974a: Fig. 6; Unpublished materials.
- 4.2 *Ground Stone Tools* Unpublished materials.
- 4.3 *Alabaster and Calcite Vases* Ciarla 1979: 327, 330–2, Figs. 1–7, 9–10, Table 5; Ciarla 1981: 53–4, Figs. 7, 8a, 8b, 10–12, 14; Tosi 1968: 57, Figs. 89–91; Tosi 1969: 369, Figs. 221, 222.
- 4.4 *Soapstone Vases* Kohl 1977: 112.
- 4.5 *Conical lamps of Calcite and Soapstone* Not represented.
- 4.6 *Stone Seals* Kohl 1977: 114–15, Figs. 5–10; Lahanier 1975; Piperno 1973; Piperno 1981; Tosi 1969: Fig. 258d.
- 4.7 *Lapis Lazuli and Turquoise Beads* Biscione *et al.* 1975: 40–4, Fig. 10, Pls. 27–30, 31a; Bulgarelli 1974: Figs. 8, 13; Bulgarelli 1979: Figs. 14–15; Bulgarelli 1981a: 65–9, Figs. 2, 2a, 3; Jarrige and Tosi 1981: 134–6, Figs. 5–6; Tosi 1969: 371–2, Figs. 249, 252–3; Tosi 1974a: Fig. 6; Tosi 1974b: Fig. 1; Tosi and Piperno 1973: Figs. 19.3, 20.1–3, 21.4–5, 26.1–2; Unpublished materials.
- 4.8 *Chalcedony Beads* Bulgarelli and Tosi 1977: Fig. 3; Lamberg-Karlovsky and Tosi 1973: Figs. 50, 51; Piperno 1973: Figs. 3–4; Piperno 1976: Figs. 5–6; Piperno 1979: 132, Fig. 6; Piperno 1981: Figs. 1–4; Tosi 1968: 60, Fig. 98; Tosi 1969: 342, 372, 379, Figs. 250–7, 258a; Tosi 1981b: 168, Fig. 111; Unpublished materials.
- 4.9 *Softer Stone Beads* Tosi 1969: 373–4, Fig. 259; Unpublished materials.

5 Shell
- 5.1 *Large Gastropod Ornaments* Biscione *et al.* 1981: 64, 82, Figs. 45, 58; Durante 1979a; Durante 1979b: 323, Figs. 3–7; Tosi 1981b: 164, Fig. 91; Unpublished materials.
- 5.2 *Small Gastropod Beads* Biscione *et al.* 1981: *Conus* 65, 67, Figs. 46–8; *Engina* 67, 76–7, Figs. 83–4; *Lyncina* 78; Unpublished materials.

6 Bone
- 6.1 *Tools* Bulgarelli 1981b; Tosi 1968: 64, Fig. 110; Unpublished materials.
- 6.2 *Beads, seals, etc.* Bulgarelli 1981b; Unpublished materials.

7 Wood
- 7.1 *Carpentry and Furniture* Not represented.
- 7.2 *Vessels, Door Sockets, Tools, Small Sculptures* Bulgarelli 1981b; Costantini 1979; Tosi 1968: 65, Fig. 115; Tosi 1969: 378–9, Figs. 197–8, 298; Tosi 1981b: 165, Figs. 102–5.

8 Leather/skin
- Bulgarelli 1977: 274; Costantini 1977a: 53–61; Costantini 1977b: 161; Costantini 1979: 116–18, Figs. 35–7; Tosi 1968: 65, Figs. 112, 114, 118–19; Tosi 1969: 364–5, Figs. 201–6, 245, 299; Tosi 1981b: 165, Figs. 100–1.

9 Textiles
- Costantini 1977a: 27–36; Costantini 1979: 109–11, 113, Fig. 31; Tosi 1969: 366, Figs. 41f–g, j–q, 207, 216–18, 220; Tosi 1981b: 160, 164, Fig. 79, 92; Unpublished materials.

10 Basketry, matting and cordage
- Tosi 1981b: 161, Figs. 4, 83–5, 88, 89.

Notes

1 It should be noted that the way a worker or artisan subdivides the manufacturing process is determined by *social* factors in addition to the more obvious physical preconditions of that particular transformation.

Acknowledgements

This study was undertaken in the summer of 1981 at the Institut für Archäologie, Seminar für Vorderasiatische Altertumskunde, Free University of Berlin, as the introductory layout of a research project and was generously sponsored by the Alexander von Humboldt Foundation. I gratefully acknowledge the generous support of Prof. Hans J. Nissen who provided excellent facilities and a most congenial environment. The theoretical part of this paper has greatly benefited from many discussions with Prof. Gregory A. Johnson and incorporates several of his suggestions, although the author alone bears the responsibility of their use and abuse. Editorial assistance has been graciously provided by Dr Margaret W. Green who invested much time and effort toward increasing the clarity of my English. Drawings and charts are the contribution of Ms Geraldina Santini whom I thank for her enduring encouragement.

Bibliography

Amiet, P. and M. Tosi. 1978. Phase 10 at Shahr-i Sokhta: excavations in square XDV and the Late 4th Millennium B.C. assemblage of Sīstān. *East and West* 28: 9–31.

AA.VV. 1977. *La citta' bruciata del deserto salato.* Venezia: Erizzo Editrice.

Biscione, R. 1979. The Burnt Building of Period IV at Shahr-i Sokhta IV. An attempt of functional analysis from the distribution of pottery types. In G. Gnoli and A.V. Rossi (eds.), *Iranica*, pp. 291–306. Napoli: Istituto Universitario Orientale.

Biscione, R., G.M. Bulgarelli, L. Costantini, M. Piperno and M. Tosi, 1975. Archaeological discoveries and methodological problems in the excavations of Shahr-i Sokhta, Sistan. In J.E. van Lohuizen-de Leeuw and J.M.M. Ubaghs (eds.), *South Asian Archaeology 1973*, pp. 12–52. Leiden: Brill.

Biscione, R., S. Durante and M. Tosi, 1981. *Conchiglie. Il commercio e la lavorazione delle conchiglie marine nel Medio Oriente dal IV al II millennio a.C.* Roma: Museo Nazionale d'Arte Orientale.

Bulgarelli, G.M. 1974. Tepe Hissar. Preliminary report on a surface survey, August 1972. *East and West* 24: 15–27.

1977. Stone working techniques and bone industry. In AA.VV. *La citta' bruciata del deserto salato*, pp. 273–6. Venezia: Erizzo Editrice.

1979. The lithic industry of Tepe Hissar in the light of recent excavation. In M. Taddei (ed.), *South Asian Archaeology 1977*, pp. 39–54. Naples: Istituto Universitario Orientale.

1981a. Turquoise working in the Helmand civilization – some
observations. In H. Härtel (ed.), *South Asian Archaeology 1979*,
pp. 65–9. Berlin: D. Reimer Verlag.

1981b. A clay-handled stone tool from Shahr-i Sokhta. In M. Tosi
(ed.), *Prehistoric Sistan I*, pp. 327–32. Rome: IsMEO.

Bulgarelli, G.M. and M. Tosi, 1977. La lavorazione ed il commercio
delle pietre semipreziose nelle citta' dell'Iran protostorico
(3200–1800 a.C.) *Geo-Archeologia* 1–2: 37–50.

Casal, J.-M. 1961. *Fouilles de Mundigak*. Paris: Mémoires de la
Délégation Archéologique Française en Afghanistan 17.

Childe, V.G. 1934. *New Light on the Most Ancient East: The Oriental
Prelude of European Prehistory*. London: Kegan Paul, 1st ed.

1942. *What Happened in History*. Harmondsworth: Pelican.

1950. The urban revolution. *The Town Planning Review* 21: 3–17.

Christensen, P. 1977. The Transformation of Nature into Commodities
(mimeo).

Ciarla, R. 1979. The manufacture of alabaster vessels at Shahr-i Sokhta
and Mundigak in the 3rd Millennium BC: a problem of cultural
identity. In G. Gnoli and A.V. Rossi (eds.), *Iranica*, pp. 319–35.
Napoli: Istituto Universitario Orientale.

1981. A preliminary analysis of the manufacture of alabaster vessels
at Shahr-i Sokhta and Mundigak in the 3rd Millennium BC. In
H. Härtel (ed.), *South Asian Archaeology 1979*, pp. 45–63.
Berlin: D. Reimer Verlag.

Compagnoni, B. and M. Tosi, 1977. The camel: its distribution and
state of domestication in the Middle East during the third
millennium B.C. in light of finds from Shahr-i Sokhta. In R.H.
Meadow and M.A. Zeder (eds.), *Approaches to Faunal Analysis
in the Middle East*, pp. 92–105. Cambridge: Peabody Museum
Bulletin 2.

Costantini, L. 1977a. *I legni lavorati di Shahr-i Sokhta*. Roma: Museo
Nazionale d'Arte Orientale Schede 8.

1977b. The plants. In AA.VV., *La citta' bruciata del deserto salato*,
pp. 168–71. Venezia: Erizzo Editrice.

1979. Wood remains from Shahr-i Sokhta: a source of information
for the ancient environment in protohistoric Sistan. In M. Taddei
(ed.), *South Asian Archaeology 1977*, pp. 87–121. Naples:
Istituto Universitario Orientale.

Costantini, L. and M. Tosi, 1975. Methodological proposals for palaeo-
biological investigations in Iran. In F. Bagherzade (ed.), *Proceedings of the 3rd Annual Symposium on Archaeological Research
in Iran*, pp. 311–31. Tehran: International Center for Archaeological Research.

1977. Population and natural resources in prehistoric Sistan. In
AA.VV., *La citta' bruciata del deserto salato*, pp. 287–93; 334.
Venezia: Erizzo Editrice.

Durante, S. 1979a. The utilization of *Xancus pyrum* (L.) at Shahr-i
Sokhta: a further evidence of cultural relations between India
and Iran in the 4th–3rd millennia B.C. In J.E. van Lohuizen-de
Leeuw and J.M.M. Ubaghs (eds.), *South Asian Archaeology
1975*, pp. 27–42. Leiden: Brill.

1979b. Marine shells from Balakot, Shahr-i Sokhta and Tepe Yahya:
their significance for trade and technology in ancient Indo-Iran.
In M. Taddei (ed.), *South Asian Archaeology 1977*, pp. 317–44.
Naples: Istituto Universitario Orientale.

Dyson, R.H., M. Tosi, R. Biscione, G.M. Bulgarelli, O. Meder, V. Pigott
and S. Howard, n.d. Excavations and re-study of Tepe Hissar.
Mesopotamia: forthcoming.

Ferioli, P. and E. Fiandra, 1979. Stamp seals and functional analysis of
their sealings at Shahr-i Sokhta II–III (2700–2200 B.C.). Part 2.
In J.E. van Lohuizen-de Leeuw and J.M.M. Ubaghs (eds.), *South
Asian Archaeology 1975*, pp. 7–26. Leiden: Brill.

Fiandra, E. 1981. The connection between clay sealings and tablets in
administration. In H. Härtel (ed.), *South Asian Archaeology
1979*, pp. 29–43. Berlin: D. Reimer Verlag.

Gupta, S.P. 1979. *Archaeology of Soviet Central Asia and the Iranian
Borderlands*. Delhi: B.R. Publishing Corp.

Hakemi, A.A. 1972. *Catalogue de l'exposition Lut. Xabis (Shahdad)*.
Tehran: International Center for Archaeological Research.

Hauptmann, A. 1980. Zur frühbronzezeitlichen Metallurgie von Shahr-i
Sokhta (Iran). *Der Anschnitt* 32: 55–61.

Jarrige, C. and M. Tosi, 1981. The natural resources of Mundigak. In H.
Härtel (ed.), *South Asian Archaeology 1979*, pp. 115–49.
Berlin: D. Reimer Verlag.

Jarrige, J.-F. 1979. *Fouilles de Pirak*. Paris: Publications de la Com-
mission des Fouilles Archéologiques. Fouilles du Pakistan 2.

Johnson, G.A. 1980. Rank-size convexity and system integration: a
view from archaeology. *Economic Geography* 56: 234–47.

In press. The changing organization of Uruk administration in the
Susiana Plain. In F. Hole (ed.), *Archaeological Perspectives on
Iran: from Prehistory to the Islamic Conquest*. Albuquerque:
University of New Mexico Press.

Kohl, P.L. 1977. A note on chlorite artefacts from Shahr-i Sokhta.
East and West 27: 111–27.

1979. The 'world economy' of west Asia in the third millennium
B.C. In M. Taddei (ed.), *South Asian Archaeology 1977*, pp.
55–85. Naples: Istituto Universitario Orientale.

1981 (ed.) *The Bronze Age Civilization of Central Asia: Recent
Soviet Discoveries*. New York: M.E. Sharpe.

Kramer, C. 1980. Estimating prehistoric populations: an ethnoarchaeological approach. In M.-T. Barrelet (ed.), *L'archéologie de l'Iraq
du début de l'époque néolitique à 333 avant notre ère. Perspective et limites de l'interprétation anthropologique des docu-
ments*, pp. 315–34. Paris: CNRS Colloque International no.
580.

Kuzmina, E.E. 1971. Earliest evidence of horse domestication and
spread of wheeled vehicles in connection with the problem of
time and place of formation of Indo-European unity. In *Les
Rapports de la Délégation des Archéologues de l'URSS, VIII
Congrès UISPP, Beograd*: 2–18. Moscow.

Lahanier, C. 1975. Note sur l'emploi de l'heulandite et de la mordenite
dans la fabrication de séaux cylindres proto-Élamites. *Annales
des Laboratoires des Musées de France*: 65–6.

Lamberg-Karlovsky, C.C. and M. Tosi, 1973. Shahr-i Sokhta and Tepe
Yahya: tracks on the earliest history of the Iranian Plateau. *East
and West* 23: 21–58.

Masimov, I.S. 1976. *Keramiceskoe proizbostvo epohi bronzy v južnom
Turkmenistane*. Ashhabad: Ylym.

Masson, V.M. 1968. The urban revolution in South Turkmenia.
Antiquity 42 (167): 178–87.

1970. *Raskopky v Altyn-depe*. Ashhabad: Ylym.

1977. Altyn-depe v epohu eneolita. *Sovetskaja Arheologija* 4: 164–
89.

1978. Gorodskie čentry ranneklassovyh obscestv. In *Istorija i
Arheologija Srednej Azii*: 73–82. Ashhabad: Ylym.

1981. *Altyn-depe*. Leningrad: Nauka.

Masson, V.M. and V.I. Sarianidi, 1972. *Central Asia: Turkmenia before
the Achaemenids*. London: Thames and Hudson.

Meder, O. 1977. Sistan: the geographical aspects. In AA.VV., *La citta'
bruciata del deserto salato*, pp. 55–64. Venezia: Erizzo Editrice.

1979. *Klimaökologie und Siedlungsgang auf dem Hochland von Iran
in vor-und frühgeschichtlicher Zeir*. Marburg/Lahn: Marburger
Geographische Schriften 80.

Mitcham, C. 1978. Types of technology. *Research in Philosophy and
Technology* 1: 229–94.

Piperno, M. 1973. Micro-drilling at Shahr-i Sokhta: the making and use
of the lithic drill-heads. In N. Hammond (ed.), *South Asian
Archaeology 1971*, pp. 119–29. London: Duckworth.

1976. Grave 77 at Shahr-i Sokhta: further evidence of technological
specialization in the 3rd millennium B.C. *East and West* 26: 9–12.

1979. Socio-economic implications from the graveyard of Shahr-i Sokhta. In M. Taddei (ed.), *South Asian Archaeology 1977*, pp. 123–39. Naples: Istituto Universitario Orientale.

1981. Bead-making and boring techniques in 3rd millennium Indo-Iran. In M. Tosi (ed.), *Prehistoric Sistan I*, pp. 319–25. Rome: IsMEO.

Redman, L.R. and P.J. Watson, 1970. Systematic, intensive surface collections. *American Antiquity* 35 (3): 279–91.

Reindell, I. and J. Riederer, 1978. Infrarotspektralanalytische Untersuchungen von Farberden aus persischen Ausgrabungen. *Berliner Beiträge zur Archäometrie* 3: 123–34.

(forthcoming). *Berliner Beiträge zur Archäometrie* 5.

Sachs, I. 1966. La notion de surplus et son application aux économies primitives. *L'Homme* 6 (3): 5–18.

Salvatori, S. and M. Vidale. In press. A brief surface survey of the protohistoric site of Shahdad: preliminary report. *Rivista di Archeologia* 4 (forthcoming).

Semenov, S.A. 1957. *Pervobytnja tehnika.* Moskva: Nauka.

Suckling, J. 1976. A naive model of a Stone Age economy. *Current Anthropology* 17 (1): 105–15.

Tosi, M. 1968. Excavations at Shahr-i Sokhta, a chalcolithic settlement in the Iranian Sistan. Preliminary report on the first campaign, October–December 1967. *East and West* 18: 9–66.

1969. Excavations at Shahr-i Sokhta. Preliminary report on the second campaign, September–December 1968. *East and West* 19: 283–386.

1970. Tepe Rud-i Biyaban. *Iran* 8: 189.

1973. Early urban evolution and settlement patterns in the Indo-Iranian borderland. In C. Renfrew (ed.), *The Explanation of Culture Change*, pp. 429–46. London: Duckworth.

1974a. The problem of turquoise in the protohistoric trade on the Iranian Plateau. In *Studi di Paleontologia, Paleoantropologia, Paletnologia e Geologia del Quaternario*: 147–62. Roma: Memorie dell'Istituto Italiano di Paleontologia Umana 2.

1974b. Gedanken über den Lasursteinhandel des 3. Jahrtausends v.u.Z. im Iranischen Raum. *Acta Antiqua* 22: 33–43.

1976. A topographical and stratigraphical periplus of Sahr-e Suxteh. In F. Bagherzade (ed.), *Proceedings of the 4th Annual Symposium on Archaeological Research in Iran*, pp. 130–58. Tehran: International Centre for Archaeological Research.

1977. The archaeological evidence for protostate structures in Eastern Iran and Central Asia at the end of the 3rd millennium BC. In J. Deshayes (ed.), *Le Plateau iranien et l'Asie Centrale des origines à la conquête islamique*, pp. 45–66: Paris: CNRS Colloque International no. 567.

1981a. Excavations at Shahr-i Sokhta 1969–1970. In M. Tosi (ed.), *Prehistoric Sistan I*, pp. 73–126. Rome: IsMEO.

1981b. Development, continuity and cultural change in the stratigraphical sequence of Shahr-i Sokhta. In M. Tosi (ed.), *Prehistoric Sistan I*, pp. 127–81. Rome: IsMEO.

Tosi, M. and M. Piperno, 1973. Lithic technology behind the ancient lapis lazuli trade. *Expedition* 15: 15–23.

Trigger, B.G. 1980. *Gordon Childe: Revolutions in Archaeology.* London: Thames and Hudson.

Chapter 4

**Towards the quantification
of productive forces in
archaeology**
Luis F. Bate

In the *Preface to a Contribution to the Critique of Political Economy*, Marx synthesizes one of the fundamental theses of the theory of historical materialism in its most general form. First of all, he maintains the materialist position that 'the mode of production of the material means of existence conditions the whole process of social, political and intellectual life'. The mode of production is characterized by the set of relations of production established among men, of a necessary character, independent of their will, which *corresponds to a definite stage of development* in their material productive forces. For Marx, the principal contradiction is that between the forces and relations of production. As he states: 'At a certain stage of development, the material productive forces of society come into conflict with the existing relations of production . . . From forms of development of the productive forces these relations turn into their fetters. Then begins an era of social revolution' (1859: 21).

Once established, these generalizations, the results of Marx's research, served as the guiding thread in his studies, coupled with the fundamental discovery of essential laws which govern the history of social processes. These in turn allow us to verify that we are dealing with specific forms of the objective existence of a system of regularities conceived as laws and dialectic categories.

In this article we refer to only one aspect of this system of objective regularities, which can be abstracted and formalized as a law converting quantity to quality and vice versa. This can better be stated as a law of *mutual correspondence* between quality and quantity, in that it concerns the fundamental relationship which makes possible the explanation of evolutionary and revolutionary forms in history, as was shown by Engels in the *Dialectics of Nature* (1934: 63).[1] The Marxist thesis involves the discovery of the correspondence between the qualitative aspects of the system of relations of production and a specific degree of quantitative development of the productive forces. A specific mode of production occurs in direct proportion to the development of productive forces. The archaeological research of authors such as Gordon Childe also supports the existence of such dialectical relationships in past societies, viewed in a long-term perspective.

In the *Preface* Marx added that material changes, occurring within the economic conditions of production, 'can be appraised with precision characteristic of the natural sciences'. From this it can be deduced that if such a relationship between quality and quantity is real, it should be equally valid, generally speaking, for every case studied in concrete reality.[2] This outlines our scientific task, meaning that our research should not only allow us to discover the specific qualities of the system of relations of production in societies studied, but also allow us to arrive at an approximate quantification of their productive forces, in order to demonstrate this mutual correspondence. When we reach this objective, we will at least be able to distinguish the range of variability in the development of the productive forces which correspond to different modes of production, characterized by the specific, essential qualities of the systems of relations of production.

Without a doubt, this represents an extraordinarily difficult, complex and long-term undertaking. As Engels points out, finding objective means of quantification is a major problem: 'The same law governs living matter, but this works under very complex conditions, and to date, it is still frequently impossible to establish quantitative measures' (*ibid.*: 64). On the other hand, if it has proved impossible to establish this in archaeology to date, it is largely because the majority of relevant data has been obtained in accordance with theoretical positions totally different from those of Marx and Engels. Nevertheless, as long as the problem is not posed with sufficient clarity, we will remain unable to guide our search for those indicators which would allow the quantification we are interested in achieving. Reality itself is complex and we must try to approach it as it is. The dialectical materialist conception opposes reductionism and this commits us to the difficult search for a more precise knowledge of this complexity and of its objective movement, that is its real concrete nature.

It can be argued, however, that it is possible to derive logical operational procedures from theoretical statements to help us quantify the degree of development of the productive forces. We can start with the information obtained in archaeology, since its data, despite mediations between the real context of living societies and the current archaeological context, are precisely the vestiges of the material transformations achieved by past societies.

For this same reason, the establishment of a range of measures corresponding to specific, essential qualities of the modes of production, along with the conditions which have a bearing on the variability of these measures, will have great methodological importance. Thus, while archaeology offers a more direct access to the study of material transformations which are the result of social production, a quantitative knowledge of the degree of development of the productive forces will allow us to formulate more consistent hypotheses based on the necessary character of correspondence concerning the quality of relations of production. We are certain, however, that this is not the only way to accomplish such inferences, nor necessarily the one that permits the greatest degree of discrimination. The degree of development of the productive forces is only a social average of the yield of labour which in turn corresponds to an organic system of different and particular forms of production, although this defines the quality of the types of essential relationships which subordinate the secondary forms of the system. The qualitative and quantitative study of material evidence of processes of distribution, exchange and consumption is also included within the scope of archaeology. Given that these and the fundamental processes of production shape a specific system of causal, reciprocal relationships, the possibility of obtaining a more precise and detailed understanding of the system of productive

relationships remains open (Bate 1977; 1981). At this point, however, we will limit ourselves to the problem of quantifying the degree of development of the productive forces.

So as to clearly situate the purpose of this brief article, it should be pointed out that resolution of all the basic problems involved in such a quantification cannot be achieved immediately. This paper endeavours only to set forth conditions which require a solution, and present proposals regarding certain points. At the same time, the lack of precision of a formula proposed in passing in a previous work on general methodological problems of historical materialist archaeology (Bate 1977) needs to be corrected.

Conditions of measurement

The possibility of achieving the quantification of productive forces is subject to diverse requirements, which must satisfy a series of organic relations, ranging from the general theoretical level to the instrumental level of actual archaeological research. The principal are the following:

1 To understand the qualities that correspond to the quantities we would like to measure. This is an obvious point which is too often overlooked by those wishing to appear scientific through the supposed impartiality and objectivity of numbers. As long as there is no intention to determine which qualities correspond to quantified variables, the display of mathematical precision in research lacks scientific relevance.

    In the present case, Marxism has succeeded in determining the degree of correspondence between the state of development of the productive forces and the essential quality of the system of social relations of production. The degree of development of the productive forces represents a social average, the result of the productivity of human labour in each concrete labour process. Even that labour socially necessary for the production of different kinds of goods or use values is an average of labour invested under technical, social and natural conditions which may be quite unequal within the same society. The essential quality of the system of social relations of production is also a synthesis of diverse, concrete social relations in regard to the objective ownership of the means of production, the conditions and forms of the division of labour, the forms and proportions of the appropriation of social wealth, or of the diverse forms and degrees of participation in exchange and consumption. All of this forms a complex concrete system of types of relations of production. If archaeology offers the possibility of arriving at a theoretical synthesis through its inferential procedure of research, it is because it has more direct instrumental access to the understanding of concrete diversity expressed by the fundamental qualities and quantities discussed above.

2 To express the logical formulation of the theoretical relationships as relationships between variables, which correspond to qualitative links that it must be possible to quantify.

3 To delimit, for comparative purposes, equivalent temporal ranges to achieve these measurements. This implies the following considerations: (a) that each historical moment of production incorporates a determined amount of past labour, which shapes the conditions of the productive forces of that moment, and, (b) that there are short, medium and long-term productive cycles, so it is desirable that temporal units limiting measurements include the complete cyclical processes. This, however, will be arbitrary in as much as any limitation on time will cut the productive cycles into initial or final phases; besides which each productive cycle is likely to generate new conditions of production.

4 To define the meaning of archaeological data as indices of the amounts of production and labour productivity for each society and each historical period studied (cf. Tosi, this volume). This implies, among other things, considerable study regarding labour socially necessary for the production of each kind of goods, in relation to historical environmental conditions, social organization, and techniques of exploitation.

5 One of the most important points left unresolved is the conventional definition of the *units of measurement for the volume of products* that human labour has objectified. These units of measurement should be sufficiently independent of historical variations of productivity of the labour force so as to allow a comparison between quantitative differences due to changes in social development.

The same problem occurs for measuring the different objective times of our own individual vital rhythms or of our cycles of social activity on the basis of a common pattern. To make them comparable and to measure their differences, it is necessary to correlate them with the characteristic objective time of phenomena occurring within a greater time—space dimension.

What all products have in common is that they constitute the objectification of a determined amount of human labour (abstract labour). Nevertheless, abstract labour in each specific historical period represents a determined amount of labour socially necessary, which is modified precisely by a change in the degree of development of productive forces. This is why we cannot measure the volume of production on the basis of indices that depend on labour socially necessary for each historical period, since productive forces are quantified for comparative purposes. In this case, for example, a measurement using input and output of energy would not serve our purpose. How can we measure the energy produced or incorporated into a society with the construction of the Sun

Pyramid of Teotihuacan, or with the production of seven Clovis type points? We can only measure human energy consumed in their production. But this amount of human energy, i.e. labour socially necessary, can vary according to technological developments in distinct historical periods, while generating the same volume of production. The problem lies in defining a way to convert the quantitative measures which theoretically interest us on an ordinal scale to an interval scale. Nevertheless, the results of this sort of research should be interpreted as relative measurements of development.[3]

For the relationships to be examined in this article, a hypothetical scale of measurement will be used for the *quantity of products* which supposes units that express equal quantities of products (labour objectified in use value), independent of the historical variation of labour socially necessary for production. We designate these hypothetical and arbitrary units as Q (quantity of products).

Formulae for measurement

The variables to be measured with the goal of mathematically formulating the logical relationships which express the concept of the degree of development of the productive forces should first be pointed out. Variables that can be evaluated in terms of measurement with the information provided by archaeology can be considered, in the hope of orienting research towards the examination of relevant indices. At present some more or less acceptable calculations are being used which could certainly be perfected. It will be necessary to weigh them adequately. These variables are:

D: *total population* of a society, or demography.

LF: the *labour force* employed by that society, expressed as a percentage of the economically active members in relation to the total population. A more precise way of quantifying this variable would be to express the percentage of time destined for work, with respect to the total amount of time available in that society. The latter should be calculated by multiplying the labour time performed by a full capacity producer by D, considered as an average.

TP: indicates the *real total production* generated by a society in the period measured (expressed by units of Q).

ISC: *individual subsistence consumption*, indicating the number of products in units of Q that an individual needs in order to subsist. The ISC should be considered a social average, subject to historical variation.

With the availability of such indices, evaluated for a defined temporal range, we can begin by calculating a *coefficient of the productive process* of a society (P.). This coefficient will express the relationship between real total production (TP) and the total volume of products destined for the subsistence of the population (*social subsistence consumption*, or SSC) on a percentage basis, so that:

$$\text{if SSC} = \text{ISC} \times \text{D}, \quad \text{P.} = \frac{\text{TP}}{\text{SSC}} \times 100$$

Thus, when a society does not produce a surplus, TP is equivalent to SSC with P. = 100; in a society with surplus, P. > 100.

Knowing the coefficient of the productive process of a society (the P. index) we can define a *coefficient of output relative to the labour force* (RPF) or relative productive forces coefficient in the following manner:

$$\text{RPF} = \frac{\text{P.}}{\text{LF}} \quad \text{or} \quad \text{RPF} = \frac{\text{TP:ISC} \times \text{D}}{\text{LF}}$$

The coefficient RPF expresses the average productivity of the labour force, in terms of how many times each producer reproduces the material conditions of subsistence of an individual member of his society. Nevertheless, the ISC can vary from one society to another, in such a way that even when the RPF is the same for two given societies with different individual subsistence consumptions (ISCs), this difference means that with the same amount of labour force, a producer can produce a greater or lesser volume of products. When this occurs, it means that such a difference arises from factors relating to productive forces such as technological development, or the natural productivity of the environment related to exploited resources.

We can consider the differences of average labour productivity with the *productive forces index* (PF), by multiplying RPF by ISC, so that:

$$\text{PF} = \text{RPF} \times \text{ISC} \quad \text{or} \quad \text{PF} = \frac{\text{P.}}{\text{LF}} \times \text{ISC} \quad \text{or}$$

$$\text{PF} = \frac{\text{TP:ISC} \times \text{D}}{\text{LF}} \times \text{ISC}$$

The productive forces index measures the average output of the labour force (expressed now by Q), which is the same as an index of the *degree of development of the productive forces*, expressed in terms of the volume of products generated by a producer and also considering how many times the producer reproduces the subsistence conditions of an individual member of his or her society.

Observe that the calculations are based on the percentage of labour force, which supposes a hypothetical average day's work of a full-time producer. Nevertheless, anthropology offers multiple proof that the time making up a day's work of an average producer can vary substantially from one society to another (cf. Sahlins 1972). The proportion or intensity of the use of the human labour force in every society is one of the aspects in which the form of relations of production reciprocally influences the development of the content of production, and labour productivity. This is why we evaluate the degree of development of the productive forces in the above manner. Nevertheless, these variations, i.e. the degree of utilization of the available labour force, can be specified more closely. For

this we can calculate production volume related to time (production/time, or QT), if we allow for the duration of a day's work of an average producer (HW = hours of daily work) in the following way:

$$\text{QT} = \frac{\text{PF}}{\text{HW}}$$

This can be calculated in a more direct manner, through the formula:

$$\text{QT} = \frac{\text{TP}}{\dfrac{\text{D}}{100} \times \text{LF} \times \text{HW}}$$

So, QT expresses the total volume of products generated during the measured period of time by an average hour of daily work.

Theoretical implications

Under the present conditions of archaeological development, the possibility of carrying out the quantification of the productive forces may seem like a subject of archaeological fiction. In reality it is a task for the future development of this science.

Nevertheless, at present, the logical mathematical formulation of the problem allows us to develop theory by outlining hypotheses that establish alternative explanations of some important questions about the development of past societies.

We propose only a few examples in the accompanying tables — hypothetical quantities for the variables that have been discussed.

a) Even within the same mode of production, the raising of subsistence consumption through technological development or an increase in natural productivity allows for the development of productive forces without varying the proportion in which a producer reproduces the subsistence conditions of an individual member of his society (RPF). We suppose that this occurs in a society of hunters and gatherers, comparing cases A and B in Table 1.

b) This explains why, during primitive communism, the development of farming and animal husbandry (barbarism) yielded impressive increases in productive forces without this leading to a generation of surplus. In its initial phase, the basic support of food production techniques assumes and demands the diversification of production; with the elaboration of new sorts of goods not previously required, and the substitution or complementing of old techniques in the production of specific use values (the construction of villages, pottery production, textile and clothing manufacturing, etc.). This means that at least subsistence consumption increases. In the same cases of A and B we can suppose that the principal technological development of the second corresponds to food production.

Besides, the demographic laws of this new society

Table 1

	Case A	B	C	D	E	F	G
ISC	10	15	10	15	15	14	15
D	1,000	5,000	10,000	10,000	10,000	10,000	100,000
TP	10,000	75,000	100,000	150,000	180,000	170,000	2,000,000
LF (%)	50	50	30	30	35	30	25
SSC	10,000	75,000	100,000	150,000	150,000	140,000	1,500,000
P.	100	100	100	100	120	121	133
RPF	2.00	2.00	3.33	3.33	3.43	4.03	5.32
PF	20.00	30.00	33.33	49.99	51.43	56.46	79.99

tend towards a large increase in population. From the beginning, this increase is facilitated by new techniques which necessitate the development of production, to assure reproduction of the economic organization as well as to defend the collective property of the natural means of production (land and/or livestock). In a society in demographic expansion, the proportion of infants increases, thereby lowering the relative proportion of full capacity producers (LF) which is why they must raise their productivity (cf. Meillassoux 1981). Even if only this single variable is considered (as in case C), the increase in the productive forces index (PF) can be appreciated. In historical reality however both aspects usually combine which is why the situation approaches that of case D.

c) The discussions on the so called 'Asiatic mode of production' have raised the possibility of surplus generation, without important technological development.[4] This is theoretically possible through the intensification of the use of the labour force. Nonetheless, this did not necessarily mean an increase in the proportion of full capacity producers (as shown in case E). The disposal of the exploitable labour force is the principal factor in the accumulation of surplus and the foundation of the mode of production. This would probably be accompanied by a demographic increase. The alternative to the development of the productive forces was probably the extension of the average day's work. In Table 2 this is illustrated by comparing a non-surplus-producing and a surplus-producing society, showing how, without a variation in the quantity of products in terms of time (QT), i.e. without an increase in technological output or natural productivity, the extension of a day's work allowed the development of productive forces, and surplus generation (cases Y and Z). It is quite probable that this variable also influenced among other things the development of the productive forces during 'barbarism' (cases X and Y).

This initial class society grew on the foundation of surplus accumulation and was widely extended in such a way that although the proportion of tributary products per producer proved to be low, the total sum represented a considerable volume. Another form of securing surplus tax tributes may have been the reduction — albeit transitory — of subsistence consumption (Table 1, case F). Although it may have been difficult to implement by the dominant class in formation for political reasons, it could certainly be imposed when a strong state system was consolidated.

In this type of society, we do not subtract the labour time of the members of the dominant class from the LF, since it would be difficult for them to maintain themselves in power as an idle class. Their character as exploiters of labour belonging to others should be measured by the proportion of the *quantity of labour that they contribute* and the *quantity of labour objectified* in products or services that they *consume*. Only the development of an extended military system which the dominant class came to require led to an important proportion of the labour force remaining unproductive. In that case (case G), as is true today, the fact that their action allowed them to obtain products through pillage, or legal or illegal plundering by dominant class sectors, does not convert them into a productive factor. Nevertheless, their existence implies that workers had to increase their productive output, either in absolute terms through the intensification or extension of a day's work, or in relative terms by raising output through technology and the rationalization of available exploited resources.

We conclude the discussion here, with the hope of having outlined a general perspective on one aspect of research in archaeology, with respect to which Marxism offers interesting alternative explanations.

Notes

1 'The law of the transformation of quantity into quality and vice versa. For our purpose, we can express this by saying that in nature, in a manner exactly fixed for each individual case, qualitative changes can only occur by the quantitative addition or quantitative subtraction of matter or motion (so called energy)' (Engels 1934).

2 In principle, dialectical reasoning requires that each research project consider even the most proven general laws as hypotheses.

Table 2

	Case X	Y	Z
ISC	12	15	15
D	5,000	10,000	10,000
TP	60,000	150,000	180,000
LF (%)	30	30	30
SSC	60,000	150,000	150,000
P.	100	100	120
RPF	3.33	3.33	4.00
PF	40	50	60
QT	7.1428	7.1428	7.1428
HW	5.6	7.0	8.4

3 There are possible solutions to this problem but there is not space to discuss them in detail here. Such a discussion does not present greater complications nor implications than the problem of transforming values into prices for the economic theory of the capitalist system. One alternative would be to calculate the amount of labour socially necessary objectified in each sort of product as a ratio of the amount of labour socially necessary that is invested in the total sum of different sorts of products, in a society more developed than the ones we would like to compare. That way, we could conventionally generalize this arbitrary index in order to quantify those products we record in each society studied. Nevertheless, we hope to find more simple solutions.

4 The first class societies should be considered an initial form of slavery in regard to the fundamental basis of property that is founded on the *labour force*. The dominant class with its established control through extra-economic forms (political, ideological and military), *does not need ownership of land nor of the instruments of production*. The fundamental condition for this is that the communal relationships between the producer and the means of production, which are mediated necessarily by the ownership of the community, not be dissolved but be maintained as a 'natural relationship'.

Acknowledgements

Our gratitude to Dr Linda Finegold who kindly translated this paper from Spanish.

Bibliography

Bate, F. 1977. *Arqueología y Materialismo Histórico*. México: Ediciones de Cultura Popular.

1981. Relación General Entre Teoría Método en Arqueologia. *Boletín de Antropologia Americana* 4: 7–54.

Engels, F. 1934. *Dialectics of Nature*. Moscow: Progress Publishers.

Marx, K. 1859. *A Contribution to the Critique of Political Economy*. Edited with an Introduction by Maurice Dobb. Moscow: Progress Publishers, 1970.

Meillassoux, C. 1981. *Maidens, Meal and Money*. Cambridge: Cambridge University Press.

Sahlins, M. 1972. *Stone Age Economics*. Chicago: Aldine–Atherton.

PART 3

Representation and ideology

Chapter 5

Social change, ideology
and the archaeological
record
Michael Parker Pearson

Social and political changes in Europe since the sixties
have included the revival and critical reappraisal of Marx's
writings as a basis for understanding social changes and direct-
ing political activity. Some preach a 'purist' orthodox doctrine
while others have developed more flexible 'revisionist' perspectives. The latter favour diversified approaches which allow the
sorting out of 'dead wood' in Marx's thinking and the investigation of issues not previously considered in depth by Marxist
analysts. The position taken here is that certain aspects of
Marx's work need re-examination. These include: to what
extent Marxist analysis should employ the methodology of the
natural or the social sciences; whether ideology is determined
by economy or exists in a reflexive relationship with it; and
whether the theory of class struggle and contradiction is
adequate for understanding social change, especially in class-
less, 'egalitarian' societies. These issues are important for
developing an archaeological theory of social change which can
be combined with existing anthropological theories of long-
term change. An analysis of archaeological material from the
Early Iron Age of Denmark explores the potential of such a
theory.

Before we develop a model of long-term change in pre-
state societies, we have to examine some of the issues within
Marxist theory which have been raised recently. A theory of
nineteenth-century capitalism will obviously require rigorous
modification for dealing with societies which existed some

2000 years ago. Furthermore, the philosophical basis of Marxist theory for understanding human actions needs to be considered. Some scholars have interpreted Marxism as a 'natural science' of society while others would question the validity of an explicitly scientific approach to the study of human consciousness and participation in society.

Marxism as science

Knowledge deemed to be 'scientific' has several features. It is methodologically pursued and systematically related, uses generalizations, allows the prediction of events (and thence the ability to exercise greater control over future events), and is objective and free of personal values and social circumstances (Walsh 1967: 37). While it is generally accepted that the study of humanity should proceed methodologically and systematically, there is some controversy over the need for generalization, prediction and objectivity for understanding ourselves.

While some scholars of the human past would refuse to admit that they use anything more than the most basic generalizations (such as the need for food, clothing and shelter) and view each event as particular and unique, the majority of philosophers, social scientists, historians, economists and politicians explicitly or implicitly use concepts such as 'common sense', 'human nature' and 'rationality' to interpret, explain and influence the course of events which they observe and participate in. Amongst archaeologists there has been a tendency to concentrate on generalizations as having primacy over particular details. One aspect of this has been the so far unsuccessful attempt to derive universal and predictive laws of human behaviour from the testing of hypotheses against empirically ascertained facts (this is exemplified by Watson, LeBlanc and Redman 1971, and criticized by Flannery 1973). Marxist writers would recognize a number of universal generalizations and generalizations that apply to particular kinds of societies, as well as recognizing that the particular and the general cannot be separated or one given precedence over the other (Carr 1961: 65).

Marx's aim to advance the possibility of a world communist society has sometimes been taken more as a prediction of the future than an outline of general guides for future action. What Marx did predict was a crisis for capitalist society resulting from its internal flaws. A distinction can be made between the prediction of general processes of change and the specific events and outcome of those processes. Unique events cannot be predicted but can be interpreted within a general understanding of change. At the same time, the recognition of processes of change allows us to intervene and change our actions accordingly. History does not repeat itself since people can and do learn from past events and may take a different course of action to avoid the same outcome from a situation similar to one which occurred in the past. We are not helpless at the mercy of natural forces but are capable of recognizing and changing the rules by which we live. 'Human nature' is not fixed forever but has the capacity to be constantly modified.

The study of the human species beyond purely biological and physical explanations involves the relationship which is peculiar to the humanities. The distinction between the subject observing and the object observed is not absolute since the social position of the observer affects the observations which are made. This is even true for the archaeological study of long-vanished societies where the people under observation obviously cannot modify their actions in response to the investigations of a modern observer. Archaeologists still draw their interpretation of these past events in terms of the experiences and values which are part of their own particular social background. However, if all knowledge is value-laden it remains important to attempt to recognize and reconcile those historically conditioned biases which the observer implicitly employs.

In conclusion, the distinction between pure science and a subjective, particularist study of humanity is not a useful one to make. Marxist theory is both science and history and uses its predictive capacity to implement alternative action and change the course of events. This has major consequences for evaluating certain propositions central to Marxism: the role of ideology in the articulation of action and belief; the understanding of class struggle and class consciousness; and the inherent contradictions behind that conflict.

Ideology

The concept of ideology was given relatively little attention by Marx and Engels, and recent commentators have argued from the original sources about its true significance for orthodox Marxist thought (McCarney 1980; Seliger 1977). The two interpretations of ideology which are generally acknowledged to have been used by Marx and Engels are that it is 'false consciousness' (a set of beliefs which distort the true nature of social relations) and that, since the material conditions of life determine consciousness, ideology is the product of human action in the world.

This deterministic notion of the relationship of social practice to ideology has more recently been reassessed. Human practice is composed of a reflexive or two-way relationship between action and thought (Giddens 1979: 49–95; Walsh 1967: 48–71; Wilson 1979). Thought is taken here to mean not only the immediate conscious thoughts and motives of the individual actor but also the set of principles which provide categories of meaning and interpretation of reality. Reality is a social construction in which principles not only provide the initiative for action but are also capable of being modified as a consequence of action (Berger and Luckmann 1967). Ideology is an active part of human practice and is not external to what humans actually do. It should be clear that ideology is not the spiritual as opposed to material reality but is present in all material practice. The ideological sphere extends to include the vast majority of our activities — the nature of our work and leisure, house forms, food preparation, our use of the past, attitudes between men and women, and our need for certain kinds of commodities and energy for consumption are just some of the areas in which we make conscious or unconscious political and ideological decisions every day. While the complexity of our reality has led us to specialize in different fields and disciplines, a properly integrative study of ourselves must break down the watertight compartments into which the social, political, economic and ideological are sometimes separated.

This has major implications for our understanding of material culture, the data source for archaeologists. Since artifacts are the product of human actions and are also used to carry out actions it follows that their meaning derives from their relationship with beliefs. Each and every artifact has an ideological component. Compare this with what Dunnell and Wenke (1980: 607) have to say on the matter:

> As a body of phenomena, the archaeological record has one great virtue for the study of human history: it records only what actually transpired, and it does so without the complications introduced by human motivations, intentions, and rationalizations that plague the use of contemporary ethnographic data. Historical documents, in common with other linguistic sources, embody elements of values, ideals, and purposes of the writers and users of the documents.

Their distinction between two types of artifacts, written and non-written, cannot be maintained in such terms. Although the recovery of the two types of information rests on different methodologies of source criticism, those methodologies should not dictate that different approaches to the study of social change are the inevitable outcome.

In conclusion, artifacts cannot be divided up according to economic, social or ideological criteria. All practice and the technology employed to implement that practice is mediated through ideology with each item taking its meaning from the whole set of material conditions, social practices and belief systems (Ingold 1980: 8–9; Sumner 1979: 211). An agricultural implement is as much the product of ideology as is a crown or a written law code; they simply have different functions.

An important corollary to the action/belief duality is the basic approach for understanding change. We should understand society as continually changing with the constant reproduction of practices creating an 'illusion' of stasis. Society and its institutions exist only in so far as they are affirmed by everyday behaviour. If the legitimacy of these social institutions is questioned then practices will be reproduced in different and modified ways. Thus every action has the potential to change the existing belief system. If action and belief are constantly reproduced in essentially the same form then only the unintended consequences of actions or the influence of an outside force will produce any change at all.

It is often stated that Marxist analyses go beyond the study of surface appearances of social phenomena and discover inner relationships between things before examining the superficial relationships (Godelier 1977: 3). As with artifacts, so institutions embody the social, the economic and the ideo-

logical (whether medieval churches or twentieth century banks). There is no direct correspondence between, say, religion and ideology or economy and subsistence, and the configuration of relationships will be different in each particular society. In many pre-capitalist societies the economy is mediated through the religion (by means of supernatural spirits, deities and ancestors) while the economy is one of the main components of capitalist ideology (Friedman 1975; Godelier 1977: 152–65).

Class struggle

An essential premise of Marxism is that humans are motivated by self-interest and motivated to accumulate power in order to extend that self-interest. People's interests become antagonistic to others' since they are involved in social relations for the production of materials and food and for the reproduction of the social institutions which articulate that production. Since the interests of many individuals will coincide, they can be said to form an interest group (this does not mean that they have the realized capacity to act together in the defence, maintenance or extension of those interests; they need not be a community or co-operating 'action group' despite having the same position in the organization of production). These interest groups are arranged in antagonistic relations with each other through their integration in the system of production, exchange and consumption. They might consist of women producing food for consumption by males in 'egalitarian' societies, or a working class producing surplus for a dominant elite. Marx's famous dictum 'The history of all hitherto existing society is the history of class struggles' (Marx and Engels 1968: 35) may now sound anachronistic and hackneyed but statements that claim it to be empirically untenable (Moore 1963: 132) result from a superficial understanding of the concept. First the term 'class' can be replaced by 'interest group' for non-capitalist societies without economically segregated classes, though it is still important to define those 'interest groups' by their relation to the production, exchange and consumption cycle. Second, tensions between groups are not always manifested through open conflicts. Returning to the statement that society exists through reproduced practices which are considered legitimate by the members of that society, we must consider how conflicts are controlled and suppressed.

While people may be controlled by direct coercive force, the most effective form of political control is essentially ideological (Carlton 1977). The position of a ruling class might be legitimated in several ways; by misrepresenting the inequalities between the surplus-producing and the surplus-consuming groups; by representing the interests of the elite as universal for the whole society; and by justifying the status quo through hierarchical conceptions of the supernatural which 'explain' the hierarchical nature of social existence (cf. Kus, this volume). Ideology, then, is also thought which serves class interests (McCarney 1980) though this does not imply that each class has its own ideologically realized identity.

Seliger has pointed out that in modern capitalism the majority of the working class adopt the ideology of the ruling class (1977: 157–66). The lack of fit between class affiliation and ideological interests should however be regarded as a changing historical phenomenon. Polarities between interest groups are reached at specific times when social tensions are aggravated to the level of open conflict. Thus while classes or interest groups are shown to exist through their relationship to the cycle of production exchange and consumption, they may not choose to actively represent that position as a conscious expression of solidarity. Hodder's work on African societies brings out this point very clearly (1979); ethnic minorities, age groups, male/female groups, elites and tribal groups emphasize their identity through clothing, portable artifacts and other forms of material culture only at times of social and economic stress (cf. Gilman, this volume).

Antagonisms are mediated and contained through the ideological categorization of the material world. This takes the form of role-playing and identity consciousness which will be manifested, in part, in material form. Where that categorization is threatened, the need to legitimate the social order will be greater (Berger 1973: 55–6). This legitimation involves the demonstration of ruling-class power in a number of ways such as by constructing monuments, destroying large quantities of prestige objects or waging war for territorial gain.

Conflict between interest groups is not limited solely to economic and social divisions within societies. The spatial dimension of domination and exploitation must also be considered. This problem has recently been framed in terms of a global system in which a core area dominates a periphery (Ekholm 1980; Wallerstein 1979). Relations of economic dependence are built up by core areas over their peripheries by accumulating surplus through unbalanced exchange (the value of commodities and labour being substantially lower in the periphery). Where relations between polities do not involve a core/periphery situation, conflicts between those polities often stem from internal tensions between interest groups. Warfare has been described as the 'property' of ruling classes; the results of expansionist aggression include greater political solidarity, advances in technology and an expansion in production (Ekholm 1980: 164). If there is a likelihood of internal social divisions threatening the power of a ruling elite, warfare between polities is one possible strategy which the elite might use in order to defuse revolutionary conflict, legitimate their position and increase prosperity and solidarity within the polity.

Contradiction

An analysis of conflict between interest groups is not complete without an understanding of contradiction, its relationship to conflict and its role in causal explanations of change. Marx and Engels identified two contexts where contradictions appear. The first is the inter-relationship between forces of production and relations of production. It is important to note that although emphasis has been placed on changes in the forces of production producing change in the relations of production, Marxism should not be taken as a technological or environmental determinism (otherwise termed 'vulgar materialism', cf. Friedman 1974). To elaborate on this, the innovation of technology capable of modifying the relations between the producers and the controllers of surplus does not occur independently of social conditions. We have to understand the existing conditions of social relations to explain why so often inventions and discoveries are made and adopted simultaneously yet independently. Once an innovation has been made and accepted, it can transform the nature of the social relations — a new subsistence technology might be contradictory to existing rules of property ownership and surplus production, with the result of transforming those rules and thereby changing the social relations. It has been suggested that contradictions between forces and relations of production have had a major effect only on capitalism and not on pre-capitalist societies (Giddens 1979: 154). There is certainly some truth in this but the difference is probably best seen as relative rather than absolute.

The second kind of contradiction exists between the appropriation and consumption of surplus and the social organization of its production. In class societies this entails the unbalanced exchange relationship which exists between the producers of a surplus and the appropriators of that surplus. The ruling class that appropriates the surplus might also control the productive technology, thereby strengthening its hold but at the same time increasing the contradictions.

There has been some confusion over the understanding of 'contradiction'. While it might appear similar to the concepts of dysfunction of maladaptation in functionalist theories (Rappaport 1978), it is in fact rooted in the action/belief duality discussed above. Contradiction and conflict are intimately linked; conflict is the active realization of contradictions, action which is related to a clash of opposed ideologies and their associated practices.

Anthropological models of social change

Although the time is ripe for a detailed critique of social evolution, I do not propose to develop it here (but see Giddens 1981). It should be sufficient to note that unilinear evolution, aspects of which were developed by Marx, Engels and Morgan (Marx and Engels 1968: 449–583; Morgan 1877), is no longer acceptable to most students of long-term change. Also subsequent multilinear theories of cultural evolution developed by the cultural evolutionists (see Service 1971; Steward 1955) can be criticized for their assumption of a causal, rather than constraining relationship between environment/technology and social organization as well as their isolation of general, ideal types of social stages (Wenke 1981: 84–7). We should be concentrating on social transformations and episodes of change and not in creating ideal stages said to lie between them. Marx's original formulation of contradictions producing conflict in the form of social revolution (Marx and Engels 1968: 181–2) is an important starting point. 'Social revolution' should be taken in a broader sense than a revolt by an oppressed class; it may be taken to be a very rapid change in social relations after a gradual build up of tensions. In other words 'revolutionary change' is defined as a rapid transformation of social relations in a relatively short timespan. Such change might take the form of warfare between polities, a political coup, or the implementation of a new productive technology, as well as a class revolution. Whatever the actual nature of this revolutionary change, it can be described as a legitimation crisis threatening the overthrow of the ruling group, who must then devise strategies to deal with that situation by demonstrating and asserting their power.

There have been a number of attempts by anthropologists to develop explanations of change to account for the patterns which they observe over a very short time during ethnographic enquiries (Bonte 1978; Friedman 1979; Leach 1954; Rappaport 1968). In most of these cases the methodology is weak. In the absence of archaeological material and with little historical information the assumption is made that the spatial variation of political forms in a region represents a collection of survivals from different evolutionary stages. This clearly requires empirical examination from the archaeologist's point of view though it does offer potential insights into the processes of transformation.

Although Rappaport employs a cultural ecology and systems theory framework in his interpretation of warfare and pig feasting rituals in the New Guinea Highlands, his evidence may be better explained within a Marxist approach (for a critique of his theoretical assumptions see Diener, Moore and Mutaw 1980). A short summary could be as follows. The social relations are centred on the antagonistic interests of males and females. Women produce the food crops and bring up the pigs (which are treated as prestige items) for the men. These contradictory antagonisms are regulated and expressed through the strong role-playing, or category definition and separation, between the sexes. This role-playing is given expression in food taboos, dress types and other forms emphasizing the differences between male and female styles of life. In such a way open conflict is prevented but tensions develop as the growing pigs require more and more food. As the women are increasingly less able to provide this food they complain to their husbands who then initiate a territorial war with neighbouring clans. After several fights a truce is called with the organization of a pig feast for all the clans in the area. Alliances are made between clans and pigs are 'sacrificed' (eaten not thrown away) to the ancestor spirits of the clan and to allies. The men manipulate the warfare and feasting in order to reaffirm clan and tribal identity, thereby healing the internal tensions between men and women. The cycle is estimated to last between five and 25 years and might possibly be a minor cycle within a much longer one which could have far-reaching effects.

Leach's study of the Kachin proposed a series of cycles each about 150 years long in which the tribal societies oscillated between egalitarian and chiefly organization. He describes the changes between hierarchical and egalitarian forms as a long-phase oscillation between polarized beliefs. Friedman's re-analysis of the same material has received strong criticism from Leach (1977: 163) but has greater explanatory value because the context of change is located not in the realm of beliefs but in the relationship between practices and beliefs. Friedman places the cycles described by Leach within a long cycle of state formation — the successive short-term discontinuities culminating in a longer-term transformation. Within each cycle contradictions build up as debts and inflation increase, along with a decrease in surplus production and greater environmental degradation. The result is a rebellion which establishes an egalitarian society. In turn the contradictions underlying the exchange of cattle and prestige items as bridewealth on the one hand and as competitive feasting on the other again result in debts accumulating between lineages. These debts are directly related to status and a chiefly status rests on the obligations due from other members of the community. These obligations are formalized in terms of relations with ancestors; in the egalitarian form all lineages mediate equally with the community ancestors (except that some will acquire greater influence over the spirits by creating debts from others); in hierarchical societies the chiefly lineage appropriates the community ancestors for its own and controls ancestral help for villagers in return for surplus as tribute.[1]

Other authors have presented similar models of transformations though in much less detail (Ekholm 1980: 156; Moore 1963: 36–9). The existence of similar transformations can be sought for in the archaeological record, a task which will be carried out below. Before doing so it is necessary to consider the relevant 'bridging' theory to link prehistoric material culture with its context of changing social practices.

Material culture, mortuary practices and ideology

Social inferences from burial practices have become increasingly common amongst archaeologists in the last 15 years (e.g. Brown 1971; Chapman, Kinnes and Randsborg 1981). A major aim has been to build law-like generalizations or universal inferences about the relationship between the variability of treatment of the dead and social factors, generally the assumed living status of the deceased (Binford 1971; Saxe 1970; Shennan 1975; Tainter 1975). Whether the status is in terms of ranking, class or kinship (Van der Velde 1979), it is generally thought to vary with differential treatment of the dead on the basis of a wide number of ethnographic observations. The recent work of social anthropologists on ritual and death rituals in particular (Bloch 1971; 1977; Huntington and Metcalf 1979; Lewis 1980) has suggested new approaches to burial studies by archaeologists. For example Klejn (1979) and Pader (1982) point out that burials are only indirectly linked to social ranking and class divisions via ritual expression. As ritual actions, mortuary practices may play an active role in the living society and influence the distribution and use of power. The empirical observation of cases where status is not overtly affirmed in death has led to developments towards a dynamic, historical perspective on mortuary variability away from the synchronic, 'snapshot' observations of ethnography (Pearson 1982a).

The relationship between society and burial practices has to be understood as the relations between living and dead before making social inferences (Pearson 1982a: 110). They can be expressed as follows:

1 Burials may be socially prescribed outlets for the advertisement and display of the social position of a group or individual. Since the dead do not bury themselves the pomp and ceremony associated with a deceased individual will reflect on the survivors. It is their decision how to stage the funeral and consequently whether to use it as a platform for acting out the social principles which they believe in. At that funeral the deceased individual's achievements are summed up not simply as a display of status but as a display in terms of certain socially acceptable values. A king may be buried as a commoner — an example which we have from modern Saudi Arabia (Huntington and Metcalf 1979: 122) — in order to show that all, whether high born or lowly, are equal before the supernatural deities, and hence support the ideological legitimation for a class society.

2 Funerary rituals, as social and political statements, embody economic as well as religious aspects. Funerals and the rituals associated with death and the ancestors are times for the transference of property and responsibilities according to the conventions of property rights and laws (Goody 1962). Also at these times agricultural surplus may be transferred into gifts for the living and the dead — funeral feasts and grave goods. Items placed with or destroyed alongside the deceased can be considered as the wasteful economic consumption of materials which might have some other socially valued capacity. Where large amounts of precious commodities are 'sacrificed', destroyed or given to the dead, or where large amounts of labour are expended on large monuments dedicated to the dead, the economic and religious spheres are inseparable.

3 Funerals can provide political legitimation through conspicuous consumption of commodities. Groups may compete in attempts to outdo each other in the lavishness and importance of a ceremony. This kind of gift exchange can take many forms — weddings, feasting, giving away precious things — and serves to build up obligations between people. However funerals are more than just one of many contexts for conspicuous consumption. The context of death is a major interface in mediations between mortals on the one hand and ancestors and deities on the other (Bloch 1977; Huntington and Metcalf 1979). It can be argued that since the funerary remains of many pre- and non-capitalist societies are far more impressive than other forms of material culture such as house forms, ancestors and deities are an important channel for the legitimation of power. Mauss's statement complements this: 'Among the first group of beings with whom men must have made contracts were the spirits of the dead and the gods. They in fact are the real owners of the world's wealth' (1954: 13). Friedman (1979) has shown that feasting among the Kachin as sacrifice to ancestors builds up debts between the living. Gregory's (1980) analysis of sacrifice in traditional societies, especially in Papua and among the Kwakiutl of north west America, concludes that gifts are given to the supernatural by groups competing against each other. He states that this competition does not put people in debt (*ibid.*: 647) though the outcome is a ranking system of differential status which surely must entail obligations from one to the other. Through processes of competition and indebtedness certain groups or individuals can gain power over others who cannot compete on similar terms. Ancestors and gods are a 'third party' through which social prestige is mediated between people. Far from being simply indicators of status, gifts to the dead may be an important part of the mechanism on which status is founded. Even if the items were possessions of the deceased in life they are still part of a gift transaction to the deceased in their new role as corpse. Like warfare, the consumption of large amounts of wealth in sacrifice can initiate increases in production. As obligations become greater and greater the prestige of one or a few individuals increases as does the capacity to procure larger surpluses (within environmental constraints) which can be transformed into more prestige goods for sacrifice or disposal with the dead.

Social change in early Iron Age Denmark

This analysis of over 600 years of change in Iron Age Jutland (a region of Denmark) incorporates all the surviving forms of archaeological evidence in order to examine the model of transformational development outlined above (a more detailed account can be found in Pearson 1984 where a full bibliography is given).

The earlier Iron Age of Denmark (c. 400 BC–250 AD) cannot be understood without considering its position in the core/periphery relations between the expanding Mediterranean world and the 'barbarian' north during the late first millennium BC and the early first millennium AD. As colonizing Mediterranean polities expanded their territory and influence (as Greek city states and later the Roman Empire) they supplied local centres on the periphery with prestige commodities (presumably in return for political co-operation and raw materials). These items, of iron, bronze, silver and gold, included drinking sets, coinage, dress fabrics and fittings and weaponry, and were supplied to a small section of the population (see Frankenstein and Rowlands 1978 on central western Europe during the sixth to fifth centuries BC). To the north of the Celtic world, in the area known as Germania from classical sources (this includes Jutland), the importation of Celtic prestige goods (drinking sets, dress styles, cauldrons, elaborate waggons and weaponry) preceded the arrival of similar Roman commodities (during the first century BC to first century AD, Celtic and Roman imports overlapped but in different areas of Denmark and the north European fringe).

The first transformational cycle that can be recognized dates from the beginning of the Pre-Roman Iron Age (c. 400 BC) until the end of the first century BC. The millennium before (the Nordic Bronze Age c. 1800–500 BC) has been interpreted as a period of hierarchical 'chiefdom' forms of social organization (Kristiansen 1981: 244–5). Towards the end of the Bronze Age the increasing shortage of bronze (*ibid.*: 248) was undoubtedly one of the factors responsible for the collapse of the ranking structure which had supported the 'chiefly' elite. The result was some kind of social revolution after which status differences were given little material expression or simply did not exist. The large-scale excavation of a settlement at Grøntoft in western Jutland (Becker 1965; 1966; 1971) revealed a cluster of farmsteads, the earliest ones undefended and the later ones enclosed in a small palisade. Each one possessed a hearth and stalling for animals. None of them possessed outbuildings and the differences in size between each farm was negligible. Assuming that the farm byres were fully occupied by cattle, that the main storage features have not escaped archaeological detection and that each farm was occupied by only one family group, the inhabitants appear to have had more or less equal productive capacity between farm units (see Fig. 1).

Fig. 1. Enclosed village at Grøntoft c. 300–150 BC. (From *Acta Archaeologica* 36 (1965): 211.)

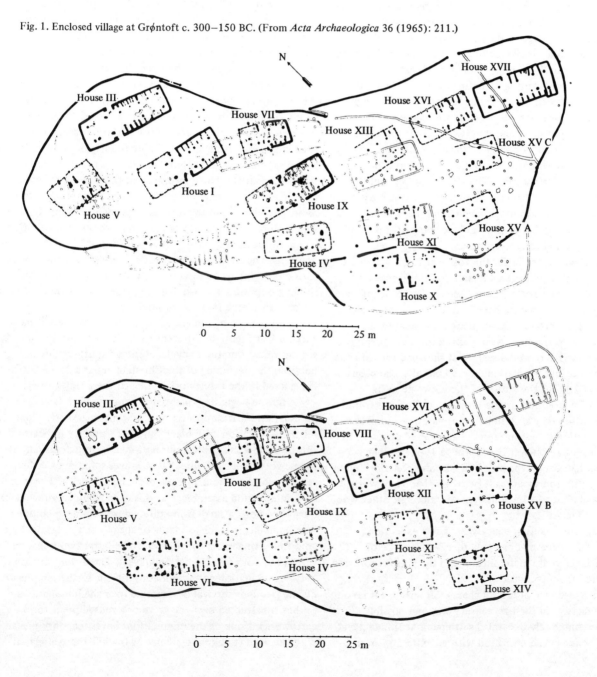

A couple of large cemeteries of this date (c. 400–200 BC) have been extensively excavated (Becker 1961), while there have been many small excavations of cemeteries in the region. The material residues of the mortuary practices indicate that for the majority of the population the death rites included cremation of the corpse and disposal of the ashes and dress remains in a clay pot which was covered by a small circular mound (mound construction appears to have ended by the first century BC). The lack of differentiation between individuals in terms of dress remains, pot types and mound types, as well as the lack of covariation of any of these features with spatial location within the cemetery, indicates a very strong conformity.[2]

Votive depositions, mainly in peat bogs and lakes, undergo interesting changes. The classes of items used as 'gifts to gods' include wooden ploughs, human sacrifices, dress fittings, neck rings, waggons and cauldrons. The ploughs and human corpses cannot individually be dated securely but date mainly between c. 400 BC and the birth of Christ on the basis of pollen analysis and carbon 14 dating. Many of the human corpses had been killed before being dumped into the bogs and lakes. An interesting feature of the well-preserved bodies is the fineness of physique and skin (Glob 1977: 163). This would indicate that at least some of these people were not involved in manual agricultural production and must have lived off other people's surplus. There are many possible interpretations of this enigmatic discovery – that captured rival elite members or witches, shamen and priests were ritually murdered, or that emerging elites living off the surplus of others were periodically overthrown.

A clear trend emerges for the votive artifacts which are relatively well dated. Between 400 and 200 BC bronze and iron dress fittings and pottery were used as gifts. Most of the dress fittings are the same as those from graves at that time. Much rarer are the bronze 'crown' neckrings. Most of the larger ones have no traces of wear and the form in general is not found in burials. It would seem that they had special ritual significance, possibly for marking some kind of social position.

Around 200 BC the nature of the votive deposits changed. A very large and ornate bronze cauldron was found in a low hill at Bra (it was definitely not part of a burial and despite its location is best interpreted as a votive deposit). In the very south of Jutland at Hjortspring a 19-metre-long wooden boat had been deposited in a lake and contained eight iron swords, 138 iron spearheads (with another 31 of wood and bone) and about 150 wooden shields, amongst other wood and metal artifacts.

Finally from the first century BC a few exceptional votive finds have been made: a gold torc, a pair of Celtic waggons with elaborate metal fittings and the famous gold and silver cauldron from Gundestrup.

There is evidence of radical changes in settlement layout and burial practices in the first century BC (and possibly earlier). The completely excavated settlement at Hodde developed initially as a single farmstead with an extra 50% more cattle space than other farms and a number of small outbuildings including a 'strong room' with its own palisade and deep foundations.[3] Around this large farm a number of small farmsteads were established (see Fig. 2) (Hvass 1975). Rare black burnished pottery was also found mainly, though not exclusively, in the compound of the main farmstead.

The changes in burial practices exhibit a similar trend. Certain cremation graves often containing the black burnished pottery were placed in new locations away from the earlier large cemeteries. Some of these contained the burnt remains of waggons and cauldrons – e.g. Kraghede (Klindt-Jensen 1949) and Husby (Raddatz 1967). Others contained large and varied weapon assemblages with finely made Celtic swords.

The changes in different contexts of material culture appear to fit together quite well. Votive deposits became increasingly elaborate and prestigious, presumably requiring more and more surplus for their production and importation. With the exception of pottery and a few of the bog corpses, these deposits finished at the same time as the same kinds of prestige goods were destroyed in individual cremation rites. If these goods had been given initially to supernatural deities, it would seem that their later occurrence in burials represents a transference of supernatural status to the ancestors of a restricted social group that was able to raise the surplus to acquire the imported commodities (either as raw material or finished product). The appearance of the large farmstead at this time complements the picture. The developing contradictory tendencies in the increasingly unequal competition for supernatural appeasement or aid produced a legitimation crisis where the egalitarian structure was infringed by incipient class divisions. The transition from 'gifts to gods' to 'gifts to ancestors' would appear to represent the stabilization of the new ruling group using its own dead to present a supernatural order which legitimated their new-found superiority.

By the end of the Pre-Roman Iron Age different parts of Jutland had begun on different social trajectories. For the second transformational cycle, events in southern Jutland between the beginning of the Christian era and 250 AD are considered in the framework of one of these trajectories.

By the beginning of the first century AD a few inhumation burials appeared as a new mortuary rite. Their regular association with black burnished pottery indicates that this new rite was adopted amongst many, though not all, of the newly established elite. These graves stand out by their relative simplicity and absence of material wealth. The standard inhumation assemblage at this time included a few black burnished pots, a small iron knife, an iron fibula, a couple of iron implements (such as razors or shears) and occasionally a gold finger ring and a pair of spurs (the latter two items are very rarely found in cremation graves). The differentiation between cremation and inhumation rites is further emphasized by the frequent survival of a mound over the inhumations (either constructed over the grave or a reused prehistoric earthwork). None of the inhumations have weaponry placed with the dead (unlike the cremations) while there is spatial

Fig. 2. Enclosed village at Hodde c. 100 BC. (From *Acta Archaeologica* 46 (1975): Figs. following p. 158.)

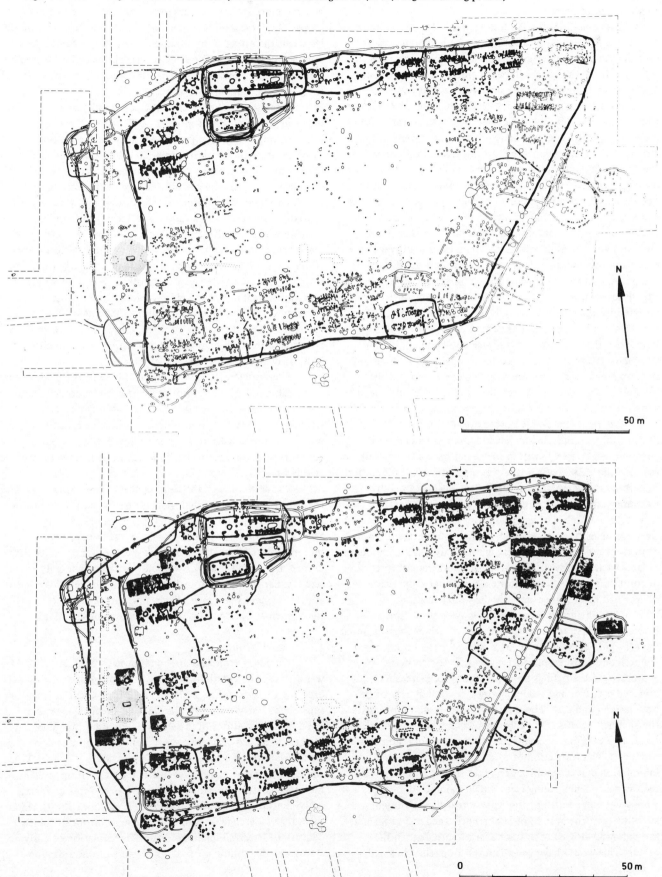

0   50 m

0   50 m

segregation of inhumation and cremation graves both within and between cemeteries.

This transition to a modest disposal of material items at funerals indicates that elites stopped competing in conventional terms of grave gift giving and now emphasized stylistic, ritual differences between elite and commoners. Rather than compete on the same terms as everyone else, they adopted a set of ritual practices which set them apart as a distinctive group. There is good evidence that the prestige items previously placed in graves and votive deposits were still in circulation yet not given as gifts to the dead. In other words the change in consumption patterns is not simply the result of declining availability of those prestige items. Settlement excavations have uncovered, at one site, the remains of a cauldron in a large farmhouse, and at another, the remains of a Celtic waggon in the first century AD levels of a large farmhouse (Jensen 1980). In addition, many cremations with weaponry date from this period but virtually all of them are accompanied by pottery which is not black burnished, indicating that other groups were now using the ritual conventions initiated by the elite a century before (cf. Miller 1982). The rejection of the need for conspicuous disposal of prestige items with the dead (though not rejected by an emulating secondary group) accompanied the imposition of ritual sanctions to demarcate social position in clearly recognizable categories. The elite, once established, did not need to legitimate their power by expending large resources.

The trend observable in cremation rites since the first century BC of separating male and female graves either in different cemeteries or within the cemetery continued into the first century AD. It was not however practised in inhumation cemeteries. Male cremations were often accompanied by weaponry although through the first and into the second century AD the number of weapon graves and the quantities of weapons in each grave declined. Swords, a prominent feature of first century BC graves, were increasingly less a component of later weapon graves. This would support the interpretation of emulation of previous ruling class mortuary practices if swords had been owned only by the upper stratum.

While the use of weaponry as grave gifts declined between the first and second centuries AD there was a gradual increase in the procurement of imported metalwork (as raw material and finished product) from the Roman world. Iron and bronze dress fittings on the corpse were increasingly replaced by silver and gold amongst a small minority of the population (Table 1). These imported items would necessitate the channelling of surplus into long-distance exchange transactions (the surplus presumably being agricultural and cattle products). The restriction of these imports predominantly to inhumation graves would suggest that their circulation was confined to a small ruling class which maintained alliances with other elites north of the Roman frontier. Although we know little of the system of land tenure, the large farms had the potential at least to extract a larger surplus than the others. This would have had the result of excluding smaller

farmers from the prestige exchange sphere. Social differences became more and more marked by this circulation of prestige items. The increase in competition for gifts to the dead would have had the effect of building up debts from small farmers unable to compete in the same terms. The tensions created by this situation of increasing inequality would have arisen out of the contradiction between the ideological acceptance of an elite protecting the interests of the community and the increasingly obvious self-interest displayed by the elite.

During this period there were also changes in the categorization of material forms. The simple ceramic designs of the early first century AD were incorporated or replaced by more elaborate and diverse motifs. The distinction between male and female cremation also changed. They were no longer spatially segregated and a number of burials had combined male and female artifact sets. Black burnished pottery became more frequent as a component of ordinary cremation graves while some cremations of the late second and early third centuries possessed all the accoutrements previously restricted to inhumations. Many of the clearly categorized organizational principles ordering funerary ritual had become blurred or redundant. Social tensions could no longer be represented and channelled through material categorization as the ideological basis of power was increasingly threatened.

The burial evidence for the last phase of the cycle points to a legitimation crisis. Many of the lavishly equipped graves were equipped with weaponry — possibly a symbolic demonstration of the ability to use force at a time of crisis. Furthermore, the graves with most items and with the greatest amounts of silver within this 250-year period were constructed at this time.

By the middle of the third century there was a rapid and total transformation of material culture (ceramics, metalwork, funeral ritual and farm construction) including the organization of production. The vast majority of burials were inhumations and displayed a much greater homogeneity than before. Likewise the farms were now of approximately equal size, similar to the previous large farms. Although this change appears to have been revolutionary, the exact form that it took (such as uprisings or external aggression) is unknown.

Conclusion

The Early Iron Age of Scandinavia (c. 400 BC−250 AD) was a time of social discontinuity after the clearly hierarchical ordering of Bronze Age society. The initially egalitarian structure of the Early Iron Age was changed through a series of rapid transformations over half a millennium into a hierarchical and class-divided system. Between c. 600 and 900 AD Denmark entered what is conventionally known as a Dark Age though the sparse material available (coins, writing, precious-metal hoards, territorial defences) points towards an increasingly centralized and powerful elite (Randsborg 1980). Documentary and archaeological evidence exists from the tenth century of large Viking kingdoms. This formation of early states was the culmination of 1500 years of discontinuous

Table 1 *Grave finds of imported prestige items, 1st century BC to mid 3rd century AD.*

	Samian ware	Gaming counter set	Bronze casserole/ladle/sieve	Bronze cauldron	Gold coin	Gold rivet/fitting/item	Gold locket	Gold ring	Silver spoon	Silver cup	Silver rivet/fitting/item	Glass bead necklace	Glass vessel	Silver fibula with gold plate	Silver fibula	Bronze fibula with gold plate	Bronze fibula with silver plate
1st century BC										1	1				1		
Early 1st century AD		1		1			1	1			1	1			3		
Late 1st–2nd century AD								1			9	3	1		7		1
2nd century AD		1		1		2	2	3	1		7		1	1	3		1
Late 2nd–early 3rd century AD	1	3	10	10				1	9	4	51	4	4	1	3	1	2

social change from a small-scale agricultural egalitarian society.

This study has attempted to outline one way of transforming material remains into social insights. The relationship of ideology and material culture has been investigated to understand how social values and identities can be given material expression and then why only at certain times. Strategies of legitimation through conspicuous consumption, manipulation of ancestors or identity consciousness are some of the forms that this expression may take. One particular aspect of social and material life, mortuary practices and the relations between living and dead, has been developed as a potential medium for the ideological manipulation of power amongst the living. The long-term changes in mortuary ritual were compared with the evidence from settlements and votive deposits and used to document and interpret a series of revolutionary watersheds which drastically transformed Scandinavian society. Comparison with similar precise chronologies for the prehistory of other parts of the world will allow us to find out whether cycles of rapid, discontinuous change have been the most important and frequent form of social development for the human species.

Notes

1 From the archaeologist's point of view it is interesting to note that Friedman omits the role of burial practices, firstly in 'creating' ancestors and secondly as a major form of feasting and conspicuous consumption through which debts are accumulated (see Gilhodes 1922; Hanson 1913).

2 Only one grave, that may date to this period (300–100 BC), stands out. It was found at Mollerup in the last century and contained two La Tene silver cups and a bronze vessel (Brøndsted 1960: 30–1).

3 Certain assumptions need to be examined. The larger byre might not have been fully used, and even if it was, the difference between it and the small farm byres might not have been enough to allow a substantial difference in subsistence output. Although there was only one hearth in the living area we cannot be sure

that there was not a larger family unit consuming the surplus of the increased production.

Acknowledgements

I would like to thank my archaeological colleagues in Denmark for their help and kindness during my field research. Professor C.J. Becker and Steen Hvass kindly allowed me to reproduce the plans in Figures 1 and 2. Parts of this paper were read and commented on by Jane Grenville, Henrietta Moore, Roger Thomas and Todd Whitelaw; they are, of course, not responsible for its final outcome.

Bibliography

Becker, C.J. 1961. *Forromersk Jernalder I Syd – og Midjylland.* København: Nationalmuseet.

1965. Ein früheisenzeitliches Dorf bei Grøntoft, Westjütland. Vorbericht über die Ausgrabungen 1961–63. *Acta Archaeologica* 36: 209–22.

1966. Das zweite früheisenzeitliche Dorf bei Grøntoft, Westjütland. 2. Vorbericht: Die Ausgrabungen 1964–66. *Acta Archaeologica* 37: 235–54.

1971. Früheisenzeitliche Dörfer bei Grøntoft, Westjütland. 3. Vorbericht: Die Ausgrabungen 1967–68. *Acta Archaeologica* 42: 79–110.

Berger, P. 1973. *The Social Reality of Religion.* Harmondsworth: Penguin.

Berger, P. and T. Luckmann, 1967. *The Social Construction of Reality.* Harmondsworth: Penguin.

Binford, L.R. 1971. Mortuary practices: their study and potential. In J.A. Brown (ed.), *Approaches to the Social Dimensions of Mortuary Practices.* Memoirs of the Society for American Archaeology 25: 6–29.

Bloch, M. 1971. *Placing the Dead: Tombs, Ancestral Villages, and Kinship Organization in Madagascar.* London: Seminar Press.

1977. The past and the present in the present. *Man* (n.s.) 12: 278–92.

Bonte, P. 1978. Non-stratified social formations among pastoral nomads. In J. Friedman and M.J. Rowlands (eds.), *The Evolution of Social Systems*, pp. 173–200. London: Duckworth.

Brown, J.A. (ed.) 1971. *Approaches to the Social Dimensions of Mortuary Practices*. Memoirs of the Society for American Archaeology 25.

Brøndsted, J. 1960. *Danmarks Oldtid. 3 Jernalderen*. København: Gyldendal.

Carlton, E. 1977. *Ideology and Social Order*. London: Routledge and Kegan Paul.

Carr, E.H. 1961. *What is History?* Harmondsworth: Penguin.

Chapman, R., I. Kinnes and K. Randsborg (eds.) 1981. *The Archaeology of Death*. Cambridge: Cambridge University Press.

Diener, P., K. Moore and R. Mutaw, 1980. Meat, markets and mechanical materialism: the great protein fiasco in anthropology. *Dialectical Anthropology* 5: 171–92.

Dunnell, R.C. and R.J. Wenke, 1980. Cultural and scientific evolution: some comments on 'The decline and rise of Mesopotamian civilization'. *American Antiquity* 45: 605–9.

Ekholm, K. 1980. On the limits of civilization: the structure and dynamics of global systems. *Dialectical Anthropology* 5: 155–66.

Flannery, K. 1973. Archaeology with a capital S. In C. Redman (ed.), *Research and Theory in Current Archaeology*, pp. 47–58. New York: John Wiley.

Frankenstein, S. and M.J. Rowlands, 1978. The internal structure and regional context of Early Iron Age society in south-western Germany. *Bulletin of the Institute of Archaeology, London* 15: 73–112.

Friedman, J. 1974. Marxism, structuralism and vulgar materialism. *Man* (n.s.) 9: 444–69.

1975. Religion as economy and economy as religion. *Ethnos* 40 (1–4): 46–63.

1979. *System, Structure and Contradiction: the Evolution of 'Asiatic' Social Formations*. Copenhagen: National Museum of Denmark.

Giddens, A. 1979. *Central Problems in Social Theory: Action, Structure and Contradiction in Social Analysis*. London and Basingstoke: Macmillan.

1981. *A Contemporary Critique of Historical Materialism, Vol. 1: Power, Property and the State*. London and Basingstoke: Macmillan.

Gilhodes, C. 1922. *The Kachins: Religion and Customs*. London: Kegan Paul, Trench and Trubner.

Glob, P.V. 1977. *The Bog People*. London: Faber.

Godelier, M. 1977. *Perspectives in Marxist Anthropology*. Cambridge: Cambridge University Press.

Goody, J. 1962. *Death, Property and the Ancestors: a Study of the Mortuary Customs of the Lodagaa of W. Africa*. Stanford: Stanford University Press.

Gregory, C.A. 1980. Gifts to men and gifts to god: gift exchange and capital accumulation in contemporary Papua. *Man* (n.s.) 15: 626–52.

Hanson, O. 1913. *The Kachins: Their Customs and Traditions*. Rangoon: American Baptist Mission Press.

Hodder, I. 1979. Economic and social stress and material culture patterning. *American Antiquity* 44: 446–54.

Huntington, R. and P. Metcalf, 1979. *Celebrations of Death*. Cambridge: Cambridge University Press.

Hvass, S. 1975. Das eisenzeitliche Dorf bei Hodde, Westjütland. *Acta Archaeologica* 46: 142–58.

Ingold, T. 1980. *Hunters, Pastoralists and Ranchers*. Cambridge: Cambridge University Press.

Jensen, S. 1980. Fredbjerg fundet: en bronzebeslået pragtvogn på en Vesthimmerlandsk jernalderboplads. *Kuml*: 169–216.

Klejn, L.S. 1979. Comments (to Van der Velde, 1979). *Current Anthropology* 20: 53–5.

Klindt-Jensen, O. 1949. Foreign influences in Denmark's Early Iron Age. *Acta Archaeologica* 20: 1–230.

Kristiansen, K. 1981. Economic models for Bronze Age Scandinavia: towards an integrated approach. In A. Sheridan and G. Bailey (eds.), *Economic Archaeology: Towards an Integration of Ecological and Social Approaches*. B.A.R. International Series 96: 239–303. Oxford: British Archaeological Reports.

Leach, E. 1954. *Political Systems of Highland Burma: a Study of Kachin Social Structure*. London: Bell and Son.

1977. A view from the bridge. In M. Spriggs (ed.), *Archaeology and Anthropology: Areas of Mutual Interest*. B.A.R. Supplementary Series 19: 161–76. Oxford: British Archaeological Reports.

Lewis, G. 1980. *Day of Shining Red: an Essay in Understanding Ritual*. Cambridge: Cambridge University Press.

McCarney, J. 1980. *The Real World of Ideology*. Brighton: Harvester.

Marx, K. and F. Engels, 1968. *Selected Works in One Volume*. London: Lawrence and Wishart.

Mauss, M. 1954. *The Gift: Forms and Functions of Exchange in Archaic Societies*. London: Cohen and West.

Miller, D. 1982. Structures and strategies: an aspect of the relationship between social hierarchy and cultural change. In I. Hodder (ed.), *Symbolic and Structural Archaeology*, pp. 89–98. Cambridge: Cambridge University Press.

Moore, W.E. 1963. *Social Change*. New Jersey: Prentice-Hall.

1970. A reconsideration of theories of change. In S.N. Eisenstadt (ed.), *Readings in Social Evolution and Development*, pp. 123–40. Oxford: Pergamon Press.

Morgan, L.H. 1877. *Ancient Society, or Researches into the Lines of Human Progress from Savagery Through Barbarism to Civilization*. London: Macmillan.

Pader, E.J. 1982. *Symbolism, Social Relations and the Interpretation of Mortuary Remains*. B.A.R. International Series 130. Oxford: British Archaeological Reports.

Pearson, M.P. 1982a. Mortuary practices, society and ideology: an ethnoarchaeological study. In I. Hodder (ed.), *Symbolic and Structural Archaeology*, pp. 99–113. Cambridge: Cambridge University Press.

1984. Economic and ideological change: Cyclical growth in the pre-state societies of Jutland. In D. Miller and C. Tilley (eds.), *Ideology, Power and Prehistory*, pp. 69–92. Cambridge: Cambridge University Press.

Raddatz, K. 1967. *Das Wagengrab der jungeren vorrömischen Eisenzeit von Husby, Kreis Flensburg*. Neumünster: Karl Wachholtz Verlag.

Randsborg, K. 1980. *The Viking Age in Denmark: The Formation of a State*. London: Duckworth.

Rappaport, R.A. 1968. *Pigs for the Ancestors: Ritual in the Ecology of a New Guinea People*. New Haven: Yale University Press.

1978. Maladaptions in social systems. In J. Friedman and M.J. Rowlands (eds.), *The Evolution of Social Systems*, pp. 49–71. London: Duckworth.

Saxe, A.A. 1970. *Social Dimensions of Mortuary Practices*. Ph.D. Thesis, University of Michigan. Ann Arbor: University Microfilms.

Seliger, M. 1977. *The Marxist Conception of Ideology*. Cambridge: Cambridge University Press.

Service, E.R. 1971. *Primitive Social Organization: an Evolutionary Perspective*. New York: Random House.

Shennan, S.E. 1975. The social organization at Branč. *Antiquity* 49: 279–88.

Steward, J. 1955. *Theory of Culture Change; the Methodology of Multilinear Evolution*. Urbana: University of Illinois Press.

Sumner, C. 1979. *Reading Ideologies: an Investigation into the Marxist Theory of Ideology and Law*. London: Academic Press.

Tainter, J.A. 1975. *The Archaeological Study of Social Change: Woodland Systems in West-Central Illinois*. Ph.D. Thesis, Northwestern University. Ann Arbor: University Microfilms.

Van der Velde, P. 1979. On Bandkeramik social structure: an analysis of pot decoration and hut distributions from the Central

European Neolithic communities of Elsloo and Hienheim. *Analecta Praehistorica Leidensia* 12: 1–242.

Wallerstein, I. 1979. *The Capitalist World Economy*. Cambridge: Cambridge University Press.

Walsh, W.H. 1967. *An Introduction to Philosophy of History*. London: Hutchinson.

Watson, P., S. LeBlanc and C. Redman, 1971. *Explanation in Archaeology: an Explicitly Scientific Approach*. New York: Columbia University Press.

Wenke, R.J. 1981. Explaining the evolution of cultural complexity: a review. In M.B. Schiffer (ed.), *Advances in Archaeological Method and Theory* 4: 79–127. New York: Academic Press.

Wilson, B.R. (ed.) 1979. *Rationality*. Oxford: Blackwell.

Chapter 6

Ideology and material culture: an archaeological perspective
Kristian Kristiansen

Introduction

In this article it will be argued that a Marxist approach to archaeology offers a convincing theoretical alternative to current approaches, and that its perception of ideology opens up a deeper understanding of the relationship between material culture and society.

Before starting, however, it may be useful briefly to discuss some of the major theoretical approaches which have been struggling for dominance throughout the last two decades, as this represents the framework against which the application of a Marxist approach in archaeology should be considered.

Recent theoretical trends in archaeology

Two trends are easily discernible: one concerned with tracing and explaining the major evolutionary stages in prehistory, another with the explanation of the structure and internal dynamics of specific social systems.

The evolutionary trend has been closely associated with various forms of neo-evolutionism in social anthropology (Fried 1960; Sahlins and Service 1960; Service 1962), whose broad evolutionary stages have served as general interpretative frameworks for much archaeological research throughout the 1960s and early 1970s. Much of this research has been aimed at correlating certain types of settlement systems (such as Renfrew's 'Early State Module'), patterns of exchange (Renfrew 1975), or grave goods diversification (Brown 1971; Tainter 1978) with certain levels of social organization on an evolutionary scale of e.g. bands, tribes, chiefdoms and states. Although such a framework serves important heuristic functions it is not adequate for explaining either change or variability in the archaeological record. On the contrary it tends to lead to a kind of 'checklist' archaeology (such as Renfrew 1973b; Peebles and Kus 1977), where static, generalized evolutionary types are imposed upon specific prehistoric sequences with the danger of obscuring the characteristics of local evolutionary trajectories (cf. Kohl, this volume). Furthermore the interaction of social systems, which have characterized all prehistoric periods, are not accounted for by such frameworks.

Thus instead of serving as a corrective for the arbitrarily constructed evolutionary typology of social anthropology the interpretation of prehistoric social evolution has rather tended to be determined by this framework, leading into a dangerous circular argument. Recent developments, however, have to some extent improved on this situation (Service 1975. For critical discussions see also *American Antiquity* 1980: 601–13; Binford 1975; Dunnell 1980; Flannery 1972; Friedman 1982).

In order to overcome some of the explanatory limitations of neo-evolutionism the 'New Archaeology' of the late sixties adopted the systemic framework of cybernetics coupled with a range of new theoretical (and methodological) approaches borrowed mainly from ecology, information theory and geography, amplified by quantitative and statistical techniques (early examples in Binford 1968; Clarke 1968: Chapters 3 and 11; Flannery 1968a; Hill 1977a; and stimulating articles and discussions in Hill 1977b). The systemic framework is often dominated by an ecological approach, especially when dealing with 'primitive' or marginal societies (Binford 1968; 1977; Jochim 1976; Zubrow 1975; several articles in Schiffer 1978–81), and by a more elaborate information theory of decision making when dealing with 'complex' societies (Flannery 1972; Johnson 1978). Ecosystemic approaches, however, are also now invading this field of research (Athens 1977; Isbell 1978; King 1978; Redman 1978; Sanders and Webster 1978).

One of the major limitations inherent in a systems framework is that it cannot account for either the genesis or the transformation of social systems in systemic terms (cf. Bender 1978; Salmon 1978; Tilley 1981a; 1981b), and the same is true of inter-systemic dynamics, e.g. trade and exchange (see the examples and discussions in Earle and Ericson 1977, especially Plog's article). Thus the sophisticated methods of spatial analysis borrowed from geography (Hodder and Orton 1976) have not yet been theoretically integrated within a systems framework. This is even more true of so-called 'normative' data, although much has been done since Binford (1965) and Clarke (1968: Chapter 9) discussed this problem, especially with respect to the analysis and explanation of stylistic variation (Blackmore *et al.* 1979; Engelbrecht 1978; Hodder 1978a; Plog 1978; Renfrew 1978; Shennan 1978; Whallon 1968; Wobst 1976).

Thus when trying to integrate the evolutionary perspective with a systems framework, explanations have tended to fall back upon single, causative factors, or so-called 'prime movers', usually population pressure (Carneiro 1970; Dumond 1965; Smith 1972; Spooner 1970). The role of trade and exchange has been linked more exclusively to the formation of highly developed and integrated social systems (Flannery 1968b; 1972; Frankenstein and Rowlands 1978; Hedeager 1978; Kohl 1978; Renfrew 1969; Webb 1975; Wright 1972). In addition so-called selective adaptive mechanisms referring to the functional compatibility between a social system and its environment have played a major role within the ecologically oriented school of Binford and his followers (see recent examples in Binford 1977; Kirch 1980; Schiffer 1978–81). Recently an attempt has been made to solve the problem of analysing transformations within a systemic framework (Renfrew and Cooke 1979), but we still await convincing applications.[1]

Underlying these theoretical developments we find a strong emphasis on a neo-positivist perception of science, originally introduced by Binford in several articles (collected in Binford 1972) and later generally accepted and applied by a whole generation of American archaeologists (see a rigorous presentation in Watson, LeBlanc and Redman 1971; discussions in Fritz and Plog 1970; Morgan 1973; 1974).

Although it would be interesting to discuss why this approach won acceptance in archaeology at a time when it had already been modified or even abandoned as a dominant philosophy of science, my point here is that such an approach is now severely hampering the theoretical development of archaeology by prescribing a rigorous one-dimensional perception of how to give meaning to and how to explain archaeological data. What at one time could be regarded as a necessary step in the process of developing and applying some scientific standards to archaeology has now turned into a paradigmatic theoretical exercise, ignoring the still many unsolved problems of interpretation and explanation and of archaeological representativity. Despite a sophisticated perception of the complicated formation processes of the archaeological record such sophistication is abandoned when it comes to explaining the relationship between the invisible social structures of prehistoric societies and their visible material remains, although some aspects of this problem have been recently touched upon by Binford in a (somewhat extreme) criticism of Schiffer (Binford 1981).

The basic problem is that structures and transformations are neither reducible to their empirical content nor their context, as I shall illustrate later in this article (cf. Tilley 1981a and 1981b).

> Thus, in archaeology, the analytical and empirical gulf between separate levels of information – e.g. site catchment and analyses of region *x*, distributional analyses of different commodities and the analysis of 'princely graves' of the same region – has to be crossed by an explanatory bridge dependent on cultural and theoretical insights rather than on analytical and deductive techniques in order to lead us towards an understanding of the structural reality that explains what happened *between* these levels.   (Kristiansen 1981a: 240)

From this it follows that the establishment of stable and predictable relationships between observable phenomena in the archaeological record and the employment of such variables in hypothesis testing represent necessary but not sufficient empirical steps on the ladder towards explanation.

Despite this criticism one should not forget that the theoretical and methodological renewal of the 1960s and 1970s represents a major breakthrough in the development of archaeology as a cultural science, comparable perhaps to the development of a chronological methodology in late-nineteenth-century archaeology in Europe. Probably the most important outcome of this process up to now has been the gradual application of a body of common methodological standards, which has been accompanied by increasing theoretical diversification. Thus one year will see the propagation of 'behavioural archaeology' as the key concept, another year 'structural archaeology' or 'spatial archaeology' competing with 'social archaeology' and 'economic archaeology'. In addition the morphogenesis of catastrophe and anastrophe in prehistory, with robust middle-range theory as a serious alternative, offer striking new solutions for the progressive archaeologist.

Although diversification and new developments should be welcomed in a period of transition, the present situation seems to reflect the impact of passive theoretical and methodological borrowing (plus talented management and promotion) and the lack of a general theoretical framework to filter, balance and restructure such borrowing. After the first stage of New Archaeology, mainly dealing with general problems and summarized in six major publications (Binford and Binford 1968; Clarke 1972; Lee and de Vore 1968; Renfrew 1973c; Ucko and Dimbleby 1969; Ucko, Tringham and Dimbleby 1972), the late 1970s have seen more attempts to explore and link together interdisciplinary 'subsystem' research (see Burnham and Kingsbury 1979; Earle and Ericson 1977; Green, Haselgrove and Spriggs 1978; Redman *et al.* 1978; Sheridan and Bailey 1981; Spriggs 1977), reflecting both the potential and the problems of the present situation. As stated by Tilley in one such recent publication: 'The central difficulty is that archaeology lacks a common problematic determining the types of problems that are posed, the form in which these problems are tackled and what is seen as being sufficient and necessary for their solution' (Tilley 1981b: 363). What we should aim at, then, is the construction of a general theoretical framework which maintains an evolutionary perspective and a systemic framework, and which is able to account for the explanation of societies in their structural and cultural totality with regard to their genesis, reproduction and transformation. When looking for such a framework we need not turn to biology, catastrophe theory or any other mechanical theory. Instead it will be suggested that Marxist theory, whose point of departure is society itself, holds a potential for developing such a framework.

Marxist theory and archaeology

It is tempting to ask, in retrospect, why earlier attempts to explain archaeological evidence in evolutionary and Marxist terms failed to exert any significant impact on the general trend of archaeological reasoning and research. Going back to the later nineteenth century, the Darwinian decades of evolutionary breakthrough where one should have expected such an integration to occur for the first time, it is easy to see today that archaeology simply was not ready.[2] At that time the primary concern was the development of an explicit archaeological method of chronological classification in order to cope with the quickly accumulating evidence (Kristiansen 1976: Fig. 1). Culture-historical interpretations, however, were constrained not only by incomplete data and dating, but also by the close relationship between archaeology, bourgeois culture and nationalism (Kristiansen 1981b; Moberg 1981; Trigger 1981) which favoured historical and ethnic interpretations. In this period the potential of prehistory for contributing to social evolution was however exclusively recognized among anthropologists, such as Morgan (1877), and Marxist historians, such as Engels (1884).

After the turn of the century most anthropological and culture-historical disciplines adopted a diffusionist and ethnic framework, which naturally supported the already prevailing trends in archaeological research (the classical presentation is Jacob-Friesen 1928). This meant that when Childe, as one of the first Western archaeologists to adopt a materialist perspective, published *Social Evolution* in 1951, his interpretations and explanations were extremely constrained by the structure of the archaeological evidence. This consisted mainly of typologically and chronologically ordered culture groups with little or no bearing upon social and economic phenomena. Childe had tried to overcome some of these difficulties by applying his framework to the more tractable Scottish evidence (Childe 1946). This attempt was later used by Piggott to show that new evidence had proven most of Childe's interpretations wrong, which in Piggott's opinion thereby demonstrated the failure of evolutionary theory (Piggott 1960: 95). Although this conclusion rather demonstrated the failure of its author to distinguish between his own (theoretical) limitations and the limitations of science, it undoubtedly reflected a general and widespread perspective among archaeologists at that time, who feared any theoretical schemes after the political misuse of ethnic interpretations during the Second World War.[3]

This general anti-theoretical approach is perhaps best demonstrated in Piggott's own work *Ancient Europe* with its lack of any consistent theoretical framework, except human nature and the nature of the evidence (Piggott 1965: 1–23). Interpretations and explanations are consequently just as inconsistent as the changing properties of the evidence – from the technological framework of the late Glacial hunters and early farmers to the diffusionist and ethnic framework of later prehistory. Where *Social Evolution* appears too simplistic because of its rigorous application of general evolutionary stage theory, *Ancient Europe* appears too kaleidoscopic because of its lack of explanatory consistency. In this way *Ancient Europe* and *Social Evolution* may be said to reflect the contradictory situation of European archaeology during the 1950s and 1960s. Here was a rich and fairly representative archaeological record – the result of 150 years of research – but analytically unsuited to support a more consistent theoretical approach such as social evolution, which was therefore wrongly refuted.[4] This further prevented necessary methodological re-orientations and developments (with the exception of ecological research). Out of this stalemate arose the 'Sceptical Tradition', as it has been appropriately labelled by Klejn (1977: 3). When these theoretical and methodological constraints were finally transcended by the development of the New Archaeology the key to explanatory status and scientific prominence had become neo-positivism because of scientific traditions and political conditions in North America.

The potential application of a Marxist framework for the explanation of prehistoric societies came up against the problem that Marxist theory has not yet developed an adequate theoretical basis for explaining the long-term changes of pre-capitalist societies.[5] This implies that the scientific potential of a wedding between Marxism and archaeology is largely unrecognized and remains to be explored. Yet recent work has strongly indicated that much previous discussion about pre-capitalist societies has been unnecessarily limited in scope, both empirically and (consequently) theoretically, by largely omitting the data of social anthropology and archaeology. This situation has to some extent been remedied by the development of French Structural Marxism with its efforts to re-define basic theoretical concepts. It has applied a framework to the explanation of pre-capitalist societies based on ethno-graphic evidence, thereby escaping the theoretical dead-ends of much Marxology (for references see Spriggs, this volume). Although this direction of structural Marxism has been rather successful in its application in social anthropology it has become increasingly clear that it suffers serious drawbacks when applied to the explanation of prehistoric long-term trans-formations operating in a wider social space than the local environment of traditional ethnographic case studies (for a general critique, see Ekholm and Friedman 1980).[6]

Recent archaeological applications of such a theoretical framework have made it apparent, first, that the long-term transformations found in prehistory and early history form a necessary basis for any serious future discussions about pre-capitalist societies, if this concept shall be given any general significance beyond that of accounting for the genesis of capitalism; secondly that such applications necessitate certain reformulations of the present theoretical concepts of struc-tural Marxism and the subsequent development of new con-cepts, especially with respect to the spatial dimensions of structural interaction and with respect to transformations (cf. Spriggs, this volume). Such attempts have already been under-taken in several studies (Bender 1978; 1981; Bradley 1981; Frankenstein 1979; Frankenstein and Rowlands 1978; Fried-man and Rowlands 1978; Kohl 1978; Kristiansen 1978a; 1981a; 1982; Rowlands 1980; Rowlands, Larsen and Kristiansen in press). In addition, works such as Rathje (1973), and the papers in Hodder (1982) are moving along somewhat similar lines, although in a more purely structural groove with less emphasis on material aspects of social reproduction.

By continuing theoretical elaboration and archaeological applications along these lines, Marxist theory may be able to offer a long-needed theoretical and explanatory 'superstruc-ture' that can cope with the impressive methodological devel-opments of the last two decades in nearly all fields of data analysis. It seems to me, therefore, that at the present moment two things are needed for a successful application of Marxist theory to archaeology:

1 More case studies along the lines referred to above. The success of any totalizing theoretical system which claims general applicability ultimately depends on its ability to account for and explain the evidence in more 'convincing' ways than previous research. This is done by subsuming earlier theories as variants of a more comprehensive general theory, as did neo-

evolutionism with respect to functionalism, ecology and history (White 1945), or structural Marxism with respect to structuralism, historical materialism and cultural ecology (Friedman 1974). Naturally this pro-cess is modified by numerous subjective factors oper-ating to maintain research traditions already estab-lished, e.g. through university teaching, control of research funding, personal and political relationships etc. There have been two decades of competing theoretical approaches and a general orientation towards endogenous development as an explanatory point of departure, combined with the local area or the region as dominant units of research. It now seems that an evolutionary structural Marxism is in a position to offer a system of theoretical concepts which links the spatial and normative dimensions of archaeological data with the prevailing, often eco-logical framework of local and regional studies to give a single model of social reproduction that accounts for both.

Thus if we want to transcend the explanatory limitations of much present research we need to study the interaction between social systems in their local, regional and even 'global' setting, in order to deter-mine the structure of such interaction with respect to local and supralocal levels of organization. How are they dependent? Who controls production and its distribution/exchange and at what levels in the sys-tem? It is only by analysing the relationships between local systems and the larger structure by which they are reproduced that one can define and explain cul-tural boundaries in a meaningful way, and define what is 'between' and what is 'within' at various levels in the system. Thus if we want to determine the locus of evolutionary change we must be able to delineate the cultural boundaries and the structural framework within which these processes are operating, by con-sidering the full scale and complexity of such pro-cesses. This implies that local and regional studies in archaeology can only be fully comprehended and explained by considering them against the structure of the larger system on which they depend. As Fried-man and Rowlands have written (1978: 205): 'A complete evolutionary model would have to be a time/space model in which transformations over time are related to variations in space. Thus the specific evolution of social formations depends on the internal properties of local systems, upon the local constraints and upon their place in the larger systems.'

2 We further need a much more systematic exploration of the relationship between the nature of the archae-ological evidence and its interpretation and expla-nation. The cultural and structural properties of extinct societies are obscured by two processes:
a) Through the ideological representation of past

social systems inherent in major parts of the material record. This is displayed in the symbolic *form and functioning of objects* (e.g. prestige goods, ritual gear and more generally in stylistic design), in the *intentional deposition of such objects* (votive offerings, hoards, grave goods) and in the *construction of symbolic structures* (often monumental constructions, barrows, temples, cult places etc.).

b) Through the subsequent transformation of the evidence after its deposition/abandonment/loss. This is dependent on *physical factors*, that is the interplay between external physical factors such as soils, climate etc. and the physical nature of the objects (e.g. stone, iron, wood etc.) which determines their rate of decay/conservation; *economic factors*, that is the later transformation of the landscape which has either preserved, destroyed or brought forth archaeological evidence; and *research factors*, that is the history of research (Kristiansen 1976; 1978b).

These factors respectively mystify and modify the information value and representativeness of the data and therefore constitute important analytical and interpretative links between theory and data. Whereas the ideological mystification of the evidence has been given little systematic attention, the transformation of archaeological data after deposition/abandonment/loss has been subject to more sustained analysis both at the general level of post-depositional formation processes (see especially Schiffer (1976), also Daniels (1972) and Clarke (1973)) and with respect to specific aspects of such processes (Foley 1981; Groube 1981; Wood and Johnson 1978). Not untypically, however, this work has neglected or been unaware of previous European research within a more traditional framework, less theoretically pretentious, but nonetheless of great value (especially the classical works of Eggers (1951: 1ff; 1959: Chapter 5); and also Torbrügge (1965; 1970—1) and Geisslinger (1967)).

While the impact of post-depositional formation processes has been dealt with rather systematically in recent years, those pre-depositional and depositional processes determining the formation and the nature of the archaeological record are much more complicated, especially those that are intentional. In the following I shall therefore deal specifically with the impact of ideology on such processes.

Ideology and material culture

It is a widely accepted assumption underlying the ecosystemic approach in archaeology that when the distortions of archaeological post-depositional formation processes have been subtracted, there exists a rather direct relationship between the archaeological record and past cultural systems when approached with relevant hypotheses and methods. Such an approach has been especially apparent in studies of mortuary practices, whose ideological manifestations are regarded as merely passive reflections of social reality. Also inherent in this tradition is the idea that society can be broken down into functional blocks or sub-systems such as religious, economic or social sub-systems and that the data can be classified accordingly (Binford 1962; 1965).

This functionalist approach arose as a necessary reaction against the traditional culture-historical perception of ideology as an independent variable that could be used to 'explain' otherwise inexplicable changes in the archaeological record (such as in stylistic design or burial practices). It was believed that criteria governing such changes first of all should be 'explained' with reference to religious ideas that might spread over large areas independently of social and economic differences. Ideological changes were thereby relegated from the organization of society to the isolated sphere of religion. Religious behaviour was consequently thought to act according to hidden, irrational (individual) preferences distributed more or less at random.

According to this approach, which reflected a twentieth-century Western perception of religion, ideological factors imposed heavy limitations on the information value of major parts of the archaeological record, perhaps most completely represented in the traditional archaeological textbook of Eggers (1959: Chapter 5). The New Archaeology tried to overcome this scepticism by re-establishing the functional relationship between society and ideology, a major step forward in understanding such phenomena. Having realized this we are in a position to take a more balanced view and reassess the relationship between ideology and material culture. This is necessary for at least two reasons, which will be further discussed in this article: first, a purely functional approach accounts only for a limited part of the ideological variation in the record. Secondly, and consequently, the functional approach has primarily been applied in areas where it seems to work best, mainly on ecological and settlement data, leaving a major part of the archaeological record unexplained.

Thus, the purely functionalist approach, which characterizes most New Archaeological research, represents a severe obstacle to the further development of archaeological interpretations and explanations. The main reason for this is its failure to distinguish between *cultural categories and material functions*. Thus: 'we should be prepared to accept the possibility that religious categories can have directly economic functions, just as "wealth objects" can be but mere ideological symbols. In terms of cultural content we can easily distinguish between religion and money, but in terms of their functioning in material reproduction we have to ask a new set of questions' (Friedman 1975b). This implies that the structures, or the dominant social relations, which organize production and reproduction may also organize other activities in a way that no cultural distinction can be drawn between the economic and the non-economic. In this way dominant social relations may cross-cut traditional institutional boundaries or the sub-systems of functional and eco-systemic models. Accordingly, 'there is no culturally defined economy, nor is there a culturally defined religion. As institutional categories these belong to our own and perhaps a few other kinds of society.

If we are to explain the functioning and evolution of social systems, it is necessary to discover the specificity of their internal structures' (Friedman 1975b). When this has been grasped, 'a vast new field of investigation opens up, namely the search for the reasons and the conditions which, in history, have brought about shifts in the locus — and hence changes in forms — of relations of production' (Godelier 1978: 765).

I believe that the principle of dominant social relations and the distinction between cultural form and material function also opens up a new field of investigation in archaeology, namely the search for the conditions that govern the cultural manifestations of material functions and hence determine the interpretation and explanation of a major part of the archaeological record, whose explanatory potential has hitherto been much neglected. Thus ideology is not considered to be a passive reflection of society, but, on the contrary, an active factor that can be used by competing individuals and social groups to establish and legitimize their dominance through an ideology bearing upon society as a whole and expressed in symbols, social norms, rules and rituals. This implies that ideology may entail both contrast and harmony on various levels. This dynamic principle may be manifested either as a reinforcement or a repression of various aspects of society, thereby further complicating the relationship between material functions and cultural form.

For example, with respect to mortuary practices, wealthy persons of high rank may be buried modestly with but a few symbols of their wealth and position, whereas members of rising and competing social groups may be buried with great symbolic manifestation of their social position. Frequently only a single social group or segment of society expresses its status in burials, whereas in some periods quite the opposite is the case: a considerably larger part of the population is buried and internal differences are equalized rather than emphasized.

At present we know very little regarding the socio-economic and ideological factors which cause these variations in mortuary practices, nor whether general rules governing these variations can be established (but see Pearson 1982). In studying mortuary practices it is therefore essential to clarify the relationship between social reality and its ideological interpretation. This can only be done by considering mortuary practices and wealth consumption within a larger framework of material production and reproduction, in order to determine how such ideological/cultural forms and norms correspond to their material functions of reproduction. Although such an approach has been employed in a few works (Bradley 1981; Ellison 1981; Kristiansen 1978a; 1981a; Randsborg 1974; 1981; Rathje 1973), it has been common to select a single period and a single region or even burial place which displays characteristic features of status (Brown 1981; Goldstein 1981; Hedeager 1978; King 1978; Shennan 1975). Those periods and regions which do not conform very well to such analysis are neglected.

In the first place this has laid not only particular explanations, but also their basic premises, open to criticism (Braun 1981; Leach 1977; Ucko 1969). Secondly, studies of mortuary practices will never contribute significantly to the explanation of social evolution if we do not try to analyse and explain their full range of variation in time and space and consider them against the larger framework of social reproduction. We further have to accept that there exists no single methodological parameter that covers all such variation, not even within a single region. The only unifying framework is theory. Therefore we will have to proceed from the rather general theoretical principles presented above and by subjective confrontation with the data deduce interpretations and explanations from which more specific hypotheses may be formulated and tested.

I shall try to demonstrate this in the following by two examples. As a starting point, however, I have tried to summarize the main theoretical concepts and principles in two diagrams (Figs. 1 and 2). The first figure shows the basic concepts and in the second figure I have tried to integrate them into a more comprehensive model of social reproduction (cf. Friedman 1975a: Fig. 1; Ingold 1981: Fig. 10.1).

Cultural representation and material function
Monuments and society in Neolithic Denmark

Why do some societies produce monumental burials and others not? And what is the relationship between monuments and society? We have been presented with several elegant answers in recent years (Chapman 1981; Fleming 1973; Renfrew 1973a; 1973b). However, the prehistory of northern Europe reveals a succession of different grave monuments — from wooden constructions to megaliths and impressive tumuli — which may help to throw some more light on these questions. In the following I shall therefore contrast two types of monuments in Neolithic Denmark — megaliths and earthen round barrows — in an attempt to outline and explain the material functions of these cultural manifestations.

The premiss for doing so is the proposition that these monuments also represent two contrasting tribal structures: the territorial chiefdoms of the Megalithic Culture (approximately 4000–2800 BC, with a climax period approximately 3500–3200 BC), and the segmentary tribes of the Single Grave or Battle Axe Culture (approximately 2800–2400 BC).[7] They further present us with very different cultural manifestations of rather similar material functions of production, at least at the level of technology and subsistence.

Thus, I shall consider the cultural and structural totality of these societies, disregarding spatial and temporal variation at the expense of constructing a general model which is able

Fig. 1. Basic theoretical concepts — a static presentation (drawn by Catherina Olesen).

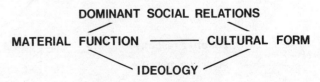

to account for such variation. By doing so, an attempt will be made to compare and confront the 'subjective' ideological evidence of ritual and religion with the 'objective' evidence of settlements, subsistence and technology.

The Megalithic Culture

Settlement, subsistence and technology. Settlements were based on local cycles of slash and burn, evidenced in pollen diagrams, opening up rather large areas which were cultivated and grassed for several centuries. In addition, areas with secondary forest were 'cultivated' by cutting for leaf fodder, building materials, etc. Broken polished flint axes regularly found around settlement areas indicate the primary importance of these tools for clearing forest for new fields throughout the period. Only a few settlement sites have been excavated. They seem to indicate a pattern of (1) hamlets of small U-shaped huts, dispersed at good fishing grounds and close to fields, (2) local central settlements, sometimes with long houses, and (3) fortified regional central places (causewayed camps) of seasonal meetings for ritual, alliances and exchange. Settlements cluster along waterways (the coast, fiords, small inland rivers and lakes) that represented the main communication system in an otherwise forested landscape. Subsistence was based on a mixed economy dominated by wheat production in cleared fields tilled by simple ard ploughing, cattle herding for milk, meat and traction, free-roaming pigs in the forest and some fishing. Although this could be described as a broad spectrum economy, I believe that this farming system should rather be characterized as intensive shifting cultivation with high productivity in relatively small open areas due to a complex cycle of cultivation, grassing, secondary forest growth and recultivation, supplemented by fishing (Tauber 1981).

The basic tools for production known to us were the polished flint axe for clearing forest, heavy timber work etc., the ard for preparing the fields, canoes of hollowed tree trunks, traps and nets for fishing, hand querns for preparing flour, a wide variety of pottery containers for holding milk products, grain etc., plus a variety of small flint tools for scraping hides, cutting and so on. Well-worked wooden axe handles, spoons and dishes give a glimpse of a highly developed tradition in carpentry. Both pottery production and flint production reveal a highly organized and skilled tradition of manufacture. Flint was extracted by mining in a few areas and distributed semi-finished (without polishing) as seen in several 'trade' hoards. The time-consuming final preparation of the long polished axes, taken far beyond practical needs, was done locally. Extraordinarily long ritual axes were also produced, but basically working and ritual axes were similarly manufactured. Later a whole tool kit for specialized timber working was developed (chisels, small flat axes, hollow axes, and so on). Also in pottery production a distinction between fine ornamented (mainly ritual) pottery and settlement pottery quickly developed and a wide variety of specialized types were produced. The same artistic quality also characterized the manufacture of the very few battle axes (originally imitating East European copper axes), mace-heads and the rather numerous amber ornaments (which also included miniature battle axes and imitations of small East European copper ornaments). Amber was used in exchange for copper tools during the early phase, but this international exchange later ceased.

Ritual and religion. The earliest monuments were heavy timber-constructed earthen long barrows, surrounded by palisades. The burials inside them were meant to hold a single chief and his family, typically a woman and one or two chil-

Fig. 2. Basic theoretical concepts — a dynamic presentation (drawn by Catherina Olesen).

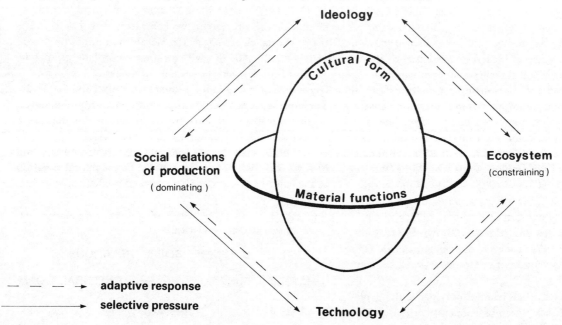

dren or very young people. Within the framework of the long barrow one chiefly family-burial could be placed along side the other, and the later megaliths — round or long dolmens with small stone chambers — continued this tradition. The megaliths typically cluster in groups, showing continued use of the same burial area for several centuries, often ending with the final stage: the big passage grave. These were constructed during the climax period and are virtually stone houses with an entrance (passage) into the chamber. After that the building of new megaliths ceased. The construction of the thousands of megaliths took place within a short time-span of 200—300 years, but they were in continued use during the following centuries. They were normally raised on agricultural land, evidenced by plough marks beneath them, and settlement material was often used in their construction.

The passage graves presented a change in burial rites, as they were meant to hold only the bones of the deceased, and one passage grave would often serve as 'temple' of the ancestors of several families, being divided into sections by stone slabs. This development towards larger communal burials (from dolmen to 'gross dolmen' to passage graves) was accompanied by the construction of the first territorial causewayed camps and later of cult-houses close to the passage graves. The causewayed camps did not serve settlement functions, but mainly ritual (and defensive?) functions, evidenced by heavy concentrations of offerings, including pottery, meals (bones and grain), a few prestige goods and also human offerings. These new ritual practices, which represent the climax period, seem to show a regional system of intercommunal ritual. Both in dolmen and passage graves a variety of goods accompanied the dead: pots, flint axes and more rarely battle axes and amber.

The megalithic monuments were quite clearly meant to hold only a very restricted number of persons, and burial took place in them rather rarely, once or twice in a generation. A complicated ritual seems to have taken place both before their construction and sometimes after. Offerings of pots etc. are sometimes documented in connection with the erection of early long barrows, and from the period of passage graves deposition of large amounts of ritual pottery took place at the entrance.

Parallel to the burial rites we find a separate religious tradition with two archaeological manifestations: the ritual hoarding or votive offering in wet places mainly of long polished axes (both singly and several together) and communal feasting. This is sometimes evidenced by large numbers of ox bones. Also single battle axes, mace heads and amber ornaments can be found as votive offerings. The tradition of ritual hoarding and feasting can be followed throughout the period. The cult places of votive offerings are normally located in the vicinity of megaliths and settlements, but during the later phase they seem to be more attached to the megaliths and the causewayed camps.

Synthesis: the social system. A close connection between

ritual, subsistence and exchange is demonstrated by the central role played by the polished flint axe in all three areas. As the basic tool in subsistence, the basic medium of exchange and the primary medium of ritual hoarding, the axe links together production, exchange and ritual consumption/feasting. This clearly resembles the production—feast—alliance cycle described by Friedman for swiddening Kachin tribes in Burma (Friedman 1975a), while axes played a similar role in New Guinea (Liep 1983; Højlund 1979; in press) (Fig. 3). As in these societies, the combination and eventual control of production, exchange and ritual must also have represented the basic source of local prestige in Neolithic Denmark and, if maintained, ranking. This was especially so as flint had to be distributed from a few source areas. Thus participation in alliances was crucial for obtaining axes (normally semi-finished products), and when finished they served both as a medium of social exchange/ritual consumption and were a precondition for increasing production by clearing new forest. This again might produce enough surplus for giving feasts, participating in alliances and ritual hoarding thus increasing prestige and ritual (= social) control. The longest and most beautiful ritual axes were undoubtedly highly valued and widely renowned, and probably had names and myths attached to them, as in New Guinea.

Thus the ritualized extension of production and prestige through feasting and ritual hoarding of polished axes reveals the primary material function of these cultural institutions. It further gives a clue as to how surplus production entered the local cycle of prestige building, embedded in alliances and exchange. But if axes were the common medium in production, ritual and exchange, then rank had to be expressed in more specific forms, as in the rare battle axes or mace heads for the living,[8] and for the dead in megalithic monuments. In order to deepen our understanding of the social system it is necessary to consider the grave monuments and their material function in social reproduction.

It is evident that the construction of monuments reveals important aspects of subsistence in such a way that one might even speak of a direct functional relationship. Thus in the early phase of forest clearance the basic material for the construction of the large monuments was the timber of big split trunks. These early structures reveal all the basic features of later megaliths and in fact bring the plan of long barrows much closer to that of the longhouses. The latter may have preceded them for ritual communal purposes, later taken over by specialized cult-houses when stones replaced timber in monument building. This change in building material may be seen as reflecting the consolidation of the settlement pattern with less forest clearance and with repeated cultivation in the cleared land. Consequently clearing the fields of stones became a major activity and they could be employed in the building of monuments for some generations. Thus in the first place the monuments symbolize the creation of agricultural land — the most valued and labour-intensive factor in slash and burn cultivation.[9] Secondly, their construction reflects the same type of social mobilization, co-operation and leadership as was needed for clearing the forest.

We may conclude, then, that the emergence of the first monumental burials, the creation and consolidation of permanent agricultural land and the development of leadership were closely related phenomena, spurred on by the mechanisms of feasting, ritual hoarding and exchange just described. We may also, with Renfrew (1973b), see the megaliths as social territorial markers of a stabilized settlement system, mobilizing an increasing population in big inter-communal building projects (rather than in settlement expansion onto poor soils),[10] thereby regulating the exploitation of land and forest resources, preventing destructive competition while sustaining the evolving hierarchical nature of society by ritual means. The culmination of these processes was reached with the construction of regional centres of inter-tribal ritual, the large causewayed camps.

Thus we see that megalithic monuments represent a ritualized extension of the organization of production. Let us, however, take a closer look at the character of monuments and burial practices in order to throw some more light, if possible, on the nature of religion and social organization.

The idea of the long barrow – presumably planned to contain the successive burials of a single chiefly lineage –

strongly indicates ascribed rank and leadership. This is clearly the case with the passage grave whose function presupposes long and repeated use by several chiefly lineages. Such chiefly co-operation might further suggest stronger integration and stability of leadership, as opposed to the frequent grouping of several dolmens in one place – rather suggesting stronger autonomy and competition between chiefly lineages. During the last centuries of the Megalithic Culture, long lines of stone-packed flat graves, sometimes extending 1–2 kilometres from the passage grave, appeared in some areas in Jutland. In other areas the bones in the chambers were constantly rearranged and even piled. Thus the passage grave seems to have served as a central religious focus for a wider settlement area of several chiefly lineages, probably descendants of the founding ancestors buried in the dolmen.

The ritualized chiefly organization of land and lineage through ancestor worship in megalithic tombs has been a recurrent phenomenon in many different parts of the world, in small-scale and more developed societies such as Madagascar (Bloch 1971; also good examples in Renfrew 1973a). Although not directly comparable with Neolithic Denmark such examples offer insights into the functional and organizational framework of these monuments. Quite clearly the megaliths do not represent burials in our sense of the word.

Fig. 3. Greenstone axe blades, shell necklaces and *Spondylus* shell money (*ndap*) in a mortuary payment on Rossel Island, Papua New Guinea. Row 1 is a solicitory gift from the gravediggers, who receive row 2 from the deceased's father's relatives. They themselves receive row 3 and necklace (a) from the deceased's own relatives. Rows 4–9 and the valuables (b)–(f) are from the deceased's spouse's relatives to the deceased's relatives. Descent on Rossel is matrilineal. The transaction illustrates the kind of ritual and social framework that produce an accumulation of primitive valuables. If buried it would resemble most neolithic hoards of western Europe. © John Liep.

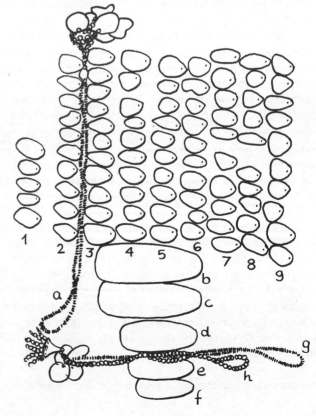

The dead were not separated from the living, but lived as ancestors in their houses among the living and could be approached when opening the chamber or contacted through rites and offerings. Thus the ancestors of the chiefly lineage rested in a stone-built longhouse, evidence for the clearing of forest and fields in their territory (Fig. 4). In this way the megaliths symbolized both the collective efforts of the community and the heroic leadership of ancestor chiefs, legitimizing and sustaining the power of their successors. This ritual practice of ancestor worship came to its full development in the passage grave (Fig. 5), now only holding the bones of the deceased, which were arranged after having been through a complicated ritual extraction of the flesh in the cult houses and causewayed camps. Skulls seem to have played a special role, and they were sometimes arranged in groups. In some cases breaking into the grave and stealing of skulls of ancestors by an enemy is strongly suggested. Thus the ancestors were present in the life of the community (not separated from it in the land of the dead) and they could be mobilized when needed.

Megalithic ritual is thus seen to represent a ritualized extension of the communal lineage structure, the chiefly lineages being direct descendants of founding ancestors, interceding with them on the community's behalf. According to this interpretation cultural institutions of feasting, ritual hoarding and ancestor worship are intricately linked with the organization of production in such a way that no clear distinction can be drawn between religion and economy. Ritual and religion served clearly material functions in the social organization of production. By transforming surplus production into ritual feasting, alliances and prestige, a ritualized hierarchical system evolved that served for more than half a millennium to organize the successful reproduction of a dispersed settlement system of intensive slash and burn agriculture.

The Single Grave Culture

Settlement, subsistence and technology. The Single Grave Culture represents an adaptation to the light soils of central and western Jutland, areas that had formerly been very scarcely

Fig. 4. Megalithic long barrow from Halskov Veenge, southeastern Denmark reconstructed after excavation (photograph: the Ancient Monument Directorate).

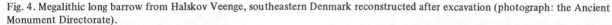

settled. These areas were characterized by a rather light open forest that could easily be transformed into grassland. Pollen diagrams indicate that permanent pastures and heathland, maintained right up to the present day, were created by a massive 'landnam' (forest clearance, literally 'land-take'). They further indicate that pastures and heathlands were dominant (as distinct from the Megalithic Culture), but with scattered secondary forest of oak and hazel and closed forests on the heavy moraines. Agriculture is demonstrated by grains of barley, the dominant crop, but stockbreeding was indisputably the basis of the economy leaving only scarce settlement traces. Settlements and barrows cluster along ecological boundaries — moraine and flat heath sand, or river-valleys and agricultural land — often in long lines kilometre after kilometre (Fig. 6). Such a settlement pattern secured access to pastures, forest and agricultural land. A few excavated (late) settlements indicate small hamlets of three to four very lightly constructed and rather small houses. They are normally close to barrows and no large central settlements have been found. Settlement material is scarce, but includes the usual small flint tools and polished axes for forest clearance (now thick butted). Small querns were also found in the later phases. Subsistence was based on stockbreeding of free-grazing cattle and sheep on extensive pastures and heathland, combined with some barley growing in small fields that were tilled with the ard. The heavy forest on the moraines and the scattered secondary forests were exploited for leaf fodder. Thus the economy should be characterized as pastoral with some agriculture.

Among the basic tools for production known to us, the polished flint axe is still the most important, plus stone wedges to help cleave tree-trunks. The ard was still used for preparing the fields, as shown by traces of ploughing beneath many barrows. For the first time wheels and wagons are introduced, evidenced both in actual finds and in trackways under or close to barrows, a response to the new open environment connecting large areas of temperate Europe at this time (Sherratt 1981). We also get glimpses of a tradition in wood and bark working — remains of dishes and boxes. In contrast to the Megalithic Culture the manufacture of the polished flint axe is rather careless and taken no further than needed for practical purposes. However, no efforts were spared to produce the beautiful and numerous battle axes, so characteristic of this culture. Pottery is also rather poor compared to the Megalithic Culture, consisting of a limited number of types dominated by the beaker. As in the Megalithic Culture we find both globular amphorae and open flat-based bowls, probably for holding and preparing milk. Amber was used for ornaments and is quite common (but becomes rare with the appearance of copper tools in the Late Neolithic).

Ritual and religion. The earliest burials were placed in the ground in a circular pit. At the bottom a single individual was buried in a timber coffin, covered with a small mound of grass or heath turf approximately 1 metre high. A wooden fence often surrounded the burial place. Later, coffins were constructed directly on the ground and again covered with a small turf mound. With repeated use new burials were added on top of the mound and covered with a new layer of turf or sand. Thus the burial practice often reveals a family succession from

Fig. 5. Three dimensional view of a passage grave from Jordhøj, Jutland (after Nielsen 1981: 83, drawn by Flemming Bau: Sesam Danmarks-historien).

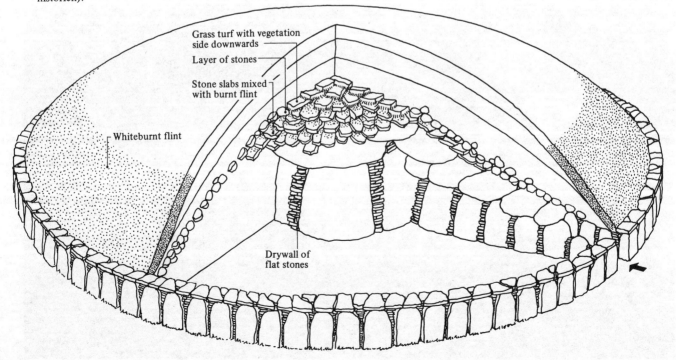

Grass turf with vegetation side downwards

Layer of stones

Stone slabs mixed with burnt flint

Whiteburnt flint

Drywall of flat stones

the earliest to the latest burials — one upon the other — but always respecting the former burials (Fig. 7). Around the periphery of the mound small child burials were dug into the barrow, completing the picture of the family mound. The rather low barrows typically cluster in long lines or groups of 10—20. Some ritual is evidenced in the early phase preceding the construction of the mound in the form of circular wooden constructions (cult-houses) standing for some time and burned down before the construction of the mound.

Both men and women are buried, sometimes in double graves or side by side. On the basis of grave goods only 25% are women, but in small well-excavated groups of barrows the female representation is seen to be higher. The evidence indicates monogamy. The position of the dead is always flexed. The males on their right side and the females on their left side, both looking to the south. Double male burials represent a distinctive feature.

Burial equipment is rather standardized: for the man a battle axe in front of the face, sometimes a beaker holding some liquor (probably mead, as in the Early Bronze Age), and also a flint axe, a few stone flakes and two round disks of amber at the belt. The latter seem to be a special distinction not found too often (perhaps symbolizing the two wheels of the wagon?). The female would normally have amber ornaments (in their hundreds) and a beaker. Children are normally without equipment but are also buried flexed.

We have very little evidence of ritual hoarding and feasting, so little that we cannot speak of a ritual tradition.

Synthesis: the social system. The connection between ritual, exchange and subsistence noted for the Megalithic Culture is dissolved. Polished flint axes are still found as grave goods in the early phase of 'landnam' but then gradually disappear, becoming smaller and more carelessly manufactured over time.

Fig. 6. Group of single barrows near Viborg in Central Jutland, photographed around the turn of the century, when the landscape still retained some of its original, open treeless character (photograph: the National Museum).

Fig. 7. Cross-section of a typical single grave (after Nielsen 1981: 118, drawn by Flemming Bau: Sesam, Danmarkshistorien).

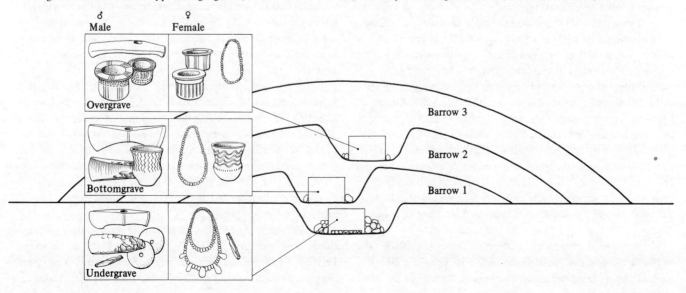

Instead we witness an enormous local production of battle axes, the standard equipment in male burials. In the early phase the axes are rather similar throughout western Europe, but are then gradually subject to local development, reflecting increasingly closed cycles of exchange and inter-marriage, with amber circulating for greater distances. The prime motive for maintaining alliances was the exchange of women and prestige goods (amber and battle axes). The open landscape, once created, was maintained by free-grazing cattle and the cutting of secondary forest for leaf fodder. Consequently land was not a scarce resource that needed to be created and maintained by ancestor spirits and their living descendants by ritual means. Productive wealth was mainly stored in cattle and sheep, needing large pastures, not in the products of the soil. Thus control of land was difficult but not important as long as it was plentiful. The decisive resource was water. Each hamlet could be self-sufficient and compete for prestige and cattle.

According to this interpretation the prime mover of leadership was exchange of prestige goods through alliances and inter-marriage, probably with cattle as a common medium of exchange and accumulation. The competitive and warlike nature of the system is shown by the hundreds of battle axes in burials. It seems, however, that certain areas were able to achieve a favoured position in the exchange system and developed slightly more hierarchical social structures, reflected in the distribution of amber. The status of females increased in areas of good soils, perhaps due to their role in agricultural production. Basically, however, the burial evidence reflects the autonomy of local lineages with the monogamous family as its smallest unit. Above this level the participation in marriage alliances created a wider territorial pattern of inter-communal tribal bonds. This is reflected in the localized distribution of certain ceramic types and battle axes, and also in a settlement pattern which shows regional clusters. Above that, wider and looser inter-regional groups are found. All in all this is a pattern very much resembling that of the segmentary lineages of African pastoralists (Sahlins 1961), although this proposition needs further testing.

These interpretations do not imply that we are dealing with a completely egalitarian system. The single graves must reflect only an upper segment of society. Since the Megalithic Culture, inherited rank and leadership had become fundamental properties of social consciousness, but larger segments of local lineages were receiving a burial in the Single Grave Culture. We are thus dealing with a ranked system of competing local lineages preventing higher levels of political hierarchization from being maintained. Hierarchization could probably be triggered if population or herds increased beyond the productive potential of land, or if prestige goods were introduced from outside the system which would also affect the processes of production, as happened later in the Bronze Age.

In order to deepen our understanding of the relationship between religion and social organization let us take a closer look at the grave monuments. The tens of thousands of barrows reflect an inversion of the megaliths in nearly all respects. Now the individual and his property are the focus of burial rites. Equipped with his personal items of rank, with liquor for feasting, he is once and for all separated from the world of the living. Leaving for another world he is socially and ritually equipped to re-occupy his place there and even brings land with him, symbolized by the half to one ha. of turf covering him. This further indicates that land was plentiful and could be taken away by and for the dead, in contrast to the megalithic monuments that reflected the opening up of new agricultural land. Later, in the hierarchical pastoral economy of the Bronze Age, monumental barrows could contain up to five ha. of land, reflecting a greater control of land by chiefly families in an increasingly dense settlement pattern. But in contrast to both megaliths and Bronze Age barrows, the barrows of the Single Grave Culture reflect no monumental ideology and were often situated on low land.

The barrow itself may be said to reflect important elements of subsistence and ecology. However, we can easily distinguish religion from economy as they are not otherwise linked up with each other by ritual means. Thus the ideology of burial rites almost exclusively reflects aspects of social organization: the transmission of personal status and property and the autonomy of the local lineage. Naturally feasting must have taken place, but as it was not linked to ritual consumption and wider inter-communal activities it is not archaeologically traceable. The subordination of religion to serve mainly social purposes and its concomitant separation from the processes of (agricultural) production seem to indicate that participation in alliances for exchange of women, cattle and prestige objects was the main prerequisite for increasing local prestige and production (accumulation of cattle).

This interpretation of Single Grave Culture social organization does not represent a unique historical case. On the contrary it entails many of the basic features of present day or historically known pastoral societies (Bonte 1978; Goldschmidt 1979; Ingold 1980). It should be stressed that pastoral societies exhibit a wide range of variation, and the Single Grave Culture is not purely pastoral. Yet certain elements seem to be more general, among them the autonomy of the household and the local lineage in production. Also an aggressive and warlike behaviour is often characteristic of a pastoral lifestyle. At marriage and death the transmission of private livestock, as distinct from land, is a decisive factor affecting both kinship systems and religion. Finally the feature of male partnership or assistant- and associateship is generally found to be linked to herding, as discussed by Ingold (1980), perhaps accounting for double male burial in the Single Grave Culture. As we have seen, all of these elements characterize the Single Grave Culture but they need to be more closely analysed in future research.

Although the Single Grave Culture represents a rather specialized adaptation to the light soils of central and western Jutland, a pastoral economy in an open environment of large permanent pastures and small rotating fields was later to dominate throughout southern Scandinavia and came to represent the basis of the Bronze Age economy. It may thus be regarded as a model of later developments (see Kristiansen 1982). During some 400 years, local cycles of expansion and regression, alliances and warfare, in a delicate environment with a low ecological threshold, kept the system in a state of equilibrium. The system's evolutionary potential was not released until the introduction of bronze.

Conclusion. By contrasting the evidence of the Mega-lithic Culture and the Single Grave Culture I have tried to demonstrate how two tribal systems with a similar technology, but a different social organization of production, may express identical cultural institutions very differently in the archae-ological record. Thus an axe is not just an axe, and a burial not just a burial. Significance is determined by their material functions, which can only be fully comprehended by consider-ing the cultural and structural totality of the evidence. The Megalithic Culture linked subsistence, social organization and religion very closely to one another in a ritualized vertical structure of reproduction. The Single Grave Culture on the other hand separated these institutions, being dominated by a competitive horizontal social structure of alliances and exchange, based on local economic autonomy, and with little evidence of communal ritual. We thus have an 'agricultural' versus 'pastoral' tribal economy. The first case produced a varied and 'rich' intentional material record, cross-cutting sub-sistence, social organization and religion, whereas the second case produced a much narrower and 'poor' intentional material record, mainly of burials. I have tried to summarize the differ-ent social dynamics of the two systems in a simplified model (Fig. 8).

These variants of tribal structure, which characterized temperate Eurasia during the fourth and third millennia BC

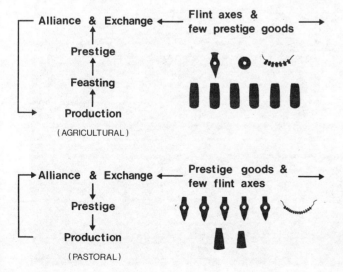

Fig. 8. Models of hierarchization in the Megalithic Culture (agri-cultural) and the Single Grave Culture (pastoral) (drawn by Catherina Olesen).

respectively, must certainly have exhibited different rules of kinship, marriage, transmission of property and so on, aspects that are not easily recognized in the archaeological record. The best way of approaching this problem is probably by structural analogy with similar systems known to us, historically or ethnographically (examples and discussion in Hodder 1978b). By doing so we may add these features as explanatory com-ponents to our models (cf. Rowlands 1980). In the following example the material manifestations of some of these phenom-ena and their temporal variation will be considered.

Consumption and sex in Bronze Age Denmark

During the Bronze Age (c. 1800–500 BC) some remark-able variations in patterns of wealth consumption can be observed, accompanied by changed rules of deposition (from burials to hoards), of burial rites (from inhumation to cre-mation) and of male/female depositions (relative increase of female wealth). As the basic cultural and organizational frame-work of Bronze Age society remained stable why then did the consumption of wealth change so markedly? In order to answer these questions, it is necessary to transcend the explanatory limitations of prevailing research traditions, deal-ing either with burials or hoards, and consider circulation and consumption within the larger cultural and structural frame-work of the Nordic Bronze Age Culture. Hopefully, this may elucidate some of the general processes responsible for vari-ations in burial practice and in patterns of wealth consumption (see also Bradley 1982). As a starting point I shall give a short account of Bronze Age social organization.[11]

The introduction of bronze finally released the evol-utionary potential of the segmentary tribes that had developed in the preceding period, based on a pastoral economy (Gilman 1981; Kristiansen 1982; for comparative pastoral evidence see Burnham 1979; Irons 1979). During the first period of the Bronze Age (1800–1500 BC) lines of long-distance exchange with central Europe were established, channelling bronze to Scandinavia. Here a stock of bronze was gradually built up and by the end of the period a local tradition of metalwork devel-oped, soon providing a wide variety of ornaments, weapons, tools and ritual gear. This tradition of Nordic metalwork con-tinued until supplies of bronze ceased, and finally disappeared with the breakdown of long-distance exchange around 500 BC. Thus, the period from approximately 1500–600 BC represents the florescence of the original Nordic Bronze Age culture (for a popular outline see Glob 1974).

With respect to social and political organization we are dealing with a hierarchical chiefdom structure with unequal access to prestige goods, characterized by intensive consump-tion of personal wealth in burials and hoards (Levy 1979; 1982; Randsborg 1974). Chiefly lineages were buried in impressive barrows of grass- and heath-turf, normally in an oak coffin. Exceptional conditions of preservation also reveal a high level of textile manufacture, sometimes deposited with the deceased in large quantities, and of carpentry, e.g. cups and stools (Fig. 9a, b and c).

Recent studies of male social organization (Kristiansen, in press) have demonstrated a rather complex system of rank. On top was the chief, also performing ritual and priestly functions[12] (plus other occupational specializations), and below him a dependant group of chiefly warriors without ritual functions. Chiefs were in control of long-distance exchange, thereby controlling both communal ritual and the distribution of prestige goods. The rather competitive and warlike nature of the system is demonstrated not only by the numerous swords, but especially by the fact that sword blades show heavy traces of actual use and sharpening, with the exception of many chiefly swords. Female members of the chiefly lineage can also be divided into those who performed priestly functions and those who did not, reflected both in clothing and in ornament types.

Large quantities of bronze and gold were stored in a wide variety of communal ritual gear, mainly found in hoards: *lurs*, shields, helmets, axes, golden drinking cups and so on (Fig. 10). Together with the ritual scenery expressed in rock carvings and bronze figures (Fig. 11), they indicate a highly organized system of communal and inter-communal ritual and feasting. The religious system was heavily influenced by Mycenaean and central European mythology and symbolism and throughout the Bronze Age new religious elements were constantly added. Thus, an elaborate religious system evolved, separated from the communal lineage structure, whose manipulation was an essential prerequisite of chiefly power.

The Nordic Bronze Age Culture is seen, then, to exhibit the basic features of a theocratic prestige-goods system, as known in Polynesia (Friedman 1982; Goldman 1955), including religious/political dualism, status rivalry and inter-chiefly competition over trade (Goldman's 'open societies'). Priestly functions were an extension and mystification of chiefly powers that were based, in reality, on the political monopolization of production, alliances and long-distance exchange. Naturally such a system exhibited considerable local and regional variation in consumption which can be shown to be linked to different regional trajectories of production, population density and exchange (Kristiansen 1978a; 1981a). In the following, however, we will concentrate on the more general temporal trends in wealth consumption, especially the relationship between male/female prestige goods, to which we shall now turn.

Male—female relationships. Fig. 12 shows the relationship between male and female prestige goods deposited in graves and hoards.[13] As can be seen, the general trend is very significant: from male dominance to female dominance. In period I female ornaments were hardly produced, but this situation drastically changed in period II. It should be added, however, that the absolute number of female depositions does not increase much after period II. Thus, the very marked difference is mainly due to a decrease in the deposition of swords. As the number of male burials without swords (indicated by the presence of razors or tweezers) remained more or less stable throughout the Bronze Age, the decrease in sword depositions reflects a changed attitude towards the demonstration of male status (see Kristiansen 1978a: Fig. 9 for sword—grave ratio). Before trying to explain this pattern, let us consider some of the changes which accompany it.

Status diversity. If we consider next the demonstration of

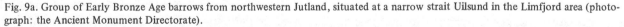

Fig. 9a. Group of Early Bronze Age barrows from northwestern Jutland, situated at a narrow strait Uilsund in the Limfjord area (photograph: the Ancient Monument Directorate).

Fig. 9b. Early Bronze Age warrior burial from Muldbjerg in western Jutland with oak coffin and clothing fully preserved.

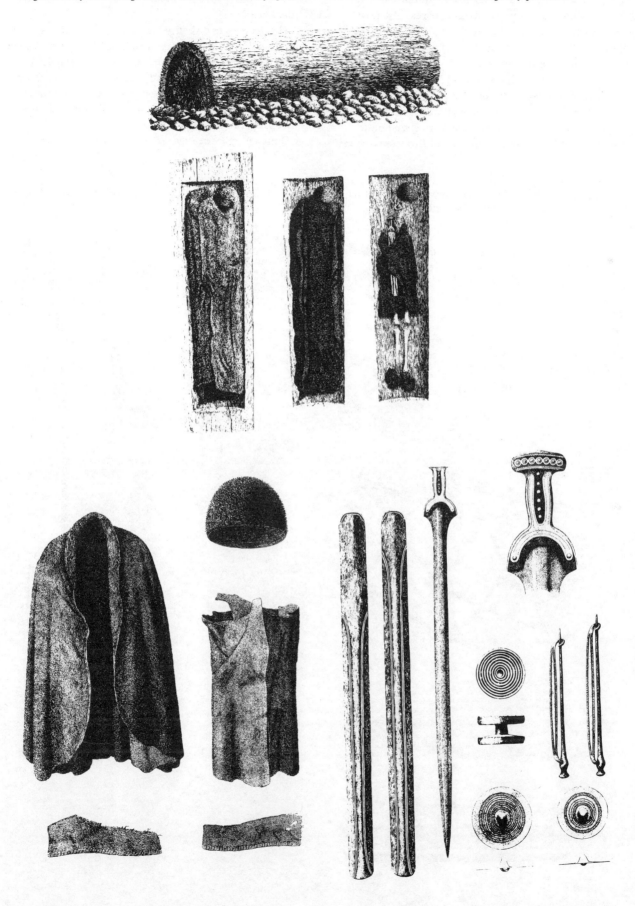

social position as reflected in numbers of different prestige goods or sumptuary goods in burials and hoards, a marked trend can be observed. According to Levy (1982: 69ff) male deposition reveals a maximum diversity in period II, then a decline, and again an optimum in period V (but lower than II), followed by a steep decline in period VI. Female depositions, however, which are more numerous, steadily increase from period II to V, and then also decline. Although these observations are rather crude, they correspond quite well to more detailed analyses of both Early-Bronze-Age male

ranking (Kristiansen, in press) and of Late-Bronze-Age hoards (Kristiansen 1974a).

The decreasing diversity index of social distinctions in male equipment is also accompanied by a blending of formerly distinct types of swords for chiefs and warriors respectively. In the Late Bronze Age such typological distinctions disappear, together with other diagnostic features of chief and warrior. In general, swords display much less artistic skill in their manufacture during the Late Bronze Age.

Quite an opposite development characterizes female

Fig. 9c. Chiefly male burial from Guldhøj in southern Jutland, the folding stool, originally with a seat of otter skin, the wooden cup decorated with tin sprags ((b) and (c) after Boye 1896).

ornaments. They maintain their artistic quality and reach a climax with respect to exaggerated and extremely impractical design in period V. The decline in diversity in period VI is due to the introduction of a new tradition of depositing pairwise neckrings, already apparent in period V, but now dominant. This is accompanied by a stylistic break with the old Nordic tradition and the introduction of a new tradition of manufacture strongly influenced by the Hallstatt Culture. The reduction in diversity is, however, to some extent compensated for by the quantity of bronze stored in each pair of

rings. It should be noticed that period I reveals very similar characteristics, but in male equipment: few and heavy forms, mostly imports or local imitations.

Let us now consider some of the accompanying changes in ritual and religion.

Ritual and religion. During period I only a few bronzes occur in burials, the greater part are found in hoards, due to the scarcity of bronze. By the end of period I the situation is gradually changing and during period II the Nordic Bronze Age

Fig. 10. Some examples of Late Bronze Age ritual gear: (a) lurs, (b) horned helmets and (c) set of golden drinking cups hoarded in an imported bronze vessel probably for holding the liquor.

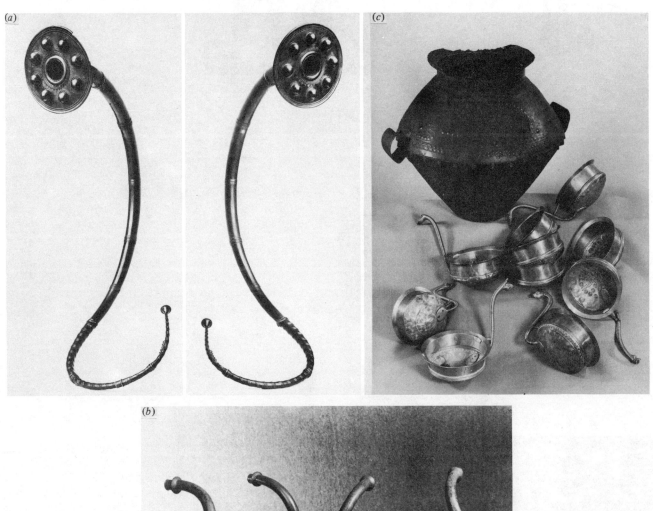

Fig. 11. Ritual scenery as presented in bronze figurines and rock carvings: (a) male warrior chief with horned helmet and ritual axe (originally a pair); (b) female priest in a short corded skirt doing ritual acrobatics; (c) drawing from 1779 of the complete set of bronze figures of which (a) and (b) are the only surviving; (d) rock carvings from Bohuslän, Sweden, of a ritual wedding; and (e) lur-blowing men with horned helmets and a ship with a life tree ((d) and (e) are from Glob 1974).

(a)

(b)

(c)
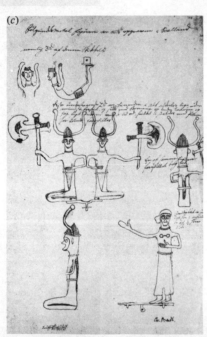

(d)

(e)

reaches its peak. The major part of the tens of thousands of impressive barrows was constructed during this period and the inhumation burials of both men and women were accompanied by rich sumptuary goods. The tradition of ritual hoarding, however, still ran parallel, mainly consisting of female ornaments, often with two or three individual sets in each hoard. But we also find a few hoards with communal ritual gear, such as double votive axes, not to forget the unique sun chariot.

Period III represents a continuation of the ritual practices of period II, although cremation is adopted. This, however, does not otherwise affect burial rites. Ritual hoarding is rare. Period III still sees the construction of quite a large number of chiefly barrows, but it becomes more common to use existing barrows for new burials, adding one or two metres to the barrow.

In periods IV and V most burials are deposited in earlier barrows. The urn is now commonly employed to hold the burnt bones, and grave goods are reduced to small personal items and finally miniatures of swords. A few big chiefly barrows with rich grave goods were built during these periods. They are situated in the centre of densely settled areas with many ritual hoards (Jensen, in press). In areas of settlement expansion, small urn barrows are constructed. Sumptuary goods are mainly deposited by ritual hoarding, often representing the equipment of several persons (Kristiansen 1974b). The manufacture and deposition of ritual gear reaches a climax. New types are employed such as horned helmets and shields,

Fig. 12. Relationship between male/female consumption of prestige goods based on swords (male) and ornaments (female) from burials (mainly Early Bronze Age) and hoards (mainly Late Bronze Age). Early Bronze Age (after Broholm (1943–4) Late Bronze Age after Thrane (1968) and author's data. The figures of period I should be regarded as an approximation (drawn by Catherina Oksen).

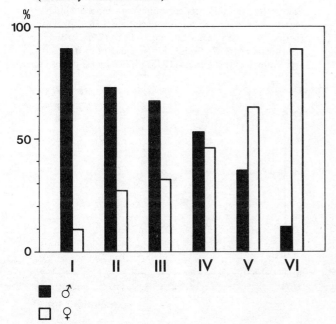

golden cups and equipment for horse-drawn wagons, just as earlier types such as the *lurs* reach their ultimate development. Period V represents the climax of these processes.

In religion the Early Bronze Age double-axe symbolism of warrior gods and sun symbolism of fertility is added to with new snake symbols of the central European mother goddess. Warrior symbolism is reinforced by the pairwise employment of ritual helmets with double ox horns, and shields. Ritual feasting is shown by drinking sets in bronze and gold (during the Early Bronze Age represented by elaborate wooden cups ornamented with tin sprags). Ritual animal symbols also include the horse, ox and swan/duck.

We may summarize the main trends as follows: the Late Bronze Age is characterized by increased ritual hoarding of prestige goods and of costly ritual gear accompanied by increased ritual and religious complexity, at least as evidenced in bronze and gold work. Much of this was probably present in the Early Bronze Age in organic material, although not all. At the same time we witness a marked decrease in mound building and in the deposition of prestige goods in burials. Thus, the hoarding frequency nearly represents an inversion of the frequency of building barrows. Period VI seems to reflect a partial reorganization of religious practices with its dominance of double neckrings and its scarce ritual evidence. Some of the communal ritual gear of period V, however, may have been deposited in this period.

When looking for factors that might have affected the above changes in ritual and consumption we should consider both the supply situation of bronze and the subsistence economy.

The supply of bronze. The supply situation is difficult to estimate without entering into a circular argument. As we are analysing fluctuations and overall changes in consumption, we can hardly then use that parameter to infer the quantity of bronze supplied by long-distance exchange from central Europe. However, the relationship between consumption and the quantity of bronze circulating above the ground may be tested by analysing the wear of prestige bronzes as an indication of how long they circulated before deposition. Such an analysis has shown that increasing circulation time reflected decreasing supplies of bronze, although the relationship is rather complex (Kristiansen 1978a). According to this, period II (especially its later part) and the beginning of period III, represent a climax in bronze supplies. Then follows a period of very scarce supplies in the twelfth century, until supplies are resumed in late period III (late twelfth, early eleventh century). The beginning of period IV witnesses another decline in supplies, and they do not increase significantly again until late period V/early period VI (800–600 BC). This is followed by a steep decline in late period VI until supplies are finally cut off with the advent of the Pre-Roman Iron Age, when iron gradually makes its appearance (c. 500 BC). However, consumption of double neckrings continues into the beginning of the Pre-Roman Iron Age, but all these rings are heavily worn.

The general picture of the supply situation throughout the Bronze Age is summarized in Fig. 13. It can be supported by independent evidence — for instance the quantity of bronze invested in casting prestige objects. By period III we see an initial trend towards saving bronze (many more swords with pommels instead of full hilts), but especially in period IV we witness an explicit concern with bronze-saving castings (hollow neckrings, thin armrings instead of massive ones and so on). It is not until late period V that prestige bronzes generally regain their weight.

Finally the relationship between the number of imports and circulation time during the Late Bronze Age was tested in three regions to see how this conformed to the above picture (Fig. 14). As can be seen, circulation time and number of imports are inversely related to each other, that is, the more imports the shorter the circulation time. This would seem to confirm our hypothesis that increasing circulation time reflects periods of declining supplies of bronze. Again we should leave both period I and VI out of consideration as they represent specific cases of foreign influence characteristic of the beginning and the end of the Bronze Age. When doing so, it is well known that both period II and period V represent climax periods with respect to the number of foreign imports and imitations.

All in all we have substantial evidence to support the picture presented in Fig. 13.

Subsistence economy. Changes in the exploitation of the landscape as reflected in pollen analyses are rather badly documented for the Bronze Age in Denmark. However, recent analyses both in Denmark and Sweden have shown that a remarkable expansion of open land and pastures took place from around 2400 BC. The permanent nature of open land is confirmed by analyses of pollen and plant remains from well-preserved Early-Bronze-Age burials. These indicate extensive hard-grassed pastures and heathlands, reflecting a pastoral economy dependent on cattle (milk, meat and hides) and sheep (wool production). Barley was the dominant crop. Generally some 30–40% of the land was settled according to the distribution of graves (Kristiansen 1978a: Fig. 13). The settled areas seem to have been heavily deforested, especially central and western Jutland, the Thy region and northwestern Zealand. In the two latter regions, perhaps the most densely settled, this is even reflected in a dominance of stone cists for

burials instead of the normal oak coffin, probably due to the scarcity of oak-mixed forests in the settled areas.

In accordance with the dominance of a pastoral economy in an open environment, light or average soils rather than heavy soils were preferred for settlements throughout the Bronze Age (Kristiansen 1978a: Fig. 11). Period III sees a trend towards heavier soils, but this was reversed again from period IV onwards. By the Late Bronze Age some changes, both in settlement and subsistence, can be observed. The settled areas are reduced due to settlement concentration, and the exploitation of the landscape consequently increased. This is reflected in pollen analyses by a further increase of open land, in the collecting of weeds from fallowed fields and in the now rapid expansion of beech on former pastures. At the same time temperature gradually declined and humidity increased, reaching a climax around 600 BC. These ecological changes, it seems, were accompanied by agricultural intensification. During the Late Bronze Age small bronze sickles are numerous, as distinct from the Early Bronze Age, and they are mainly found in female burials and hoards. Also ploughing is made more efficient by the introduction of the compound bow-ard. In periods V–VI wooden double-spades occur in northern Jutland, also reflecting intensified agricultural exploitation.

Thus, the Late Bronze Age is characterized by agricultural intensification and settlement concentration within the light soils of the old settlement areas. At that time, or perhaps a little later, agricultural production was reorganized, and settlements became more stable, reflected in the appearance of 'Celtic fields' all over southern Scandinavia. This was accompanied by the adoption of iron technology (for a discussion, see Kristiansen 1978a; 1981a; Stumann 1979; Windelhed 1977).

Fig. 13. Graph suggesting the quantity of bronze supplied to northern Europe during the Bronze Age (periods I–IV) (drawn by Catherina Oksen).

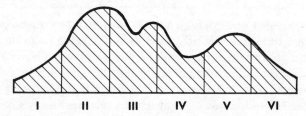

Fig. 14. Relationship between number of imports (minus imitations) and circulation time during the Late Bronze Age (period IV–V) on Zealand (Zone 1), Fuen (Zone 2) and northern Jutland (Zone 3). Circulation time decreases from left to right. Imports after Thrane (1975) (drawn by Catherina Oksen).

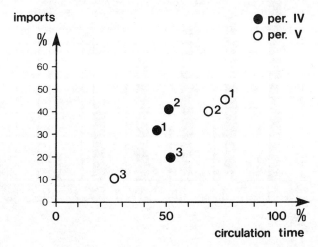

Interpretations and explanations. As will be clear from the above outline, no simple answer can be given to our original question: what determines changes in ritual and wealth consumption in an otherwise stable social organization characterized by cultural continuity? It can also be seen that some marked changes occur in the Final Bronze Age, period VI, which link this period closely to the first period of the Pre-Roman Iron Age. But let us first consider the unbroken tradition of the Nordic Bronze Age down to period VI.

As no single hypothesis accounts for the variation in the evidence, let us start by rejecting the more simple and obvious interpretations, one by one, and then in the end piece together what is left over.

1 It is clear that the change in burial practices from inhumation to cremation does not account for the reduction of male prestige goods, although it may explain why prestige goods in general are consumed by ritual hoarding rather than in burials from period IV onwards. Yet, cause and effect are not easy to determine. However, occasional ritual hoarding is a much cheaper method of consumption than the regularity of burial consumption, and that may be the more significant point (Kristiansen, in press).

2 This raises the question of the effects of the supply situation. For many years it was believed that the frequent hoarding and the decline in burial consumption during the Late Bronze Age reflected a situation of abundance, bronze being so common that it was no longer employed for personal prestige items that were therefore frequently hoarded and remelted. As has been demonstrated, however, this is not the case, rather the opposite. The decreasing supplies do seem to conform quite well with the shift from burial consumption to ritual hoarding, as a means of maintaining chiefly consumption and display in a period of scarcity (since period IV). Hoarding during periods II–III on the other hand was a complementary practice to burial consumption (Randsborg 1974: Fig. 6). When supplies increased during late period V, the ritual system had adopted ritual hoarding and urn burials without prestige goods as consistent features. But again, we are still left with the decrease in male consumption unexplained. Perhaps we should look more closely at the relation between decreasing social attributes and increase of ritual gear and ritual hoarding. Do these changes reflect a 'real' change in male social structure or an ideological change of representation?

3 It has been shown that the decrease in male status diversity and in the consumption of prestige goods had already begun with the advent of period III, that is shortly *before* the supply situation worsened. At the same time the number of female burials increased and they also witnessed an increase in status diversity. It would seem, then, that the need to signal male

wealth and status in burials had decreased, due to a stabilization of the hierarchical social structure which had evolved during late period I and flourished during period II. This argument is supported by the fact that male burials in northern Germany (Mecklenburg) reach a climax both with respect to consumption and status diversity in period III, at the same time as this area was integrated into the alliance and exchange system of the Nordic Bronze Age.

Thus, the decline in male status diversity and prestige consumption did not in the first place reflect a real decline in social complexity, but rather a change in the ideological manifestation of wealth and status. This can be interpreted as reflecting a stabilization of male social structure. The continuity of chiefly burials is further testified by the unbroken employment of razor and tweezer in burial equipment throughout the Late Bronze Age.

At the same time, however, the investment in ritual gear was heavily increased, as was its consumption by ritual hoarding. Whereas, in the Early Bronze Age, ritual gear, such as double axes or early *lurs*, were rarely deposited, we are suddenly presented with a widespread hoarding of such implements. In the Early Bronze Age they might just as often have occurred in male burials, they are now almost exclusively deposited in an isolated ritual context of hoarding. It should be noted that most of these rather elaborate and extremely valuable sumptuary goods were attributes of male priestly and chiefly functions – *lurs*, shields, horned helmets, and probably also the golden drinking cups. It would seem then that the focus of male display and competition did shift from *personal attributes* of chiefly, mainly warrior functions, to chiefly, mainly priestly, more *communal functions*. The reinforcement of priestly functions would conform well with a situation of scarce supplies of bronze leading to increased competition of alliances on the one hand and to communal display, rather than personal display, on the other. Also the continuous accumulation of new religious impulses from central Europe can be seen to be part of chiefly, priestly control and ritual competition. Such communal ritual competition and display served to regulate and compensate for destructive inter-communal warfare in a period of declining supplies of bronze. (Otherwise, personal weapons should have been relegated from status display and consumption due to their regular use.)

Having now shed some light on the change in male status display we are still left with the increase of female consumption unexplained. Let us, however, bridge our analyses by first considering the construction of chiefly barrows and their implications for our analyses.

4 The decline in the construction of chiefly barrows during period III, and the employment of existing barrows for secondary burials during the Late Bronze Age would seem to conform quite well with the proposed explanation of increasing social stabilization with less need to exaggerate and legitimate chiefly superiority. The need was rather to emphasize the unbroken rule of chiefly lineages by employing the barrows of the chiefly ancestors for their successors. Later the rise of regional political centres and new ruling chiefly lineages during the Late Bronze Age resulted in the construction of a few monumental chiefly barrows, whereas subordinate local lineages in new settlement areas employed small urn barrows. Such centralization processes and the concomitant employment or revival of old traditions of display would conform well with the above proposition that wealth consumption and monumental barrows are closely linked to the legitimation of rising elites, based on the political and military success of male chiefly lines. That might also account for the pronounced male dominance in the early phases of social stratification (period II and III).

5 Although this is probably true, there is more to it than social dynamics. Barrows, it should be remembered, also relate very closely to the exploitation and control of land, and ultimately to subsistence, by the repeated removal of the fertile upper layers of soil for their construction. In fact, the 40,000–50,000 or so Bronze Age barrows represent the devastation of several hundred thousand hectares of good soil in a period of a few centuries. In a situation of continuous expansion this would scarcely harm production. However, the settlement territories of the Early Bronze Age had for the greater part been continuously exploited since the Single Grave Culture (in Jutland) and the Late Neolithic (in eastern Denmark). Although this exploitation formed part of a gradual cyclical movement of fields and pastures, the overall productive potential of the settled areas must have decreased. Owing to increasing soil degradation, marginal lands were given up and from the Late Bronze Age settlements clustered. The pressure on land was further increased, leading to an intensification of production. Consequently, the final decline in mound building (from period IV) can be explained as a function of increasing contradiction between ritual/political and economic demands, demonstrating the intricate interaction between social, economic and ecological factors in the decline of mound building and the stabilization of social hierarchies.

The development of chiefly, communal ritual and ritual hoarding would also seem to represent a ritual/political response to a situation of increasing social and economic contradictions — the reinforcement of the mythical and religious powers of chiefly lines served to legitimize and stabilize the political superstructure of an increasingly degraded economic base, reflected in among other things the decline of the construction of monumental barrows. We are led finally towards the sphere of production and the question of its impact on changes in male/female status consumption.

6 As demonstrated earlier, the Late Bronze Age is characterized by gradual changes in settlements, climate and ecology, leading to intensification of production and increased exploitation of the landscape. The character of this intensification is more precisely indicated by technological innovations, such as the compound bow-ard, and by the increase of cereals in pollen diagrams. All in all a heavier dependency on agricultural production is evident. The giving up of some marginal lands and the spread of the beech point in the same direction — pasture land was given up. This trend would gradually lead to a more stable and permanent settlement pattern, and a regulation of fields and pastures. In the end the transmission of land, rather than livestock, would become a major focus.

With this background the widespread occurrence of small bronze sickles in both hoards and burials makes sense. Harvesting and the preparation of fields now became a major activity which, according to the find context of sickles, was mainly carried out by women. It would seem then that the changed position of women should also be related to a gradual shift from a pastoral economy towards a more agricultural economy — or at least that agricultural production became more important in a period of ecological degradation and the lowering of productive potential of the settled areas. The dependence on agricultural land rather than pastures also changed the focus of male prestige from alliances/warfare and the accumulation of livestock towards the preservation and maintenance of productive land.

Thus, the rise of female ranking and wealth display should probably be related both to the stabilization of male ranking, allowing wealth to be invested in wives and daughters, and to the increased importance of females in production and alliances.

The exchange of females in regional alliance politics can be demonstrated already from late period I between northern Germany and Zealand and such alliance politics seems to have been an important aspect of political expansion and control of the exchange of bronze (Kristiansen 1981a: 254ff). This would account for the development of female ranking and wealth display, but not for the decline in male wealth display from period IV onwards. However, in a period of declining supplies of bronze, females might have increased their importance as a medium for establishing alliances and maintaining the flow of bronze. Thus, the increase in female ranking and wealth display and the concomitant decline in male display can be explained as a function of decreasing supplies of bronze.

I thus propose that the decline in male display – or rather the conversion from social to communal ritual wealth – and the increase of female display of wealth from late period III onwards should be seen as a combined result of declining supplies of bronze, intensification of agriculture and increased import- ance of females in alliance politics and in agricultural production. It may further be suggested that these changes were accompanied by changed rules of inheritance and transmission of land through both male and female lines. The details of the ultimate consequences of this development, leading to the final collapse of the theocratic prestige-goods system of the Bronze Age and the reorganization of both settlements and economy during the Pre-Roman Iron Age, are beyond the scope of this article (see Kristiansen 1980; Pearson, this volume).

7 As will be clear from the above analysis, we are deal- ing with a complex interplay between processes of social, economic and ritual change, some of them general and some of them more specific. I have tried – by scientific trial and error (falsification) – to con- struct a processual chain of events (1–6 above). As general processes I have considered the concomitant rise of ruling elites/monumental barrows/display of male wealth, followed by consolidation, decline of monumental barrow building/of male wealth display and increase of female wealth display. These pro- cesses, however, are accompanied by changed con- ditions of production (ecological degradation and agri- cultural intensification), leading to decreasing supplies of bronze and further changes in wealth consumption from burial to hoarding, and an increase of communal ritual and of female wealth display. It may further be suggested that this sequence should be regarded as irreversible, triggered by the social and political dynamics of the Bronze Age prestige-goods system, and constrained by the ecological and technological conditions of a small-scale economy in a temperate habitat.

With respect to the proposed general processes of the rise and consolidation of ruling elites and their archaeological correlates, we find a rather similar pattern during the Iron Age. Thus, after the reorganiz- ation of settlements and economy during the Pre- Roman Iron Age (500–100 BC) accompanied by settlement expansion into previously forested heavy soils, we suddenly find a horizon of rich male weapon burials from 100 BC, reflecting long distance contacts

with the Celtic world. During the following Early Roman period (0–200 AD) rich female burials also make their appearance, together with Roman imports, and from 200–400 AD, the Late Roman period, male weapon burials disappear and rich female burials dominate (Hedeager 1978; 1980; Hedeager and Kristiansen, in press; cf. Pearson, this volume). Huge depositions of weapons in moors demonstrate conflict and war between competing regional kingdoms. From 400–800 AD, after the collapse of the Roman Empire, wealth disappears from burials and is hoarded instead. At the same time, pollen diagrams reflect marked changes in the exploitation of the landscape – pastures are given up and agricultural production is probably intensified, a development that had begun by 200 AD.

This sequence – although taking place within a different social and economic framework – has much in common with the Bronze Age sequence and might indicate that we are dealing with a more general pattern. The rise of Viking kingdoms during the ninth and tenth centuries also reveals an initial sequence of male warrior burials as well as runic monuments (Randsborg 1981).

Thus, I believe that the Bronze Age of northern Europe highlights some of the general conditions and developmental processes that govern the relationship between material function and cultural form in ranked and stratified societies.[14]

Conclusion

Some questions have been posed, some answers pro- posed and the reader may now deliver his or her judgement. When doing so, however, the ultimate purpose of this article should be remembered – to demonstrate the necessity of dis- tinguishing between material function and cultural form as a prerequisite for interpreting and explaining social organization in archaeological terms. This can only be done by considering cultural form within a larger framework of production and reproduction in order to determine its material functions. I have tried to illuminate the potential and the necessity of such an approach by examples from later European prehistory (4000–500 BC). It is suggested that archaeologists should be searching more consistently for the conditions that govern cultural manifestations of material functions in societies at various levels of social complexity and in various stages of their development. This determines the interpretations and explanation of a major part of the archaeological record.

Notes

The general theoretical position adopted in this article is derived mainly from structural Marxism as it has been developed and applied in recent works by Jonathan Friedman and Mike Rowlands especially, heavily influenced, however, by Maurice Godelier's version of structural Marxism and the World System theory of Emmanuel Wallerstein. I have not considered other

Marxist directions, partly because of my ignorance of them and partly because I have not found them useful in an archaeological context. This is the case, for example, with respect to the German 'Frankfurt School', as it is mostly concerned with sociology, although a (rather primitive) historical and evolutionary perspective has been taken up in recent years (Eder 1976; Habermas 1976; discussed in Götze and von Thienen 1981). Also I have not considered the application of Marxist theory to archaeology in the communist countries (discussed in Klejn 1977), in part due to my lack of knowledge of the Russian literature, but especially due to the fact that in most East European countries so-called Marxist explanations normally consist of a few mechanical statements at the end of an otherwise traditional archaeological analysis. To my knowledge it is only in East Germany that one finds an explicit concern to combine Marxist theory with archaeological method (Herrmann 1965; 1979; Herrmann and Sellnow 1973; Otto and Brackmann 1975) and social anthropology (e.g. the journal *Ethnographisch–Archäologische Zeitschrift*).

1 One of the basic problems in a mathematical approach to transformations is methodological/empirical. In most cases of major social transformations in prehistory and early history the nature of the empirical evidence changes drastically just as we witness major breaks in cultural continuity. This implies that it is rarely possible to apply methodological parameters that cover 'both sides' of such transformations. One may apply specific parameters designed for, let us say, the evidence of the Bronze Age or the Iron Age, but not for both periods. This empirical and methodological incompatibility implies that explanations remain within the realm of intelligent interpretation and theoretical deductions. Mathematical approaches to transformations consequently remain a heuristic device — a tool for thinking rather than for concrete analysis. This is apparently also the position taken in Renfrew's suggestive introductory article (Renfrew 1979). With respect to the scientific framework of New Archaeology — generally more rigorously prescribed than performed — I still find that some of the best critical discussions of the limitations of such a framework are a handful of earlier articles by Adams (1974), Flannery (1972; 1973), Freeman (1968), and Kushner (1970), going far beyond the trivialities of ideographic/nomothetic and induction/deduction debates.

2 I consider C.J. Thomsen's Stone, Bronze, Iron Age scheme, and Worsaae and de Mortillet's discovery of the Old Stone Age mainly as empirical observations, fundamental, but with little or no bearing upon evolutionary theory, except in very general terms.

3 The methodological and theoretical hangovers of German archaeology are evident in the historical self-critique in Eggers's book of 1959, which should be compared with Jacob-Friesen's book of 1928. See also Hachmann, Kossach and Kühn (1962) and Klejn's review of this general research tradition (1971; 1974) which primarily failed because it was unable to develop common criteria for different types of migration, invasion and diffusion (examples and discussion in Adams 1968; Myhre and Myhre 1972. For an interesting New World attempt, see also Thompson 1958).

4 Willey and Phillips's *Method and Theory in American Archaeology* (1958) and Clarke's *Analytical Archaeology* (1968) represent related attempts at an alternative solution through the analytical and methodological refinement of the traditional framework, in Clarke's book supported by quantitative methods and statistics.

5 I am here especially thinking of 'primitive' or small-scale societies (bands and various forms of tribal structures) and not the more developed systems, such as asiatic or feudal states, with a long and outstanding Marxist research tradition not taken into consideration in this article.

6 The same explanatory limitations characterize ethnoarchaeology. Although the experience gained from such fieldwork has proved extremely valuable with respect to understanding the nature and the properties of the archaeological record one should be very careful not to infer general explanations from such local studies, just as their social significance for archaeology is to be understood in the context of the present day world economic system, a point which is generally not sufficiently realized. A good critical discussion of the theoretical framework of ethnoarchaeology has recently been offered by Schiffer (1978).

7 In an earlier paper I have attempted to outline some basic features of the evolution of tribal systems in temperate northern Europe 4000–500 BC (Kristiansen 1982), and the reader is referred to this article for references to relevant literature (note 1). For valuable advice and discussions on neolithic ritual I want to thank Sven Thorsen, the Ancient Monuments Directorate and Klaus Ebbesen, University of Copenhagen.

8 A clue to the social and ritual value attached to battle axes is given by the fact that only one had been ritually buried at the regional causewayed camp at Sarup (Andersen 1980: Fig. 24).

9 We lack any systematic analysis of the average quantity of stones contained in undisturbed megaliths and the amount of virgin stone-scattered land needed to supply this quantity. If we make a conservative guess of 5–10 ha. per megalith and estimate the original number of megaliths as approximately 20,000 the implications are quite suggestive.

10 This argument is further supported by the fact that megaliths cluster distinctively on the best soils in southern Scandinavia and are very scarce or absent on the poorer, light soils.

11 With respect to literature, the reader is referred to the bibliography in Kristiansen (1981a) with the addition of a forthcoming conference report from a Bronze Age seminar held in Lund, May 1982.

12 Chiefly male double burials might indicate a division of 'priestly' and 'political' functions, originating in the Single Grave Culture. This pairing is also strongly evidenced in religious symbolism.

13 For a definition and analysis of ritual hoards, see Levy (1982). From this it is clear, however, that ritual hoarding can be regarded as an alternative way of depositing personal sets of sumptuary goods.

14 After the completion of the manuscript, the book *Ranking, Resource and Exchange* has appeared (Renfrew and Shennan 1982) with a collection of stimulating papers, many of them bearing upon the problems discussed in this article. With respect to the Danish evidence Shennan's paper elegantly revives the old problem of amber (Shennan 1982). This I deliberately avoided in my earlier papers, as I wanted to show that the major factors were rather rooted in subsistence and the organization of production, with amber on top of that as a dependent variable (otherwise northwestern Europe should not have seen a decline during the Late Bronze Age). Shennan's paper, however, puts the Bronze Age evidence into a refreshing long-term perspective that seems compatible with such a view. Randsborg's paper (1982), on the other hand, although it has some stimulating ideas, must be rejected for its simplistic climatic determinism, an approach lately taken to its extreme by Bouzek (1982). Also Hodder (1982) *Symbolic and Structural Archaeology* and Renfrew, Rowlands and Segraves (1982) *Theory and Explanation in Archaeology* appeared after the completion of the manuscript. References have therefore been determined by my knowledge of the manuscripts in draft versions.

Bibliography

Adams, R.McC. 1974. Anthropological perspectives on ancient trade. *Current Anthropology* 15: 239–58.

Adams, W.Y. 1968. Invasion, diffusion, evolution? *Antiquity* 44: 115–29.

Andersen, N.H. 1980. Sarup. Befaestede neolitiske anlaeg og deres baggrund. *Kuml*: 63–98.

Athens, J.S. 1977. Theory building and the study of evolutionary process in complex societies. In L.R. Binford (ed.), *For Theory Building in Archaeology*, pp. 353–84. New York: Academic Press.

Bender, B. 1978. Gatherer–hunter to farmer: a social perspective. *World Archaeology* 10: 205–22.

1981. Gatherer–hunter intensification. In A. Sheridan and G. Bailey (eds.), *Economic Archaeology: Towards an Integration of Ecological and Social Approaches*. B.A.R. International Series 96: 149–57. Oxford: British Archaeological Reports.

Binford, L.R. 1962. Archaeology as anthropology. *American Antiquity* 28: 217–25.

1965. Archaeological systematics and the study of culture process. *American Antiquity* 31: 203–10.

1968. Post-Pleistocene adaptations. In S. Binford and L.R. Binford (eds.), *New Perspectives in Archaeology*, pp. 313–42. Chicago: Aldine.

1972. *An Archaeological Perspective*. New York: Seminar Press.

1975. Comments on evolution. In L.R. Binford (ed.), *An Archaeological Perspective*, pp. 105–13. New York: Seminar Press.

1977 (ed.). *For Theory Building in Archaeology*. New York: Academic Press.

1981. Behavioral archaeology and the 'Pompeii premise'. *Journal of Anthropological Research* 37: 195–208.

Binford, S.R. and L.R. Binford (eds.) 1968. *New Perspectives in Archaeology*. Chicago: Aldine.

Blackmore, C., M. Braithwaite and I. Hodder, 1979. Social and cultural patterning in the Late Iron Age of southern Britain. In B.C. Burnham and J. Kingsbury (eds.), *Space, Hierarchy and Society*. B.A.R. International Series 59: 93–112. Oxford: British Archaeological Reports.

Bloch, M. 1971. *Placing the Dead*. London: Seminar Press.

Bonte, P. 1978. Non-stratified social formations among pastoral nomads. In J. Friedman and M.J. Rowlands (eds.), *The Evolution of Social Systems*, pp. 173–200. London: Duckworth.

Bouzek, J. 1982. Climatic changes and Central European prehistory. In A. Harding (ed.), *Climatic Change in Later Prehistory*, pp. 179–82. Edinburgh: Edinburgh University Press.

Boye, V. 1896. *Fund af Egekister fra Bronzealderen i Danmark* (Trouvailles de cercueils en chêne de l'âge du bronze en Danemark). Copenhagen: Høst og Søn.

Bradley, R. 1981. Various styles of urn cemeteries and settlement in southern England c. 1400–1000 BC. In R. Chapman, I. Kinnes and K. Randsborg (eds.), *The Archaeology of Death*, pp. 93–104. Cambridge: Cambridge University Press.

1982. The destruction of wealth in later prehistory. *Man* (n.s.) 17: 108–22.

Braun, D.P. 1981. A critique of some recent North American mortuary studies. *American Antiquity* 46 (2): 398–416.

Broholm, H.C. 1943–4. *Danmarks Bronzealder*, Bind 1–2. Copenhagen: Nyt Nordisk Forlag–Arnold Busck.

Brown, J. (ed.) 1971. *Approaches to the Social Dimensions of Mortuary Practices*. Memoirs of the Society for American Archaeology 25.

1981. The search for rank in prehistoric burials. In R. Chapman, I. Kinnes and K. Randsborg (eds.), *The Archaeology of Death*, pp. 25–38. Cambridge: Cambridge University Press.

Burnham, B.C. and J. Kingsbury (eds.) 1979. *Space, Hierarchy and Society*. B.A.R. International Series 59. Oxford: British Archaeological Reports.

Burnham, P. 1979. Spatial mobility and political centralization in pastoral societies. In Équipe Écologie et Anthropologie des Sociétés Pastorales (eds.), *Pastoral Production and Society*, pp. 349–61. Cambridge: Cambridge University Press.

Carneiro, R.L. 1970. A theory of the origin of the state. *Science* 169: 733–8.

Chapman, R. 1981. The emergence of formal disposal areas and the 'problem' of Megalithic tombs in prehistoric Europe. In R. Chapman, I. Kinnes and K. Randsborg (eds.), *The Archaeology of Death*, pp. 71–82. Cambridge: Cambridge University Press.

Childe, V.G. 1946. *Scotland Before the Scots*. London: Methuen.

1951. *Social Evolution*. London: Watts.

Clarke, D. 1968. *Analytical Archaeology*. London: Methuen.

1972 (ed.) *Models in Archaeology*. London: Methuen.

1973. Archaeology: the loss of innocence. *Antiquity* 47: 6–18.

Daniels, S.G.H. 1972. Research design models. In D. Clarke (ed.), *Models in Archaeology*, pp. 201–29. London: Methuen.

Dumond, D.E. 1965. Population growth and cultural change. *Southwestern Journal of Anthropology* 21: 302–24.

Dunnell, R.C. 1980. Evolutionary theory and archaeology. In M. Schiffer (ed.), *Advances in Archaeological Method and Theory* 3: 35–99. New York: Academic Press.

Earle, T. and J.E. Ericson (eds.) 1977. *Exchange Systems in Prehistory*. New York: Academic Press.

Eder, K. 1976. *Die Entstehung Staatlich organisierter Gesellschaften, Ein Beitrag zu einer Theorie der Sozialen Evolution*. Frankfurt/Main: Suhrkamp.

Eggers, H.J. 1951. *Der römische Import im freien Germanien*. Atlas der Urgeschichte 1. Hamburg: Museum für Völkerkunde und Vorgeschichte.

1959. *Einführung in die Vorgeschichte*. München: R. Piper.

Ekholm, K. and J. Friedman, 1980. Towards a global anthropology. In L. Blusse, H.L. Wesseling and G.D. Winius (eds.), *History and Underdevelopment*, pp. 61–76. Leiden: Center for the History of European Expansion.

Ellison, A. 1981. Towards a socioeconomic model for the Middle Bronze Age in southern England. In I. Hodder, G. Isaac and N. Hammond (eds.), *Pattern of the Past*, pp. 413–38. Cambridge: Cambridge University Press.

Engelbrecht, W. 1978. Ceramic patterning between New York Iroquois sites. In I. Hodder (ed.), *The Spatial Organization of Culture*, pp. 141–52. London: Duckworth.

Engels, F. 1884. *The Origin of the Family, Private Property and the State*. New York: International Publishing Company, 1940.

Flannery, K. 1968a. Archaeological systems theory and early Mesoamerica. In B. Meggers (ed.), *Anthropological Archaeology in the Americas*, pp. 67–87. Washington DC: Anthropological Society of Washington.

1968b. The Olmec and the valley of Oaxaca: a model for interregional interaction in formative times. In E.P. Benson (ed.), *Dumbarton Oaks Conference on the Olmec*, pp. 119–30. Washington DC: Dumbarton Oaks Research Library and Collection Trustees, for Harvard University.

1972. The cultural evolution of civilizations. *Annual Review of Ecology and Systematics* 3: 399–426.

1973. Archaeology with a capital S. In C. Redman (ed.), *Research and Theory in Current Archaeology*, pp. 47–58. New York: John Wiley.

Fleming, A. 1973. Tombs for the living. *Man* (n.s.) 8: 177–93.

Foley, R. 1981. Off-site archaeology, an alternative approach for the short-sited. In I. Hodder, G. Isaac and N. Hammond (eds.), *Pattern of the Past*, pp. 157–84. Cambridge: Cambridge University Press.

Frankenstein, S. 1979. The Phoenicians in the Far West: a function of Neo-Assyrian imperialism. In M.T. Larsen (ed.), *Power and Propaganda. A Symposium on Ancient Empires*, pp. 263–94. Copenhagen: Akademisk Forlag.

Frankenstein, S. and M.J. Rowlands, 1978. The internal structure and regional context of Early Iron Age society in south-western Germany. *Bulletin of the Institute of Archaeology, London* 15: 73–112.

Freeman, L.G. 1968. A theoretical framework for interpreting archaeological materials. In R.B. Lee and I. de Vore (eds.), *Man the Hunter*, pp. 262–7. Chicago: Aldine.

Fried, M.H. 1960. On the evolution of social stratification and the state. In S. Diamond (ed.), *Culture and History, Essays in Honor of Paul Radin*, pp. 713–31. New York: Columbia University Press.

Friedman, J. 1974. Marxism, structuralism and vulgar materialism. *Man* (n.s.) 9: 444–69.

1975a. Tribes, states and transformations. In M. Bloch (ed.), *Marxist Analyses and Social Anthropology*, pp. 161–202. London: Malaby Press.

1975b. Religion as economy and economy as religion. *Ethnos* 40 (1–4): 46–63.

1979. *System, Structure and Contradiction: the Evolution of 'Asiatic' Social Formations*. Copenhagen: National Museum of Denmark.

1982. Catastrophe and continuity in social evolution. In C. Renfrew, M. Rowlands and B. Segraves (eds.), *Theory and Explanation in Archaeology: The Southampton Conference*, pp. 175–96. London: Academic Press.

Friedman, J. and M. Rowlands (eds.) 1978. *The Evolution of Social Systems*. London: Duckworth.

Fritz, J.M. and F.T. Plog, 1970. The nature of archaeological explanation. *American Antiquity* 35: 405–12.

Geisslinger, H. 1967. *Hörte als Geschichtsquelle*. Offa-Bücher 19. Neumünster: Karl Wachholz Verlag.

Gilman, A. 1981. The development of social stratification in Bronze Age Europe. *Current Anthropology* 22: 1–23.

Glob, P.V. 1974. *The Mound People*. London: Faber.

Godelier, M. 1978. Infrastructures, society and history. *Current Anthropology* 19 (4): 763–71.

Götze, B. and V. von Thienen, 1981. Archaeological remarks on a revised theory of evolution. In A. Sheridan and G. Bailey (eds.), *Economic Archaeology: Towards an Integration of Ecological and Social Approaches*. B.A.R. International Series 96: 77–86. Oxford: British Archaeological Reports.

Goldman, J. 1955. Status rivalry and cultural evolution in Polynesia. *American Anthropologist* 55: 680–97.

Goldschmidt, W. 1979. A general model for pastoral social systems. In Équipe Écologie et Anthropologie des Sociétés Pastorales (eds.), *Pastoral Production and Society*, pp. 15–27. Cambridge: Cambridge University Press.

Goldstein, L. 1981. One-dimensional archaeology and multi-dimensional people: spatial organization and mortuary analysis. In R. Chapman, I. Kinnes and K. Randsborg (eds.), *The Archaeology of Death*, pp. 53–70. Cambridge: Cambridge University Press.

Green, D., C. Haselgrove and M. Spriggs (eds.) 1978. *Social Organization and Settlement*. B.A.R. International Series 47. Oxford: British Archaeological Reports.

Groube, L. 1981. Black holes in British prehistory: the analysis of settlement distributions. In I. Hodder, G. Isaac and N. Hammond (eds.), *Pattern of the Past*, pp. 185–210. Cambridge: Cambridge University Press.

Habermas, J. 1976. *Zur Rekonstruktion des Historischen Materialismus*. Frankfurt/Main: Suhrkamp.

Hachmann, R., G. Kossach and H. Kühn, 1962. *Völker zwischen Germanen und Kelten*. Neumünster: Karl Wachholz Verlag.

Hedeager, L. 1978. Processes towards state formation in Early Iron Age Denmark. In K. Kristiansen and C. Paludan-Müller (eds.), *New Directions in Scandinavian Archaeology*, pp. 217–23. Copenhagen: National Museum of Denmark.

1980. Besiedlung, soziale Struktur und politische Organisation in der älteren und jüngeren römischen Kaiserzeit. *Praehistorische Zeitschrift* 55: 38–109.

Hedeager, L. and K. Kristiansen, in press. Bendstrup. En fyrstegrav fra aeldre romertid, dens sociale og historiske miljø. *Kuml*.

Herrmann, J. 1965. Archäologische Kulturen und sozialökonomische Gebiete. *Ethnographisch–Archäologische Zeitschrift* 6: 97–128.

1979. *Ökonomie und Gesellschaft an der Wende von der Antike zum Mittelalter: Zum Problem der Herausbildung der ökonomischen Grundlage der Feudalgesellschaft im mittlern und westlichen Europa*. Berlin: Academie-Verlag.

Herrmann, J. and I. Sellnow (eds.) 1976. *Beiträge zur Entstehung der Staates*. Berlin: Academie-Verlag.

Hill, J.N. 1977a. Systems theory and the explanation of change. In J.N. Hill (ed.), *Explanation of Prehistoric Change*, pp. 59–103. Albuquerque: University of New Mexico Press.

Hill, J.N. (ed.) 1977b. *Explanation of Prehistoric Change*. Albuquerque: University of New Mexico Press.

Hodder, I. (ed.) 1978a. Social organization and human interaction: the development of some tentative hypotheses in terms of material culture. In I. Hodder (ed.), *The Spatial Organization of Culture*, pp. 199–269. London: Duckworth.

1978b. *The Spatial Organization of Culture*. New Approaches in Archaeology. London: Duckworth.

1982. *Symbolic and Structural Archaeology*. Cambridge: Cambridge University Press.

Hodder, I. and C. Orton, 1976. *Spatial Analysis in Archaeology*. Cambridge: Cambridge University Press.

Højlund, F. 1979. Stenøkser I Ny Guineas Højland. *Hikuin* 5: 31–48. (English translation in press: The function of prestige weapons in the reproduction of New Guinea highland tribal society. *Oral History*.)

Ingold, T. 1980. *Hunters, Pastoralists and Ranchers*. Cambridge: Cambridge University Press.

1981. The hunter and his spear: notes on the cultural mediation of social and ecological systems. In A. Sheridan and G. Bailey (eds.), *Economic Archaeology: Towards an Integration of Ecological and Social Approaches*. B.A.R. International Series 96: 119–30. Oxford: British Archaeological Reports.

Irons, W. 1979. Political stratification among pastoral nomads. In Équipe Écologie et Anthropologie des Sociétés Pastorales (ed.), *Pastoral Production and Society*, pp. 361–74. Cambridge: Cambridge University Press.

Isbell, W.H. 1978. Environmental perturbations and the origin of the Andean state. In C. Redman *et al.* (eds.), *Social Archaeology. Beyond Subsistence and Dating*, pp. 303–14. New York: Academic Press.

Jacob-Friesen, K.H. 1928. *Grundfragen der Urgeschichtsforschung. Rassen, Völker und Kulturen*. Hannover: Helwingsche Verlagsbuchhandlung.

Jensen, J. in press. Bosaettelse og rigdomscentre i Østdanmark i slutningen af yngre bronzealder. Conference Report from Lund, ed. B. Stjernquist.

Jochim, M.A. 1976. *Hunter–Gatherer Subsistence and Settlement: a Predictive Model*. New York: Academic Press.

Johnson, G.A. 1978. Information sources and the development of decision-making organizations. In C. Redman *et al.* (eds.), *Social Archaeology. Beyond Subsistence and Dating*, pp. 87–112. New York: Academic Press.

King, T.F. 1978. Don't that beat the band? Nonegalitarian political organization in prehistoric Central California. In C. Redman *et al.* (eds.), *Social Archaeology. Beyond Subsistence and Dating*, pp. 225–48. New York: Academic Press.

Kirch, P.V. 1980. The archaeological study of adaptation: theoretical and methodological issues. In M. Schiffer (ed.), *Advances in Archaeological Method and Theory* 3: 101–56. New York: Academic Press.

Klejn, L.S. 1971. Was ist eine archäologische Kultur? *Ethnographisch–Archäologische Zeitschrift* 12: 321–45.

1974. Regressive Purifizierung und exemplarische Betrachtung. Polemische Bemerkungen zur Integration der Archäologie mit der schriftlichen Geschichte und Sprachwissenschaft bei der Ethnischen Deutung. *Ethnographisch–Archäologische Zeitschrift* 15: 223–71.

1977. A panorama of theoretical archaeology. *Current Anthropology* 18: 1–41.

Kohl, P.L. 1978. The balance of trade in southwestern Asia in the third millennium BC. *Current Anthropology* 19: 463–92.

Kristiansen, K. 1974a. Late Bronze Age hoards of Denmark: representativity, chronology and interpretation. Unpublished Ph.D., University of Aarhus.

1974b. Glerupfundet. Et depotfund med kvindesmykker fra bronzealderens femte periode. *Hikuin* 1: 7–38.

1976. A source-critical analysis of hoards from Late Danish Bronze Age (Period IV–V). Summary. *Aarbøger for nordisk. Oldkyndighed og Historie*. 1974: 119–60.

1978a. The consumption of wealth in Bronze Age Denmark. A study in the dynamics of economic processes in tribal societies. In K. Kristiansen and C. Paludan-Müller (eds.), *New Directions in Scandinavian Archaeology*, pp. 158–90. Copenhagen: National Museum of Denmark.

1978b. The application of source criticism to archaeology. *Norwegian Archaeological Review* 11 (1): 1–5.

1980. Besiedlung, Wirtschaftsstrategie und Bodennützung in der Bronzezeit Dänemarks. *Praehistorische Zeitschrift* 55: 1–37.

1981a. Economic models for Bronze Age Scandinavia: towards an integrated approach. In A. Sheridan and G. Bailey (eds.), *Economic Archaeology: Towards an Integration of Ecological and Social Approaches*. B.A.R. International Series 96: 239–303. Oxford: British Archaeological Reports.

1981b. A social history of Danish archaeology (1805–1975). In G. Daniel (ed.), *Towards a History of Archaeology*, pp. 20–44. London: Thames and Hudson.

1982. The formation of tribal systems in later European prehistory: northern Europe 4000–500 BC. In C. Renfrew, M. Rowlands and B. Segraves (eds.), *Theory and Explanation in Archaeology*, pp. 241–80. London: Academic Press.

in press. Kriger og Høvding i Danmarks Bronzealder. Conference report from Lund, ed. by B. Stjernquist.

Kushner, G. 1970. A consideration of some processual designs for archaeology as anthropology. *American Antiquity* 35: 125–32.

Leach, E. 1977. A view from the bridge. In M. Spriggs (ed.), *Archaeology and Anthropology: Areas of Mutual Interest*. B.A.R. Supplementary Series 19: 161–76. Oxford: British Archaeological Reports.

Lee, R.B. and I. de Vore (eds.) 1968. *Man the Hunter*. Chicago: Aldine.

Levy, J. 1979. Evidence of social stratification in Bronze Age Denmark. *Journal of Field Archaeology* 6: 49–56.

1982. *Social and Religious Organization in Bronze Age Denmark. An Analysis of Ritual Hoard Finds*. B.A.R. International Series 124. Oxford: British Archaeological Reports.

Liep, J. 1975. Regnskab efter døden. *Jordens folk* 11. årgang (1): 1–12.

1983. Ranked exchange in Yele (Rossel Island). In E.R. Leach and J.V. Leach (eds.), *The Kula: New Perspectives in Massim Exchange*. Cambridge: Cambridge University Press.

Moberg, C.A. 1981. From artefacts to timetables to maps (to mankind?): regional traditions in archaeological research in Scandinavia. *World Archaeology* 13 (2): 209–21.

Morgan, C.G. 1973. Archaeology and explanation. *World Archaeology* 4: 259–76.

1974. Explanation and scientific archaeology. *World Archaeology* 6: 133–7.

Morgan, L.H. 1877. *Ancient Society*. New York: Henry Holt.

Myhre, B.M. and B. Myhre, 1972. The concept 'immigration' in archaeological contexts illustrated by examples from west Norwegian and north Norwegian Early Iron Age. *Norwegian Archaeological Review* 5 (1): 45–61.

Nielsen, P.O. 1981. *Danmarkshistorien. Oldtiden. Stenalderen. Bondestenalderen*. Copenhagen: Sesam.

Otto, K. and H.J. Brackmann (eds.) 1975. *Moderne Probleme der Archäologie*. Berlin: Akademie-Verlag.

Pearson, M.P. 1982. Mortuary practices, society and ideology: an ethnoarchaeological study. In I. Hodder (ed.), *Symbolic and Structural Archaeology*, pp. 99–113. Cambridge: Cambridge University Press.

Peebles, C.S. and S.M. Kus, 1977. Some archaeological correlates of ranked societies. *American Antiquity* 42 (3): 421–48.

Piggott, S. 1960. Prehistory and evolutionary theory. In S. Tax (ed.), *Evolution after Darwin vol. II. The Evolution of Man*, pp. 85–97. Chicago: University of Chicago Press.

1965. *Ancient Europe*. Edinburgh: Edinburgh University Press.

Plog, S. 1978. Social interaction and stylistic similarity: a reanalysis. In M. Schiffer (ed.), *Advances in Archaeological Method and Theory* 1: 144–82. New York: Academic Press.

Randsborg, K. 1974. Social stratification in Early Bronze Age Denmark. A study in the regulation of cultural systems. *Praehistorische Zeitschrift* 49: 38–61.

1981. Burial, succession and early state formation in Denmark. In R. Chapman, I. Kinnes and K. Randsborg (eds.), *The Archaeology of Death*, pp. 105–22. Cambridge: Cambridge University Press.

1982. Rank, rights and resources. In C. Renfrew and S. Shennan (eds.), *Ranking, Resource and Exchange*, pp. 132–9. Cambridge: Cambridge University Press.

Rathje, W.L. 1973. Models for mobile Maya: a variety of constraints. In C. Renfrew (ed.), *The Explanation of Culture Change*, pp. 731–57. London: Duckworth.

Redman, C. 1978. Mesopotamian urban ecology. The systemic context of the emergence of urbanism. In C. Redman *et al.* (eds.), *Social Archaeology. Beyond Subsistence and Dating*, pp. 329–48. New York: Academic Press.

Redman, C. *et al.* (eds.) 1978. *Social Archaeology. Beyond Subsistence and Dating*. New York: Academic Press.

Renfrew, C. 1969. Trade and culture process in European prehistory. *Current Anthropology* 10: 151–60.

1973a. *Before Civilization*. London: Jonathan Cape.

1973b. Monuments, mobilization and social organization in Neolithic Wessex. In C. Renfrew (ed.), *The Explanation of Culture Change*, pp. 539–58. London: Duckworth.

1973c (ed.) *The Explanation of Culture Change: Models in Prehistory*. London: Duckworth.

1975. Trade as action at a distance: questions of integration and communication. In J. Sabloff and C.C. Lamberg-Karlovsky (eds.), *Ancient Civilization and Trade*, pp. 3–59. Albuquerque: University of New Mexico Press.

1978. Space, time and polity. In J. Friedman and M. Rowlands (eds.), *The Evolution of Social Systems*, pp. 89–114. London: Duckworth.

1979. Transformations. In C. Renfrew and K.L. Cooke (eds.), *Transformations: Mathematical Approaches to Cultural Change*, pp. 3–44. New York: Academic Press.

Renfrew, C. and K.L. Cooke (eds.) 1979. *Transformations: Mathematical Approaches to Cultural Change*. London: Academic Press.

Renfrew, C., M. Rowlands and B. Segraves (eds.) 1982. *Theory and Explanation in Archaeology.* London: Academic Press.

Renfrew, C. and S. Shennan (eds.) 1982. *Ranking, Resource and Exchange. Aspects of the Archaeology of Early European Society.* Cambridge: Cambridge University Press.

Rowlands, M. 1980. Kinship, alliance and exchange in the European Bronze Age. In J. Barrett and R. Bradley (eds.), *Settlement and Society the British Later Bronze Age.* B.A.R. British Series 83: 15–55. Oxford. British Archaeological Reports.

Rowlands, M., M.T. Larsen and K. Kristiansen (eds.) forthcoming. *Centre, Periphery and Dependency in Prehistory.* Cambridge: Cambridge University Press.

Sahlins, M.D. 1961. The segmentary lineage: an organization of predatory expansion. *American Anthropologist* 63: 322–45.

Sahlins, M.D. and E.R. Service (eds.) 1960. *Evolution and Culture.* Ann Arbor: University of Michigan Press.

Salmon, M.H. 1978. What can systems theory do for archaeology? *American Antiquity* 43: 174–83.

Sanders, W.T. and D. Webster, 1978. Unilinealism, multilinealism and the evolution of complex societies. In C. Redman *et al.* (eds.), *Social Archaeology: Beyond Subsistence and Dating*, pp. 249–302. New York: Academic Press.

Schiffer, M.B. 1976. *Behavioral Archaeology.* New York: Academic Press.

1978. Methodological issues in ethnoarchaeology. In R. Gould (ed.), *Ethnoarchaeology*, pp. 229–47. Albuquerque: University of New Mexico Press.

1978–1981. (ed.) *Advances in Archaeological Method and Theory*, vols. 1–4. New York: Academic Press.

Service, E.R. 1962. *Primitive Social Organization.* New York: Random House.

1975. *The Origins of the State and Civilization.* New York: Norton.

Shennan, S.E. 1975. The social organization of Branč. *Antiquity* 49: 279–88.

Shennan, S.J. 1978. Archaeological 'cultures': an empirical investigation. In I. Hodder (ed.), *The Spatial Organization of Culture*, pp. 113–39. London: Duckworth.

1982. Exchange and ranking: the role of amber in the earlier Bronze Age of Europe. In C. Renfrew and S. Shennan (eds.), *Ranking, Resource and Exchange*, pp. 33–45. Cambridge: Cambridge University Press.

Sheridan, A. and G. Bailey (eds.) 1981. *Economic Archaeology: Towards an Integration of Ecological and Social Approaches.* B.A.R. International Series 96. Oxford: British Archaeological Reports.

Sherratt, A. 1981. Plough and pastoralism in prehistoric Europe: aspects of the secondary products revolution. In I. Hodder, G. Isaac and N. Hammond (eds.), *Pattern of the Past*, pp. 261–305. Cambridge: Cambridge University Press.

Smith, P. 1972. Land-use, settlement patterns and subsistence agriculture. In P.J. Ucko, G.W. Dimbleby and R. Tringham (eds.), *Man, Settlement and Urbanism*, pp. 409–25. London: Duckworth.

Spooner, B. (ed.) 1970. *Population Growth: Anthropological Implications.* Cambridge, Mass. and London: MIT Press.

Spriggs, M. (ed.) 1977. *Archaeology and Anthropology. Areas of Mutual Interest.* B.A.R. Supplementary Series 19. Oxford: British Archaeological Reports.

Stumann, S. 1979. Nogle aspekter omkring ejendomsformer og social arbejdsdeling i Danmarks yngre bronzealder og aeldre jernalder. *Kontaktstencil* 16.

Tainter, J.A. 1978. Mortuary practices and the study of prehistoric social systems. In M. Schiffer (ed.), *Advances in Archaeological Method and Theory* 1: 106–43. New York: Academic Press.

Tauber, H. 1981. 13 C evidence for dietary habits of prehistoric man in Denmark. *Nature* 292: 332–3.

Thompson, R.H. 1958. *Migrations in New World Culture History.*

University of Arizona. Social Science Bulletin 27, vol. 29. Tucson: University of Arizona Press.

Thrane, H. 1968. Eingeführte Bronzeschwerter aus Dänemarks jüngerer Bronzezeit (Periode IV–V). *Acta Archaeologica* 39: 143–218.

1975. *Europaeiske forbindelser. Bidrag til studiet af fremmede forbindelser i Danmarks yngre bronzealder (periode IV–V)* (with a summary in English). Nationalmuseets skrifter: Arkaeologiks-historisk raekke. Bind 16. Copenhagen: National Museum.

in press. Indledende overvejelser om strukturudviklingen i Sydskandinaviens bronzealder. Conference Report from Lund, ed. by B. Stjernquist.

Tilley, C. 1981a. Economy and society: what relationship? In A. Sheridan and G. Bailey (eds.), *Economic Archaeology: Towards an Integration of Ecological and Social Approaches.* B.A.R. International Series 96: 131–48. Oxford: British Archaeological Reports.

1981b. Conceptual frameworks for the explanation of sociocultural change. In I. Hodder, G. Isaac and N. Hammond (eds.), *Pattern of the Past*, pp. 363–86. Cambridge: Cambridge University Press.

Torbrügge, A.W. 1965. Vollgriffschwerter der Urnenfelderzeit. Zur methodischen Darstellung einer Denkmalergruppe. *Bayerische Vorgeschichtsblätter* 30: 71–105.

1970–1. Vor- und frühgeschichtliche Flussfunde. *Bericht der römisch-germanischen Kommission*, 51–2.

Trigger, B. 1981. Anglo-American archaeology. *World Archaeology* 13 (2): 138–55.

Ucko, P.J. 1969. Ethnography and archaeological interpretation of funerary remains. *World Archaeology* 1: 262–81.

Ucko, P.J. and G.W. Dimbleby (eds.) 1969. *The Domestication and Exploitation of Plants and Animals.* London: Duckworth.

Ucko, P.J., G.W. Dimbleby and R. Tringham (eds.) 1972. *Man, Settlement and Urbanism.* London: Duckworth.

Watson, P., S.A. LeBlanc and C.L. Redman, 1971. *Explanation in Archaeology.* New York: Columbia University Press.

Webb, M. 1975. The flag follows trade: an essay on the necessary interaction of military and commercial factors in state formation. In J. Sabloff and C.C. Lamberg-Karlovsky (eds.), *Ancient Civilization and Trade*, pp. 155–209. Albuquerque: University of New Mexico Press.

Whallon, R. 1968. Investigation of late prehistoric social organization in New York State. In S. Binford and L.R. Binford (eds.), *New Perspectives in Archaeology*, pp. 223–44. Chicago: Aldine.

White, L.A. 1945. History, evolutionism and functionalism: three types of interpretation of culture. *Southwestern Journal of Anthropology* 1: 221–48.

Willey, G.R. and P. Phillips, 1958. *Method and Theory in American Archaeology.* Chicago: University of Chicago Press.

Windelhed, B. 1977. *The Transition from Extensive to Intensive Farming in the Early Iron Age and its Effect on Settlement.* Department of Human Geography, University of Stockholm.

Wobst, H.M. 1976. Stylistic behavior and information exchange. In C.E. Cleland (ed.), *Culture Change and Continuity: Essays in Honor of James Bennett Griffin*, pp. 317–42. New York: Academic Press.

Wood, R.W. and D.L. Johnson, 1978. A survey of disturbance processes in archaeological site formation. In M. Schiffer (ed.), *Advances in Archaeological Method and Theory* 1: 315–87. New York: Academic Press.

Wright, H.T. 1972. A consideration of interregional exchange in Greater Mesopotamia 4000–3000 BC. In J. Wilmsen (ed.), *Social Exchange and Interaction.* Anthropological Papers 46: 95–105. Museum of Anthropology, University of Michigan.

Zubrow, E.B. 1975. *Prehistoric Carrying Capacity: a Model.* Menlo Park: Cummings.

Chapter 7

The spirit and its burden: archaeology and symbolic activity
Susan Kus

Only now, after having considered four moments, four aspects of the fundamental historical relationships, do we find that man also possesses 'consciousness'; but, even so, not inherent, not 'pure' consciousness. From the start the 'spirit' is afflicted with the curse of being 'burdened' with matter . . .

(Marx and Engels, *The German Ideology*)

Marx and a theory of consciousness

Whether it be phrased as 'ideal and material', as 'mind and body', as 'spirit and nature', or as some other similar opposition, a categorical split of the world underlies the western intellectual and artistic tradition and the reconciliation of such paired terms has provided this tradition with a major leit-motif. Those social thinkers of Marxist persuasion interested in the most 'immaterial' of humanity's creations —literary critics (e.g. Williams 1977) and philosophers of 'critical theory' (e.g. Schmidt 1973) — have easily recognized and valued such a thematic concern in the work of Marx. In contradistinction those who accept a strict material—economic interpretation of Marx's thought discredit this problematic theme within the material determinism of an abstract base—superstructure model of society. In a social and intellectual milieu under-pinned by the logic of pragmatism and empiricism, the burden of reasserting the critical nature of the theme of matter and idea in social theory, and of rejecting a facile material deter-minism as solution to this problem, is upon those who poten-tially stand to be accused of subjective idealism.

The rebuttal to a reductive and material-determinist cultural theory begins with an understanding of the critical role that concepts of the individual and creative social practice played in the formation of Marx's thought. As Williams argues:

At the very centre of Marxism is an extraordinary emphasis on human creativity and self-creation. Extra-ordinary because most of the systems with which it contends stress the derivation of most human activity from an external cause: from God, from an abstract Nature or human nature, from permanent instinctual systems, or from an animal inheritance.

(Williams 1977: 206)

The rejection of a strict material determinism is an attempt to prevent the loss of a 'human quality' from the social theoreti-cal object of study and to appreciate the creative and 'mean-ingful' nature of being-in-the-world. It is an attempt to prevent the evacuation of the problem of the subject in social theoreti-cal discourse. Such an attempt to understand the relationship of individual to society necessitates a dialectical appreciation of the relationship of matter to idea. It demands a reassess-ment of the traditionally understood relationship of individual to society so as to understand this relationship as one of sub-jective experience and expression ('practical consciousness') never divorced from an historical context of inter-subjective (social) relations, social products, and material environment.[1]

Marx's work is predicated upon a consideration of subjectivity and the individual consciousness. It was the immediate focus of his earliest works, it underpinned his social theory, and it directed his social praxis. Marx's initial involvement in philosophy was under the influence of the Young Hegelian wave of interest in Reason and the social order. Marx's doctoral dissertation was a comparison of 'Natural Philosophy' as espoused by Democritus and by Epicurus. Marx was attracted to the 'idea of freedom of self-consciousness' in the work of Epicurus (Kolakowski 1978: 101), but it is in his criticism of Epicurus that there is a real foreshadowing of the focus of his later works. Epicurus was concerned with the attainment of *self*-knowledge through the recognition of the consciousness of individual freedom. Epicurus was not interested in knowledge of the world. Marx, in contrast, sought the actualization of this individual freedom within nature and in the creation of the social world.

The concepts of freedom and consciousness are essential to an appreciation of Marx's continuing discourse because they underpin his characterization of the social order. It was the loss of awareness by social beings of their creative role in the construction of the social order that provided Marx with a theoretical problem. His interest in this problematic theme eventually focused his attention at the level of the social and material context of being-in-the-world, rather than at the level of individual consciousness. As a consequence, a theory of consciousness was left underspecified in the thought of Marx. Too often the theory of consciousness that has been supplied by students of Marx has been in the form of empiricist epistemological arguments. Such a theoretical choice, however, strips meaning from 'practical consciousness' (by rendering meaning as idiosyncratic, anonymous, or epiphenomenal to socio-cultural processes) and fosters a material reductionist interpretation of Marx (Kus 1979).

The archaeologist confronted with the most 'material' of humanity's creations is perhaps the most sorely tempted of social scientists to adopt an empiricist epistemology and a strict materialist interpretation of Marx so as to render tractable Marxist theory in the context of archaeological information. V. Gordon Childe, in his attempt to integrate Marxist social theory with available archaeological data and archaeological research directions, was fully aware of the temptation to the archaeologist of adopting what has often been called a 'vulgar' materialist interpretation of Marxism. Childe insightfully reworked various epistemological arguments in defining a concept of knowledge so as to overcome the constraints of the positivist school of thought. However, his adherence to certain basic empiricist tenets reduced the question of creative social practice to one of pragmatic activity. It is valuable to the present discussion to give closer attention to the problem of matter and idea within the context of archaeology and social theory and, in particular, to Childe's formulation of and solution to this problem.

Archaeology and a domain of ideas

For the anthropologist, images of wo/man the tool-maker and wo/man the symbol-user have been variously employed to characterize the quality of the social and the cultural object of study. Yet, as noted above, it is perhaps the archaeological record that presents the most unique stage for a stark confrontation of matters material and ideal in the social and the historical sciences. Childe recognized the challenge that archaeological information offers to a body of social theory when he remarked: 'As an archaeologist I deal with concrete material things as much as any natural scientist. But as a pre*historian* I must treat my objects always and exclusively as concrete expressions and embodiments of human thoughts and ideas — in a word of knowledge' (Childe 1956: 1). Among contemporary archaeologists, it is not only an increasing concern to view their discipline as a social science, but also an increasing methodological and analytical sophistication which has fostered an appreciation for the considerable empirical weight carried by symbolic behaviour and materials in cultural descriptions. The situation serves to underscore the theoretical challenge of Childe's insight regarding archaeological information.

Archaeologists have always recognized a category of sumptuary goods, magico-religious items, ritual structures, symbolic behaviour, etc., but more often than not this category has been considered as a *residual* cultural category. With sophisticated advances in analytical and statistical techniques, this archaeologically defined category of symbolic items and activities has the potential for increased and diversified content, as well as increasingly elaborate description. For example, there are ethno-botanical and physiochemical techniques that can potentially retrieve such ephemeral material evidence of ritual activity as the leaving of flowers and the placing of food as grave offerings. There are increasingly sophisticated applications of statistical analyses to patterns recoverable in archaeological deposits which contribute to refined descriptions of 'ritual' behavioural practices such as mortuary rites of prehistoric populations. Certainly, the methodological and the analytical challenges to the archaeologist in the *identification* and *description* of symbolic concerns in the archaeological record are far from insignificant. Yet, perhaps the more critical challenge to the archaeologist is the *theoretical* assessment of symbolic matters in the move from the use of natural science methods (which are far from theoretically neutral) to social theoretical arguments.

Childe, as quoted above, put his finger on the problem of the articulation of method and theory in archaeology. The methods of the natural sciences are eminently convenient to the acquisition and descriptive analysis of archaeological data. However, the 'objects' which confront the archaeologist fit less adequately than do the 'objects' which confront the natural scientist classical empiricist assumptions. In particular, they do not fit the assumption that would consider such 'objects' to be completely specified in objective space and time. Rather, the 'objects' of the archaeologist are produced and finally specified in a symbolic and a meaningful context of human practice. Archaeologists have employed alternative theoretical strategies that recognize the symbolic as a facet of the material social and cultural context. Yet, more often than not, their strategies leave the symbolic as epiphenomenal to a determinant material or an abstract systemic order.

Most often archaeologists adopt a classical materialist or empiricist stance which focuses on a reified concept of society where society, as actor or as entity, is defined in terms of its material reproduction and evolution. Within such a perspective a notion of subjective experience and expression is translated into a reified concept of the psycho-biological individual. As a consequence the problem of the symbolic, though adding historical colour and specificity to cultural description (i.e. adding bulk to the 'reconstruction of extinct lifeways'), is theoretically defused for archaeology (i.e. is extraneous in the 'search for cultural processes') as it becomes a problem of psychological mechanics and/or a subject of philosophical speculation as traditionally conceived. For the archaeologist who has adopted a systems approach to society, the definition of society as object of study is expanded to include not only a concept of material production but also of energy and information processing. Within this alternative perspective symbolic activity is granted a functional status as the 'code' necessary to effect the organization of matter, energy, and information. However, symbolic content, considered as the ideational production of a society with a less-than-perfect understanding of its own operational logic, is left superfluous to abstract systemic laws and operations. Such materialist and systemic perspectives reify and oppose concepts of society and individual. They foster an understanding of society which Marx has warned against; they set society above and oppose it to the individual by endowing society with goals and an *élan vital* of its own. This genre of theoretical solution given to the problem of the nature of the social form was turned around by Marx — turned from solution into question — into the historical question of how and why it is that society has been 'alienated' from 'practical consciousness' and thus appears as owing its existence and meaning to factors outside of the human condition.

This problem of history is challenging within a Marxist perspective. If meaning is ultimately referent to the human situation and to consciousness, it is also the case that meaning is not purely subjective. Consciousness is not idealized but practical. This is to say that though the final context and thus the final dimensioning of meaning is in subjective experience and expression, it is not the case that meaning is defined only in terms of subjective intention and action. Meaning necessarily encompasses the consequences of expressive action for ideally the individual is capable not only of volition but of accepting responsibility for the consequences of her/his actions, consequences which are aspects of the inter-subjective (social) context and of material processes. For Marx human praxis was both the context and the creator of meaning and humanity was recognized to be 'self-present as an Absolute in its own finitude' (Kolakowski 1978: 80). If we grant that meaning is dependent on an existential context, then we must

grant that its context is historical as well. If we recognize ourselves to be participants in a self-constituting reality then we must recognize the historical subject and context similarly.

Childe's work *Society and Knowledge* (1956) is an interesting work in light of the above discussion in that the thematic foci of meaning, the social context, history, and praxis are evoked in his arguments on Marxist theory and archaeology. Childe addressed these thematic issues cited above using concepts of knowledge, society, progressive change, and pragmatism. Yet, these concepts employed by Childe are defined and related by various empiricist epistemological arguments that, however removed from a positivist position, still allow meaning to slip from the existential and historical subject. In essence, Childe defines a concept of knowledge as relative to an historical and a social context, but evacuates the problem of the subject in his social theory. Society, conceived (as by Childe) as context for the progressive accumulation of knowledge, does not admit of a finality of knowledge in the existential human situation and thus meaning becomes the property and problem of the future and/or of an ahistorically removed objective spectator.

Childe and a concept of knowledge

V. Gordon Childe, as an archaeologist and as a social theoretician, made a concerted effort to apply Marxist theory to archaeology. This effort was an attempt to carry archaeological research beyond the level of artifact description and historical particularism to a level of social theory. As noted earlier, Childe was aware of the threat of a material-reductionist interpretation of Marx. At one point he expressed this concern *vis-à-vis* a concern for the need of a concept of knowledge to be relevant to a social and historical context. To approach the problem of 'human thoughts and ideas' (Childe 1956: 1), Childe recognized that issues of knowledge, belief and epistemology become critical to social theory. He directly addressed these concerns in his work *Society and Knowledge*.

To define a concept of knowledge as relevant to the historical context, suitable to the study of archaeological materials, and adequate to his Marxist theoretical directions, Childe realized that he would have to overstep the restrictive bounds of a logical positivist definition of this concept. The *social* and the *historical*, the critical dimensions of the archaeological object and the archaeological context, were ignored, if not rendered insignificant, in the positivist definition of knowledge. It was the recognition and the valuation of these dimensions that underpinned Childe's definition of knowledge and that rescued his arguments from reaching the same impasse that eventually led to the decline of the positivist school.

Childe viewed knowledge as historically dependent, thus recognizing the positivist goal of absolute certainty as unobtainable. He also viewed knowledge as socially relative arguing that absolute knowledge is meaningless in practice because 'the best of reasons' on which beliefs are based are those reasons that society declares as 'best'. Yet, Childe's understanding of society and history in the definition of a cultural object of study are open to theoretical questioning. He came to narrowly equate the socially significant with the pragmatic and to view history simply as the temporal dimension of error thus leaving meaning external to a given social and historical context.

For Childe the term 'practical' in the Marxist concept of 'practical consciousness' was not employed in the encompassing sense of 'praxis' − sensuous human activity − but in the more narrow sense of 'pragmatic' or 'practical' − useful; capable of being turned into use or account. He stressed a normative and utilitarian definition of knowledge contrasting this with the domain of personal beliefs. To give credit to Childe, his understanding of 'practical' must be seen as a significant theoretical coup. It guaranteed that the material inventory of archaeological data (viewed as overwhelmingly technological in significance) was, to a major degree, mappable onto the symbolic and ideational domain which carried theoretical relevance. Yet, the theoretical valuation of archaeological information that results from Childe's arguments is accompanied by the loss of the meaningful dimension of his object of study. A 'human quality' is present only as individual error and belief. To state this argument another way, Childe, in his attempt to make the Marxist proposition that 'social being determines consciousness' tractable in the archaeological context, formalized that proposition to read: 'knowledge held by the individual is socially determined'. One might understand this position of Childe in the context of his attempt to tailor Marxist theory to available archaeological data and methods. However, there is an underlying confusion in this attempt. It is the confusion of a methodological question − the question of the identification of particular *individuals* in the archaeological record − with a theoretical question − the question of the psycho-biological dimensions of the *individual* as they relate to the character of the social object. The Marxist perspective that 'social being determines consciousness' does not necessarily demand the identification of individuals; rather, it demands that both a 'subjective' and an 'inter-subjective' constituent are recognized as contributing to the form as well as content of social activity and representation.[2]

It is not really the case that Childe has misread various directions of thought outlined in Marx's works. Williams's assessment of Marx's handling of the issues of consciousness, individual, and society makes this point.

> Consciousness is seen from the beginning as part of the human material social process, and its products in 'ideas' are then as much part of this process as material products themselves. This, centrally was the thrust of Marx's whole argument, but the point was lost, in this crucial area, by a temporary surrender to the cynicism of 'practical men', and, even more, to the abstract empiricism of a version of 'natural sciences'.
>
> (Williams 1977: 59−60)

Sahlins has recognized that the critical issue at stake in adhering to 'practical theories of culture' (Sahlins 1977) is the problem of 'meaning' and, in particular, its locus. If we equate meaning to knowledge and knowledge to the pragmatic, then 'the final logic of cultural form is beyond the character and relativity of any human conception' (Sahlins 1977: 15). Today, it is still a pragmatic problem focus and a classical empiricism that plague the social theory of archaeologists and orient their Marxist analyses.

Traditional applications of Marxist thought to archaeological analyses often impose a rigid dichotomy on matter and idea and thus on activity and representation. Such an understanding of Marxist thought often results in the theoretical move of assigning matter and activity to a 'determinant' base and idea and representation to a 'determined' superstructure. It is also the case that oftentimes in the Marxist tradition the 'ideational' (i.e. symbol, representation, etc.) has been subsumed by the category of ideology. Ideology, in turn, has been employed synonymously for 'false consciousness'. Concepts such as 'false consciousness', dogma, etc., are certainly useful, and questions on the content and role of ideology in class-organized societies are important and interesting. However, a traditional concept of ideology is too limited to handle effectively a more encompassing realm of ideation. What is needed is a more comprehensive term, such as 'social representation' for instance, that can encompass such diverse concerns as that of the role of belief in the structuring of behaviour and as that of the dialogue between exponents of dogma and heresy whose vested interests might entail considerations other than their personal beliefs. If we recognize such concerns as those evoked by a concept of social representation, then the traditional handling of ideational matters in a base−superstructure model of social formation is suspect. The next section will examine more closely this base−superstructure model of a society that often serves as a point of orientation in Marxist analyses in sociocultural anthropology and archaeology.

Mode of production

The most sensitive and insightful handlings of the base−superstructure model and a concept of mode of production begin with the understanding that a notion of ideology does not encompass all ideational concerns in a given cultural form. The resulting reassessment of the concept of mode of production (e.g. Friedman 1974; Godelier 1975), the concept which has, in certain hands, helped to foster a harsh materialist dimension in Marxist theory, clarifies this point. Such a reassessment emphasizes the particularization of this concept into its constituent elements: 'forces of production' and 'relations of production'.

'Forces of production' are generally defined as the technical and material conditions of social reproduction. 'Relations of production' are those social relations which dominate the material processes of the production, distribution, and consumption of resources and social products in a given techno-ecological context (Friedman 1974). 'Relations of production' are not determined by 'forces of production'. These two conditions of the production and reproduction of the material conditions of social existence are in a relationship of mutual constraint. What this reassessment of the concept of mode of production has done is brought social relations and 'ideation' into the base or infrastructure. This is accomplished, for example, by recognizing that in certain societies the relations of kinship function as 'relations of production' (Godelier 1975), while in other societies it might be the religious organization that functions as 'relations of production' (Godelier 1978). This interpretation of mode of production avoids a strict material—economic definition of a social formation, but it destroys the integrity of a concept of 'practical consciousness'.

The burden of the interpretation of mode of production as outlined above is the theoretical justification, on functional grounds, of the separation of certain 'organizational' from 'representational' features within the social object of study. This interpretation separates the question of the activity necessary to 'render unto Caesar the things that are Caesar's and to God the things that are God's' from the representational question of why Caesars and why Gods exist and demand such action. An order of activity (the transformation of matter, energy, and information, if you prefer) in society is effected *and* understood by individuals in a context of human perception and conception, a context of meaning. For the subject and thus for society understood as individuals engaged in creative social praxis, organization is never given without representation (Augé 1975; Touraine 1977); human activity is first and foremost symbolic activity. To separate action from representation is to alienate 'practical consciousness' from itself.

Practical consciousness

The question that we seem to be facing at this point is whether to undertake, once again, the task of reassessing the concept of mode of production so as to accommodate an understanding of society and culture as meaningfully constituted. It is perhaps more expedient and theoretically satisfying to adopt an alternative conceptual focus within a Marxist perspective. Williams has suggested this in his work *Marxism and Literature* by encouraging us to: 'begin from [the] proposition which originally was equally central, equally authentic [in the thought of Marx]: namely the proposition that social being determines consciousness' (Williams 1977: 75). The strength of this focus within Marxist theory is that it sets up an immediate theoretical unity of the concepts of individual/ subjective consciousness and society/social context, the two concepts most critical in the definition of a social and cultural object of study. Further, by emphasizing the dialectical nature of this relationship, it salvages the anthropological project both from a simple psychological reductionism and from a reification of society as system opposed to the individual.

To argue that considerations of the individual subject and of consciousness are critical, if not central, to Marx's thought may give some archaeologists cold feet in their trenches. However, the issue is not really one of forsaking the spade for the spirit medium and armchair philosophy. It is rather one that encourages us to reassess the sufficiency of the traditional repertoire of questions that we bring to the archaeological record and to reassess our social theoretical pronouncements.

At a certain point in our analyses it is necessary to address such issues as ecological balance, surplus material production, information processing, organizational effectiveness of control hierarchies, etc. However, we must supplement our traditional repertoire of questions on the character of a society with questions on the nature of subjective experience and expression within particular social and historical contexts. Merleau-Ponty made such a point when he argued that: 'the process of joining objective analysis to lived experience is perhaps the most proper task of anthropology' (Merleau-Ponty 1974: 116), for at some point the variables of anthropology must be recognized as having an immediate level of human significance.

To approach this question of 'practical consciousness' it is clear that we cannot simply rely on categories supplied by classical psychological theory, as we wish to avoid psychological reductionism. We must begin to explore an alternative set of 'emergent' concepts and their changing content as they relate to the formulations and solutions of the enduring problems of the human situation, the relation of society to nature and the relation of individual to individual. Various thematic foci of such concepts are already to be found in our traditions of social thought, such conceptual foci as 'authority', 'power', 'sacredness', 'hierarchy', and 'legitimacy'. Others we will have to supply.

Consider by way of illustration a notion of 'legitimacy'. Legitimacy is not a descriptive attribute of a society reified and understood in terms of abstract systemic operations. Within a theoretical perspective which defines society as an abstract system or imbues society with an *élan vital* of material reproduction and growth, the question of legitimacy is theoretically non-essential, and when addressed within such a perspective it can only be seen as adding historical colour or descriptive specificity to a given society under consideration. However, if we understand society as Marx did, as consisting of individuals engaged in creative social practice, then a question of legitimacy becomes a critical issue, particularly in the case of 'complex' societies, with regard to an understanding of a given society's capacity for self-creation and change. The sociologist, Touraine, in his work *The Self-Production of Society* (1977) puts forth the convincing argument that the capacity for change of a given society (here the term society is shorthand for individuals engaged in creative social practice and is not to be understood in terms of society reified as actor) is dependent not only on its potential for surplus material production and accumulation, but also on the 'image' it has of its capacity to act upon itself. As Marx asserted, where there exists an historical materialist understanding of the constitution of a social order, the capacity of a society for self-creation opens onto a rich field of individual and social/

historical choice. On the other hand, for example, a society which defines itself as an element of an ahistorical and immutable cosmological order, and which legitimates its socio-political order through reference to such a cosmological order, places restrictions on the form and direction social change can take. It potentially renders problematic the initiation of change by means other than divine inspiration, exegetical clarification, and cosmic cataclysm.

The question of socio-political legitimation is contained within the larger problem-focus on a given society's capacity for change and the form such change can take. In this larger problem-focus we are encouraged to pursue various themes addressed in the works of Marx: nature in relation to human activity and the forms and 'logic' of social relations within the historical context. The question of society and nature is in part, but only in part, a question of available technology and organizational potential as they relate to surplus material production and accumulation. It is also a question of society's understanding of its capacity to interact with and intervene in an order of physical nature as it is conceived within a given historical context. It is a question of society's creative capacity, a capacity which includes that of self-creation through self-definition. This self-definition is referent not only to a confounding with or a distancing from an order of physical nature, but also referent to the understood logic of its internal make-up, the logic of social relations. If we begin to give serious consideration to this latter conceptual theme in a society's order of representation, then it becomes clear that a simple listing of dominant ideologies, that is, a listing of a mythic evolutionary sequence of gods, kings, and politicians, is insufficient to appreciate the form and dynamics of activity, cultural categories, and conceptual schemes as they relate to form and change in societies (Kus 1979).

Archaeology and practical consciousness

Cultural categories, concepts and representational structurings necessarily find their expression in activities, material symbols and institutional forms. Merleau-Ponty remarked upon this when he said:

> ... the spirit of society is realized, transmitted, and perceived through the cultural objects which it bestows upon itself and in the midst of which it lives. It is there that the deposit of its practical [in the sense of Marx's use of this term] categories is built up, and these categories in turn suggest a way of being and thinking to men.   (Merleau-Ponty 1974: 180)

If this is indeed the case then the archaeological record should permit the archaeologist to pursue, albeit with difficulty, such themes central to social theory as symbol, representation and 'practical consciousness', themes which upon first approach appear as anathema to one interested in material cultural products. A recent volume edited by Hodder (1982) on *Symbolic and Structural Archaeology* contains exploratory studies examining the theoretical and practical implications of this direction in archaeology.

Consider for a moment the concept of legitimacy as introduced in the discussion above. 'Legitimacy', considered as a conceptual node, brings into discussion such terms as 'tradition', 'pattern', 'authority', 'lawfulness' and 'order'. If it is possible to understand a notion of the maintenance and/or creation of *order* as an aspect of the question of the legitimation of a socio-political order, then *space*, as one of the most immediate dimensions of order as lived and thought, can be considered as a critical element in the definition and legitimation of a socio-political order. Higher-order settlements and urban centres, considered as socially 'created' space, offer a prime field for the representational mapping of social and cosmological orders as is witnessed in the significant degree of planning characteristic of early urban centres.

The higher-order settlements of socio-political orders which seek their legitimation in a confounding of their principles of ordering and activity with the principles of a defined order of physical nature, might symbolically map this adherence to an ahistoric cosmological ordering by reference to a schema of 'ecological' balance, a schema of calendrical divisions, or a representation of a dynamic equilibrium involving primal elements or forces of the cosmos. Socio-political orders that effect a distancing from an order of physical nature must have recourse to alternative principles of ordering, that is, they must define and make reference to prerogatives of the socio-political order. Such prerogatives must focus on those issues denied in the ahistoric repetitiveness of the natural order, the issues of temporality and change — history (Kus 1979).

It is possible to understand a concept of history in various ways. One alternative is to view an historical past as normative and as a model for the social present. The spatial representation of such an understanding of history might involve the valuation of special activity centres which focus on historically invested items, individuals and locations. However, if history is understood as conformity with the past, the question of innovation and creation remains problematic. It is possible, alternatively, to understand history in terms of a dynamic principle. This is accomplished by a valuation of the future (Eliade 1949), and thus the *creation*, rather than the maintenance, of order becomes a central theme in socio-political legitimation. This creation of order in certain cases might be presented in terms of an ideal of political unification, and its representational mapping. Such representation might involve a small-scale mapping of the geographical divisions of a 'kingdom' onto the urban centre through the residential organization of individuals identified with respect to geographical or ethnic affiliation within the centre, or it might involve the mapping of an abstract ideal of a whole created through the unification of its parts (e.g. a central location of secular authority considered as *axis mundi* to the four cardinal directions). Of course, it would be convenient if the representational schemes of various means of socio-political legitimation were conceptually straightforward and mutually exclusive, but this is probably not the case in any given social and historical context (see Kus (1982) for an extended discussion of these concerns).

If in archaeology we wish to handle the insight of Childe that recognizes that the objects confronting the archaeologist are to be treated 'always and exclusively as concrete expressions and embodiments of human thoughts and ideas' (Childe 1956: 1), we must keep in mind that we are looking at features of an *objectified* material social context that serves as the context of subjective experience and expression. Such features must be recognized as *material* elements relevant to one pole of a complex dynamic of conceptual ordering and activity that finds its complement in the 'opposite' pole of the *embodiment* of meaning in 'practical consciousness'. Archaeological information is thus placed in a more complex theoretical perspective than has been traditionally recognized, a theoretical perspective that precludes any simple causal opposition or identity of material and ideal matters. Within this perspective archaeologists would do well to begin to explore such conceptual tools offered by Marx as 'objectification', 'materialization', 'reification' and 'alienation' within his theory of historical materialism considered as 'a revolutionary theoretical step' in an attempt to integrate individual praxis with structural and material causation (Brown 1978: 16).

Concluding remarks

Archaeologists, with reference to the historical form and content of alternative social contexts to which they have access, can contribute to the exploration of central themes in the work of Marx, themes of subjective experience and expression understood as equally central to both a concept of 'practical consciousness' and to a theory of social form. In this latter concern it is subjective experience and expression that determines the character of meaning in any given social and historical context and thus serves to give dimension to activity and representation in society. Yet, in dialectical fashion, subjective experience and expression are dependent on a social and historical context. It is the generalization of subjective experience and expression that can occur in such a context that often leads to the reification of concepts and the objectification of patterns of behaviour, to their valuation as ahistorical, and to their characterization as referent to an order existing independent of the immediate 'practical'/existential context. Often concepts and behaviour are further ordered and institutionally appropriated by (alienated in) such 'ideological' forms as religion, politics and academic philosophy. Thus invested with a seeming cosmological or 'essential' character, it becomes easy to lose sight of their origins and the factors determining their continued existence. It is easy to lose sight of their human scale and their dependence on the lived human drama. It was this the central concern of Marx to understand how individuals become alienated from their creations so as to be able to re-establish the creative freedom of 'practical consciousness' in the social world. This is to restore to individuals their *history*. As Marx recognized, it is by no means an easy task, and as an anonymous graffitist wrote in a Paris metro station: 'Mon Dieu, c'est longue la préhistoire!'

Notes

1 The terms 'experience' and 'expression' are used to emphasize the existential nature and volitional aspects of the human situation, of being-*in-the-world*. This is in contrast to the decontextualized and essentialist quality of the terms 'action' and 'idea'. These latter terms do not necessarily invoke notions of intention or of conceptual structuring and restructuring which are necessary to a discussion of meaning and meaningful activity.

2 'Representation' here refers to a dynamic conceptual scheme or ordering which is symbolic in quality. Its field of reference encompasses both individual symbolic elements and orthodox belief systems.

Acknowledgements

This article is a reworking of ideas originally presented in a paper delivered at the annual meetings of the Society for American Archaeology in 1979 at Vancouver. I would like to thank Margaret Saint John and Rohn Eloul for their help and encouragement in the writing of this paper.

Bibliography

Augé, M. 1975. *Théorie des pouvoirs et idéologie.* Paris: Hermann.

Brown, R.H. 1978. Symbolic realism and sociological thought: beyond the positivist–romantic debate. In R.H. Brown and S.M. Lyman (eds.), *Structure, Consciousness, and History*, pp. 13–37. New York: Cambridge University Press.

Childe, V.G. 1956. *Society and Knowledge.* London: Allen and Unwin.

Eliade, M. 1949. *Le mythe de l'éternel retour.* Paris: Librairie Gallimard.

Friedman, J. 1974. Marxism, structuralism, and vulgar materialism. *Man* (n.s.) 9: 444–69.

Godelier, M. 1975. Modes of production, kinship and demographic structures. In M. Bloch (ed.), *Marxist Analyses and Social Anthropology*, pp. 3–27. New York: John Wiley.

1978. Economy and religion: an evolutionary optical illusion. In J. Friedman and M.J. Rowlands (eds.), *The Evolution of Social Systems*, pp. 3–11. London: Duckworth.

Hodder, I. (ed.) 1982. *Symbolic and Structural Archaeology.* Cambridge: Cambridge University Press.

Kolakowski, L. 1978. *Main Currents in Marxism*, vol. 1. Oxford: Clarendon Press.

Kus, S. 1979. *Archaeology and Ideology: The Symbolic Organization of Space.* Ph.D. Thesis, University of Michigan. Ann Arbor: University Microfilms.

1982. Matters material and ideal. In I. Hodder (ed.), *Symbolic and Structural Archaeology*, pp. 47–62. Cambridge: Cambridge University Press.

Marx, K. and F. Engels, 1970. *The German Ideology* (The Marxist–Leninist Library). London: Lawrence and Wishart.

Merleau-Ponty, M. 1974. *Phenomenology, Language, and Sociology: Selected Essays.* London: Heinemann.

Sahlins, M. 1977. The state of the art in social/cultural anthropology: search for an object. In A.F.C. Wallace *et al.* (eds.), *Perspectives on Anthropology 1976*, pp. 14–32. Washington: American Anthropological Association.

Schmidt, A. 1973. *The Concept of Nature in Marx.* London: New Left Books.

Touraine, A. 1977. *The Self-Production of Society.* Chicago: University of Chicago Press.

Williams, R. 1977. *Marxism and Literature.* London: Oxford University Press.

Chapter 8

**Objectivity and
subjectivity in
archaeology**
Mike Rowlands

Does it require deep intuition to comprehend that man's ideas,
views and conceptions, in a word, man's consciousness, changes
with every change in the conditions of his material existence, in
his social relations, and in his social life?

(Marx and Engels, *Selected Works* Vol. 1 (1959), p. 49)

Introduction

It was a guiding idea of Marx that our knowledge of the
world is limited by the historical epoch within which we live.
Understanding is thus itself both produced and constrained by
historical process. Such an apparently paradoxical and relativistic view is deeply pessimistic of the attainment of objective, timeless knowledge. However, like Hegel, Marx envisaged
a utopian future when the distinctions between essence and
appearance and subjectivity and objectivity would be obliter-
ated in an historically achieved condition of social awareness.
The attainment of 'knowledge' of the world for Marx was
therefore progressive; a process of 'seeing through' surface
appearance to underlying reality which, rather like personal
development, was temporally ordered.

In this respect, Marx differed little from the other
thinkers of his day. But unlike Hegel, Dilthey or Weber, he did
not believe that progressive understanding would be achieved
by greater conceptual clarity. Only by practice could reality be
made to expose to the observer its own immanent logic, and
reveal the ideas of previous epochs as particularistic distortions.

To observe that the dominant ideas of any period which claim
to be universal truths were those of the 'ruling class' was to
expose their ideological nature and to gain knowledge of the
structure of domination which they conceal.

Thus, the past has always to be viewed retrospectively;
in reverse of how it is written. Objective knowledge of the past
is a viewpoint of the present and, in turn, current claims to
universal truths are open to future accusations of particularistic distortion. Marx has thus been accused of presentism; of
projecting on to the past categories that are relevant only for
understanding the present. History, in the Marxian scheme,
becomes a simple mirror image of the present. Baudrillard
claims, for example, that all non-capitalist societies are
regarded by historical materialists through 'the mirror of production' (Baudrillard 1975). Thus Marx's analysis of modern
capitalism distorts the reality of the past by imposing upon the
latter concepts of our political economy in a form of temporal ethnocentrism. In a less sanguine age, Marx's notion that
our interpretation of the past is always guided by contemporary interest, that the 'human anatomy holds the key to the
anatomy of the ape', not only does not strike a sympathetic
chord but is actually forgotten (Leach 1977). The unintended
consequence of a viewpoint such as Baudrillard's, which Marx
was concerned to avoid, is extreme relativism; historical
epochs must be understood on their own terms, regardless of
the impossibility of achieving such a state of affairs.

Objective structures without a subject

To recognize that the past is always studied from a presentist point of view is therefore not only to acknowledge 'revisionism' but also to differ as to its basis in subjectivity and objectivity. A 'history for' some purpose (discontinuous) is contrasted with a 'history of' some entity existing in real historical time (continuous). In the former, historical consciousness implies the possibility of multiple histories (personal, group, class, etc.) and multiple times (linear/cyclical; reversible/non-reversible) consistent with the interiorization of time experience. In the latter, a unified historical process is implied which lies outside human conscious activity (in the sense, no one could have woken up one morning and said the Hundred Years' War is starting today; the ability to do this lies not in individual experience but in the historian's or prehistorian's use of time and the validity of their claim to construct retrospective 'objective knowledge').

We can continue further with this contrast since it is quite prevalent in contemporary archaeology. Applying Nadel's distinction between ideological and scientific history (Nadel 1942: 72), in the former the past is characterized as an infinity of events resulting from past human actions. The extent to which any of them have any meaning depends on contemporary conscious ordering of past events into process. This ordering process is guided by present interests and the ideological role played by images of the past in society. The distinction between reality and ideas is thus largely suppressed in favour of the latter. Hence there can be no kind of historical process outside of human conscious experience, i.e. no process which is not anchored in collective memory (Halbwachs 1980). (It may be worth pointing out here that the subjectivist characterization of the past as an unknown concatenation of events is no less real than the notion of conscious process. Reflection of personal experience should tell one that we interiorize the past in both these guises; as personal events and as periods of self-classification although temporally separated from each other. A surer guide to this particular version of the process/event:culture/society dichotomy is thus Freud's logic of primary and secondary process: Sullaway 1979: 340.)

For those archaeologists who have a more vested interest in supporting the idea that a prehistory *of* some entity is more than an image to serve contemporary ideological purposes, holding to the notion that through a certain mode of thought, some segment of a past reality can be established, is probably fairly essential. When dealing with long time periods, it might be assumed that processes operate which lie outside human consciousness. In this case, either human actors will not figure at all, except as 'props', or will act as 'encompassed' characters; this is implied by Marx's statement that 'Men make history but not under conditions of their own choosing, but under conditions directly inherited from the past' (Marx 1954: 10). We can assume that Marx is claiming some more complex relation between social system and social action. Thus, social system implies the presence of objective structures, and social action the presence of conscious activity operating within these historically inherited constraints. The materialism/idealism debate was resolved, so Marx believed, by denying both the status of the transcendental subject (Hegelian world spirit, etc.) and the primacy of objective material conditions (Feuerbach's materialism). Instead, historical process was defined as a struggle between human deeds and historically derived structures which alone enables human beings to move beyond their present objective conditions of existence.

Two crucial problems were 'left over' by Marx in resolving, to his own satisfaction, the idealism/materialism dispute. The first centres on the status of objective conditions. How can the consequences of human subjective actions have objective effects that 'take on a life of their own'? The second is how can we gain knowledge of such objective conditions which is not relativistic and illusory; a product of living within them? Marx thus bequeathed, as unresolved, questions which continue to dominate twentieth-century social thought. Not perhaps because of intellectual incapacity on his part but simply, following his own epistemology, because the social conditions of his time did not permit their resolution and those existing today still may not do so.

One solution to the first problem is to deny the presence of objective conditions altogether. Here, the dichotomies between structure and action or reality and thought are suppressed by positing the primacy of objective structures of the mind (categorization processes). Objective conditions have no reality except as the products of forms imposed on the world either consciously (idealism) or unconsciously (structuralism) as guides to human action. Objective conditions and social actions are unified as the result of cognitive structuring in which both 'reality' and 'truth' are socially relativistic and temporally shifting concepts (although Lévi-Strauss is hesitant on drawing this conclusion, cf. 1966: 117).

A second solution is exemplified by Althusserian Marxism. Althusser simplifies matters by retaining a strict reality/thought dichotomy. Neither can be reduced to the other and he assigns each to a different branch of knowledge (historical materialism and dialectical materialism, respectively). Following Freud on the timeless logic of the unconscious, Althusser denies superstructure a history; only infrastructure possesses the capacity for social change. The thinking subject is unimportant in the latter and Althusser has to assume that 'history is blind: a process without a subject' (Althusser 1969: 167–8). In his work on ideology, on the other hand, he takes the knowing subject as central and denies that ideas are simply reflections of reality but are integral to it (Althusser 1969: 231–2). This apparent paradox he attributes to analytic perspective which defines for him different fields of enquiry within social reality.

The Althusserian solution is by no means novel. It codified what had already become a fundamental cleavage in the Marxist tradition. Since Engels simplified Marx by claiming that ideas are only a reflection of the reality of social relations, the development by Plekhanov to Lenin and Stalin of a crude, mechanical materialism became inevitable. The humanist reaction to this trend by Lukacs and Gramsci created a countercurrent which came to regard ideas as the common assumptions through which a group or society conceptualizes the values and beliefs that allow it to operate effectively. Thus, to Althusser, an ideology consists of a system of representations which form an organic and vital part of every social structure (Althusser 1969). Whilst ideas, actions and interests are inseparably combined, yet the conditions within which they exist are derived historically.

A third solution would therefore be to place ideas, actions and interests back into history, as part of a developmental process. One example is found in Popper's theory of World 3. Here, objective structures are the consequences, not necessarily intentional, of actions which, once produced, exist independently of them and take on 'a life of their own' (Popper 1972: 118). Although they are the products of human actions, objectified structures exist independently of any knowing subject. This is due to the fact that social actions have unintended consequences that are not in the consciousness of the actors and which 'generate institutional dynamics with a frequently high degree of autonomy' (Berger and Kellner 1982: 70). Such creations come to occupy a central place in human social and physical environments. They have to be adapted to and thus shape the actions of successive generations. Each generation has to evaluate, criticize, revise or revolutionize them as part of a transactional relation between it and the structures of unintended consequences of actions inherited from previous generations. Objective structures thus have histories; they are by nature open to change, both as the result of some internal logic, and as the result of the criticism generated by their inability any longer to satisfy human needs. The mediatory role of criticism is thus the process of knowledge formation, which may be subjective (sets of dispositions) or, preferably, objective (problems, theories and arguments) and exists independently 'of anybody's claim to know' (Popper 1972: 109). It is the role of criticism in the promotion of social change which Bourdieu and Habermas have also recently converged upon in their critiques of objectivist knowledge and the need for a third-order knowledge which grounds knowledge of objective conditions in practical thought (Bourdieu 1977: 18–19; Habermas 1971).

This overlaps with solutions to the second problem left unresolved by Marx. Can we gain knowledge of objective conditions which is not a product (a rationalization of) of living within them? To answer this question in the affirmative is to be on the side of science. It would assume that objective knowledge is not something produced by a particular method but is the product of a critical mode of thought which evades ideology and gains some definite purchase on reality. (Hence, Marx's well-known phrase: 'scientific thought differs from ideology as real knowledge differs from empty talk'.) The result is to soften the distinction between modes of thought and to recognize their common cognitive basis, even though we may give priority to one mode over others as superior in its practical implications. The distinction between science and

ideology (or objective versus subjective knowledge) is thus displaced by a stress on the unity of theory and practice, and critical evaluations of the former in terms of its practical effectivity in the operation of the latter (a potentially relativistic argument). The resulting reduction of theory to practice thus runs the danger of excluding the possibility of detached knowledge (universal truths) which is not immediately relevant in the serving of immediate interests. On the other hand, to assume the existence of a theoretical consciousness existing independently of living *praxis* (an explicandum) is to indulge in arid speculation. A reasonable alternative would be to postulate that theoretical understanding, whilst initiated in the particularity of concrete, historical situations, remains an act striving towards a universality which necessarily surpasses the action at hand.

What has been said so far supports the assumption that a 'prehistory of' some entity has some basis in reality. The study of the past is not limited to the results of past human actions which, as Collingwood put it, can only be apprehended from within the event (Collingwood 1946: 213–14). On the contrary, we need not assume that objective structures were in the minds of contemporary actors at all and can claim instead that they are only detectable retrospectively as the result of a particular mode of critical enquiry. The language of evolution, transformation, cyclical trends and other totalizing models are useful, if insecurely based, metaphors in any provisional attempt at grasping their meaning. Handling social process in the very long term is still a problem that remains unresolved, and will remain so as long as insecurity exists as to whether such problems exist in reality and are relevant concerns in contemporary consciousness.

Sense of past — sense of place

Up till now, we have accepted the traditional view that the construction of a history entails the imposition of form on the past as a retrospective act of will by the present. Any epistemology which attempts to reconstruct the past 'as it really was' is therefore flawed in its initial assumptions concerning the irreducibility of historical facts. But the claim to have escaped from contemporary relativism by arguing for the existence of objective structures outside the knowing subject, is not a central issue in current theorizing of 'history for some purpose'. Subjective interpretations of the past are equally 'presentist' but in a different way.

The primary motive is to establish a sense of past, upon which members of a community in the present can project a common sense of unity. All community, national, pan-national and world histories share this motive in common. Politics and archaeology are therefore inseparably bound to each other at the regional and national levels as competing interpretations of past experience are brought to bear on questions of ethnic and regional separatism, subnationalism and nationalistic integration enforced by the modern state. Historical consciousness is thus used as a means of cohering mass sentiment either in support of dominant authorities or, more often, to organize resistance against them, with the rationalization that the uniqueness and particular identity is in danger of being lost. The histories of different units are irreducible; a number of local histories cannot combine to form a national history and the latter cannot be colligated into supranational historical accounts. Each of these forms may be pursued concurrently, roughly corresponding with an ascendancy from the popular to the increasingly academicized and specialist practitioner. Each projects its own beam of light on to the past in the search for unique, particularistic and endlessly regressive sequences of historical events which serve to define identity at ascending levels of cultural and political integration. In the words of Huizinga: 'the past is limited always in accordance with the kind of subject which seeks to understand it. Every civilisation has a past of its own . . . History is the intellectual form in which a civilisation renders account to itself of its past' (Huizinga 1963: 7).

Societies are thus believed to be enriched or impoverished by the amount of history they interiorize. Cases range from the fragmented historical consciousness of ex-slave societies in the Caribbean where anything of any substance is of the moment (Wylie 1982), to China, India and Egypt which claim descent from ancient civilizations and base a contemporary sense of national unity on millennial heritage (Wallerstein 1978). This willingness to interiorize history lies behind the famous distinction made by Lévi-Strauss between hot and cold societies (Lévi-Strauss 1966). As Lévi-Strauss later made clear, he was not referring to the objective fact that some societies have and others do not have a past (Charbonnier 1969: 38–9). All societies have a past. But some societies are surrounded by their past and remain impervious to it. Others, particularly those superficially termed complex, research it and actively interiorize it as a necessity for the maintenance of identity and a sense of unity.

The principle at stake, therefore, is not whether political and ideological context acts to expand, truncate, distort or suppress 'real' history. The fact that this is so is made no clearer by positing objective 'pure' history on the one hand, and the existence of conditions promoting its distortion on the other. In reality, objective and subjective views of the past are not so neatly separated in this way. The issue is rather that what exists to be manipulated is a principle of historical understanding which asserts that past and present are unified through a mental act of 'objectification'. In order for the present to discover itself (assuming it has the reflective need to do so), it must confront itself with a like object in the past with which unity can be established in order to discover a common sense of time and place. Historical understanding is grounded upon and built upon the continuous exchange of inner experience with objects outside of oneself. Hence the emphasis on intuition and imagination as the mode in which historical events are incorporated into present thoughts (Collingwood 1946: 218–19). The act of reconstructing the past becomes a personal creative one limited to a commonly held definition of a unique entity (defined by sense of place

and time) within which an infinite regression into detailed knowledge is the sure path to historical enrichment.

Certain general features of traditional archaeological practice are clarified once these points are recognized. As is well known, archaeology, more than most disciplines, has a popular base. This is due partly to the fact that access to its product by the non-*cognoscenti* is less restricted by the mysticism of its practice and by recognition of acknowledged difficulties in decoding its texts; and also, because archaeology's data base is embedded in individualized capitalist property relations which makes its possession a matter of personal ownership. To varying degrees, archaeology provides a particularly efficient access to a sense of past, as a fairly free resource, upon which personal, community, national and supranational forms of identity can be established and changed.

In Europe, archaeology only gradually came to be separated from other activities such as folklore and custom, all of which were associated with the quickening interest in 'national culture' in the eighteenth and early nineteenth centuries. Historical consciousness and nationalism are indissolubly bound up with each other in modern European thought. Moreover, nationalism is not something which the modern state invented in order to bind its members to it through mass cultural sentiment. The former usually preceded the latter and, depending on the form taken, has as often as not acted as a source of resistance to the expansion of state power and the rationalization of modern life. The development of archaeology in Europe has in large part been on the side of nationalism, and its relation to the state (and the extent to which the latter has encouraged its development) has been both variable and ambiguous. In recent times, archaeology has been encouraged to produce a sense of past to bolster monolithic state identity (German national socialism and Soviet communism); has been discouraged due to the fear that it would promote regional separatist movements and undermine nation–state integration (modern France); or has been left as a largely free resource at the local level as long as 'official' national history remained the prerogative of the state (Great Britain).

Since the Second World War, the relation between archaeology and nationalism in Europe has been strongly de-emphasized. The reasons for this lie both in the repugnance felt towards the role of archaeology in promoting German nationalism and in the appeal of a 'prehistory of Europe'. In reaction to the ugly reality that extreme nationalism can result in fascism, historical consciousness was shifted to continental proportions in Europe. The desire for European political unity has thus been preceded by a search for commonality in a unified sense of past as a response to the horrors of two world wars, blamed on political disunity, and resistance to the prospect of a political future of either indirect hegemony of market forces administered by the USA or direct rule by the Soviet Union.

If pan-national sentiment and search for identity exist as a strong motivation for archaeological research in Europe and elsewhere at the present time, this would account for the apparent lack of enthusiasm amongst many of its practitioners for comparative and generalizing goals. It is for this reason that culture-history cannot be polemicized away and remains a principal organizing force in archaeological research and will do so for as long as it operates as a form of repressed motivation rather than an acknowledged and investigable regularity in social life.

Objectivity versus subjectivity

Objectivist versus subjectivist accounts of the past thus lead to two distinct modes of enquiry for which the terms social evolution and culture-history are metaphorical expressions. The relative merits of each were central to positivist versus relativist debates in the philosophy of history (compare Hempel 1974 and Collingwood 1946) and in the early polemics of the 'new archaeology' (Binford 1962).

Some of the logical implications of these two categories are summarized in Table 1.

The social origins of this conventional dichotomy can, no doubt, be traced back, in the case of objectivism, at least to the French and Scottish schools of eighteenth-century Enlightenment philosophy, and subjectivism to German romantic idealism. The codification of these different principles for interpreting the past is thus not unrelated to the presence of strong nation-states in the case of the former, and the absence of statehood and the search for cultural unity in the case of the latter. Divorced from their particular contexts, however, these two principles have striven for universality by defining each other as either empirical, physical and scientistic, or as mental, intuitive and particularistic.

Archaeological practice appears to deny such overt categorization. In studying European prehistory, Gordon Childe, for example, consistently asserted that his purpose was to understand the origins of a unique set of social conditions which led to the development of modern capitalism in Europe and nowhere else in the world. Yet he is probably most well known for arguing equally forcefully that archaeology should study regularities and correlations in the past (Childe, e.g. 1958). As an example of a more overtly humanist tradition in British archaeology, in *Ancient Europe*, Piggott declares that 'every civilisation should be evaluated on its own terms' and yet he denies that facts speak for themselves and argues that the latter are selected by general concepts and models (Piggott 1965: 5).

The conclusion seems inescapable that archaeology is firmly in the grip of clearly demarcated intellectual positions – positions that have to be characterized as either/or, in some cases regardless of actual personal practice. Either archaeology must be explanatory, empirical and capable of obtaining objective truth or it is intuitive and particularistic and a matter of personal interpretation. The result is an archaeological practice polarized between the pursuit of generalizations at the level of objective structures or the reconstruction of subjectively defined entities, the meaning of which for the present

Table 1

	Objective	Subjective
Synchrony	Present as frozen time	Present as mental construct of sedimented memories of the past
Diachrony	Linear, continuous chronology	Multiple time scales, constructed according to interests. Change fortuitous
Context	Generalization and comparison of an object of study	Particularization and detailed knowledge of a unique past
Aims	Explanation	Understanding

is by no means devoid of political importance and social generalization. The resulting tragic gap between 'a history which explains more and teaches us less and a history which teaches us more and explains less' (Lévi-Strauss 1966) has been an object of concern, and some mirth, in recent surveys of the subject (Flannery 1982; Renfrew 1982).

Many of these difficulties can be traced back to the misguided attempt to isolate history from the study of regularities and correlations in social life, as a necessary step in harnessing its subject matter to the creation of nationalist histories in the nineteenth century. Aspirations in archaeology to escape from such constraints and to achieve stability in some more generalizing mould were achieved only by avoiding any critical assessment of the distortions of its intellectual past and adopting an antagonistic and negative attitude towards it. The resulting dualism between a 'traditional' (subjective) archaeology and a 'new' (objective) archaeology left the former intact in its implicit and tacit practices and the latter deprived of insight into the nature of some of the basic motivating forces in the construction of their subject.

Archaeological epistemology has been renegotiated in recent years in terms of two distorted categories, inherited from the nineteenth century, which are no longer viable in contemporary contexts. On the one hand, the past is an object without a subject and on the other it is a subject without an object. Neither carries great conviction and often produces meaningless results and a disconnection between stated aims and achieved practice. Whilst neither the reality of objective structures nor the opacity of social goals to actors is in doubt, in archaeology this too easily takes on the appearance of the 'iron cage' of evolutionary determinism, closed off to any critical awareness. Absorbed by the present, this kind of 'sense of past' encourages political fatalism and acquiescent acceptance of blind historical forces beyond the knowledge and control of the individual. Subjectivity without an object, on the other hand, reduces the past to the present as varying forms of ideologies held by different groups to legitimize their interests. This promotes a frankly cynical view of the role of archaeology in contemporary political contexts. Both are the products of the uncritical acceptance of historically inherited, outmoded and distorted categories of thought. The deconstruction of these categories and the construction of new ones to take their place is an act of intellectual labour still to be achieved in contemporary archaeology.

Conclusion

Objectivity and subjectivity are thus opposed to each other as exclusive choices when, in the final analysis, it is their internal relationship to each other in a single field of enquiry which needs to be achieved. But as Marx taught us, the history of culture develops by the assertion and pursuit of what appear to be irreconcilable conflicts and oppositions. As we work through these movements, we learn how what is true in each of them can be integrated into a more comprehensive understanding that enables us to reject what is false, partial and one-sided. Put differently, recognition that knowledge is socially constructed exposes the social particularity of claims to universal and timeless understanding in archaeology. It permits us to interrogate the intellectual conditions in Western thought which made such divisions both necessary and reasonable; to ask how these have affected claims to knowledge in archaeology and to turn such enquiries into a source of generalization concerning the role of history in society as well as the history of societies.

Bibliography

Althusser, L. 1969. *For Marx*. Harmondsworth: Penguin.
Baudrillard, J. 1975. *The Mirror of Production*. St Louis: Telos Press.
Berger, P. and H. Kellner, 1982. *Sociology Reinterpreted*. Harmondsworth: Penguin.
Binford, L. 1962. Archaeology as anthropology. *American Antiquity* 28: 217–25.
Bourdieu, P. 1977. *Outline of a Theory of Practice*. Cambridge: Cambridge University Press.
Charbonnier, G. 1969. *Conversations with Claude Lévi-Strauss*. London: Cape.
Childe, V.G. 1958. Retrospect. *Antiquity* 32: 74.
Collingwood, R.G. 1946. *The Idea of History*. Oxford: Oxford University Press.
Flannery, K. 1982. The golden marshalltown: a parable for the archaeologist of the 1980s. *American Anthropologist* 84: 265–78.
Habermas, J. 1971. *Knowledge and Human Interest*. Boston: Boston Press.
Halbwachs, M. 1980. *The Collective Memory*. New York: Harper.
Hempel, K. 1974. Reasons and covering laws in historical explanation. Reprinted in P. Gardiner (ed.), *The Philosophy of History*. Oxford: Oxford University Press.
Huizinga, J. 1963. A definition of the concept of history. In R. Klibansky and H.J. Paton (eds.), *Philosophy and History*, pp. 1–11. New York: Harper.
Leach, E.R. 1977. A view from the bridge. In M. Spriggs (ed.), *Archaeology and Anthropology*. B.A.R. Supplementary Series 19: 161–76. Oxford: British Archaeological Reports.
Lévi-Strauss, C. 1966. *The Savage Mind*. London: Weidenfeld and Nicholson.
Marx, K. 1954. *The 18th Brumaire of Louis Bonaparte*. Moscow: Progress Publishers.
Marx, K. and F. Engels, 1959. *Collected Works*, Vol. 1. London: Lawrence and Wishart.
Nadel, S.R. 1942. *A Black Byzantium*. Oxford: Oxford University Press.
Piggott, S. 1965. *Ancient Europe. A Survey*. Edinburgh: Edinburgh University Press.
Popper, K. 1972. *Objective Knowledge*. Oxford: Oxford University Press.
Renfrew, C. 1982. Explanation revisited. In C. Renfrew, M.J. Rowlands and B.A. Segraves (eds.), *Theory and Explanation in Archaeology. The Southampton Conference*. London: Academic Press.
Sullaway, F.J. 1979. *Freud, Biologist of the Mind*. New York: Basic Books Inc.
Wallerstein, I. 1978. Civilisation and modes of production. *Theory and Society* 5: 1–12.
Wylie, J. 1982. The sense of time, the social construction of reality and the pursuit of nationhood. *Comparative Studies in Society and History* 24: 438–66.

PART 4

Social transformations

Chapter 9

**Explaining the Upper
Palaeolithic Revolution**
Antonio Gilman

Any attempt to provide a Marxist account of the social
processes of pre-class societies (including the extinct ones
known to us through the archaeological record) faces the
serious difficulty that the works of Marx and Engels provide
little sure guidance for the enterprise. The founders of historical materialism were familiar with European pre-capitalist
social formations, but with respect to pre- and early class
societies they could only know what was just beginning to be
discovered and synthesized. The views of Marx and Engels
were, accordingly, subject to continual review through their
lifetimes as new information became available. Thus, the
'Asiatic Mode of Production' of the *Grundrisse* (Marx 1965
[orig. 1857—8]), a construct developed on the basis of early-
nineteenth-century British accounts of India, was set aside in
the *Origin of the Family* (Engels 1972 [orig. 1884]), which
relied on the more up-to-date ethnology of Morgan. At the
same time, Engels dropped the functionalist account of the
origins of ruling classes which he had set forth in the *Anti-
Dühring* (1935 [orig. 1877]: 181—3) in favour of a conflict
model stressing the importance of commodity exchange in
generating social divisions. We have every reason to suppose,
therefore, that the masses of prehistoric and ethnographic
information and analysis made available over the course of the
past century would have led to even greater changes of
position. Marxists today must make their own prehistory aided

by only the most general guidelines provided by historical materialism (cf. Meillassoux 1972).

The difficulty of constructing a properly Marxist account of pre-class social systems is exacerbated by the fact that these are fundamentally different from the social formations with which historical materialism has typically concerned itself. 'The history of all hitherto existing society is the history of class struggles', says the *Communist Manifesto* (Marx and Engels 1968 [orig. 1848] : 35) and Engels's footnote to this slogan ('That is all *written* history') only serves to emphasize that the quintessence of Marxism is class analysis. To propose to conduct such an analysis on social systems in which social positions are determined by age, sex and achievement (that is to say, in which social classes as usually defined do not exist) is paradoxical, if not problematical. It is clear that an analysis of the end of pre-class societies (of their transformation into or inclusion within class societies) can be conducted along more or less orthodox Marxist lines. Marxism leads one to distinguish straightforwardly between 'tributary' and 'kin-ordered' modes of production (cf. Wolf 1981). It is not so clear, however, that the contrasts and changes between and within kin-ordered societies can be subjected to an analysis which remains Marxist as such. Leacock (1972: 246) has noted, for example, that Engels's (1972 [orig. 1876] : 251–4) treatment of the role of tools in early human evolution anticipates Washburn's ideas on the same subject 80 years later (e.g. Washburn 1960): this shows not that Washburn is a Marxist, but that Engels understood Darwinism and could apply it creatively. The question, then, is whether an analysis of pre-class societies can be developed which, apart from its jargon, is specifically Marxist, as opposed to being generically evolutionist, structuralist or functionalist.

In any attempt to construct a distinctively Marxist account of the social dynamics of pre-class societies, an essential first step must be to emphasize the archaeological record. Marxism seeks to explain/predict/direct social change, and the rate of such change in pre-class societies is not high. Almost inevitably, then, Marxist accounts of such societies based on ethnography have tended to emphasize the social statics of the systems they examine. It is not surprising, therefore, that ethnographically oriented Marxists have converged with cultural ecology (e.g. Lee 1979) — a tendency criticized as 'vulgar' Marxism — or with structuralism (e.g. Godelier 1975) — a tendency for which the appropriate critical designation might be 'effete' Marxism (T.K. Earle, personal communication). The time-span over which ethnographic evidence has been collected is hardly sufficient to provide evidence to test hypotheses concerning the dynamics of social change within a still egalitarian social system. The very forces which make ethnographic research possible bring to an abrupt end the 'kin-ordered' nature of the society under study. The only way out of this practical and theoretical impasse is to place at the centre of our attention the archaeological record. With all its defects this provides the only (and thus the best) evidence for

the long-term trajectories of societies which remain kin-ordered.

Since Marxism is primarily a theory of social change, we must look at those segments of the archaeological record which give manifest evidence for universal and pervasive transformations in social arrangements. There are two such metamorphoses within the time-span in which kin-ordered modes of production were universal. One is the Neolithic Revolution, associated with the introduction of farming and initially defined within a Marxist framework (Childe 1951 [orig. 1936]). This has been one of the central objects of archaeological research in the past 35 years, and the many empirical studies devoted to its elucidation are complemented by a variety of theoretical positions, some idealist (e.g. Isaac 1962), many ecological materialist (e.g. Flannery 1968), and a few attempting to trace a Marxist path between these (e.g. Bender 1978; Kohl and Wright 1977). The other great social change before the emergence of class societies is the Upper Palaeolithic Revolution (Feustel 1968; cf. the 'Broad Spectrum Revolution' of Flannery 1969). Although the transformation in human political economies associated with this latter process is no less fundamental than the changes associated with the Neolithic Revolution, theoretical work on the nature of the dynamics involved remains scanty and rudimentary. As part of the task of seeing how far one can go in building a distinctively Marxist prehistory, it will be useful, then, to outline briefly the changes involved in the Upper Palaeolithic Revolution and to review the general explanatory accounts which are currently proposed in the literature.

Main features of the Upper Palaeolithic Revolution

The transition from the Middle to the Upper Palaeolithic involves changes in all aspects of the archaeological record, in artifact technology and typology, in the evidence for subsistence patterns, in the nature and distribution of habitation sites, in burial patterns, in the regional configuration of artifact type distributions, and in the material expression of symbolic behaviour. Similar changes occur throughout the Old World, but are best documented in southwest France. Mellars's (1973) description of the transition in the classic area of Palaeolithic research and White's (1982) updating of Mellars's work provide the basis of the following summary.

Archaeologists have traditionally concentrated their attention on artifacts, so that changes in the stone and bone implements are the best documented features of the Upper Palaeolithic Revolution. As far as the stone tool industry is concerned, the Revolution is characterized by a complete shift in predominant artifact types. The tool categories which form the overwhelming bulk of Mousterian assemblages — sidescrapers, denticulates, etc. — are in the minority in all Upper Palaeolithic assemblage types except the Chatelperronian (Chung 1972); they are replaced by endscrapers, burins, etc., tool classes which in the Mousterian had been rare. This change in typology is facilitated by the greater use of the blade core to produce blanks for artifact manufacture. The bone industry changes even more dramatically. In contrast to the rudimentary bone implements found in Mousterian assemblages, the Upper Palaeolithic has a sophisticated range of production: the groove-and-splinter technique of splitting bone and antler into workable pieces is the first step in the all-over shaping of a variety of points, awls, harpoons, mobiliary art, etc. These general changes in the bone and stone industries are accompanied by the constant development of novel, specific artifact types (e.g. split-based bone points, Noailles burins, laurel leaf points) with restricted spatial and temporal distributions. The Middle Palaeolithic completely lacks such a rich variety of specialized types. In the Upper Palaeolithic bone and stone are combined into composite tools much more complex than the simple hafted instruments which may have been made in the Mousterian. In the later Upper Palaeolithic, furthermore, there appear the first mechanical devices to assist human muscle power: spearthrowers and bows. The stylistic and technical perfection of the best Upper Palaeolithic arti-facts strongly suggests, as Binford (1973) has pointed out, that tools were 'curated' rather than expediently made and dis-carded. Upper Palaeolithic industries are more elaborate stylistically and functionally than their Mousterian prede-cessors, and it is fair to conclude that they were more effective in handling nature.

Faunal remains from Middle and Upper Palaeolithic habitation sites have, until recently, been collected and studied for their environmental rather than economic significance, so that it is difficult to evaluate systematically the shifts in sub-sistence patterns associated with the Upper Palaeolithic Revol-ution. Reviewing the available evidence from the Périgord, Mellars (1973: 260–4) concludes that (a) in the Upper Palaeo-lithic there was greater concentration on single species (usually reindeer) as the main food resource, and (b) in later phases the hunting repertoire expanded to include fishing and fowling. Recent detailed studies of Middle and Upper Palaeolithic assemblages from Cantabria (Freeman 1973a; Straus 1977) reveal a somewhat different pattern. In the Upper Palaeolithic the range of fauna regularly exploited expands to include Alpine species, nocturnal animals (which must have been trapped), and molluscs (which in the final phases are even overexploited: Straus *et al.* 1980), but evidence of specializ-ation on a particular species seems to be restricted to just one Magdalenian site (red deer at El Juyo). Throughout the Upper Palaeolithic, however, faunal collections reveal a 'catastrophic' mortality profile (dead animals are of all ages) (Klein *et al.* 1981); this suggests that hunters were not restricted in their kills to the weaker of their prey. The accomplished technique such a killing pattern implies would naturally translate itself both into exploitation of a wider range of species and into specialization on a single, wild-harvested species, as conditions rendered either strategy more cost-effective.[1] It would seem, then, that the greater techno-environmental control suggested by Upper Palaeolithic tool kits is also reflected in hunting patterns.

If indeed the Upper Palaeolithic exhibited broad advances in technique with respect to the Mousterian, the resultant increase in adaptive effectiveness should be reflected in increased population densities. This is confirmed in the Périgord where, as Mellars (1973) has indicated, the number of sites per unit time is some ten times larger for the Upper than for the Middle Palaeolithic. Similar results are reported from Cantabria, another well-canvassed region (Straus 1977). This increase in the number of sites cannot be wholly attributed to the loss of earlier sites over time and is not compensated by any decrease in site size. On the contrary, the much larger size of some Upper Palaeolithic occupation horizons suggests not only that population was higher, but also that it was grouped into larger aggregates.

The development of technique which characterizes the shift from Middle to Upper Palaeolithic is accompanied by extensive changes in the archaeological evidence for social organization. The comparison of Middle and Upper Palaeo-lithic burial practices by Binford (1968a), systematically reviewed and updated by Harrold (1980), shows that the latter exhibit a greater variety of ritual contrasts, possibly reflecting a greater complexity in the social arrangements requiring certification when the participants died. Another facet of the social aspect of the Upper Palaeolithic Revolution is mani-fested archaeologically in the profound change in the way in which assemblage types are differentiated spatially and chronologically. The Middle Palaeolithic assemblage types distinguished by Bordes (1953) are characterized by variability in the proportion of major tool classes and by differences in the proportions of flakes manufactured by different tech-niques. The various Upper Palaeolithic assemblage types also differ in the proportions of major tool classes and in various technological respects, but in addition each assemblage type is characterized by differing proportions of the specialized arti-fact types discussed above. In spite of the abundance of stratified sequences of assemblages, the general absence of such type fossils has led directly to the failure to establish a clear, widely accepted cultural sequence within the time-span of 40,000 years or more covered by the Mousterian (cf. Binford 1973; Bordes and de Sonneville-Bordes 1970; Mellars 1969; Rolland 1981). By contrast, the general outlines of the Upper Palaeolithic succession have been accepted since the beginning of the century (Breuil 1912). Spatially, the contrast is equally striking: Upper Palaeolithic assemblage types form distinct regional groups, but experts who shun references to a 'Solutrean' or 'Gravettian' in, say, the Near East find no difficulty in identifying the Near Eastern Middle Palaeolithic as 'Mousterian' (e.g. Bordes 1968; cf. Rolland 1981).[2] The contrast in pattern has been concisely summarized in diagram-matic form by Isaac (1972: 401). The 'stylistic and artisan investment' (Binford 1973: 251) in artifact production (which permits the prehistorian to differentiate assemblages spatially and temporally) is also manifested in the personal ornaments and in the artistic representations which constitute the most

striking novelties of the Upper Palaeolithic. These, together
with the annotated bone pieces studied by Marshack (1972),
are often interpreted vitalistically as expressions of emergent
human cognitive capacities. More significantly, however,
spatially clustered, stylistically distinctive material remains
are, as Wobst (1977) points out, a by-product of (and useful
contributor to) the maintenance of communication within
the social groups that manufacture them. That 'cultures', in
Childe's (1929: v–vi) classic definition of the term, do not
appear until the Upper Palaeolithic can, then, be interpreted
as indicating that, before then, 'ethnicity may not . . . have
been a component of the cultural environment of man'
(Binford 1973: 244; cf. Freeman 1973b: 131; Leroi-Gourhan
1964: 221). The appearance of art and ornament, the more
elaborate burial patterns, the change in archaeological systematics, the production of highly stylized artifacts, all are
manifestations of the appearance in the Upper Palaeolithic of
a 'new form of social organization, one in which greater corporate awareness . . . played a role' (Binford 1968a: 148).

The Middle to Upper Palaeolithic transition is best
documented in western Europe, but it is apparent that after
about 40,000 years ago changes in the lithic and bone industries similar to those just discussed occur in eastern Europe
and Africa. In each of these, furthermore, some at least of the
additional innovations associated with the Upper Palaeolithic
are definitely present, e.g. ornaments and art in southern
Russia (Klein 1973), intensification of faunal exploitation in
southern Africa (Klein 1979), etc. Thus, in every area of the
world where reliable assemblages are numerous enough to
permit systematic comparisons, the occurrence of an Upper
Palaeolithic Revolution is the salient feature of the Upper
Pleistocene archaeological record. But while the Upper Palaeolithic Revolution is widespread, it is not abrupt. Conceptually,
it may be a 'quantum advance' (Klein 1973: 122) and, cumu-
latively, it is certainly far-reaching, but the transition is
nothing if not gradual. The slow nature of the change can be
illustrated in two ways. First, most Upper Palaeolithic innovations in fact occur with lesser frequency or intensity in the
Middle Palaeolithic. This is clear in the lithic industry, where
the major Upper Palaeolithic tool categories, as well as the
blade technology used to make them, all occur (in low fre-
quencies) in Mousterian assemblages. Likewise, worked bone is
not altogether lacking in the Mousterian. Hafted (composite)
tools are probably present as well. Burials may be simpler, but
they are, after all, a Mousterian innovation. Some regionalization of distinctive style zones is apparent in later phases of
the Middle Palaeolithic (e.g. the Aterian). Even decorated and
inscribed pieces are not unknown (e.g. Freeman 1978). Second,
the characteristic features of the Upper Palaeolithic often only
achieve full expression in its later phases. Expansion and/or
intensification of faunal exploitation only becomes manifest
in the Solutrean and Magdalenian, both in Cantabria and in the
Périgord (Mellars 1973; Straus 1977); earlier Upper Palaeolithic faunal exploitation does not differ markedly from that
of the Mousterian (cf. Gamble 1979). Regionalization of

assemblage types is less pronounced in the earlier than in the
later Upper Palaeolithic: Aurignacian assemblages cover a
wider geographical area than Magdalenian ones. The climactic
phase in the development of Palaeolithic art is, once again, the
Magdalenian. As a result of these two tendencies, it is not
surprising that at the chronological dividing point between
Middle and Upper Palaeolithic there are often 'transitional'
cultures: in France, the 'B' facies of the Mousterian of
Acheulian tradition and the Chatelperronian; in east-central
Europe, the Szeletian; in southern Africa, the Umguzan complex (Sampson 1974). All of these share Middle and Upper
Palaeolithic features. The Upper Palaeolithic Revolution, like
the Neolithic Revolution later on, encompasses the entire
inhabited world in a gradual process of immense significance.

Current explanatory approaches

Apart from being consistent with the content and tempo
of the changes involved, a successful account of the Upper
Palaeolithic Revolution must meet two requirements. First, it
must be comprehensive enough to link together all the various
technical and social features of the transition into a single,
causally plausible explanatory web. Second, the account must
be structurally basic enough to be able to explain the occurrence of the Revolution in all the very diverse areas in which it
took place. There are three major approaches to the problem
of the Middle to Upper Palaeolithic transition and it will be
instructive to examine them with these requirements in mind.

The biological approach

Mousterian artifact assemblages are mostly associated
with skeletal remains of *Homo sapiens neanderthalensis*, Upper
Palaeolithic assemblages mostly with *Homo sapiens sapiens*. In
Europe transitional specimens are unknown. Before the Second World War, when the outlines of the Middle to Upper
Palaeolithic transition were well known in Europe and when
very little information was available from other regions, the
generally accepted explanation of the cultural changes
involved was to attribute them to the associated biological
changes. As Sackett (1968: 66–7) has pointed out, artifact
types were considered to be analogues to biological fossils and
differences in artifact types were seen as indicative of biological differences. A wholesale change in typology, such as
that associated with the Upper Palaeolithic Revolution, could
only be brought about by a wholesale change in biology. The
idealist inclinations of artifact connoisseurs converged with
an abject biological reductionism in a nice example of the
unity of opposites.

After the Second World War the biological approach to
Palaeolithic culture change was fairly generally abandoned (see
below), but recently it has been revived, notably by Richard
Klein:

> [The] physical characters [of Neanderthals], in com-
> bination with such cultural facts as the absence of
> undoubted art objects in Mousterian sites, suggests that
> they *may* have been 'primitives' in the narrowest imagin-

able sense of that word. Thus, in addition to possessing simpler cultures than we do, they may have been bio-physically less complex.   (Klein 1973: 123)

The people who appeared 35,000 years ago knew how to do an awful lot of things their predecessors didn't. Something quite extraordinary must have happened in the organization of the brain . . . I'm quite convinced . . . that in Europe it was a physical replacement of one kind by another. And I'm prepared to bet that that's what happened in Africa too and at about the same time . . . I would think that the behavioral gulf between these two very different kinds of people would have been so great that there would have been no desire at all to mate.

(Klein, quoted in Rensberger [1980: 7, 8])
A somewhat more subtle version of this approach explains the cultural changes of the Middle to Upper Palaeolithic transition in terms of biological changes permitting the development of full linguistic competence.

Whether it was only with the appearance of *Homo sapiens* or before, that the lowered larynx and mobile tongue developed, . . . at whatever point in human evolution the symbolic mode of communication . . . became established as a regular component of human behavior, the adaptive advantage it conferred upon its users must have been significant . . . Not only is it a plausible hypothesis that a cultural informational transformation contributed to the 'replacement' of Neanderthals by fully sapiensized populations, but also it is easy to see how a communication advantage could have enhanced the learning of new adaptive tasks.

(Conkey 1978: 73—4; cf. Isaac 1972: 403; 1976: 286)
In short, the Upper Palaeolithic Revolution is the technological and social manifestation of the biological achievement of a full capacity for culture.

Empirically, the biological approach to explaining the Middle to Upper Palaeolithic transition faces the difficulty that the skeletal differences between *Homo sapiens neanderthalensis* and *Homo sapiens sapiens* have no direct bearing on their respective intellectual/cultural capacities. The changes in facial and cranial morphology have no clear explanation (certainly not an intellectual one) and the decrease in robustness in the post-cranial remains can be plausibly interpreted as the *result* of more effective extrasomatic adaptations (Trinkaus and Howells 1979).[3] Even if, for the sake of argument, one were to allow that *Homo sapiens sapiens* was biologically more capable of cognitive representations such as language than his immediate predecessors, however, one would still not be able to use his increased abilities as a sufficient explanation for the new elements in his cultural repertoire. To say, for example, that Cro-Magnons were capable of painting caves (and that Neanderthals were not) does not explain why they painted them. Conversely, if painting caves is part of a more effective adaptive system, then one need not appeal to the capability of painting them in order to explain why the paint-

ing took place. Because biological changes underdetermine cultural ones, the biological approach fails to establish a plausible link between the assumed causes and the known manifestations of the Upper Palaeolithic Revolution.

The particularist approach

The overtones of *Rassengeschichte* inherent in the biological approach to Palaeolithic culture change led to a widespread revulsion among prehistorians. After the Second World War the focus of much of the research was to emphasize the continuities between the Middle Palaeolithic and its successors: the existence of intermediate cultures in a number of areas and the presence of Upper Palaeolithic elements in earlier contexts (Bordes 1971; Bricker 1976: 139—43) were deployed as evidence to debunk the catastrophism implicit in the classic biological model. Like other cultural particularist responses to racialist evolutionary theories, this approach has the great merit of encouraging the detailed documentation of variation in the anthropological record and the defect of blurring broad contrasts which still demand an explanation. Thus, although Bordes does not deny that differences exist in the nature and distribution of assemblage types between the Middle and the Upper Palaeolithic, he considers them to be the material expression of 'tribes' in both instances (e.g. Bordes 1968: 144—5, 157—8). In his last statement on the subject, Bordes clearly reveals the thrust of his position: 'Il est d'ailleurs curieux que [certains] auteurs dénient aux Moustériens tout sentiment d'identité ethnique au moment où les paléontologues rattachent l'homme du Néanderthal à l'espèce *Homo sapiens* comme une simple race . . . ou démontrent que certaines industries moustériennes ont été l'oeuvre d'*Homo sapiens sapiens*' (Bordes 1981: 87). This simply turns the biological argument on its head. The existence of detailed similarities and continuities between the Mousterian and its successors does not obliterate the major differences which exist and require explanation.

The cultural materialist approach

Sally Binford (1968b; 1970) has put forward the theory that the changes involved in the Upper Palaeolithic Revolution were brought about by the hunting of herds of migratory herbivores. First proposed tongue-in-cheek as the achievement of 'a level of primary predation efficiency' (Binford and Binford 1966), the central idea is expressed as follows:

The cooperative hunting of a few males to capture one or two animals characterized human subsistence from at least Mindel times . . . , but the large-scale systematic exploitation of migratory herd mammals is a qualitatively different kind of activity, one that makes totally different structural demands on the human groups involved. This kind of hunting is known to characterize Upper Palaeolithic adaptations, and it is proposed . . . that . . . not only did this hunting pattern appear before the Upper Palaeolithic, but that the formal changes documented from Neanderthal to

modern man and from Mousterian to the Upper Palaeolithic occurred in response to this basic structural change
in ecological relationships.   (Binford 1968b: 714)
The detailed steps in the model as applied to the Near East are
summarized in flow-chart form in Fig. 1, but its essential
features might be replicated in other areas with appropriate
changes in empirical variables. The central thrust is to provide
an ecological explanation for the development of the group
co-operation which is the practical basis of the hunter—
gatherer band in the classic model of Service (1962).

    The co-operative hunting account of the 'origin of Band
Society' has been amplified by Wobst's (1976) interpretation
of the significance of the appearance of style zones in the light
of his simulations of Palaeolithic demographic processes
(Wobst 1975). The latter show that a local exogamous group
(the 'minimal band' of c. 25 individuals) must be part of a
mate exchange network (a connubium: Williams 1974) of
some 500 individuals in order to survive. At population
densities of Palaeolithic sparseness this means that travel time
to maintain necessary social contacts would constitute a significant cost. The existence of style zones is interpreted as the
material expression of the demarcation of its social identity by
a closed connubium (cf. the 'dialectical tribe' of Birdsell
1953). Because peripheral groups within a closed connubium
must forego mates obtainable from 'alien' neighbours, the
travel cost of maintaining the exchange of mates is higher than
in an open connubium. Therefore, the appearance of style
zones is interpreted to mean (a) that population densities had
become high enough to make the longer travel for mates
feasible, and (b) that the closed connubium conferred practical
benefits which compensated for the higher cost of procuring
mates.

    It was at this time that work groups, requiring more per-
sonnel than a single local group could provide, had
achieved a sufficient pay-off to have become a predictable part of the seasonal round of activities and . . . that
additional pay-off could be gained by minimizing the
turn-over in this personnel. Such pay-offs may well have

Fig. 1. The Upper Palaeolithic Revolution according to Binford (1968b; 1970).

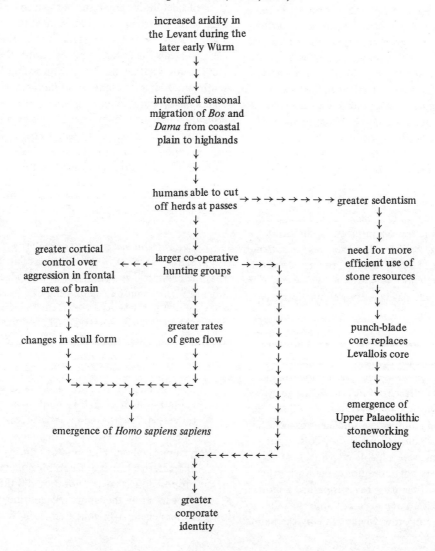

derived from large scale game drives that effectively exploited the windfall of the spring and fall migrations of large herbivores.   (Wobst 1976: 55)

The causal chain involved in Wobst's elaboration of the Binford model is summarized in flow-chart form in Fig. 2.

The cultural materialist accounts just outlined have the merit of focusing research on subsistence techniques, demography, and social organization, aspects of the archaeological record too often neglected in Palaeolithic studies, but the specificity which gives the approach its heuristic value is carried to the point of becoming a theoretical defect. On the one hand, the argument is tied to specific ecological settings, those where co-operative hunting of large, seasonally migratory herd animals would have been advantageous in mid-Würm times. Even assuming that such opportunities had the predicted consequences for *Bos* and *Dama* hunters in the Levant or for *Rangifer* hunters in the Périgord, how can the model help us understand the transition to the Upper Palaeolithic in Cantabria (where quite different faunal exploitation patterns are attested), let alone in the Maghreb or southern Africa? The Upper Palaeolithic Revolution is an Old-World-wide event and cannot be explained by local ecological gimmicks. On the other hand, even where the ecological conditions are arguably appropriate for the co-operative hunting theory, the causal links between the change in hunting patterns and the remaining cultural changes have an implausible, Rube Goldberg-like quality. It is proposed, for example, that the increased sedentism required in order to cut off migrating herds at fixed localities would encourage the adoption of the more parsimonious punch-blade technique in order to husband the relatively scarcer flint resources locally

available (Binford 1970: 282). Would this mean that Middle Palaeolithic techniques survived longer, *ceteris paribus*, in areas with abundant flint resources, like the Périgord? Similarly, the link between co-operative hunting and the closed connubium proposed by Wobst depends on an assessment of the relative effectiveness of set v. pick-up hunting teams which is hardly supported by the available ethnographic record on hunting practices.[4] Cultural materialism, here as elsewhere (cf. Friedman 1974), fails to link technical and social changes in a convincing causal sequence.

The available literature on the Middle to Upper Palaeolithic transition, in so far as it transcends a purely descriptive level, does not contain a satisfactory account of the nature of the processes involved. We are left to choose between positions which reduce the cultural changes to epiphenomena of undocumented biological changes, positions which minimize the significance of the transformation (and thereby suggest that no explanation is necessary), and positions which explain the transformation in terms of mechanically conceived ecological devices. It is clear that there is room for a more convincing approach, Marxist or otherwise.

Theory, discussion, and conclusions

Wobst (1976), Conkey (1978), and White (1982) are correct in emphasizing that the key feature which requires explanation in the Upper Palaeolithic Revolution is the appearance of style in its various manifestations. The changes in artifact and subsistence technology constitute straightforward adaptive improvements, but the development of art and tools worked with an elaboration far beyond functional requirements and the increased regional clustering of types of such objects reflect social changes whose causes are not so immediately explained in terms of Darwinian rationality.[5] The widespread interpretation of these changes as reflecting the appearance of increased corporate solidarity, the development of closed connubia, or more generally the introduction of ethnicity constitutes a major first step in understanding the processes involved, but this idea has not been articulated satisfactorily with the techno-environmental aspects of the Upper Palaeolithic Revolution. The proposed explanations to date — that these social changes are epiphenomena either of biological changes in the human species or of technical changes in ways of exploiting the environment — are demonstrably inadequate. As Bender (1981: 153) has suggested, in order to connect the social and technical changes of the Upper Palaeolithic Revolution in a plausible framework, it will be useful to review some of the principal conclusions of alliance theory in social anthropology, since this provides us with a basic understanding of the social relations of production in the primitive social formations which emerged in the Late Pleistocene.

The adaptive necessity for local groups to maintain alliances with their neighbours was expressed aphoristically by Tylor (1889: 267) as 'the simple, practical alternative between marrying out and being killed out'. Tylor's dictum emphasized a group's need for alliances in order to maintain access to its

Fig. 2. The development of Upper Palaeolithic style zones according to Wobst (1976).

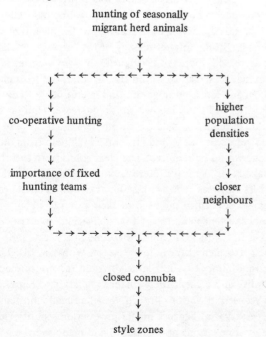

own territory, but subsequently the utility of alliance was recognized to include the assurance of access to the territory and resources of others in times of shortage. Alliances established by means of the exchange of spouses (by exogamy) promote security by preventing conflict and facilitating economic assistance between groups. Beyond a certain social distance, however, the costs of alliance outweigh its benefits. As Lévi-Strauss (1969 [orig. 1949]: 46) notes: 'A very great number of primitive tribes simply refer to themselves by the term for "men" in their language . . . In all these cases, it is merely a question of knowing how far to extend the logical connotation of the idea of a community, which in itself is dependent on the effective solidarity of the group.' The occasional and dispensable contacts with strangers can be governed by the norms of what Sahlins (1965) has termed 'negative reciprocity'.

Within the circle of the co-operative, maximally endogamous group (the connubium), mutual assistance is not absolute, however. Members of the same household and their close kinsmen may entertain relations governed by 'generalized' reciprocity, but, as Sahlins (1972: 123–30) has emphasized, the sphere of 'balanced' reciprocity is replete with variable and grudging co-operation, especially in moments of crisis. Within the 'Domestic Mode of Production' relations between households are governed by contradictory forces: on the one hand, the household desires to establish external ties in order to insure against inevitable failures in its own production; on the other hand, it desires to limit its external ties in order to husband its resources. Beyond the intimate domestic sphere of unquestioning mutual assistance, the household establishes ties whose scope and intensity are inversely proportional to the security of its autonomous production. To the extent that the household assures its production security by its own efforts, it both diminishes its need for the assistance of other households and increases the likelihood that it will be subject to the importunities of other households. Maintaining the necessary web of social relations requires the balancing of contradictory interests and it is this that makes ritual reinforcement of reciprocity necessary.

Archaeologists have tended to interpret the existence of style zones as the material expression of actual co-operation between local groups (see Brown and Plog 1982 for a well-developed expression of this view). Indeed, the diagram by which Wobst (1977: Fig. 1) expresses the functional sphere of artifact style in facilitating the transmission of information corresponds precisely to the sphere of balanced reciprocity as expressed diagrammatically by Sahlins (1965: Fig. 1). But the solidarity of households engaged in balanced reciprocity must be sanctified by ritual (or, in the material expression of ritual in artifacts, by style) not because co-operation between households exists, but because it is liable to break down.[6] The lesson of alliance theory is, therefore, that rituals expressing corporate solidarity came to have increasing salience in Upper Palaeolithic material culture, not because co-operation between local groups/households/minimal bands had

increased, but because, although co-operation was necessary, the basis for it had become more problematical.

Alliance theory suggests how the technical and social aspects of the Upper Palaeolithic Revolution may be integrated into a single, coherent, plausible account. A local group in the Palaeolithic would have obtained the wherewithal with which to survive, on the one hand, from its own co-operative efforts assisted by whatever level of technique was known to it and, on the other hand, by pooling its resources (or risks, as Wiessner [1982: 173] puts it) with those of neighbouring groups. No group would have been able to dispense with outside assistance, but the frequency with which it would have to make appeal to other groups and the number of needed allies would be inversely proportional to the effectiveness of its own techniques. Thus, as technique improved, relations between groups would become more problematical: the need for positive co-operation would be balanced by the defensive needs indicated by Tylor. The Upper Palaeolithic Revolution involves, then, a critical change in the balance of social security, a change brought about by the development of the forces of production.

The low level of technology possessed by Lower and Middle Pleistocene human groups logically would have had two consequences. First, local groups would often require the help of their neighbours: the local production shortages which are not uncommon among ethnographically documented hunter–gatherers (Colson 1979) can only have been more frequent for foragers with more limited equipment. Second, population densities must have been very low, so that any particular local group would have had little choice in its allies. All help would be welcome and, conversely, help would be granted to all. The give-and-take of mutual aid would have been so essential that it would have known no social boundaries. In the Upper Pleistocene there was continual and accelerating improvement in the level of human technology. The innovations vary from region to region, but to the extent that the techno-environmental efficiency of the forces of production increased, there would logically be two outcomes. First, population densities would rise. Second, the frequency with which any local group would find itself unable to obtain the necessities of life on its own would decrease. Thus, as more neighbours became available (to whom help might have to be given), fewer occasions would arise on which help from one's neighbours would be required. The clear solution to this shift in the balance of a group's interests would be to restrict the scope of its alliances. The establishment of closed circles of mutual aid would fulfil the need of each group to obtain occasional assistance and to limit its obligations to assist others. Given the increase in population density, this shift could be performed at fairly low cost (cf. Wobst 1976). The closed connubium of friends-in-need would require ceremonies to symbolize and cement their alliance and style to represent it, not because innovations in technique had made mutual aid more necessary, but because higher production security (made possible by innovations in technique) had made social co-operation more unstable.[7] The overall process is summarized in flow-chart form in Fig. 3.

The approach just proposed to account for the salient features of the Upper Palaeolithic Revolution has several points to recommend it. First, it is consistent with the empirical record of change in the prehistoric remains. The pace of change assumed by the model is a gradual one and the correlative technological and social aspects predicted by it are confirmed archaeologically. Thus, many of the characteristic technical advances of the Upper Palaeolithic are present in a small way in the Mousterian, while the first foreshadowing of the elaborate collective representation of the Upper Palaeolithic are the formal burials of the preceding period. The model proposed here sees in the Upper Palaeolithic Revolution gradual cumulative processes which eventually culminate in critically significant qualitative changes.[8] Second, the model links the technical and social aspects of the Revolution in a manner structurally basic enough to accommodate the diversity of ecological circumstances in which it took place, and concrete trajectories by which it took place. The changes in social organization attendant on the cumulation of technical

advances are not tied, as in the cultural materialist accounts of Binford or Wobst, to specific settings, but rather to an overall increase in production security.[9] The changes in technology are seen as primary adaptive improvements to be explained within a Darwinian framework of the kind elucidated by Hayden (1981). The changes in social organization arise from a shift in group interests ultimately caused, but not specifically determined, by more effective technologies. That is to say, the materialist determination of social structure is in the last, not the first, instance. Finally, unlike other accounts, this theory embodies specific suggestions concerning the nature of 'pre-Band Society' social structure. The idea that the social structure of human groups before the Upper Palaeolithic was based on unlimited co-operation is in accord with the emphasis on sharing which Isaac (1971) has made the basis of his social analysis of the earliest known human cultural remains.

To date, explanations of the Upper Palaeolithic Revolution have been characterized by a considerable theoretical poverty. We have been left to choose between an idealism that considers the cultural information of the Upper Palaeolithic so much more complex than that of preceding periods that it necessarily reflects genetic changes in the capacity for culture and a mechanical materialism that reduces the social and ideological developments of the Upper Palaeolithic to instruments necessary to make new technologies effective. By focusing on the social relations of production, I have tried to steer a course between these extremes. Such an approach is characteristically, but not exclusively Marxist. The central ideas of alliance theory go back, after all, to Durkheim and Tylor, who were not Marxists. What is muted in the work of Durkheim and of most of his successors, however, is any emphasis on the tensions and divisions underlying the corporate solidarity of the social group. Sahlins's essentially Marxist addition to alliance theory is to show how internal economic tensions served as a stimulus for the change from egalitarian to complex social systems (Sahlins 1972: 123–48). It is this same emphasis on conflict and contradiction, cast backwards so to speak, that permits one to arrive at a better account of the Upper Palaeolithic Revolution.

This essay is Marxist, not only in its analytical approach, but also in its conclusions. Marx and Engels took up the idea that primitive communism was the pristine form of human social organization in order to show, as Pershits (1981: 85) puts it, 'the historically conditioned and, therefore, transient character of [the] basic institutions of class society'. Morgan provided Marx and Engels with the opportunity to convert a philosophical theory into a scientific one. In response, opponents of Marxism have tended to emphasize the great differences between pre-class societies. This criticism has been all the more effective in that Marxist syntheses of prehistory have tended to emphasize the stages, rather than the processes, of social evolution. To articulate the archaeological evidence for the earliest human social formations to a coherent account of the social dynamics of pre-class societies will contribute, I

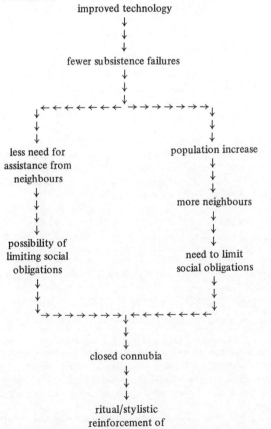

Fig. 3. The relation between technological improvements and social change over the course of the Upper Palaeolithic Revolution.

hope, to the revitalization of the basically correct notion of primitive communism.

Notes

1 Bahn (1978) even defends the hypothesis that Upper Palaeolithic animal exploitation practices included incipient forms of husbandry.
2 At the same time, raw materials at Upper Palaeolithic sites are sometimes procured from distant sources, which may indicate, as White (1982: 176) says, more 'structured relationships between the inhabitants of different geographic areas'.
3 In fact, of course, the only evidence for *Homo sapiens sapiens'* biological superiority is his cultural production. The evidence for the assumed cause is its supposed effect. It is this circularity that makes the biological approach irrefutable.
4 Among the !Kung San, for example, 'the composition of the hunting party is not a matter of strict convention or of anxious concern. Whoever the hunters are, the meat is shared and everyone profits. The men are free to organize their hunting parties as they like . . . Men from different bands may hunt together' (Marshall 1976: 357). In Australia, 'collective hunting can be carried out by men who are not clansmen, and knowledge of animal behaviour and personal skill are more important than detailed local knowledge in most conditions' (Peterson 1975: 63).
5 The question of the nature and pace of Upper Pleistocene human biological evolution (which may include local population replacement events) is an interesting research area, but (for the reasons noted earlier) not one which can easily contribute to an understanding of the cultural changes of the period.
6 The notion that ritual serves to alleviate uncertainty is, of course, a functionalist commonplace, but one contemporary example may be to the point: in American society the increasing prevalence of rituals (in which artifacts play no little part) asserting the sanctity and permanence of the nuclear family (Mother's and Father's Days, wedding anniversaries, renewed wedding vows, etc.) does not reflect any increasing unity of the family in fact. Rather, these practices are meant to ward off whatever disruptive forces have led to a rising divorce rate.
7 Wiessner's (1982) useful analysis of the social relations of hunter–gatherer production helps define the nature of the changes brought about by improvements in technique. Of the four approaches used to reduce the variance in mean subsistence income – prevention of loss, storage, negative transfer of risk (expropriation), and pooling (sharing) – the first two would be immediately and directly affected by increases in technological effectiveness. Improvement in these strategies, however, would tend to affect the social approaches to risk prevention by increasing the feasibility and profitability of expropriation and by reducing the incentive to share. In short, technological improvements in the security of production would lead to potential decreases in social security, a recurrent pattern in social evolution (cf. Gilman 1981). The emergent social tensions would be mediated by stylistic intensification. Pfeiffer (in White 1982: 184) points in the right direction when he sees 'the spectacular increase in . . . art and ceremony' as 'an effort to reduce conflict'.
8 My model implies that technological and social changes unfold over the course of both the Middle and the Upper Palaeolithic. Evidence for such 'progress' is available for the latter period, but remains to be developed for the former.
9 The idea of 'primary hunting efficiency' lampooned by Binford and Binford (1966) may not, after all, be such a bad one.

Acknowledgements
Earlier drafts of this paper received useful criticisms from Harvey Bricker, Glynn Isaac, Susan Kus, Paul Mellars, Kathryn Maurer Trinkaus, Keith Morton, Erik Trinkaus, and Gregory Truex. All remaining errors are of course mine.

Bibliography
Bahn, P.G. 1978. The unacceptable face of the West European Upper Palaeolithic. *Antiquity* 52: 183–92.
Bender, B. 1978. Gatherer–hunter to farmer: a social perspective. *World Archaeology* 10: 205–22.
  1981. Gatherer–hunter intensification. In A. Sheridan and G. Bailey (eds.), *Economic Archaeology: Towards an Integration of Ecological and Social Approaches*. B.A.R. International Series 96: 149–57. Oxford: British Archaeological Reports.
Binford, L.R. 1973. Interassemblage variability – the Mousterian and the 'functional' argument. In C. Renfrew (ed.), *The Explanation of Culture Change: Models in Prehistory*, pp. 227–54. London: Duckworth.
Binford, L.R. and S.R. Binford, 1966. The predatory revolution: a consideration of the evidence for a new subsistence level. *American Anthropologist* 68: 508–12.
Binford, S.R. 1968a. A structural comparison of the disposal of the dead in the Mousterian and the Upper Palaeolithic. *Southwestern Journal of Anthropology* 24: 139–54.
  1968b. Early Upper Pleistocene adaptations in the Levant. *American Anthropologist* 70: 707–17.
  1970. Late Middle Palaeolithic adaptations and their possible consequences. *Bioscience* 20: 280–3.
Birdsell, J.B. 1953. Some environmental and cultural factors influencing the structure of Australian aboriginal populations. *American Naturalist* 87: 171–207.
Bordes, F. 1953. Essai de classification des industries 'moustériennes'. *Bulletin de la Société Préhistorique Française* 50: 457–66.
  1968. *The Old Stone Age.* London: Weidenfeld and Nicolson.
  1971. Du Paléolithique moyen au Paléolithique supérieur, continuité ou discontinuité. In F. Bordes (ed.), *The Origin of Homo sapiens*, pp. 211–18. Paris: UNESCO.
  1981. Vingt-cinq ans après: le complèxe moustérien revisité. *Bulletin de la Société Préhistorique Française* 78: 77–87.
Bordes, F. and D. de Sonneville-Bordes, 1970. The significance of variability in Palaeolithic assemblages. *World Archaeology* 2: 61–73.
Breuil, H. 1912. Les subdivisions du Paléolithique supérieur et leur signification. *C.R. XIV Congrès International d'Anthropologie et d'Archéologie Préhistoriques, Genève*, pp. 165–238.
Bricker, H.M. 1976. Upper Palaeolithic archaeology. *Annual Review of Anthropology* 5: 133–48.
Brown, D.P. and S. Plog, 1982. Evolution of 'tribal' social networks: theory and prehistoric North American evidence. *American Antiquity* 47: 504–25.
Childe, V.G. 1929. *The Danube in Prehistory.* Oxford: Clarendon Press.
  1951. *Man Makes Himself.* New York: Mentor Books.
Chung, Young-Wha, 1972. L'outillage de type archaïque dans le Paléolithique supérieur du sud-ouest de la France. Thèse Dr. de l'Université Bordeaux 1.
Colson, E. 1979. In good years and bad: food strategies of self-reliant societies. *Journal of Anthropological Research* 35: 18–29.
Conkey, M.W. 1978. Style and information in cultural evolution: toward a predictive model for the Paleolithic. In C. Redman *et al.* (eds.), *Social Archaeology: Beyond Subsistence and Dating*, pp. 61–85. New York: Academic Press.
Engels, F. 1935. *Herr Eugen Dühring's Revolution in Science.* Chicago: Charles H. Kerr.
  1972. *The Origin of the Family, Private Property, and the State.* New York: International Publishers.

Feustel, R. 1968. Evolution und Revolution im Ablauf der Steinzeit. *Ethnographisch—Archäologische Zeitschrift* 9: 120–47.

Flannery, K. 1968. Archaeological systems theory and early Meso-america. In B. Meggers (ed.), *Anthropological Archaeology in the Americas*, pp. 67–87. Washington, DC: Anthropological Society of Washington.

1969. Origins and ecological effects of early domestication in Iran and the Near East. In P.J. Ucko and G.W. Dimbleby (eds.), *The Domestication and Exploitation of Plants and Animals*, pp. 73–100. London: Duckworth.

Freeman, L.G. 1973a. The significance of mammalian faunas from Paleolithic occupations in Cantabrian Spain. *American Antiquity* 38: 3–44.

1973b. El Musteriense. In J. González Echegaray *et al.* (eds.), *Cueva Morín: Excavaciones 1969*, pp. 15–140. Santander: Patronato de las Cuevas Prehistóricas.

1978. Mousterian worked bone from Cueva Morín (Santander, Spain): a preliminary description. In L.G. Freeman (ed.), *Views of the Past: Essays in Old World Prehistory and Palaeoanthro-pology*, pp. 29–51. The Hague: Mouton.

Friedman, J. 1974. Marxism, structuralism, and vulgar materialism. *Man* (n.s.) 9: 444–69.

Gamble, C. 1979. Hunting strategies in the central European Palaeo-lithic. *Proceedings of the Prehistoric Society* 45: 35–52.

Gilman, A. 1981. The development of social stratification in Bronze Age Europe. *Current Anthropology* 22: 1–23.

Godelier, M. 1975. Modes of production, kinship, and demographic structures. In M. Bloch (ed.), *Marxist Analyses in Social Anthro-pology*, pp. 3–27. New York: John Wiley.

Harrold, F.B. 1980. A comparative analysis of Eurasian Palaeolithic burials. *World Archaeology* 12: 195–210.

Hayden, B. 1981. Research and development in the Stone Age: tech-nological transitions among hunter—gatherers. *Current Anthro-pology* 22: 519–48.

Isaac, E. 1962. On the domestication of cattle. *Science* 137: 195–204.

Isaac, G. 1971. The diet of early man. *World Archaeology* 2: 278–99.

1972. Chronology and the tempo of culture change during the Pleistocene. In W.W. Bishop and J.A. Miller (eds.), *Calibration of Hominoid Evolution*, pp. 381–400. Edinburgh: Scottish Academic Press.

1976. Stages of cultural elaboration in the Pleistocene: possible archaeological indicators of the development of language capabilities. *Annals of the New York Academy of Sciences* 280: 275–88.

Klein, R.G. 1973. *Ice Age Hunters of the Ukraine.* Chicago: University of Chicago Press.

1979. Stone Age exploitation of animals in southern Africa. *American Scientist* 67: 151–60.

Klein, R.G., C. Wolf, L.G. Freeman and K. Allwarden, 1981. The use of dental crown heights for constructing age profiles of red deer and similar species in archaeological samples. *Journal of Archae-ological Science* 8: 1–31.

Kohl, P.L. and R.P. Wright, 1977. Stateless cities: the differentiation of societies in the Near Eastern Neolithic. *Dialectical Anthropology* 2: 271–83.

Leacock, E.B. 1972. Editor's introduction to 'The part played by labor in the transition from ape to man'. In Engels 1972: 245–9.

Lee, R.B. 1979. *The !Kung San: Men, Women, and Work in a Foraging Society.* Cambridge: Cambridge University Press.

Leroi-Gourhan, A. 1964. *Le Geste et la Parole.* vol. 1: *Technique et Langage.* Paris: Albin Michel.

Lévi-Strauss, C. 1969. *The Elementary Structures of Kinship.* Boston: Beacon Press.

Marshack, A. 1972. Cognitive aspects of Upper Palaeolithic engraving. *Current Anthropology* 13: 445–77.

Marshall, L. 1976. Sharing, talking, and giving: relief of social tensions among the !Kung. In R.B. Lee and I. DeVore (eds.), *Kalahari Hunter—Gatherers: Studies of the !Kung San and Their Neigh-bors*, pp. 349–71. Cambridge, Mass.: Harvard University Press.

Marx, K. 1965. *Pre-Capitalist Economic Formations.* New York: International Publishers.

Marx, K. and F. Engels, 1968. *Selected Works in One Volume.* New York: International Publishers.

Meillassoux, C. 1972. From production to reproduction. *Economy and Society* 1: 93–105.

Mellars, P.A. 1969. The chronology of Mousterian industries in the Perigord region of southwest France. *Proceedings of the Pre-historic Society* 35: 134–71.

1973. The character of the Middle-Upper Palaeolithic transition in southwest France. In C. Renfrew (ed.), *The Explanation of Culture Change: Models in Prehistory*, pp. 255–76. London: Duckworth.

Pershits, A.I. 1981. Ethnographic reconstruction of the history of primitive society. In E. Gellner (ed.), *Soviet and Western Anthro-pology*, pp. 85–94. New York: Columbia University Press.

Peterson, N. 1975. Hunter—gatherer territoriality: the perspective from Australia. *American Anthropologist* 77: 53–68.

Rensberger, B. 1980. The emergence of *Homo sapiens. Mosaic* 11 (6): 2–12.

Rolland, N. 1981. The interpretation of Middle Palaeolithic variability. *Man* (n.s.) 16: 15–42.

Sackett, J.R. 1968. Method and theory of Upper Palaeolithic archae-ology in southwestern France. In S.R. Binford and L.R. Binford (eds.), *New Perspectives in Archaeology*, pp. 61–83. Chicago: Aldine.

Sahlins, M.D. 1965. On the sociology of primitive exchange. In M. Banton (ed.), *The Relevance of Models for Social Anthropology*, pp. 139–236. London: Tavistock.

1972. *Stone Age Economics.* Chicago: Aldine—Atherton.

Sampson, C.G. 1974. *The Stone Age Archaeology of Southern Africa.* New York: Academic Press.

Service, E.R. 1962. *Primitive Social Organization.* New York: Random House.

Straus, L.G. 1977. Of deerslayers and mountain men: Paleolithic faunal exploitation in Cantabrian Spain. In L.R. Binford (ed.), *For Theory Building in Archaeology: Essays on Faunal Remains, Aquatic Resources, and Systemic Modeling*, pp. 41–76. New York: Academic Press.

Straus, L.G., G.A. Clark, J. Altuna and J.A. Ortea, 1980. Ice Age sub-sistence in northern Spain. *Scientific American* 242 (6): 142–52.

Trinkaus, E. and W.W. Howells, 1979. The Neanderthals. *Scientific American* 241 (6): 118–33.

Tylor, E.B. 1889. On a method of investigating the development of institutions: applied to laws of marriage and descent. *Journal of the Royal Anthropological Institute* 18: 245–72.

Washburn, S.L. 1960. Tools and human evolution. *Scientific American* 203 (3): 3–15.

White, R. 1982. Rethinking the Middle/Upper Palaeolithic transition. *Current Anthropology* 23: 169–92.

Wiessner, P. 1982. Beyond willow smoke and dogs' tails: a comment on Binford's analysis of hunter—gatherer settlement systems. *American Antiquity* 47: 171–8.

Williams, B.J. 1974. A model of band society. *Memoirs of the Society for American Archaeology* 29.

Wobst, H.M. 1975. The demography of finite populations and the origins of the incest taboo. *Memoirs of the Society for American Archaeology* 30: 75–81.

1976. Locational relationships in Palaeolithic society. *Journal of Human Evolution* 5: 49–58.

1977. Stylistic behavior and information exchange. In C.E. Cleland (ed.), *For the Director: Research Essays in Honor of James B.*

    Griffin, pp. 317–42. Ann Arbor: Museum of Anthropology,
    University of Michigan.
Wolf, E.R. 1981. The mills of inequality: a Marxian approach. In G.D.
    Berreman (ed.), *Social Inequality: Comparative and Develop-
mental Approaches*, pp. 41–57. New York: Academic Press.

Chapter 10

**Force, history and
the evolutionist
paradigm
Phil Kohl**

... it may still be permissible to ascribe changes in the central Mexican culture trajectory in the sixteenth century A.D. *at least in part* to the sudden and decisive arrival of the Conquistadores.
(Renfrew 1978: 203; emphasis added)

As for the vast mainland, ... we are sure that our Spaniards, with their cruel and abominable acts, have devastated the land and exterminated the rational people who fully inhabited it. We can estimate very surely and truthfully that in the forty years that have passed, with the infernal actions of the Christians, there have been unjustly slain more than twelve million men, women, and children. In truth, I believe without trying to deceive myself that the number of the slain is more like fifteen million.
(Bartolome de Las Casas 1974 (1542): 40–1)

One of the major features of contemporary archaeology in the English-speaking world has been the nearly universal acceptance of an evolutionary perspective to explain cultural change. The conflict between diffusionary and evolutionary explanations in archaeology dates back at least to the nineteenth century when de Mortillet and his disciples battled Montelius and adherents of the *ex oriente lux* model of development for prehistoric Europe. Although this dichotomy frequently has been described as anachronistic, overdrawn, or even silly, it has resurfaced today in the victory of evolution or processual over anti-processual, particularistic, or historical explanations. Binford, for example, is adamant on the subject, entitling a critique of Willey and Sabloff's argument for a

Central Mexican invasion at Seibal 'Some Comments on Historical *versus* Processual Archaeology' (1972: 114–21, emphasis added). Similarly, Renfrew's mathematical modelling of discontinuity and sociocultural collapse, cited at the beginning of this essay, views itself as an attack on 'the last stronghold of the anti-processualists'. The polemic is so deliberate that one must ask the question whether or not these currently popular evolutionary or processual explanations really represent an advance over the nineteenth-century debates. This paper hopes to explore this question by critically evaluating the positive and negative aspects of accepting an evolutionary paradigm for understanding prehistory and by examining a specific case of prehistoric contact that involved the deliberate use of political, military, and economic coercion to modify and change local evolutionary trajectories. A distinction will be made between *social evolution* or the theory that societies qualitatively change over time, exhibiting a general tendency to become larger and more complex in ways that can be determined objectively, and *evolutionism* or the degeneration of this theory into the description of an automatic, inevitable, and universal process, characterized by pure stages or ideal types of sociocultural development.

The development and utility of the evolutionary paradigm
The renaissance of an evolutionary paradigm in archae-

ology has occurred for numerous justifiable reasons. On the one hand, the growth of evolutionary thought in archaeology slightly follows its reacceptance into the mainstream of social anthropology, as reflected in the writings of White, Steward, Harris, and Service. Numerous studies, like that of Sanders and Price (1968), consciously adopt typologies proposed by these neo-evolutionists, perhaps the most widely utilized being Service's (1962) original quadripartite division of levels of sociopolitical integration. On the other hand, the acceptance of evolutionary models must be seen as the product of a reaction against overworked diffusionary accounts that prevailed earlier in this century, as well as the result of the more complete documentation of the prehistoric record that unequivocally demonstrated the existence of local evolutionary sequences and multiple paths leading towards complex forms of society. For all intents and purposes, it became impossible to adhere to Raglan's famous dictum that the 'savage never invents or discovers anything' after MacNeish had shown that pre-Columbian civilizations ultimately were based on the indigenous development of native cultigens. In the Old World, new data, particularly calibrated radiocarbon determinations suggestive of a chronological fault line making Europe older relative to the Near East, led to the ready acceptance of evolutionary models by European prehistorians who had long laboured under the unsatisfying shadow of Childe's supposed doctrine of modified diffusionism (Daniel 1976).[1] Finally, co-operation between natural scientists and archaeologists has also promoted the growth of evolutionary models; the retrieval of ecological data and concentration on the natural setting of archaeological sites necessarily and properly leads to interpretations of the material record in terms of local adaptations to the environment. From a materialist perspective, the orientation gained from this development must also be evaluated positively; emphasis has been directed to the daily activities of most members of prehistoric agrarian societies.

The growth of the evolutionary paradigm in archaeology has promoted a comparative approach in which societies clearly separated historically or genetically from one another are analysed together for purposes of detecting similar courses of cultural development. As diffusionary models historically degenerated into nationalistic myths of superior or gifted peoples, bestowing their innovations upon less well-endowed neighbours, the rise of evolutionary models has had the undeniably positive and important effect of combatting this racism by demonstrating that all cultures develop or modify their own technologies and adapt to local conditions.

Also undeniably progressive within the evolutionary paradigm is the implicit assumption that societies change and qualitatively differ from one another. For example, the state, *contra* Lowie (1929), is not always with us, but is the product of a complex evolutionary process in which society is differentiated into distinct classes having different access to the means by which social life is reproduced; in state societies formal institutions are developed to enforce and maintain this class structure. Correspondingly, as White (1960: vi) recog-

nized, a belief in social evolution implies that society has not reached some final or natural form but can evolve further into a qualitatively distinct formation in which such class divisions need not exist.

While always abstractions from reality, typologies are necessary to order the evolutionary record (Leacock 1972: 12), and those currently accepted by contemporary archaeologists, such as bands, tribes, chiefdoms, and states, have the singular advantage of focusing inquiry upon society, not upon its technology or method of food procurement. In this sense — though not, unfortunately, in terms of facility for archaeological reconstruction — the utilization of these levels represents a distinct advance over earlier ordering schemes, such as the Three Age system.

Evolutionism or the degeneration of evolutionary thought

Similar to the modified diffusionary views they replaced, evolutionary models in archaeology have been overutilized and employed uncritically, resulting in their own caricature or the near parody of the positive features adumbrated above. Let us proceed in reverse order. First, the conceptual nature of the evolutionary typology has been forgotten, stages have been reified and determination of the presence or absence of a given evolutionary level has become a final goal of archaeological research. Thus, we have tiresome disquisitions on whether the Olmec were a chiefdom or state society, whether the Halafian culture represents the world's first chiefdom (Watson and LeBlanc 1973), or whether Middle Horizon Huari should be elevated to state status (Isbell and Schreiber 1978). The game is simple: define criteria that supposedly are indicative of a given evolutionary level; examine the archaeological evidence for the society under review; and assign this society to its appropriate rank. Evolutionary levels, in short, devolve into another cultural trait to be listed with the other more tangible material indices of the given society. Far from being processual, the procedure is descriptive and dangerously simplifies reality. In Yoffee's (1979: 6) terms, the evolutionist paradigm has been simply accepted 'as revealed truth through which data must be interpreted', or, more tellingly:

> The purpose of such typing seems designed to make possible the extrapolation from a trait or single characteristic of a whole congeries of sociocultural functions thought to characterize a type — *no matter that these may be completely unindicated in the material record* or that functions vary exceedingly among ethnographically described representatives of a type. Thus archaeological reconstructions of the evolutionist stages of the rise of civilization have sometimes read less like science than science fiction.   (1979: 25; emphasis in original)

Moreover, since the perspective of this exercise is comparative, the reification of typological tools inevitably leads to a search for similarities, not differences, among societies ranked at the same evolutionary level. The terms have become ideal types, a tendency devastatingly criticized by Legros

(1977). Clearly, the attempt to draw comparisons among different societies is a legitimate and appropriate exercise, but this effort should not obscure or gloss over fundamental differences that distinguish societies and that must be explained in terms of each society's specific historical development. Following Terray's interpretation of Marx, Legros insists that all societies combine several distinct modes of production in different ways, precluding any rigid classification scheme into pure stages or ideal types:

> Marx's analysis provides the concepts that render possible the formulation of why, and in what respect, each society has to be treated as an irreducible specificity (a 'rediscovery' of Boas' cultural relativism; relativism for which Boas unfortunately provided no theory). From the Marxist point of view, one can explain, for example, why France, Germany, and England are each unique social formations despite the fact that all three are dominated by the capitalist mode of production . . . With Marxism, what is at stake is not a classification of societies, but an understanding of the specificity of each actual concrete society as a unique synthesis of heterogeneous modes of production.   (1977: 37–8)

It can be argued further that we need an historical perspective on our own attempts at comparison. Harris (1968: 171, 173), for example, defends Morgan's scheme for classifying societies into discrete stages on the grounds that: 'The first step in the development of any science must be the assumption that the phenomena to be studied are related in an orderly fashion'. Likewise it follows that it was appropriate for the Boasians to criticize this rigidly proposed order. Today, neo-evolutionary accounts have held sway long enough, and documentation of the differences among equivalently classified societies will prove more illuminating than the formulaic listing of commonly shared traits. The point is not to advocate a return to historical particularism but to argue for the abandonment of what has become a largely sterile exercise. Theory cannot be forsaken, and concepts must be defined and utilized that are universal in scope. Whether such tools are primarily typological as in the evolutionary paradigm or analytical as with those defined by Marx, they are useful only in so far as their essentially conceptual nature is not forgotten (cf. also Thompson 1978: 235). To parody Lévi-Strauss, states (or bands, etc. or, for that matter, modes of production) have little to do with empirical reality but are to do with models which we build up after them. These types can prove to be useful tools for analysis, but they do not exist as such.

Finally, evolution's positive historical role of combatting diffusionary myths of national superiority also can be undermined and reversed. According to the evolutionist paradigm, all societies essentially evolve independently of one another; this tenet makes possible an interpretation that attributes specific technical innovations or unusual social institutions to the genius of a peculiarly gifted people. Such highly nationalistic and chauvinistic interpretations of prehistory are commonplace in countries such as the Shah's Iran,

Israel or China. The evolutionary paradigm is particularly stressed in the case of China: Chinese civilization evolved almost totally independently of borrowings from the West, and, when contact was established, it was Chinese discoveries, such as silk, that diffused west, more than the reverse. However understandable this reaction might be to the earlier western formulated myth of secondary development, it still simplifies an extremely complex, reciprocal process. The point is that both diffusionary and evolutionary models have been and will continue to be used for narrowly defined political purposes; that diffusionary prehistoric accounts of racial supremacy achieved particular notoriety in this century must itself be explained historically and not in terms of diffusion's assumed inherent reduction to racism.

If we examine the prehistoric record carefully, we see that attempts to interpret cultural developments solely as adaptations to local conditions are as unsatisfactory as the diffusionary explanations they replaced. The Tehuacan Valley was never isolated from other regions, and some of the earliest cultigens, such as avocados (MacNeish 1967: 292), were not indigenous but introduced into the valley. Even the productivity of maize (and the subsequent appearance of permanent villages) is supposed to have increased as the result of its introduction to diverse areas far removed from its original highland home. European prehistorians must consider the circulation of goods, particularly metals, to explain the development of Bronze Age cultures in Europe (Kristiansen 1981; Rowlands 1973). In systems parlance, cultures are open-ended and must be viewed in relation to other cultures. The statement is trite but bears repeating to counter the dominant theories of evolutionism.

The dichotomy between diffusion and evolution, of course, is false since both processes nearly always operate simultaneously. One does not wish to return to the classic search for efficient causes but to postulate mechanisms or principles of contact that relate directly to internal structural features of the societies that are interacting with each other. Thus, in a detailed examination of models for understanding the Scandinavian Bronze Age Kristiansen distinguishes between local economic growth or 'expanded reproduction' and more general forms of surplus accumulation which can be derived by external means principally through trade and war. According to Kristiansen, one must examine societies' adaptations to local environmental conditions, their setting, and the political, military and exchange alliances that linked them to one another. The former act as a negative determinant in the sense that they impose 'a hierarchy of constraints on the functioning of the social system', while focus on the latter allows one to interpret the dynamic changes that occur on a large inter-regional scale. A similar attempt to unite internal and external factors characterizes Ekholm and Friedman's stimulating study (1979) of imperialism in ancient world-systems. While numerous, perhaps insuperable, difficulties remain in applying Wallerstein's concept of a world-economy (1974; 1980) directly to antiquity, this study's preliminary

delineation of common principles of expansionism and
attempt to explain developments on a macro-historical scale
are admirable.[2] In short, though our concepts for understanding contact among prehistoric social systems require further
refinement, rejection of evolutionism does not imply a return
to sterile, non-explanatory searches for agents of change.

Forcible incorporation into historical processes

The fruitless evolution–diffusion debate only continues
if we create a strawman antagonist or caricature contemporary
evolutionary reconstructions beyond recognition. Nearly all
evolutionary presentations of anthropologists admit significant
contact among different societies that promoted internal cultural change. In fact, several theories on the origin of the state
emphasize such variables as warfare (Carneiro 1970) and conquest (cf. the ethnographic examples of state formation discussed by Service 1975). However, these models are less
popular with or downplayed by archaeologists (e.g., Flannery
1972: 405), perhaps due to their former overuse in archaeological reconstructions.[3] Adams has criticized this tendency
of archaeologists to gloss over evidence for sudden, possibly
violent transformations of the social order and to prefer
models emphasizing gradual, adaptive change:

> The models of sociocultural development that most
> influence our thinking are framed in terms of endogen-
> ous change. An external event or influence may be
> thought of as triggering a progressive increase in scale
> and complexity, but the latter is assumed to have a
> smoothly unfolding internal inevitability of its own.
> Surely, however, it is absurd to think of this as the path
> that at least the more complex societies have normally
> followed. They dominate weaker neighbors, coalesce,
> suffer from varying forms and degrees of predation,
> develop and break off patterns of symbiosis – all in
> dizzyingly abrupt shifts.   (1974: 249)

It also must be said that the absurdity of insisting upon
gradual, smoothly unfolding evolutionary processes more
often than not reflects a profoundly conservative political bias,
as explicitly attested, for example, in Clark's recent denial of a
Neolithic revolution (1980).[4]

The fact is that even a cursory examination of any historical sequence cannot overlook the effects of sudden,
decisive events, particularly the coming together or conjunc-
ture of separately evolving historical trajectories. There clearly
exist historical periods – a renaissance or an industrial revolution – notable for accelerated development or collapse. The
remainder of this essay wishes to present an example of such a
period that is known to us from Central Asia and discuss its
implications for understanding historical processes. The purpose is to show that models which fail to account for deliberate, frequently violent, or coercive impositions of complex
societies (themselves, needless to say, composed of groups
with diverse, often opposed interests) on one another or on
simpler, less powerful societies are inadequate. Traditional
diffusionary agents of change that we know were important

historically also existed – sometimes at markedly different
levels of development – in prehistory. A satisfactory interpretation of their role in significantly modifying local evolutionary
sequences must not refer to them as efficient causes, but
analyse their internal structural features that promoted conquest, imperial expansion, colonization, mass migration, or
other means of coercive incorporation into larger historical
processes. Such explanations cannot meaningfully be based on
paradigms derived from natural history or biology, but must
consider human history *sui generis*, as the product of
deliberate, conscious acts that often – and always in the long
run – lead to unforeseen consequences.

Central Asia provides an ideal laboratory for consideration of such historical processes. Situated between three
major cultural areas, its history is punctuated by sudden
reversals, conquests, and long-distance trade. Reference to the
Silk Route, the Mongol invasions and state formation, or the
penetration of Buddhism and Islam should suffice to show the
importance of large-scale developments that significantly
altered the history of the entire area. If we examine the prehistoric record as reconstructed by Soviet archaeologists working in their Central Asian republics and northern Afghanistan,
we can detect the co-occurrence of evolutionary and diffusionary processes. The latter, particularly those examples suggesting the use of force or violent incorporation, are our concern
and are well documented. Predictably, the Soviets have been
criticized by Western scholars for stressing exogenous factors,
such as tribal movements from Iran or the northern steppes,
and the criticism is justified in so far as certain Soviet scholars
do not attempt to explain why such movements occurred or
why they were successful. However, a noticeable paradigmatic
shift, paralleling that in the West, is occurring in which evolutionary models supplant the traditional exogenous explanations. Masson, for example, today emphasizes the internal
emergence of urban society at Altyn-depe in southern Turkmenistan during the fourth and third millennia BC (Masson
and Kiyatkina 1981; Masson 1981). It is beyond the scope of
this essay to discuss why this shift is occurring or to what
extent it imitates developments in Western archaeology; one
obvious factor is that as more data have accumulated internal
features of continuity have become more apparent, obviating,
in many instances, reference to external factors.

Yet striking discontinuities remain during certain
periods, particularly the Late Bronze Age or Namazga VI
period, which can be dated to the end of the third and beginning of the second millennium BC. Settlements in the piedmont strip of southern Turkmenistan become smaller or are
totally abandoned at approximately the same time that scores
of planned, fortified, indeed, almost standardized sites appear
to the east in the former deltaic extension of the Murghab
river and on the Bactrian plain of northern Afghanistan and
southern Uzbekistan (Askarov 1977; Masimov 1981a; Sarianidi
1977, 1981). Bactria is particularly interesting in that earlier
third millennium sites, including Harappan-related settlements
on the Shortughai plain (Francfort and Pottier 1978), are

recorded on its easternmost extension, while the known record of earlier sites in the western centre or classical Bactrian heartland consists only of scattered stations containing relatively simple Neolithic and earlier chipped stone tool assemblages. In other words, there is practically no evidence for post-Neolithic cultural developments in Margiana and western Bactria or in two of southern Central Asia's historically most productive and important regions before the sudden appearance of the Late Bronze settlements.[5] The picture of a relatively rapid colonization of Margiana and Bactria from the west is complicated by numerous features, including the apparent retreat of Harappan influence to the south, a possible West Asian wide shift from overland to maritime long-distance trade (Dales 1977), the appearance of steppe-related ceramics on the elaborately fortified sites in Margiana, and unquestionably significant technological advances, such as the advent of mounted pastoral nomadism at approximately the same period of time (Kuzmina 1980). The record simply cannot be interpreted as an autonomous response to local environmental conditions; some degradation of the hydrological regime in the Kopet Dagh piedmont strip may have occurred (Dolukhanov 1981), but the entire shift and expansion of settlements took place on a scale and in areas not explicable by consideration of ecological data alone (cf. Tosi, this volume). The massive fortifications of the major sites and their obvious planning suggests that the colonization did not take place under totally peaceful conditions. Similarly, the metallurgical industry, including sophisticated weapons, evolved much more rapidly throughout Central Asia and the Indo-Iranian borderlands during the Late Bronze and Early Iron Age than in immediately preceding periods; these developments must be associated with advances in transportation, the rise of mounted pastoral nomadism, and the subsequent apparent instability that seems to have prevailed during the second millennium BC. Critical technologies existed, the acceptance of which was not accidental but essential to the societies caught up in the larger historical process.

This colonization or establishment of sites in previously unoccupied areas does not represent a continuous evolutionary advance in social terms from previous developments in Central Asia. In many respects, the societies inhabiting the lowland sites in Margiana and Bactria seem less complex than their Middle and Early Bronze predecessors in southern Turkmenistan. Thus, excavations at Sapalli-tepe (Askarov 1973) in southwestern Surkhandarya province (Uzbekistan) of a central fortified area (82 × 82 m) revealed the presence of eight separate multi-room complexes, each of which apparently were inhabited by several families and contained separate pottery kilns with little internal specialization distinguishing one complex from another. The documentation of domestic pottery production at Sapalli contrasts sharply with the presumably earlier evidence of a special potters' quarter, containing more than 60 two-tiered potters' kilns, at Altyn-depe in southeastern Turkmenistan (Masson 1981: 141).

Similarly, there is less evidence for social differentiation in the mortuary remains from Sapalli than from Altyn despite the excellent preservation of elaborate metal artifacts, semi-precious stones, seal amulets, and even textiles, including the remains of silk clothing, at the former site. The graves at Sapalli included 125 individual and 13 collective burials (Askarov 1977: 38) in contrast with the graves from Altyn where roughly 2/3 of the adult burials occur in collective graves (Kircho, personal communication). The richest tombs at Sapalli only contained about 50 objects, primarily pottery vessels, and females usually were buried with more objects than males. The number of goods in the graves seemed to depend upon the age of the deceased with infant and children's graves containing fewer gifts, possibly suggesting that status was achieved, not ascribed nor inherited. Although numerous finely fashioned artifacts indicative of craft specialization occur, the distributional evidence in the Sapalli graves suggests little social differentiation beyond that of sex and age.

Craft production, particularly metallurgy, continues to evolve at the same time that society appears to have become less complex and internally differentiated. At Shortughai in northeastern Afghanistan, for example, metal artifacts are more common and impressive in the post-Harappan periods III and IV when architecture (and other evidence for social complexity) appears to have declined in quality and scale of workmanship (Francfort, personal communication). Other sites in southern Bactria, such as a circular 'temple' complex at Dashli 3 (Sarianidi 1977: 34–40), are more difficult to interpret, and current excavations on the largest urban sites in Margiana, particularly Gonur 1 (Sarianidi, personal communication), undoubtedly will change our understanding of the character of these lowland settlements. But a model of evolutionary progression from simple to complex social orders will remain invalid or represent a gross simplification of what must have been an extremely complex historical process.

The Central Asian data also reveal another anomaly difficult to interpret from a narrowly conceived evolutionary view of social reality. Excavated village sites contain the same range of goods and record the same activities as are documented for the larger urban sites. Thus, excavations at the earlier Middle Bronze site of Taichanak-depe (Shchetenko 1968) (c. 1 ha.) in the central piedmont zone of southern Turkmenistan uncovered more than 20 rooms over a 400 sq. m excavated area which formed three separate domestic complexes; three rooms (17–19) in the northwestern complex, one of which was thought to be used for grain storage, contained female figurines and one a silver Maltese-cross-shaped seal. Male figurines, generally a rarer item in the material cultural assemblage of Namazga-related sites, also were found as were agate, carnelian, and lapis lazuli beads, a leaden artifact, and part of another compartmented bronze seal; pottery kilns and slag fragments and clay ladles were discovered suggesting local metallurgical production. These data (cf. Shchetenko 1970: 50), as well as those from later sites like Sapalli, imply that the urban/rural dichotomy was not particularly pronounced relative to what is known of the Mesopotamian pattern (and would that there were more excavated Meso-potamian villages) as, for example, attested by the contrast in funerary remains from the Early Dynastic village settlement of al-Ubaid with that of the neighbouring city of Ur (cf. Adams 1966: 100–1). It is perhaps reminiscent of the pattern now known from Indus Valley sites, as at the small village site of Allahdino (Shaffer 1982) where metal artifacts made from silver, gold, and lead – though interestingly and in contrast to Taichanak-depe no evidence for local production – were found together with seals with Harappan script and standard-ized Harappan pottery.

Simple models of internal growth and differentiation cannot explain the Central Asian data, particularly the late third–early second millennium establishment of settlements throughout Margiana and Bactria. Analogies must be drawn to later historical periods in which peoples, like the Yueh Chih, moved into Central Asia, initiating a reaction and displacement far to the south on the Indian subcontinent (for a recent in-depth analysis of early nomadic state organization in Central Asia cf. Barfield 1981). Archaeological data suggests that this pattern of penetration began in the late prehistoric period, though, of course, the details and relative strengths of the interacting groups were different. The historical record, how-ever, only provides a clue as to the complexity of the pro-cesses involved. The archaeological data must be examined from a broad inter-regional perspective, taking account of Late Bronze Age developments from Baluchistan and the eastern Iranian plateau north to the steppes of Kazakhstan. This data should be compared to later historical evidence, but more importantly analysed by reference to structural studies on the dialectical tensions and interactions between settled and nomadic societies, perhaps best exemplified in the writings of Lattimore (1951). Correspondences and disjunctions then will emerge which will help us reconstruct the Late Bronze Age pattern of expansion.

Historical events and structural factors should not be confused, but the tendency among contemporary processual archaeologists as well as among historians of the *Annales* school (cf. Kinser 1981) is to minimize the importance of the former. Human-willed history is reduced to natural history and rendered incredible as a result. The logic of events must be appreciated through analyses of the structural bases of the societies that came into contact or formed the given conjunc-ture. A difficulty with contemporary archaeological expla-nations for change, such as population pressure, trade, or the like, is that as commonly employed they overlook or dismiss the role of intentionality in the process. To return to the Central Asian example, the expansion of Late Bronze Age peoples from Turkmenistan and possibly Iranian Khorassan east and south into neighbouring, apparently less developed regions could be interpreted as being due to population pressure or to the need for materials from other regions. It would be easy to 'prove' either hypothesis. What is missing is reference to the political calculus that stimulated and made possible either or both demographic growth and control of

trade routes. Population may have increased in the presumed Turkmenistan heartland for the simple reason that there was room to expand at the expense of weaker neighbours; the opportunity generated the expansion as much as, if not more than, any inherent tendency explained by reference to favour-able and productive agricultural conditions. Similarly, an explanation focusing on access to or control of trade routes must note how the movement into Bactria or Baluchistan seems to coincide with the disappearance or retraction of Harappan remains; again, an opportunity was seized which was the result of conscious, self-motivated action. All other aspects of this Late Bronze phenomenon, including the fortifi-cations and presence of steppe-like ceramics, must be interpreted in a manner which emphasizes the political nature of the processes involved, particularly the desire for different societies or elites within complex societies to conquer, exploit, or somehow benefit from the relations they establish with neighbouring peoples. To a great extent, human history con-sists of deliberate, frequently brutal, and forcible attempts to seize or maintain power.

In *Capital* Marx's discussion of the effects of the Great Discoveries on the birth of capitalism follows and is logically secondary to his analysis of the expropriation of the agricul-tural population and emergence of a dispossessed wage-labour class in medieval Europe. The analysis of events stimulating and facilitating the transition to capitalism are treated only after the internal structural bases for this development have been examined. The priority given to structural factors, how-ever, does not lead to a dismissal of the seemingly fortuitous conjuncture of events that profoundly affected the subsequent 'culture trajectories' of both Old and New World civilizations:

> The discovery of gold and silver in America, the extir-pation, enslavement and entombment in mines of the aboriginal population, the beginning of the conquest and looting of the East Indies, the turning of Africa into a warren for the commercial hunting of black-skins, signalized the rosy dawn of the era of capitalist pro-duction. These idyllic proceedings are the chief moments of primitive accumulation . . .
>
> These methods (or momenta) depend in part on brute force, e.g., the colonial system. But they all employ the power of the State, the concentrated and organized force of society, to hasten, hothouse fashion, the process of transformation of the feudal mode of production into the capitalist mode, and to shorten the transition. Force is the midwife of every old society pregnant with a new one. It is itself an economic power.   (1906: 823–4)

We need only add that midwives sometimes engage in life-saving operations.

Notes

1 Unfortunately, this article cannot document how Childe's views were distorted by these practitioners and later unfairly cari-catured by those interested in overturning this doctrine. It is appropriate in the context of a book on Marxism and archae-

ology, however, to at least note ironically that the discipline's supreme prehistorian has been typed as an evolutionist by anthropologists (e.g. Harris 1968) and a modified diffusionist by archaeologists.

2 The subject is worth a separate detailed study. Some difficulties include: the processes of and purposes for capital accumulation among early states; the scale of surplus production and exchange in antiquity; the transferability of critically important technologies, such as metal working and horse breeding, from core to peripheral *or* peripheral to core areas; and the simultaneous existence of multiple world-systems and their effect on analysing core–core and core–peripheral relations. While their interpretations are not without difficulties, both Weber (1976) and Finley (1973) have discussed at length the limited character of capital formation in 'ancient economies'. Difficulties with the Wallersteinian model that can be documented archaeologically are presented in my forthcoming article entitled 'The ancient economy, transferable technologies, and the Bronze Age world-system: a view from the northeastern frontier of the ancient Near East'. Some scholars (e.g. Ekholm 1980), however, prefer to lump ancient, medieval, and capitalist world-systems into a single overarching type, exhibiting identical evolutionary and devolutionary patterns. While such a general perspective may provide insights, a focus on differences between pre-capitalist world-systems seems to me to be a more useful and illuminating way to proceed.

3 Yoffee's important and admirable critique of evolutionism is, I believe, fundamentally mistaken on this point. Although he admits that 'it would be fatuous to discount totally the occurrences of discontinuities produced by exogenous developments' (1979: 10), he argues that the tendency of evolutionary models is to explain development internally but collapse externally. My assessment is that archaeological reconstructions of both evolutionary and devolutionary processes today emphasize internal variables. The classic Mayan collapse, for example, is interpreted as a process internal to the Mayan cultural system, and references to Mexican invasions are denounced as heretical. Culture change and decline in the American Southwest similarly are viewed as responses to local ecological conditions, and unequivocal evidence for contact, economic exchange and possible political dependency upon Mexico (Weigand 1977; Weigand, Harbottle and Sayre 1977) again receives little notice. It would be easy to continue this list, and I am forced to consider Yoffee's opposite opinion as clouded by or as a reaction to the egregious abuse of invasions, marauding peoples, and the like for explaining cultural collapse in Mesopotamia by earlier archaeologists and Assyriologists. His illuminating discussion of internal factors leading to the collapse of Old Babylonian society serves as a valuable corrective to such accounts.

4 Clark's writings are exceptional in this respect. In *Mesolithic Prelude*, for example, he not only belatedly acknowledges that N.Ya. Marr and K. Marx were separate individuals, but also argues for a vision of history almost diametrically opposed to that of Adams (Clark 1980: 101). In an earlier essay (1979) the political implications of this vision are made more explicit: ancient temples are likened to banks and mutual assurance corporations as 'mechanisms of social well-being' (*ibid*.: 10); ruling classes need to live luxurious and sophisticated lives in order that artisans produce masterworks (*ibid*.: 12); in short, 'if our common aim is to enhance our lives, our guiding light must surely be . . . hierarchy rather than equality . . . ' (*ibid*.: 19). It is refreshing to find such a political viewpoint so explicitly and well articulated. Would that younger processual or positivist archaeologists were as straightforward or *thought through the political implications of their view of history and society as consistently* as the former Disney Professor at Cambridge. For a

similar explicit formulation of the political implications of evolutionary theory compare Cohen (1981: 207).

5 This statement ignores small scatters of Namazga III related materials in the northernmost Kelleli oasis in Margiana, a possible Early Bronze or Namazga IV occupation at Kelleli 4 (Masimov 1981b: 466), and is based on the presently known distribution of settlements in Bactria. Drs J.-C. Gardin and H.-P. Francfort (personal communication) believe that the absence of earlier remains in Bactria reflects the lack of systematic exploration in northwestern Afghanistan, particularly in the northern foothills of the Hindu Kush. Their argument is complex and should serve as a working hypothesis for future research, but I remain unconvinced that additional investigations will alter significantly the general picture presented in this essay. A sudden peopling or colonization also seems to characterize northern Bactria (or southern Uzbekistan) where adequate reconnaissance and survey work has been conducted. Northwestern Afghanistan must contain an additional record of indigenous developments or even possibly sequences with affinities to Aeneolithic and Bronze Age sites excavated south of the Hindu Kush, such as Mundigak. But the weight of the evidence for Bactria – as is becoming clear for northern Baluchistan (Jarrige and Meadow 1980) as well – argues for a massive shift in relations, suggesting the actual movement of peoples south and east from Turkmenistan and possibly Iranian Khorassan at the end of the third millennium BC. Even if I am mistaken and future surveys reveal a totally different picture, there exist other areas in Central Asia, such as Khoresmia and the Fergana valley, that exhibit sharp chronological and regional discontinuities to allow us to construct a theoretically similar process of sudden, externally induced change or forcible incorporation into larger historical processes.

Bibliography

Adams, R.McC. 1966. *The Evolution of Urban Society*. Chicago: Aldine.
   1974. Anthropological perspectives on ancient trade. *Current Anthropology* 15: 239–58.
Askarov, A. 1973. *Sapallitepa*. Tashkent: FAN.
   1977. *Drevnezemledel'cheskaya kul'tura epokhi bronzi yuga Uzbekistana*. Tashkent: FAN.
Barfield, T. 1981. The Hsiung-nu imperial confederacy: organization and foreign policy. *The Journal of Asian Studies* 41: 45–61.
Binford, L. 1972. *An Archaeological Perspective*. New York: Seminar Press.
Carneiro, R.L. 1970. A theory of the origin of the state. *Science* 169: 733–8.
Clark, G. 1979. Archaeology and human diversity. *Annual Review of Anthropology* 8: 1–19.
   1980. *Mesolithic Prelude*. Edinburgh: Edinburgh University Press.
Cohen, R. 1981. Evolutionary epistemology and human values. *Current Anthropology* 22: 201–18.
Dales, G. 1977. Shifting trade patterns between the Iranian plateau and the Indus Valley in the third millennium BC. In J. Deshayes (ed.), *Le plateau iranien et l'Asie centrale des origines à la conquête islamique*, pp.67–78. Paris: CNRS. Colloque International no. 567.
Daniel, G. 1976. *A Hundred and Fifty Years of Archaeology*. Cambridge: Harvard University Press.
Dolukhanov, P. 1981. Ecological prerequisites of early farming in southern Turkmenia. In P.L. Kohl (ed.), *The Bronze Age Civilization of Central Asia: Recent Soviet Discoveries*, pp. 359–85. New York: M.E. Sharpe.
Ekholm, K. 1980. On the limitations of civilization: the structure and dynamics of global systems. *Dialectical Anthropology* 5: 155–66.

Ekholm, K. and J. Friedman, 1979. 'Capital' imperialism and exploitation in ancient world systems. In M.T. Larsen (ed.), *Power and Propaganda: A Symposium on Ancient Empires*, pp. 41–58. Copenhagen: Akademisk Forlag.

Finley, M.I. 1973. *The Ancient Economy*. London: Chatto and Windus.

Flannery, K. 1972. The cultural evolution of civilizations. *Annual Review of Ecology and Systematics* 3: 399–426.

Francfort, J.-P. and M.-H. Pottier, 1978. Sondage préliminaire sur l'établissement protohistorique Harapéen et post-Harapéen de Shortugai (Afghanistan du N.-E.). *Arts Asiatiques* 34: 29–79.

Harris, M. 1968. *The Rise of Anthropological Theory*. New York: Crowell.

Isbell, W.H. and K.J. Schreiber, 1978. Was Huari a state? *American Antiquity* 43: 372–89.

Jarrige, J.-F. and R.H. Meadow, 1980. The antecedents of civilization in the Indus Valley. *Scientific American* 242: 122–33.

Kinser, S. 1981. *Annaliste* paradigm? The geohistorical structuralism of Fernand Braudel. *The American Historical Review* 86: 63–105.

Kristiansen, K. 1981. Economic models for Bronze Age Scandinavia: towards an integrated approach. In A. Sheridan and G. Bailey (eds.), *Economic Archaeology: Towards an Integration of Ecological and Social Approaches*, pp. 239–303. B.A.R. International Series 96. Oxford: British Archaeological Reports.

Kuzmina, E.E. 1980. Etapi razvitiya kolesnovo transporta Srednei Azii v epokhu aeneolita i bronzi. *Vestnik Drevnei Istorii* 4: 11–35.

Las Casas, B. de, 1974. *The Devastation of the Indies: A Brief Account*. New York: Seabury Press.

Lattimore, O. 1951. *Inner Asian Frontiers of China*. Boston: Beacon Press.

Leacock, E.B. 1972. Editor's introduction. In F. Engels, *The Origin of the Family, Private Property, and the State*, pp. 7–67. New York: International Publishers.

Legros, D. 1977. Chance, necessity, and mode of production: a Marxist critique of cultural evolutionism. *American Anthropologist* 79: 26–41.

Lowie, R. 1929. *The Origin of the State*. New York: Harcourt, Brace and World.

MacNeish, R.S. 1967. A summary of the subsistence. In D.S. Byers (ed.), *The Prehistory of the Tehuacan Valley*, vol. 1: *Environment and Subsistence*, pp. 290–309. Austin: University of Texas Press.

Marx, K. 1906. *Capital: A Critique of Political Economy*. New York: The Modern Library.

Masimov, I.S. 1981a. The study of Bronze Age sites in the Lower Murghab. In P.L. Kohl (ed.), *The Bronze Age Civilization of Central Asia: Recent Soviet Discoveries*, pp. 194–220. New York: M.E. Sharpe.

1981b. Raskopki v Kellelinskom oazise. *Arkheologicheskie Otkritiya – 1980 goda*: 466–7.

Masson, V.M. 1981. Urban centers of early class society. In P.L. Kohl (ed.), *The Bronze Age Civilization of Central Asia: Recent Soviet Discoveries*, pp. 135–48. New York: M.E. Sharpe.

Masson, V.M. and T.P. Kiyatkina, 1981. Man at the dawn of urbanization. In P.L. Kohl (ed.), *The Bronze Age Civilization of Central Asia: Recent Soviet Discoveries*, pp. 107–34. New York: M.E. Sharpe.

Renfrew, C. 1978. Trajectory discontinuity and morphogenesis: the implications of catastrophe theory for archaeology. *American Antiquity* 43: 203–22.

Rowlands, M. 1973. Modes of exchange and the incentives for trade, with reference to later European prehistory. In C. Renfrew (ed.), *The Explanation of Culture Change: Models in Prehistory*, pp. 589–600. London: Duckworth.

Sanders, W.T. and B.J. Price, 1968. *Mesoamerica: The Evolution of a Civilization*. New York: Random House.

Sarianidi, V.I. 1977. *Drevniye Zemledel'tsii Afghanistana*. Moscow: Nauk.

1981. Margiana in the Bronze Age. In P.L. Kohl (ed.), *The Bronze Age Civilization of Central Asia: Recent Soviet Discoveries*, pp. 165–93. New York: M.E. Sharpe.

Service, E.R. 1962. *Primitive Social Organization*. New York: Random House.

1975. *Origins of the State and Civilization: The Process of Cultural Evolution*. New York: Random House.

Shaffer, J. 1982. Harappan culture: a reconsideration. In G.L. Possehl (ed.), *Harappan Civilization: A Contemporary Perspective*, pp. 41–50. New Delhi: Oxford and IBH, and American Institute of Indian Studies.

Shchetenko, A.S. 1968. Raskopki poseleniya epokhi bronzi Taichanakdepe. *Karakumskie Drevnosti* 2: 18–24.

1970. Raskopki melkikh poselenii epokhi bronzi. *Karakumskie Drevnosti* 3: 33–50.

Thompson, E.P. 1978. *The Poverty of Theory and Other Essays*. London: The Merlin Press.

Wallerstein, I. 1974. *The Modern World-System: Capitalist Agriculture and the Origins of the European World-Economy in the Sixteenth Century*. New York: Academic Press.

1980. *The Modern World-System II: Mercantilism and the Consolidation of the European World-Economy, 1600–1750*. New York: Academic Press.

Watson, P.J. and S.A. LeBlanc, 1973. Excavation and analysis of Halafian materials from southeastern Turkey. Paper presented at the seventy-second annual meeting of the American Anthropological Association, New Orleans.

Weber, M. 1976. *The Agrarian Sociology of Ancient Civilizations*. London: New Left Books.

Weigand, P. 1977. The prehistory of the state of Zacatecas. In C.E. Sánchez (ed.), *Anuario de Historia Zacatecana*. Zacatecas: Universidad Autónoma de Zacatecas.

Weigand, P., G. Harbottle and E.V. Sayre, 1977. Turquoise sources and source analysis: Mesoamerica and the southwestern U.S.A. In T.K. Earle and J.E. Ericson (eds.), *Exchange Systems in Prehistory*, pp. 15–34. New York: Academic Press.

White, L. 1960. Foreword. In M. Sahlins and E.R. Service (eds.), *Evolution and Culture*. Ann Arbor: University of Michigan Press.

Yoffee, N. 1979. The decline and rise of Mesopotamian civilization: an ethnoarchaeological perspective on the evolution of social complexity. *American Antiquity* 44: 5–35.

Chapter 11

**The transformation of
Asiatic formations:
The case of Late
Prehispanic Mesoamerica**
John Gledhill

Introduction

It would be hard to accuse Mesoamerican archaeologists generally of being atheoretical. If the cultural-ecological and cultural-materialist research strategies have been pushed to their limits anywhere it is here. 'Marxism' itself has come to embrace such a diverse range of positions that those who do not share the present writer's sympathy for Marx's political conclusions might now be able to adopt terms drawn from Marxist theory without any additional embarrassment. There is no need here to rehearse the arguments against vulgar materialism and against the identification of Marxist theory with vulgar materialism. What the uncommitted reader expects to be shown is how the employment of Marxist concepts can lead to the advance of theory.

This paper is addressed to what I see as two central and inter-related weaknesses in the mainstream of North American work on the explanation of cultural process in later Meso-american prehistory. First there is a continuing tendency to advocate demo-techno-ecological determinist explanations for sociocultural change despite, in some cases, the acceptance of arguments which undermine a reductionist approach to social and political process. The recent statement by Sanders *et al.* (1979) on the role of irrigation illustrates this rather well. Secondly, there has been a marked tendency to attempt to understand pre-colonial Mesoamerican reality in terms of ahistorical categories, through the uncritical employment of con-

cepts of 'economic stratification' and formal economic categories whose use outside the capitalist system must be qualified.[1] Marxist theory can, I think, be usefully employed to point out these difficulties and to pose alternative conceptualizations. So can some facets of Weberian theory. It is not my intention here to try to appropriate archaeology, or rather prehistory, for Marxism and thereby replicate some of the problems which have dogged the so-called 'Marxist anthropology' (Gledhill 1981a). This is a paper about Mesoamerican prehistory and general theoretical problems in the analysis of pre-capitalist social formations, not an exercise in Marxology; and I do not believe that Marx himself ever set out to provide a comprehensive theoretical account of pre-capitalist formations, let alone a theory of social evolution. Even had he done so, he would have been the first to insist that his work should be judged solely on its scientific merits. Although discussion will begin with some of Marx's own writing, it is pointless to debate issues in terms of the fidelity or otherwise of any substantive thesis to Marx's own position.

In 1519 the *Conquistadores* began the process of subsuming a non-European civilization in Mexico which, in terms of their own experience, presented a paradoxical blend of the barbarous and the magnificent. The Aztec ruler Moctezuma Xocoyotzin presided over an empire apparently held together more by terror than by administrative sophistication and ideology, from a capital city which did not compare unfavourably with its occidental counterparts. Neo-evolutionist theory has made it almost a habit of mind to conceptualize the pre-colonial states of highland Mesoamerica as the crucial test of the hypothesis of the existence of structural regularities in the processes of social evolution in historically independent regions. Yet it is perhaps open to question whether we in fact dispose of an adequate set of concepts to make these broad cross-cultural comparisons effectively. Before he read Morgan, Marx's response to this question was to include the New World states among those formations characterized under the 'Asiatic' mode of production (AMP). As is well known, ortho-dox Marxism came to reject the AMP, whilst Wittfogel (1957) partially resurrected it in the form of 'Oriental Despotism' and turned it back on Marxism in the form of a critique of the Soviet Union. Wittfogel's influence on Mesoamerican pre-history requires no further comment, and this has complicated discussion of the AMP in particular, and Marxist theory in general, ever since (Carrasco 1978).

The concept of an Asiatic Mode of Production (AMP)

In Marx's formulation of the AMP, there can be no pri-vate ownership of land, only private (and communal) possession (Marx 1959: 791; Marx 1973: 472–4). In contrast to the feudal mode, there is no landlord class distinct from the state. Since the state combines sovereignty with a monopoly of ultimate title to land, the appropriation of the surplus product from the direct producer requires no special political or economic pressure 'beyond that common to all subjection to the state', and tribute as a form of pre-capitalist ground-rent therefore coincides with state taxation in the AMP. Marx's emphasis on the clan/village 'commune' in the *Formen* text might seem to underline a distinction between Asiatic and Feudal formations, in so far as feudal landlordism is seen as incompatible with the community's retention of effective con-trol over the allocation and distribution of its lands to its members. The scheme of distinctions developed in the text itself is, however, one which generates the set Asiatic, Ancient and Germanic Modes (Marx 1973: 486). The discussion is structured by the question of the historical preconditions for the development of the capitalist mode of production. His-torical developments in medieval Europe are treated in a con-crete way, not as expressions of the inner dynamic of a 'Feudal Mode of Production' construct associated uniquely with Europe, but in relation to antecedent Ancient and Ger-manic forms.

This is important in the light of subsequent debates within Marxism. Despite the valuable textual observations made by Godelier (1970) on the development of Marx's own thought, it remains clear that in practice the AMP lends itself to the 'stagnation'/'dynamism' dichotomy between East and West which is so deeply ingrained in European thought (Hindess and Hirst 1975: 201–6). Given the cellular structure of autarkic village communities as the socio-economic foun-dation on which the state is superimposed, Marx's construct can generate a long-term dynamic for Asiatic social formations in which political boundaries shift and empires and dynasties rise and fall, whilst basic socio-economic conditions remain stationary across millennia (see, for example, Marx 1959: 796). Taken literally, such a view would clearly be absurd empirically. Wittfogel, who had a clear ideological stake in arguing for structural continuity in 'Oriental' regimes, almost reverses the argument. Oriental societies can and do experience the development of private property in land, commodity pro-duction and mercantile capitalist elements; they are dis-tinguished historically by the fact that the state remains 'stronger than society', centralized political control placing limits, after a point, on private capital accumulation and the effective political representation of private economic interests (Wittfogel 1935).

Much recent Marxist writing has been opposed to the ideological connotations of the 'Asiatic' label for obvious reasons (Bailey 1981), but many have remained reluctant to adopt the solution of supplanting the AMP construct entirely with a generalized feudal mode. Amin has proposed the con-cept of a 'tributary' mode as the 'normal' successor of a uni-versal 'primitive-communal' mode (Amin 1976: 9–16). The feudal mode represents a 'developed' form of this, where the village community loses its *dominium eminens* over the soil to a landowning class. Among Mesoamericanists writing within a Marxist framework, Carrasco (1978) is somewhat more influ-enced by Wittfogel's ideas, though his starting point is classically Marxist: where the direct producers retain possession of their means of economic reproduction, surplus can only be appropriated through 'extra-economic' coercion. Carrasco contends that both 'feudal' and 'Asiatic' systems share the characteristic that political relations organize the distribution of means of production and effect the extraction of surplus product. He concludes that: 'The differences between the two systems are fundamentally differences between distinct forms of political organisation and the state' (1978: 71). Here the emphasis seems to have shifted towards the degree to which political power (and hence, derivatively, economic control) is centralized in the social formation, with 'despotism' and 'feudalism' representing simply two poles of variation along a continuum (*ibid.*: 72). This line of argument leads us back not simply to Wittfogel, but also to Weber.

Since ideal-type constructs are essentially heuristic, Weber's methodology permitted him considerable scope for varying his definitions, and it would be pointless to catalogue his different accounts of feudalism and related concepts such as 'patrimonialism', 'sultanism' and so forth here. It is import-ant, however, to note that Weber's definition of feudalism as a 'structure of domination' (distinguished from patrimonialism and charisma) severs any necessary connection with landlord-ism (Weber 1951: 33). In the case of the type of feudalism based on fiefs (*Lehensfeudalismus*), we are dealing, in Weber's terms, with a system of administration in which rights to exercise authority are delegated in return for services of a military or administrative character through a contractual relationship of personal loyalty between lord and vassal

(Weber 1978: 255–7). Fiefs may involve the granting of economic rights over land and labour, fiscal rights (to tax) or political powers, juridical and military authority (*ibid.*: 257). Naturally, the granting of these different powers is often separated, and few overlords in fief-based feudal regimes permit the system to develop to its ideal-typical extent, since their own authority becomes increasingly precarious as this state of affairs is approximated.

Weber distinguished *Lehensfeudalismus* from a set of other variants, chief of which was prebendalism. Here, within otherwise patrimonial, often highly politically centralized regimes, rulers grant benefices (rights to appropriate income) primarily, Weber suggested, as a matter of fiscal considerations. Benefices are granted 'on a personal basis in accordance with services, thus involving the possibility of promotion' (Weber 1978: 260). In concrete cases these distinctions tend to become somewhat blurred, and Weber was at pains to point out that the fief, though characteristic of the Occident, was not unique to it. Nevertheless, the primary function of the separation of the prebendal type was that of emphasizing the distinctive features of such formations as those of the Islamic Near East, Moghul India and Manchu China. This is therefore one approach to discussing the kind of variation to which Carrasco refers. It is not, however, likely to prove a very useful one unless we can move beyond ideal-typical constructs towards an understanding of the dynamic processes which generate variation in terms of effective political, administrative and political-economic centralization. Moreover, these questions are complicated theoretically by recent work which has rejected the kind of model of the relationship between the state and the economy offered by Wittfogel for the Chinese case (Moulder 1977).[2]

Since Marx did not elaborate substantive theories of his pre-capitalist modes of production, we should briefly consider the claim that Marxism provides a theory of history in the form of 'historical materialism'. Carrasco's approach focuses on political variation, arguing that relations of production 'are' political relations in Asiatic and feudal systems (1978: 71). This view leads to a number of theoretical difficulties, since it does not, as it stands, tell us what distinguishes the feudal mode of production, say, from the ancient mode within Marxist theory or any other framework. Is it something to do with the form of the polity or with the role played by politics with respect to the economy? This brings us to fundamental issues regarding the way we should conceptualize and explain the structure of social formations as totalities.

Orthodox Marxism founds its analysis of politics and the state on the concept of class. Marx's own historical writings throw doubt on explanations for historical change which reduce politics to the simple expression of economic interests and power.[3] In the case of pre-capitalist formations, the issues seem doubly complex, given the general consensus among western Marxists today that 'non-economic instances are dominant', despite their differing views on what determines the total structure of social formations (Kahn and Llobera

1981; Gledhill and Rowlands, 1982). All forms of property relations, capitalist and pre-capitalist, evidently depend on specific legal and political conditions. The base of the capitalist mode of production is a particular form of economic subsumption of the direct producer, but this does not prevent other modes resting on different forms of economic subsumption, as Hindess and Hirst suggested in denying that serfdom is a necessary characteristic of the feudal mode of production (Hindess and Hirst 1975: 234–42). Whilst this approach yields some genuine insights into the reproduction of feudal formations, it leaves the political dimension quite indeterminate. The landlord *class* is politically dominant in the sense that the feudal state guarantees their property rights and defends feudal exploitation, representing the interests of landlords *vis à vis* peasants. Yet landlords may lack local or national political power, or at least be subordinated politically to the centre. Furthermore, it might be argued that the exigencies of combatting tendencies to political decentralization might prompt a centralized state to take measures which would damage the economic power of landlords were these feasible. The simple deterministic relationships between socioeconomic structure and polity posited by orthodox Marxism clearly cannot obtain.

For Weberians, some of these problems are resolved *a priori*. Economic or social class (Weber 1978: 302–5) is only one possible modality of stratification, the distinction between 'status groups' and classes lending itself with evident facility to the discussion of pre-capitalist societies. Besides removing stratification from any necessary economic basis, Weber rejected 'class struggle' as the invariant force beneath macrosocial change. This is perhaps the crucial issue, since it can be argued that the notion that change must be the product of concrete class struggle is the way in which Marxist theory avoids a teleological conception of history. In criticizing Althusserian Marxism for precisely this vice, Poulantzas (1975) argued that an objective definition of class structure must involve political and ideological as well as economic criteria. Even in the capitalist mode of production, the capitalist class cannot confront the working class in a 'purely economic' way. Unfortunately, Poulantzas was then forced to concede that it was impossible to predict the political behaviour of a given stratum of a class in a concrete struggle from a supposedly 'objective' account of their economic class interests and situation (Cutler *et al.* 1977: 189–206).

Again, such problems seem to be magnified in precapitalist contexts. Here considerable attention has been paid to the extent to which the exploited classes are incapable of constituting classes 'for themselves', and are thus unable to achieve forms of consciousness and autonomous political organization which would permit them to transform society in their own interests (Godelier 1977a; Islamoğlu and Keyder 1977; Terray 1975). Many writers on the AMP have accordingly come to posit *intra*-class contradictions as the positive impetus to change, whilst the distinction between 'principal' (rich versus poor citizens) and 'fundamental' (master–slave) contradictions has been used similarly in literature on the ancient world (Vernant 1976). These reformulations do not necessarily imply that inter-class conflict without *für sich* consciousness plays no role in shaping the destiny of pre-capitalist formations. They do, however, make it all the more difficult to explain change in conventional class terms. As the links between political process and the economy become more indirect, it is tempting to reverse the lines of causality associated with materialist theories of social evolution.

That little would be achieved by a negation of the 'economic interpretation of history' through the substitution of logically equivalent 'political' or even 'cultural' determinism can be illustrated in preliminary fashion with the classic case of Imperial China. Under the Manchus, centralized administration was effected through scholar-officials (*literati*), in theory openly recruited through the examination system. If we emphasize the prebendal nature of the system, power and authority seem to stem from the monopolization of official posts and to be unconnected with landlordism; the larger part of the income of the *literati* derived from unaudited surcharges on the taxes they collected (Weber 1951; Wang 1973). Marxists who reject the AMP maintain that the Chinese system was, in fact, feudal. As well as the Manchu noble households and officials of various grades who derived their income from peasant corvée on state land grants or taxation, China also had a lower ranking upper class stratum of private landlords. The latter were urban absentees who lived from rents extracted from peasants cultivating widely dispersed and relatively small landholdings scattered through different villages and regions, along with profits from usury and commerce. The two categories of tax-dependents and landlords also partially overlapped: many of the *literati* were also landlords, and the 'gentry' landlords, who held degrees but were not necessarily officials, in turn derived material advantage from a closer relationship with the state apparatuses in terms of the enforcement of rent payments (Chang 1962: 132—6). The gentry probably also held a disproportionate share of the private land-base.

Although landlords and *literati* remain distinct, there were clear indirect structural relationships between landlordism and bureaucracy, as Barrington Moore (1968) has observed. In practice, the achievement of official rank demanded the support of a wealthy family, so that directly or indirectly, landed property predominated in the recruitment of *literati*. The wealth accumulated by office-holding could be translated back into landed wealth, so that the private wealth accumulation of the gentry probably, on aggregate, exceeded the disposable resources of the state, with evident political implications. Although the degree of effective bureaucratization of administration in the modern sense was severely limited (Moulder 1977: 55—6), the Chinese state did take measures to prevent its fiscal-administrative agents from establishing local ties: they were repeatedly moved around from region to region, and forbidden to hold posts in areas where their family had lands (Weber 1951). But this strategy also limited their effectiveness as agencies of central authority in the face of

powerful local landlord cliques, who could also manipulate officials in the centre through private ties (Ch'ü 1969). The Chinese state defended the rights of landlords and merchants in the face of rioting over levels of rent or prices, and it may be argued that the state's representation of private economic interests was an index of its weakness relative to local landlord-gentry economic power (Moulder 1977: 61—2).

Both from the public order standpoint and from the standpoint of effecting a greater centralization of power, the state should have sought to curb private excesses. Successful state interventions of this kind are, however, rare in Chinese history. The empires periodically succumbed to the 'feudalizing', centrifugal tendencies in their political economy, the imbalance between centre and periphery created by the localized, class control of resources. Diminution of internal trade and revenue crisis brought increases in tax demands. Now the central authority became the primary target of peasant revolts, and landlord—peasant class alliance was possible. Yet despite this so-called 'dynastic cycle', an imperial polity was always reconstituted after the short-lived but signal achievements of the Ch'in were stabilized by the Han in the first century BC.

Two distinct lines of inquiry seem germane to resolving the apparent paradox of Chinese unification. The first, a world-systems approach, would ask whether the tendency to recentralize was a function of the limitations or even non-viability of more localized political economies, from the standpoint primarily of elements of the ruling class. Secondly, we could examine the extent to which the type of economic class stratification found in China was itself dependent in the long term on the coercive powers of central authority. This second issue clearly entails analysis of inter-class relationships, and an analysis that is dynamic, focusing on the processes of class struggle in the countryside within the matrix of contradictions between landlord and state, centre and periphery. It is the balance of social forces created by the totality of these conflicts and oppositions, played out historically subject to varying ecological and geographical conditions,[4] which determines the long-term configuration and developmental possibilities of the formation concerned. An extended analysis aimed at determining the conditions underlying the balance of social forces in the Chinese case cannot be attempted here. But the analysis of the Aztec case will permit us to examine some of the basic issues raised by the Chinese example in more depth in another historical context. No resolution of the crucial problems of historical determination discussed above can, of course, be reached on the basis of only two or even several cases. Only exhaustive controlled cross-cultural comparison would be an appropriate methodology for that daunting task.

The Aztec social formation in 1519

The multiplicity of historical sources from the immediate post-conquest period, ranging from chronicles and ethnographies to administrative reports and archival data, seems to make an introductory static description of aboriginal institutions quite straightforward. In fact, of course, there are numerous methodological problems in ethnohistorical research, only a few of which can be touched on here. They do not, however, differ qualitatively from those generally encountered in historical or ethnographic research, and it is regrettable that few Mesoamerican archaeologists yet share the awareness of Sanders *et al.* (1979) that an integrated, co-operative blending of historical and archaeological research is the key to real advance. The fact that much of the supposed 'history' of the Aztecs is an essentially ideological construct may be off-putting to hard-boiled positivists. I suspect that most social anthropologists would feel that this is precisely why it is illuminating.

At the time of the conquest the Aztec empire was the dominant power in Mesoamerica. Michoacán and Oaxaca retained political autonomy in the highland regions, whilst the nature of Aztec dominance (and the substance of the term 'empire' perhaps) changed significantly beyond its core zone in the Basin of Mexico (Adams 1979; Barlow 1949; Katz 1978). The Yucatan Maya were outside the Aztec sphere of political incorporation, but these lowland centres were arguably crucial components of a larger world-economy whose structure is central to understanding the 'internal' political economy of the Aztecs (Gledhill and Larsen 1982). I will begin with a brief idealized account of the Aztec land tenure system as it existed at the time of conquest. The ruler of Tenochtitlan was theoretically but one of the heads of the Triple Alliance comprising the city-states of Tenochtitlan, Texcoco and Tlacopan. In practical terms the supremacy of the Aztec monarch was clearly established under Moctezuma Xocoyotzin (Ixtlilxochitl 1975: 450–1). Indeed, the political trend since Tenochtitlan overthrew Azcapotzalco hegemony had been one of continuous attempts to centralize power in the hands of the Aztec monarchy, within the structure of the state as well as within the alliance (Calnek 1974; 1978a; and see below). Authority within the state was distributed between holders of secular administrative offices, the priesthood and the military. To this structure corresponded 'Asiatic' forms of appropriation.

Lands worked by the corvée of free members of peasant communities (*macehualtin*) were assigned to the maintenance of the three departments of state. Lands designated for temple maintenance were called *tecpantlalli*, those for army provisioning were termed *milchimalli* (Carrasco 1978; Hicks 1974). With regard to the first category, lands dedicated to the support of secular administration, the indigenous terminology is more complex. Gibson (1964: 257) glosses the category *tecpantlalli* 'land of the community houses', but it clearly had the connotation of lands assigned to the palace of the king and the households of provincial governors. Such lands were inhabited and worked by a named category of persons, *tecpanpouhque*, who paid no tribute (Gibson 1964: 259; Hicks 1974: 244). This status seems to have been hereditary, but with the possibility of removal. It is unclear whether *tecpantlalli* was worked in common (Gibson 1964), but the labour system associated with it distinguishes it from another category of land set aside for secular administration,

tlatocamilli. This was land in each community assigned to supporting local office-holders and tribute collectors, worked by the *macehualtin*. In their struggles to combat Spanish expropriations, the Indians placed all the above types in the category 'land of the community'. The ruler's *tecpantlalli* might be seen as a form of patrimonial domain, but the other types unambiguously display the principle of attachment to the office, implying that the incumbent lacked rights of alienation.

Beside the plots dedicated to provisioning the state organizations, communities of *macehualtin* worked their own *calpullalli*. This community land pertained to the *barrios* (*calpultin*) into which residential communities were subdivided, individual households enjoying use-rights. It is quite clear that land rights within the *calpulli* corporations were distributed unequally in a way which does not correlate with household size (Carrasco 1978: 37; Gibson 1964: 267–8), and economic differentiation within peasant communities will be examined in more detail below. Priority must be given, however, to discussion of two further indigenous land categories, *pillalli* and *tecuhtlalli*.

After the conquest, the Indians correlated these 'lands of the nobility' *pillalli* and *tecuhtlalli*, with private, and therefore alienable, land in the Spanish sense. There is, however, no *a priori* justification for the assumption that this equation implies the substantive identity of European and aboriginal notions of property. The fact that native sources blur distinctions between 'renting' and 'buying' (Carrasco 1978: 27), for example, is quite predictable in a system in which it is frequently use-right rather than ultimate title which is theoretically being transferred. Nevertheless, many writers see *pillalli/tecuhtlalli* as sufficient to establish the existence of class relations based on landownership.

Following Zorita (1963), Katz argues that *pillalli* constituted private landed domains cultivated by a specific category of persons, the *mayeque*, who were tied to the land and transferred with it. He regards the combination of private landowning and 'bondsman' labour as 'feudalistic', though he doubts whether the trend was towards a fully feudalistic society (1972: 225–6). Others display less concern for the total structure of the formation, and concentrate on the evidence for land sales and purchase as part of a wider debate on the role of 'the market' in Aztec society (see Gledhill and Larsen 1982). An extreme version of this attitude is represented by Offner (1981), who argues for a 'lively real estate market' in Texcoco. Both lines of interpretation are challenged by Carrasco (1978; 1981). Whilst he does not deny the possibility of land sales, he argues against the notion of a significant market in land on the grounds that 'free' alienation was hedged about by political and status restrictions (Carrasco 1978: 27–8; 1981: 63–4). The distribution of land and labour is effected primarily through political and administrative channels. Land is appropriated by the nobility in the first instance by virtue of their status and public functions as a stratum (1978: 26), and *pillalli* constitutes 'generalized' office land, as distinct from land attached to the performance of specific duties like *tlatocamilli* (1981: 63). Similarly, Adams (1979) has defined the Aztec nobility as an 'Ottoman-style nobility of function' rather than a landowning class, although he focuses his analysis on a type of landed benefice assigned to tribute-collectors and does not discuss *pillalli* explicitly.

Whilst there clearly were mechanisms for the transfer of rights over land, and members of the merchant stratum (*pochteca*) are recorded as owning '*tierras propias*' (Gibson 1964: 263; Torquemada 1969, II: 546), *pillalli* was first and foremost patrimonial land of the nobility. The status of 'noble' (*pilli*, pl. *pipiltin*) was ascriptive and inherited bilaterally. Persons promoted to *pilli* status for valour were distinguished as *quauhpipiltin* (Calnek 1974: 202–3). In theory, the hereditary nobility of Tenochtitlan were descendants of the first king. Calnek (1978a) has argued that intermarriage between 'dynastic groups' which governed the warring city-states of pre-imperial times led to the consolidation of a pan-Basin aristocratic stratum. Bilateral status transmission permitted status claims to be made in different polities and succession was unstable; the system reflected underlying factionalism. Calnek suggests, however, that political centralization was ultimately effected through the mobilization of these cross-cutting ties: the authority of the rulers of subject states was gradually undermined through the distribution of largess to lower-ranking aristocrats with links to Tenochtitlan (Calnek 1978a: 467). All royal dynasties were closely related, however, and the opportunity to share in the imperial tribute base gave the lower-ranking nobles an interest transcending local loyalties.

Membership of the *pilli* category was not based on holding office or one of a proliferating series of titles, which only influenced an individual nobleman's rank (Calnek 1974: 193). Furthermore, the kinship system of the nobility clearly reflects political developments, but does not give us a clear picture of the social basis of the power and status of the dynastic groups in the first instance. Noble houses were headed by persons of *tecuhtli* status, whose households formed private redistribution centres and who assigned lands in their patrimonial domain to dependent *pipiltin* (Carrasco 1978: 25; Hicks 1974: 245). The 'seigneurial' appearance of this system should not be taken as implying an effective control of the distribution of *pillalli* by members of the *tecuhtli* stratum, but it does raise the general question of the role of control over land in the 'private sector', however defined, with respect to both the distribution of power and the appropriation of surplus product.

At this point it is essential to stress that private landholdings in Late Horizon Mesoamerica rather closely resemble the Chinese system described above. Owners held lands in many distant communities, whilst single communities contained holdings of multiple, urbanite absentee landlords (Gibson 1964: 263–4). Holdings were relatively small, scattered parcels. Yoatzin, *cacique* of Cuernavaca, held a total of up to 120 ha. in Morelos, plots ranging in size from 1 or 2 to 6.8 ha. (Riley 1978: 52). There was no intervention in the labour process by the landowner, and the primary structural significance of *pillalli* and *tecuhtlalli* seems to have been that landowning provided the nobility with a permanent means of appropriating dependent labour and its surplus beyond the income-yielding offices allocated by the state to individuals. The extent of this form of landholding is difficult to determine empirically from the historical data (mostly court cases), since in the confusion and opportunism which followed the conquest, Indian nobles deliberately blurred the distinction between land attached to offices and patrimonial holdings (Riley 1978: 55–6). The policies of Cortés also rapidly changed the pre-colonial pattern of dispersed distribution (Gibson 1964: 264). But up to one third of the rural population in areas for which archival data has been analysed were classified as 'tenants on the lands of *caciques*' rather than *calpulli* members in the 1530s (Hicks 1974: 257; Katz 1972: 225).

This brings us to the question of the lower orders in Aztec society. As noted above, Zorita's report on Indian rural organization associated *pillalli* with the named category *mayeque*, although Hicks has observed that this term does not appear in Nahuatl sources, and may have been an artifact of Zorita's need to explain why some peasants were exempted from tribute to the state (Hicks 1974: 255). There is no real evidence for the tenants of nobles being tied to the land, though the assumption that serfdom is an essential characteristic of occidental feudalism which underpins Katz's comparison between the two systems is erroneous empirically and theoretically anyway. Calnek rejects the idea that the *macehual*–*mayeque* distinction corresponds to a difference of social class on the grounds that both were exploited in the same way, payment of rent as a share of the crop, whether they worked office-land or *pillalli* (Calnek 1974: 193–4). He also includes *tlacotin* ('slaves') in this equation, despite their different juridical status. Hicks recognizes distinctions in class situations, but similarly denies that the native categories correspond to distinct classes, although he views the employment of slaves as a separate, primarily urban, phenomenon (Hicks 1974: 259–60). *Tlacotin* were in any event only around 5% of the population (Katz 1972: 225).

In juridical and status terms, indigenous categories seem to represent gradations rather than sharp breaks, as was also the case in the Ancient Near East (Finley 1973). Yet there do seem to be important structural implications in the fact that a substantial part of the rural population lacked access to community land, *calpullalli*. Tenants of the nobility performed personal services, offered their female labour for spinning and weaving items destined for the nobility's redistribution–retainership system, acted as burden carriers or messengers, and were in some cases skilled artisans. Armed with an economic means of appropriating dependent labour and surplus product, the nobility as landowners enjoyed a private tributary system independent of state-controlled modes of appropriation and, indeed, extracted many rural producers from the public tribute net. The long-term capacity for wealth accumulation by the nobility, as distinct from the state, was therefore in part tied to their share of the land base, which represented the extension of their patrimonial revenues. Landlord—tenant relationships also existed within joint households in rural *calpultin*, and some *barrio* residents lived from providing specialized services to officials and nobles, receiving their land rights from them (Carrasco 1976: 57).

Whilst this situation illustrates a relationship between peasant household organization and the tribute system, it also suggests that the community as such played no role in distributing usufruct rights at this time and that economic differentiation might lead to some households becoming effectively landless were other community members not willing to reassign use-rights to part of their own land. As in the colonial period, there may have been sanctions against transfer of rights to outsiders, although it is just conceivable that outsiders might sometimes have gained effective possession of community plots piecemeal following an initial transfer of use-rights.[5] But the individualization of rights of possession at the household level is of broader interest in relation to the organization of production in urban centres, where the bulk of the population at this time was non-agricultural (Sanders *et al.* 1979: 179).

In Tenochtitlan, mass demand was supplied by petty-commodity producers organized in a corporate (*calpulli*) framework which could be glossed as a 'guild' system, with market place provisioning dominant (Calnek 1978b; Sahagún 1950—69, IX: 91—2; Zorita 1963: 157—9). Peasant producers (together with professional traders) supplied commodities to substantial urban markets, and this is significant. Even if most rural households remained self-sufficient, and most land and labour remained locked away from mercantile relationships, these were far from being simply residual, as Carrasco's formulation implies. It is difficult to argue convincingly that the state regulated trade and the market system administratively in Polanyi's sense (Gledhill and Larsen 1982). State foreign-trade monopolies probably increased the wealth of the upper ranking, wealthier stratum of the merchant category, the *pochteca*, but it seems clear that the corporate merchant organization preceded the establishment of the empire, and continued to organize a mercantile system of trade, in which the state participated indirectly. Again, this implies both potential for private wealth accumulation outside the state sector, and limitations on the share of the social surplus appropriated by the state.

Although this attempt at static reconstruction could be deepened and extended considerably, such an exercise would begin to yield diminishing returns from the theoretical point of view. Questions such as the way the nobility acquired their lands and originated as a stratum demand diachronic answers. Attempts to produce simple formulae to 'characterize' the total structure of the Aztec formation evidently fail to capture the complexity of the system. A more dynamic approach may fare better in explaining observed structure and postulating trends.

Contradictions within the dominant class: short and medium term dynamics

It is well known that the upper-ranking *pochteca* rose in status in Aztec society and began to share some of the privileges of the nobility (Chapman 1957). If the accumulation of mercantile wealth offered the possibility of achieving social and political status, it did not ensure success. *Pochteca* asserted their status claims by feasting the nobility and military orders, who reacted with significant antagonism (Sahagún 1950—69, IX: 31—3). Their promotion was clearly an act of state policy, designed to strengthen the position of the ruler against the nobility politically as well as to aid the revenue needs of the palace. The state here cannot be seen simply as an agency mediating conflicts arising from the particularistic interests of a series of differentiated upper-class fractions. Though conflicts of this type were characteristic of Aztec conditions, the functionalist view of Engels (1968) is inadequate. Political centricity itself is constantly threatened in imperial systems, and competition and conflict at the top of the social hierarchy underpin change at the politico-administrative and socioeconomic levels. Whilst the ruler's power stems initially from a particular base, his activities take on an increasingly specialized role relative to the structure being reproduced overall, leading to what Eisenstadt (1963) has defined as the increasing autonomy and 'disembedding' of the political domain. Two implications of this ideal-type are clearly in evidence in the Aztec case: the emergence of discrepancies between the ruler's goals and those of 'traditional', ascriptive hierarchies, and the emergence of specific organs of political struggle, such as court cliques.[6]

This does not, however, imply that the dynamic of change is 'purely' political. Political goals, strategies and processes serve as the means by which power distributions stemming from access to different sources of wealth accumulation are, or are not, regulated. Objectively and historically, the 'autonomy of the state' rests on the state of the underlying material power balances, the extent to which political centralization is possible and can be maintained. One of the major political events in late Aztec history was the so-called 'aristocratic reaction', where Moctezuma Xocoyotzin expelled commoners from state offices (executing many in the process). This, together with a concomitant series of 'populist' gestures towards the peasantry (Katz 1972: 239—41), in fact reflected a significant strengthening of the power of the monarchy, since Moctezuma's initiatives represented a reduction in the decision-making (political) functions of the *pipiltin* (Calnek 1974: 203). Aside from their immediate political significance, attempts to bureaucratize administration (and the nobility) were part of a package of measures equally intended to enhance the economic power of the state (Katz 1972). This brings us to the relationship between the state and private landholding.

Durán (1951) and other writers using the source called 'Crónica "X"' recount that the lands of Azcapotzalco were expropriated after her defeat, and distributed as shares by area amongst the Aztec nobility. The commoner *calpultin* were excluded, and this story performs rather obvious ideological functions, since the nobility are credited with doing all the fighting. Katz (1972: 226) argues that all land expropriated in conquered territories continued to be cultivated by the original *macehualtin* and was outside the *pillalli/tecuhtlalli* categories. Similarly, Adams (1979) stresses the prebendal nature of grants of land made to tribute collectors in the provinces, noting that cultivation was supervised by a separate state functionary, and the office-holder was granted only a rental income. Evidently systems of this type were optimal from the state's point of view, not only restricting the growth of patrimonial lands, but also reinforcing office-holding and state service as a route to private wealth and high rank.

Gibson, however, sees some state land-grants as adding to private Indian properties (1964: 263) whilst Hicks (1974: 254–5) sees *macehualtin* as being evicted from expropriated land and replaced by a new population, who became *mayeque*. Cortés remarked that the plots of *mayeque* tenants were of uniform size (note the emphasis on area in expropriations above), and that such communities lacked kinship ties (Hicks 1974: 253). All this should refer to lands acquired outside the Triple Alliance territory, but the contradictory picture presented by the historical sources may also reflect contradictions between state policy and actual practice, together with change through time, as the state effected greater centralization and bureaucratization. We have also noted possibilities of other modes of acquisition of former *calpullalli*, relating to economic differentiation within *calpultin*. Pawning family members was, however, the characteristic response to crisis in the rural community, a crisis which seemed to be growing judging by the rising curve of activity by slave dealers through the imperial phase (Hicks 1974: 257; Katz 1972: 242). There is also the question of references to land purchases by *pochteca* in the sources, noted earlier. Possibly lesser *pipiltin* might be forced to alienate land under economic adversity. If this were so, it might also raise the question of whether, as in China, access to the fruits of office might not be inextricably linked to rank maintenance for noble families. The right to acquire land was supposedly one of the main privileges the state granted the *pochteca*, and here we can see the value of Carrasco's stress on the mediating role of politics. Mercantile capital remained subordinated politically. Gibson insists that *calpullalli* plots might also be purchased by private individuals (1964). What 'purchase' might mean here has already been discussed, but where such transfers occurred, merchants might well have been involved.[7]

These observations from historical sources give us no real index of the scale and prevalence of the phenomena con-cerned, and no clear picture of trends through time beyond, perhaps, suggesting that the state sought to check the further expansion of noble patrimonial domain. More work on local archives would help, but it is really essential to complement this with the longer-term picture offered by archaeology. Paucity of excavation limits the conclusions which can be drawn at present, but the comprehensive survey data encourages us to believe something which the historical sources often imply: that people termed *mayeque* were originally migrants and refugees, and noble landholdings began before the formation of the empire. This would imply a relationship between political decentralization and the development of private domains which requires more detailed examination.

The long term: cycles, trends and structural transformation

The archaeological record for the Basin of Mexico reveals quite massive demographic shifts and displacements during the period between the collapse of Teotihuacán and the rise of the Aztecs (Parsons 1976; Sanders *et al.* 1979). A virtual gap in occupation appears in the central Basin as supra-regional dominance passes to Tula to the north and Cholula to the south between 950 and 1150 AD (Sanders *et al.* 1979: 149). In the periods preceding and following this phase, the pattern of settlement is consistent with city-state decentralization, but there are significant changes in the nature of rural settlement after 1150. In particular, Sanders and his colleagues postulate that a dispersed type of rural occupation correlates with the settlement of landless tenants (1979: 178–9). There is a clear morphological and distributional distinction between this and another contemporary form which is more clustered and structured. Sanders *et al.* therefore associate the latter with *calpulli* organization. The dispersed type predominates in the *chinampa* cultivation zone, the Zumpango region and the southern piedmont, areas where previous occupation had been minimal. It appears before the fifteenth century, although the later period sees major growth of population from modest beginnings. The notion of 'state-directed agricultural intensification and resettlement' used by Sanders *et al.* could thus be applied to city-states, their dynastic groups offering lands claimed by their constituent houses to people uprooted by the effects of inter-state conflict and civil wars.

This archaeologically-inspired hypothesis cannot account for Aztec land tenure in its full complexity, but it may help to explain how one third of the imperial rural population could be classified as tenants of the nobility despite the existence of the *calpulli* communities. No expropriation of community land would initially be involved directly, and some of the resettled land would also no doubt be *tecpantlalli*. As a class, the military aristocracies of the city-states were expropriating the peasantry, but collectively and indirectly, as the by-product of inter-state conflict, rather than individually by direct action against their own immediate subjects. These circumstances would not seem conducive to a mobilization of the free peasantry against the *pipiltin*, representing themselves locally as protectors. Famines occurred in 1454 and 1505 according to the chroniclers (Sahagún 1950–69, VIII; Tezozomoc 1975). These 'natural' disasters reflected the existence of exploitative relations in general, but more specifically the development of the urban economies and mercantile relations, which their social effects in turn reinforced. Although the state promoted agricultural intensification, it did not use the tribute system to remedy deficits in the market place (Calnek 1974: 191), and merchants—slave dealers and wealthier *calpulli* members seem to have become the targets of popular unrest in 1505 (Katz 1972: 240).

Despite its own contributions to the processes weakening the peasant communities (Hicks 1974), the 'orientalizing' monarchic state had a political incentive to devise modes of exploiting them itself which would help combat further tendencies to private expropriation, in the interests of its own revenue base, aside from considerations of public order. Judging from Cortés's experience of resistance in the imperial core area, Moctezuma's measures were successful, at least in the short term. New private appropriations of land by the nobility beyond the core regions would seem to become impractical, given the necessity of state backing for expropriations, once the state was strong enough to enforce a prebendal system and dominated the local aristocracies. Within the core zone, the trend was also influenced by the political strength of the state versus the nobility, in conjunction with factors weakening the capacity of free peasant households to defend their rights of possession and retain their social independence. The development of internal economic stratification may have weakened the corporate solidarity of the *calpultin*, but the state had a strong interest in defending communal tenures as a bulwark against feudalization, just as in the colonial period.

Structural factors promoting feudalizing tendencies in the formation have already been touched on. There were significant weaknesses in the economic base of centralized power, and the predatory nature of Aztec imperialism has often been seen as implying the impossibility of such a system achieving long-term stability. The preceding cycles of expansion and collapse of extended territorial control would seem to reinforce this view, although it is clear that there are significant structural developments between Teotihuacán and Tenochtitlan (Gledhill and Larsen 1982). As we have seen, the upheavals caused by this long-term cycle probably played a crucial part in the transformation of the highland zone formations.

Although the determinants of the long-term cycle cannot be fully evaluated here, it does seem possible to argue that each episode of centralization was related to a core zone's establishment of direct policito-military controls over a wider, pre-existing 'world-economy' network,[8] at least after Teotihuacán. Tenochtitlan pursued a policy of encouraging craftsmen to migrate to the core, and adjusted the international division of labour through the tribute system to suit its own commercial purposes (Bray 1977). The importance of this wider resource network is political, in the sense that appropriation of resources flowing through it becomes essential for the exercise of political control. In phases of decentralization, both the maintenance of local political hierarchies in city-states and political expansion remain tied to 'success' in extracting a share of the wealth being generated in the larger system, and since the political environment is competitive, even survival implies continuous attempts at expansion. This emphasis on the 'world-economy' unit of analysis should not be interpreted as a rejection of arguments concerned with agricultural intensification and unequal access to productive resources. I would not wish to deny, for example, that water control reinforces and deepens local power relations, or that access to lands of differing productive potential relates to uneven accumulation of wealth. We must, of course, also recognize that there are different bases for appropriating surplus from the direct producers and that these imply different social processes of reproduction of the exploitative relationship, different kinds of contradiction and dynamic effects. But the point I want to stress here is simply that these factors are insufficient to explain how and why empires formed and collapsed. The suppression of city-state centrifugalism was clearly an extended process in the final precolonial period, and was a matter of its becoming politically feasible to introduce more centralized measures of politico-administrative control over subject states, whilst securing stability in the core itself (Calnek 1978a).

The underlying dynamic of expansion and collapse illustrates the way in which political and economic developments are inextricably linked together. On the one hand, the structures of the Mesoamerican polities became increasingly differentiated as problems of political control became more complex with larger populations to be administered and a more complex economic base to be regulated, partly as a result of the growth of the 'world economy' infrastructure. On the other hand, the elaboration of political structures itself provided the dynamic behind the evolution of the world-economy, since increasing levels of resource mobilization were in essence inputs into processes fuelling competition between different upper-class fractions as well as provisioning the organs of government and political hierarchization in general. Fractions within the state become political agencies, and the problem of maintaining centralization is at issue.

This, as we have seen, is where the extent of direct state appropriation of resources becomes crucial. Despite its moves towards the bureaucratization of administration, the Aztec state was faced with a situation in which a considerable proportion of the social surplus was being appropriated as private revenue, in the form of rents and mercantile profits. Landlordism of the kind found in the Basin of Mexico could probably have endured in a city-state framework. The Aztec nobility enjoyed their share of the revenues of empire through holding office, a unifying force which does, however, rather highlight the principle that the state lacked the power and resources to create an administrative system staffed by personnel more directly dependent on itself. The fact that the monarchs do seem to have made land grants which were added to noble patrimonial domains also suggests that autonomous state power was precarious. Despite Moctezuma Xocoyotzin's successes, the political aspirations of the nobility cannot have been effectively suppressed structurally.

The political integration of the empire remained congenitally weak beyond its core zone, its dominance resting on the massive economic and demographic superiority established in the unified Basin of Mexico. Weakening of that unity would rapidly have destroyed it. Peasant resistance to increasing exploitative pressures in downswing phases of the highland agricultural cycle combining with internal rivalries within the dominant stratum under a weaker monarch would provide a scenario for such breakdown. Even the vastly more integrated imperial structure of the Spanish conquerors found that Mexico was a difficult country to govern. Yet despite all the pressures towards decentralization, it still seems necessary to be precise about the exact nature and limits of the 'feudalization' processes formations such a pre-colonial Mesoamerica could experience. The significance of this will become apparent if we return to our original discussion of the AMP and the comparison with China. Now, however, these cases should be placed in a wider comparative context.

Conclusion: the AMP and the quest for theoretical generalization

This discussion began with the possibly startling idea that a useful comparison might be made between Aztec Mesoamerica and the coeval civilization of China. Much of it has perhaps not seemed terribly reminiscent of what Marx had to say on these matters in *Grundrisse*, one kind of formulation which was originally intended to bring such apparently disparate cases together. Nor, I imagine, will the reader find too much similarity between the kind of analysis I have offered of the Aztecs and Godelier's account of the Inca, particularly in his more recent work (Godelier 1977b, but see also the earlier paper reprinted in 1978). I have criticized Godelier's approach extensively elsewhere (Gledhill 1981a), but it may be worthwhile to emphasize one point on which we might share broad agreement.

Before their encounter with Morgan, the founders of Marxism seemed to be offering a rather clear-cut emphasis on the distinctiveness of the line of development pursued by non-European and non-Mediterranean civilizations. My choice of negative definition here is deliberate. The long ideological trajectory of European political manipulation of the concept of 'Oriental Society', combined with Marx's rather specific and non-evolutionist theoretical project, no doubt had a somewhat deleterious effect on their treatment of these issues. Yet Marx at any rate, Morganism notwithstanding, continued to display a strong commitment to a 'multi-linear' universal history up to the moment of his death.

An emphasis on 'multi-linearity' (and indeed 'history') can easily become an emphasis on historical specificity to the point of particularism. My contention here is that this is not the only alternative to the 'historico-philosophical' theories which Marx so emphatically rejected. In this paper I have implicitly rejected the adequacy of conceptualizing either the Mesoamerican or Chinese cases in terms of the conventional neo-evolutionist category of 'pristine state formation'. I am suggesting instead that the evolution of these agrarian civilizations is a process which requires periodization in just the same way as capitalist development requires periodization. The particular approach I have adopted emphasizes that both China and Mesoamerica were imperial societies, and that both require analyses focused on the contradictions generated by partial transformation of an 'Asiatic' regime; that is, the structure of domination constituted by the state ceases to preserve a strict identity with the bases for class domination. From this standpoint, the two cases I have discussed appear to be at opposite poles of such a process of transformation. Had I included Mesopotamia in the discussion, I might well have created the illusion of an 'intermediate stage' in some evolutionist model. This would, however, simply have been an illusion, as would be immediately apparent if we considered other cases, such as Egypt and Peru, or the possibility of cycles within individual areas which are not linear in the direction of transformation. The real issue is rather how we can account, in terms of dynamic, generative processes, for the distribution of elements of stability and change over the long term in the development of those civilizations which were created and re-created over millennia outside the northwest European and Mediterranean zones.

In some respects, the contrasts between Graeco-Roman civilization and the 'Asiatic' formations are clear enough to justify Marx's separation of these cases as distinct 'epochal' modes of production, though it is worth bearing in mind the significant structural continuities that obtained in the 'Oriental' parts of the empires with Mediterranean cores (Gledhill 1981a). On the other hand, our attention has often been focused theoretically on the common characteristics of 'imperial societies' when such characteristics had been contrasted with the peculiarities of western Europe as the site of the 'original' industrial capitalist transformation. The most obvious recent variant on this theme is Wallerstein's distinction between 'world economies' and 'world empires' (Wallerstein 1974; 1980), though that author would be the last to claim complete originality for the thesis in question. From the point of view of the present discussion, it is worth noting that the analysis presented here supports other recent work which suggests that it is necessary to modify the propositions which Wallerstein advances on the relationships between polity and economy in the two types of 'world system' contexts.

As Moulder (1977) observes, the European core state is a quite novel historical formation, because its adoption of 'mercantilist' rather than 'provisioning' policies promotes, for the first time, the development of a *national* economy and 'nationalizes' capital accumulation on a world-scale to an unprecedented degree. Linking the genesis of the European type of *truly* centralized, truly bureaucratic, state to the continuity of geo-political military competition within the European world-economy, Moulder's analysis implies that the world-system which came to be centred on Europe was structured by the development of national states whose apparatuses were far stronger than those of the central powers of world-empires. She shares Wallerstein's emphasis on the importance of a multi-state arena in European development, but there are important differences in the arguments which emerge from her comparison between the 'imperial' and 'national' state. Instead of treating the world-system as some kind of integrated economic unity, defined in terms of an encompassing international division of labour, we might place more emphasis on the existence of politically structured economic sub-systems centred on national states and their colonial empires. The multiplicity of these sub-systems would then be the key to the rapid escalation of capital accumulation on the basis of production in the nineteenth century. Inter-state politico-military competition would therefore be central to explaining both the development of the 'modern' type of state and the evolution of a capitalist world-economy, seen, *contra* Wallerstein, as a relatively recent historical phenomenon (Gledhill 1981a).

The politico-military dimension is certainly central. But it in turn requires explanation, and it is here that the comparative issues raised in the present discussion become relevant. The overall failure of imperial society in Europe might be linked to the very complete form of 'feudalization' set in train by the fall of the Roman empire in the West, but not perhaps fully consummated until the post-Carolingian epoch. In the West, decentralization of politico-juridical and military power enters into an unprecedented combination with a specific type of localized, class control of resources in the sphere of agricultural production (Anderson 1973). In 'Asiatic' regimes it seems difficult to defend private property relations at the local level in the long term without the guarantee of support by a political organization at a higher level. Furthermore, long-term structural continuities in agrarian organization must in part reflect the somewhat limited degree of economic control over the peasant labour process achieved or achievable within 'Asiatic' systems.

Large-scale production on the basis of servile labour was never really practicable in the private sector, because the way in which private domain over land was realized was seldom, if ever, conducive to the development of an extensive 'demesne' economy. The form of landlordism which developed fully in China and was only emergent in Mesoamerica represents, in effect, the establishment of privatized tributary relationships between a segment of the peasantry and members of urban elites, outside the state systems of tax and corvée. The essence of these relationships was their parcellization: many landlords to a single community, many communities participating in the formation of individual private domains. Even if landlord–tenant relations became purely mercantile, as they did in China, where the peasants were subordinated through debt, this situation was almost the antithesis of what would have

been required for a thorough-going transformation of agrarian structure. The European 'manoral' economy should not, of course, be equated with the demesne as a landlord enterprise (Gledhill 1981b). But the landlordization of China and Mesoamerica was not even comparable to the other polar case of a manor farmed entirely by tenants. All variants of the European type of landlord–tenant relationship could, and did, have transformative effects on rural economies irrespective of the results of rural class struggle by the peasantry against economic subsumption by landlords. Such effects were of necessity minor and even reversible in 'Asiatic' systems, and in this sense the emphasis which Marx, along with many of his predecessors and contemporaries, placed on the 'stationary' nature of the agrarian systems of such formations has a genuine element of truth.

The emphasis placed by so many archaeologists on the technological dimension of agricultural systems has tended to override the potentially more valuable focus on agrarian systems defined in terms of social relations of production. The focus of this paper has been on the way in which agrarian systems both condition and are conditioned by the political structures and dynamics of 'Asiatic' societies, defined in terms of the processes which distribute power to social classes and political elites. In 'Asiatic' regimes 'class' and 'elite' remain, to a degree, conceptually separate, not necessarily in terms of concrete social groups, but as bases for conflicts concerned with power relations.

If we consider the case of China, it seems clear that the *literati* shared with the landlords a direct material interest in the long-term preservation and extension of the system of private property relations based on mercantile mechanisms of class subordination. At the same time, the development of this system was structured in accordance with the dependence of the imperial regime on a tax-base which was largely peasant. In both China and Mesoamerica a centralized state had to inhibit the complete parcellization of its revenue base, and it is clear in the Chinese case that incoming dynasties did promote a limited measure of 'land reform' to redress the imbalances created by decentralization. This, of course, also pacified the peasantry. The more interesting comparative questions therefore lie at the other pole of the cycle, the limited nature of the 'feudalization' which occurred with the collapse of the central power.

As I noted in my introduction, analytical attention has often been placed on the extent to which 'peasants' cannot constitute a class 'for themselves'. There clearly is a sense in which this is generally true, despite the fact that the evidence strongly suggests that the rural populations of ancient civilizations are a far from passive element in their history, as my argument has continually emphasized (see also Adams 1981). Struggles in the countryside tend, of necessity, to be relatively particularistic and local, even where they are widespread in occurrence at particular times, as in the Chinese case. (Only in the period of European imperialist penetration does it seem possible to argue that new processes were set in motion which created the conditions for the wider-ranging 'mass movements' of the kind experienced in recent history.) Yet it seems equally necessary to recognize that the effectiveness of local upper-stratum 'class' power was limited by the circumstances of its creation and its resultant nature. The very weak form of economic control which was established in China was scarcely a viable basis for a sudden innovation in the military—political dimension of landlord—peasant relationships which would have laid the basis for a radical change of course.

In the case of Mesoamerica, it has been suggested here that the emergence of private tributary domains was initially a feature of the decentralized situation. Mercantile forms of domination would be much less significant than in the Chinese case, and at most a secondary development. Whether Meso-america was embarking on a path of development which would eventually have produced a formation similar to China is evidently a fairly meaningless question, and in many respects the two cases are poles apart in complexity and sophistication. Yet the emergent Mesoamerican pattern of private domain was broadly similar to that of China. This is not really para-doxical. In the decentralized period, local elite power in city-states must have required the active support of the commoner population and 'unfree' categories of people would have represented those excluded from and marginalized by par-ticularistic ties of kin and class. Transformation in political (and possibly military) structure brought about in the pro-cesses of empire formation did not, I have argued, create fundamentally new potentials for transformation of the local situation in a future phase of decentralization.

In a real sense, even in the core zone where the Aztec elite were not simply alien expropriators, class power was sub-ject to developmental constraints which reinforced its long-term dependence on the existence of an overarching state. The peasant community could suffer, it could be partially trans-formed, but it was not subjected to the kinds of processes which could have finally brought its elimination as a social force. Thus, in both China and Mesoamerica, the tripartite relationship between state, 'private sector' and peasantry preserved a kind of dynamic equilibrium. The mercantile element in unequal social relationships, and mercantile insti-tutions, could undergo significant development. But they could not fuse effectively with other modes of decentralized social power. Thus the larger structure preserved its 'Asiatic' characteristics in more than a formal sense.

The role of agrarian structure does therefore seem crucial in comparative, multi-linear evolutionary terms. In 'Asiatic' regimes, the state's primary revenue source is the peasant community (cf. Tosi, this volume). (The collapse of the agrarian revenue base in a definitive manner, given the different nature of Roman landlordism in the West, is there-fore the first step in the processes which created modern Europe.) While this base is preserved, the mercantile—commercial sectors of the economy are neither victims nor beneficiaries of state policies on balance. The overall effect can be neutral, because these sectors are not, in the last analysis,

the basis for state finance. This is not to say that Asiatic regimes eschew the opportunities presented by commercial growth to add to their revenues, but the controls which undoubtedly were exercised over commercial economy were probably primarily political in motivation, and in practice scarcely crushing (Moulder 1977; Gledhill and Larsen 1982).

A system which feudalizes completely, in political, military and economic domains, creates a new situation. The very weak state may become a very strong state in the long term as a result of economic and geo-political competition. But in making this transformation, would-be centralizers must foster a radically new type of relationship between state and economy, that is, merchant capital. We cannot begin to appreciate the extent to which European development rep-resented a fundamental historical departure simply by assum-ing this to be the case and searching, piecemeal, for factors which singly or in combination define some essential and sufficient difference. The dynamic and complex determinants of other lines of evolution is not something which can be residualized analytically. Marx's simple sketch-map did nothing more than define a problem. Yet it may have been an important one. To this extent, the notion of an AMP may be worth defending, not because it is impossible to find simi-larities between European feudalism and other systems and construct more general classificatory concepts such as Amin's 'tributary mode', but because it remains unclear whether such a construct would represent an improved point of departure.

Notes
1 See Gledhill and Larsen 1982.
2 Moulder makes the important distinction between 'mercantilism' as the positive promotion of mercantile accumulation by its nationals in modern nation states and what she sees as the 'neutral' impact of the centre in other cases.
3 See in particular Marx 1968.
4 It is essential to recognize, however, that the effects of these 'natural' conditions on social change are also determined by social processes.
5 Alienation of communal land certainly did occur in the colonial period, before the imposition of a private property regime on the Indians under the liberal *Reforma* (Gledhill 1981b; Tutino 1975). Mercantile capital had a freer hand in the colonial period, how-ever, whilst the fiscal crises of the imperial centre ensured that a fully-fledged latifundist estate structure would be consolidated in the seventeenth century.
6 Katz (1972) gives a lively account of Aztec politics, though he is perhaps guilty of overliteral treatment of the sources for early Aztec history.
7 In contemporary Mexico, land distributed to peasants under the agrarian reform legislation cannot be alienated, yet nevertheless private capital sometimes secures effective control over such plots through rental, often employing the 'landlord' as a day-labourer (Díaz-Polanco and Montandon 1977).
8 See Ekholm and Friedman (1979) for an elaboration of this point, although the present writer does not accept the whole of the broader thesis they present here.

Bibliography
Adams, R.McC. 1979. Late Prehispanic empires of the New World. In M.T. Larsen (ed.), *Power and Propaganda. A Symposium on*

Ancient Empires, Mesopotamia 7: 59–73. Copenhagen: Akademisk Forlag.

1981. *Heartland of Cities: Surveys of Ancient Settlement and Land Use on the Central Floodplain at the Euphrates*. Chicago: University of Chicago Press.

Amin, S. 1976. *Unequal Development. An Essay on the Social Formations of Peripheral Capitalism*. Hassocks: Harvester Press.

Anderson, P. 1973. *Passages from Antiquity to Feudalism*. London: New Left Books.

Bailey, A.M. 1981. The renewed discussions of the concept of the Asiatic Mode of Production. In J.S. Kahn and J. Llobera (eds.), *The Anthropology of Pre-Capitalist Societies*, pp. 89–107. London: Macmillan.

Barlow, R.H. 1949. *The Extent of the Empire of the Culhua Mexica*. Ibero-Americana 28. Berkeley: University of California Press.

Bray, W. 1977. Civilising the Aztecs. In J. Friedman and M.J. Rowlands (eds.), *The Evolution of Social Systems*, pp. 373–98. London: Duckworth.

Calnek, E.E. 1974. The Sahagún Texts as a source of sociological information. In M.S. Edmonson (ed.), *Sixteenth Century Mexico. The Work of Sahagún*, pp. 189–204. Albuquerque: University of New Mexico Press.

1978a. The city-state in the Basin of Mexico: late prehispanic period. In R.P. Schaedel, J.E. Hardoy and N.S. Kinzer (eds.), *Urbanization in the Americas from its Beginnings to the Present*, pp. 463–70. The Hague: Mouton.

1978b. El sistema del mercade de Tenochtitlan. In P. Carrasco and J. Broda (eds.), *Economía Política e Ideología en el México Prehispánico*, pp. 97–114. México: Nueva Imagen.

Carrasco, P. 1976. The joint family in Ancient Mexico. In H.G. Nutini, P. Carrasco and J.M. Taggart (eds.), *Essays on Mexican Kinship*, pp. 45–64. London: University of Pittsburg Press, Feffer and Simons.

1978. La economía del México prehispánico. In P. Carrasco and J. Broda (eds.), *Economía Política e Ideología en el México Prehispánico*, pp. 15–76. México: Nueva Imagen.

1981. Comment on Offner. *American Antiquity* 46: 62–8.

Chang Chung-li, 1962. *The Income of the Chinese Gentry*. Seattle: University of Washington Press.

Chapman, A. 1957. Port of trade enclaves in Aztec and Mayan civilisation. In K. Polanyi, C. Arensberg and H.W. Pearson (eds.), *Trade and Market in the Early Empires*, pp. 114–53. Chicago: Free Press.

Ch'ü T'ung tsu, 1969. *Local Government in China under the Ch'ing*. Stanford: Stanford University Press.

Cutler, A., B. Hindess, P.Q. Hirst and A. Hussain, 1977. *Marx's Capital and Capitalism Today*, vol. 1. London: Routledge and Kegan Paul.

Díaz-Polanco, H. and L.G. Montandon, 1977. *La burguesia agraria de México: un estudio de caso en el Bajío*. México: Cuadernos del CES 22. El Colegio de México.

Durán, Fray D. 1951. *Historia de las Indias de Nueva España*. México: Editora Nacional.

Eisenstadt, S.N. 1963. *The Political Systems of Empires*. New York: Free Press.

Ekholm, K. and J. Friedman, 1979. 'Capital', imperialism and exploitation in ancient world-systems. In M.T. Larsen (ed.), *Power and Propaganda. A Symposium on Ancient Empires*, pp. 41–58. Copenhagen: Akademisk Forlag.

Engels, F. 1968. The Origin of the Family, Private Property and the State. In *Marx and Engels: Selected Works in One Volume*, pp. 461–583. London: Lawrence and Wishart.

Finley, M. 1973. *The Ancient Economy*. London: Chatto and Windus.

Gibson, C. 1964. *The Aztecs under Spanish Rule: A History of the Indians of the Valley of Mexico 1519–1810*. Stanford: Stanford University Press.

Gledhill, J. 1981a. Time's arrow: anthropology, history, social evolution and marxist theory. *Critique of Anthropology* 16: 3–30.

1981b. Agrarian change and the articulation of forms of production: the Mexican Bajío 1800–1910. *Bulletin of Latin American Research*, 1:1, 63–80.

Gledhill, J. and M.T. Larsen, 1982. The Polanyi paradigm and the dynamics of archaic states: Mesopotamia and Mesoamerica. In C. Renfrew, M.J. Rowlands and B. Segraves (eds.), *Theory and Explanation in Archaeology. The Southampton Conference*, pp. 197–229. London: Academic Press.

Gledhill, J. and M.J. Rowlands, 1982. Materialism and socio-economic process in multilinear evolution. In C. Renfrew and S. Shennan (eds.), *Ranking, Resource and Exchange*, pp. 144–50. Cambridge: Cambridge University Press.

Godelier, M. 1970. Preface. In *Sur les Sociétés Précapitalistes. Textes choisis de Marx, Engels, Lénine*. Paris: Centre d'Études et de Recherches Marxistes, Éditions Sociales.

1977a. Politics as infrastructure. In J. Friedman and M.J. Rowlands (eds.), *The Evolution of Social Systems*, pp. 13–28. London: Duckworth.

1977b. *Perspectives in Marxist Anthropology*. Cambridge: Cambridge University Press.

1978. The concept of the 'Asiatic Mode of Production' and Marxist models of social evolution. In D. Seddon (ed.), *Relations of Production: Marxist Approaches to Economic Anthropology*, pp. 209–57. London: Frank Cass.

Hicks, F. 1974. Dependent labour in prehispanic Mexico. *Estudios de cultura náhuatl*, 11: 243–66.

Hindess, B. and P.Q. Hirst, 1975. *Pre-Capitalist Modes of Production*. London: Routledge and Kegan Paul.

Islamoğlu, H. and C. Keyder, 1977. Agenda for Ottoman History. *Review* 1 (1): 31–55.

Ixtlilxochitl, A. de, 1975. *Obras Históricas*. Edited by E. O'Gorman. México: Universidad Nacional Autónoma de México.

Kahn, J.S. and J. Llobera, 1981. Towards a new anthropology or a new marxism? In J.S. Kahn and J. Llobera (eds.), *The Anthropology of Pre-Capitalist Societies*, pp. 263–329. London: Macmillan.

Katz, F. 1972. *The Ancient American Civilisations*. London: Weidenfeld and Nicolson.

1978. A comparison of some aspects of the evolution of Cuzco and Tenochtitlan. In R.P. Schaedel, J.E. Hardoy and N.S. Kinzer (eds.), *Urbanization in the Americas from its Beginnings to the Present*, pp. 203–14. The Hague: Mouton.

Marx, K. 1959. *Capital*, Vol. 3. Moscow: Progress Publishers.

1968. The Eighteenth Brumaire of Louis Bonaparte. In *Marx and Engels: Selected Works in One Volume*, pp. 96–179. London: Lawrence and Wishart.

1973. *Grundrisse*. Harmondsworth: Penguin Books.

Moore, Barrington Jnr. 1968. *Social Origins of Dictatorship and Democracy*. Harmondsworth: Penguin Books.

Moulder, F.V. 1977. *Japan, China and the Modern World Economy*. Cambridge: Cambridge University Press.

Offner, J.A. 1981. On the inapplicability of 'Oriental Despotism' and the 'Asiatic Mode of Production' to the Aztecs of Texcoco. *American Antiquity* 46: 43–61.

Parsons, J.R. 1976. Settlement and population history of the Basin of Mexico. In E.R. Wolf (ed.), *The Valley of Mexico. Studies in Pre-Hispanic Ecology and Society*, pp. 69–100. Albuquerque: University of New Mexico Press.

Poulantzas, N. 1975. *Classes in Contemporary Capitalism*. London: New Left Books.

Riley, G.M. 1978. El prototipo de la hacienda en el centro de México: un caso del siglo XVI. In E. Florescano (ed.), *Haciendas, Latifundios y Plantaciones en América Latina*, pp. 49–70. México: Siglo Veintiuno Editores.

Sahagún, Fray B. de, 1950–69. *Florentine Codex, General History of the Things of New Spain.* Edited by J.O. Anderson and C.E. Dibble, 12 volumes. Santa Fé: School of American Research and University of Utah.

Sanders, W.T., J.R. Parsons and R.S. Santley, 1979. *The Basin of Mexico. Ecological Processes in the Evolution of a Civilisation.* New York: Academic Press.

Terray, E. 1975. Classes and class consciousness in the Abron Kingdom of Gyaman. In M. Bloch (ed.), *Marxist Analyses and Social Anthropology*, pp. 85–135. London: Malaby Press.

Tezozomoc, H.A. 1975. *Crónica Mexicana.* México: Editorial Porrúa.

Torquemada, Fray J. de, 1969. *Los Veinte i un Libros Rituales i Monarquía Indiana*, 3 volumes. México: Editorial Porrúa.

Tutino, J.M. 1975. Hacienda social relations in Mexico: the Chalco Region in the Era of Independence. *Hispanic American Historical Review* 55: 496–528.

Vernant, J.P. 1976. Remarks on class struggle in Ancient Greece. *Critique of Anthropology* 7: 21–34.

Wallerstein, I. 1974. *The Modern World System: Capitalist Agriculture and the Origins of the European World-Economy in the Sixteenth Century.* New York: Academic Press.

1980. *The Modern World System II: Mercantilism and the Consolidation of the European World-Economy, 1600–1750.* New York: Academic Press.

Wang, Yeh-chien, 1973. *Land Taxation in Imperial China, 1750–1911.* Cambridge, Mass.: Harvard University Press.

Weber, M. 1951. *The Religion of China.* New York: Free Press.

1978. *Economy and Society*, 2 volumes. Berkeley: University of California Press.

Wittfogel, K.A. 1935. The foundations and stages of Chinese economic history. *Zeitschrift für Sozialforschung* 4: 26–58.

1957. *Oriental Despotism: A Comparative Study of Total Power.* New Haven: Yale University Press.

Zorita, A. de, 1963. *Life and Labour in Ancient Mexico.* New Brunswick: Rutgers University Press.

PART 5

Epilogue

Chapter 12

A consideration of
ideology
Peter Gathercole

In his recent essay, 'Archaeology and Human Diversity'
(1979), Grahame Clark states:

If a main part of this essay is given to an examination of
the process of cultural enrichment, this should not be
taken to endorse the ideas of progress as this has commonly been understood, still less the complacent doc-
trines of liberal humanism. On the contrary, it is offered
as a reminder of the heritage that mankind stands in
imminent danger of losing in the name of science and
social justice. From this standpoint archaeology by no
means stops short at validating contemporary trends and
goals. *Instead it poses questions more radical than those
commonly asked by political science or sociology
because they are framed in an ampler perspective.*

(Clark 1979: 5; my emphasis)

As an archaeologist of great distinction, well known for
his writings on the place of archaeology within society, Clark's
views inevitably command respect. For this reason alone, it is
relevant to note that in this essay he rates archaeology of such
importance as a discipline to place it firmly within the domain
of social theory, alongside and of more importance than either
political science or sociology. I am concerned here not so
much with the largeness of Clark's claim, but with the fact
that he has made it at all. Among other things, it indicates a
considerable shift in his attitude towards the social responsibilities of archaeologists, a matter he has always taken very

seriously. For example, in the second edition of *Archaeology and Society* (1947), when discussing the need for the subject to remain free from state control, he said:

> The primary task of archaeologists is to enlarge and deepen man's knowledge of his own development. The results of their labours, wisely used, may subserve great social ends, fostering love of country and in the end promoting a deeper realisation of human solidarity, but the motive of their researches ought to be no more and no less than the acquisition of knowledge. *There is a very real sense in which archaeologists can only discharge their highest social function by ignoring society.*
>
> (Clark 1947: 214; my emphasis)

Clark's change of view, incorporating the 'ampler perspective' which archaeology can bring to the consideration, for example, of 'the idea of progress as this has been commonly understood', surely implies that the subject should be seen today, if it was not before, as an ideological discipline. Archaeologists should no longer regard themselves (if they ever did) as able to 'ignore society', but must be firmly within it, having some form of ideological commitment to its existence, and treating more explicitly the ideology of their discipline.

These comments may seem self-evident. After all, Marx, Mannheim and others have made us sufficiently aware of the need to take the concept of ideology seriously. Yet the extent of dispute among archaeologists today over their own basic concepts suggests that a discussion of the place of ideology within the discipline would be in order. In this respect, because he considers the matter in a closely related discipline, I follow the views of the historian Gordon Leff, and adopt the definition of ideology given in his book *History and Social Theory*:

> The problem of ideology is central to historical — as to all social — understanding. If men govern the rest of nature in virtue of their reason and technological power, they are themselves governed by their beliefs. All human action . . . belongs to a frame of reference, however unconsciously formulated. It is this framework of assumptions and intentions, habits and ends, interests and ideals, values and knowledge which constitutes an ideology — or, to use a less rebarbative term, an outlook.
>
> (Leff 1969: 155)

In other words, in the years since Clark urged archaeologists to 'discharge their highest social function by ignoring society', the latter have become sufficiently rebarbative to justify a more ideological attitude towards their discipline. This paper, then, deals with certain aspects of the frame of reference, whether or not consciously formulated, which archaeologists use when they practise their craft. It assumes that to understand the influence of ideology in archaeology is indeed central to archaeological understanding, and that the particular character of the subject casts its practitioners in roles which emphasize the usefulness of making more conscious the nature of archaeological knowledge. One might say that without the archaeologist there would be a form of legendary prehistory but no archaeology. Sufficient, therefore, be the need for self-awareness.

As Leff remarks, an ideology is composed of various elements, but in the context of this paper its most significant one is knowledge. Here I also follow Leff, who distinguishes two kinds of knowledge: scientific (or formal) and social:

> This distinction between scientific and social knowledge is central to the problem of ideology. For if all knowledge is ideological in the sense of having some framework, the validity of scientific and formal knowledge remains independent of its antecedents . . . The criteria of the human studies [i.e. social knowledge] on the other hand, are human experience in greater or lesser immediacy; they can therefore only be judged by how far their propositions accord with that experience; and since it will — through new experience, changed values, increased knowledge and so on — differ from epoch to epoch, so will assessments of it . . . But whereas the beauty of a mathematical proof or scientific experiment lies precisely in establishing propositions which we do not experience as such, we can only fully comprehend a Gothic Cathedral or the *Divine Comedy* through recreating its context. In contrast to the need to refine a scientific process we have in some measure to re-enact the original meaning in any work of human experience, whether it is a system of banking or a musical score.
>
> (Leff 1969: 211–12)

I shall return to Leff's more extended points later. For the moment I wish only to elaborate on his basic distinctions with regard to archaeology. One might therefore distinguish between scientific archaeological knowledge, embracing concepts relating to the technical terms and procedures common to the subject worldwide, and social archaeological knowledge which is less empirical and more wide-ranging. The latter is concerned mainly with the comprehension and interpretation of evidence; it is more responsive to individual experience, and it is more reflective of the idiom of a particular period or occasion. In the sense that social knowledge is more closely tied than scientific knowledge to specific historical and sociological factors affecting the use of concepts in a particular society, it is perhaps more 'ideological' than its counterpart. But this difference is relative; these forms of knowledge are dialectically related to each other, so much so that at times scientific and social knowledge might, or might seem to, interpenetrate, or even merge together.

Merge together? I say this because one of the linking elements of our two kinds of knowledge is language. I do not have the occasion to develop the point in this paper, but one of the problems involved in any consideration of archaeological knowledge is the status of its language as a vehicle fit to express its meaning at both scientific and social levels of knowledge. To take an obvious example, if I say a certain archaeological culture comprises so many elements with a number of characteristics, this statement can be checked and understood by any archaeologist, regardless of time and place.

If, however, I say the same culture therefore represents society X, with the following economic, social, ideological, etc. characteristics, this statement is bound to be more contentious because of the diverse attitudes archaeologists necessarily have towards what defines and constitutes any society, past or present. Obviously, inherent in the use of language which has reference to the past is the danger of employing solecisms. Some archaeologists would seek to escape from this danger by trying to evolve a special archaeological language and a list of linguistically precise archaeological concepts to go with it. But precisely because one kind of archaeological knowledge is social knowledge, intimately linked to the criteria of human experience, etc., such efforts must be futile. Thus scientific archaeological knowledge may well be clear and relatively unambiguous (as Leff says, 'independent of its antecedents'), but because of its nature social archaeological knowledge is likely to be contentious, even — to anticipate an argument developed below — *unstable*.

By way of illustration I return briefly to Clark's essay of 1979. It is likely that most archaeologists would agree with his statement that '[Man's] artefacts have until quite recently displayed an ever greater increase in diversity as well as mere complexity' (1979: 3). But it is less likely that many would endorse his claim 'that danger threatens [that cultural diversity] not merely from the homogenizing pressures of natural science and mass production, but also and perhaps even more from an ideology that seeks to justify the destruction not merely of our heritage but of our very humanity in the name of economics and an ostensibly liberal philosophy' (1979: 1). Opinion among his colleagues might also be divided over some of his other remarks, e.g.: 'Archaeology shows very plainly that we have achieved our humanity only to the extent that we have constrained our animal natures by means of artificial conventions acquired in the course of history and incorporated in cultural traditions. The most palpable index of progression from mere animality is provided not merely by the increasing complexity but still more by the cultural diversity of the artefacts which constitute the archaeological record of human history down to quite modern times' (1979: 5). When, however, Clark turns to modern European history to press his case, he engages in a form of argument which, by the standards of any reasonable present-day criteria, reduces his thesis to a piece of unabashed special pleading: 'Anyone traveling through a territory as restricted as Europe as recently even as 1914 could have savoured a diversity not merely of material products but of social and political styles transcending that available today in the entire world. The texture of life was so immeasurably richer then, that to experience even an inkling of it today people have to resort as they do in their millions to monuments, museums, illustrated books, or the theater' (*ibid.*: 13). Although this strange epitaph for the world of the Hapsburg Empire invokes as part of its justification the thirst of modern Europeans for popular education and enlightenment (itself an admirable sentiment), it nonetheless assumes that only by the perpetuation of 'vertically structured societies'

(*ibid.*: 9) can civilization, as Clark perceives it, continue. He might perhaps have chosen a happier example than the Europe of marked class privilege, mass poverty and extreme nationalistic rivalries to exemplify that rich (and, of course, quintessentially human) 'texture of life', the apparent passing of which he so much deplores.

I am not really concerned here, however, with the validity of Clark's argument. My point is that his language (or, in the idiom of this essay, his use of social knowledge) is contemporary and, from one point of view, sectarian. In an argument which could be interpreted as rich in false antitheses, he makes a fundamental and, no doubt, to some of his readers, questionable distinction between the concepts of diversity and of homogeneity. All Clark's power of evocative language, especially by the use of such words as 'heritage', 'cultural tradition', 'humanity' and 'animality', is harnessed to present a picture of Man on the brink of disaster. It would be ridiculous to suggest that the author of *World Prehistory* is using archaeology as the buttress of such archaeologically derived special pleading as one finds, for example, in the work of Von Däniken. But he is here writing in order to justify his own vision of Armageddon. Of course, just as he can expect to be criticized for this, so, alongside Von Däniken, and, for that matter, the Flat-Earthers and the Mormons of Utah, he has every right to interpret archaeology in whatever way he chooses. This is the inescapable result of both living in the sort of contemporary world that Clark deplores, and accepting its consequence that archaeology is ideological. To put the point in another way, archaeology is a product of nineteenth-century Western thought. Its conceptual tools, particularly at the interpretative level, derive from a language evolved for other uses. Its employment of formal or scientific language to describe or analyse empirical information probably rests on a rough and ready plateau of agreement among archaeologists. Less empirical, more social or metaphorical language relating mainly to interpretation may not fare so easily — and might not ever do so, given the contentiousness of the source of our social knowledge, i.e. social theories and the variety of social forms these theories seek to understand.

Does this mean, therefore, that archaeology, in the last analysis, must operate only at the level of mere guesswork, or as one of my old New Zealand colleagues, a social anthropologist, used to say, as 'a fascinating intellectual exercise'? He had more than a point. Here, however, it is useful to recall some remarks by Mellor in his critique of Leach's use of the 'black box' doctrine to limit the extent of archaeological theorizing:

> No doubt the data will always be flimsy, the tests inconclusive the scope for imaginative alternative theories great. None of this reduces archaeological theorizing to the level of guesswork. The complexity of the subject and the relative paucity of data may well be part of what makes archaeology, like cosmology, endlessly fascinating *and likely to be endlessly unsettled* [my emphasis]. But it is a great mistake to suppose that what is endlessly

fascinating and unsettled therefore cannot be scientific. If that were so, there would be very few sciences.

(Mellor 1973: 498)

I agree with Mellor, particularly when he says that archaeology is likely to be endlessly unsettled. Compared, for example, to history or sociocultural anthropology, the data *are* flimsy, the tests *are* inconclusive, and the scope for imaginative alternative theories *is* great. The subject has a fascinating fragility and open-endedness which does lead one to treat it at times merely as an intriguing intellectual exercise, where opportunities for the play of subjective assumptions and prejudices are enormous (and are great fun too). The rest of this paper, therefore, is a commentary on this unsettled discipline, where I use aspects of Marxist theory to explore whether or not archaeology might usefully become more settled, more homogeneous in its core assumptions, or more united in its ideology. In this setting Marxism becomes a metaphor, or, if you like, a form of symbolic analogy, employed to underscore certain problems in the relationship between archaeology and any ideology to which archaeologists might subscribe.

It might be asked, 'Why Marxism?' My answer is not simply that archaeology has pragmatic and historical links with one or more versions of materialism, of which Marxism is probably the most vocal and best documented. It is also (and this may not be accidental) that I have found it — during more than 30 years — to be as endlessly fascinating and unsettled as archaeology itself. More specifically, there appear to be such obvious, almost trite, conjunctions between archaeology and that aspect of Marxism defined as historical materialism, at least at the level of social theory, to make this exploration of a particular ideology worthwhile. Each is concerned with the interpretation of the human past. Each seeks to define social forms and to explain their means of transformation over time, in order to understand how societies have become what they are today. Each has to employ particular conceptual and linguistic tools of the present in essentially historiographical contexts, and to be aware of attendant dangers of solecisms and related errors. On the face of things, historical materialism might be able to offer at least a reasonably stable starting point for materialist interpretations of archaeological information. This is especially so, given the well-known formulations set out by Marx in his *Preface To A Contribution to the Critique of Political Economy* (1859). The conjunction seems particularly clear if one can assume that much of the archaeologist's evidence corresponds to Marx's material base of society, and that the area for interpretation refers predominantly (though not, of course, wholly) to his ideological superstructure. Childe put the case with characteristic succinctness in *Piecing Together the Past*:

> [Marx] argued quite convincingly that means of production and relations of production are interdependent in the sense that technology can only function within an appropriate economy or system for distributing the product and that the relations of production in turn determine in the long run the ideological superstructure —

codes of morality and law, superstitions and religious beliefs, artistic expression and so on. Briefly this is equivalent to saying that what we have called material culture determines spiritual culture.   (Childe 1956: 53)

Childe makes the matter seem so straightforward and obvious that one wonders what has prevented ideology-questing archaeologists, newly converted to historical materialism, from signing up in their droves. But, indeed, the snags are considerable, and they are ideological. I hope that I need not labour the otiose point that to adopt a Marxist standpoint is in the eyes of some of one's colleagues to invite questions concerning one's wider political affiliations etc. Yet the contentious history of Marxism as a political philosophy does have great bearing on the present validity of Marx's famous *Preface*. Indeed, from one point of view, the history of historical materialism, at least in so far as it stems from Marx's formulations of 1859, has been remarkably unstable. Today one can question it on several grounds, of which two are particularly relevant to this discussion.

Firstly, as Giddens has recently pointed out, Marx expressed himself somewhat differently on these matters in the *Formen* (Forms which Precede Capitalist Production), which were part of the *Grundrisse*, the draft notes of *Capital*. The *Formen*, which dates to the same period as the *Preface*, is 'by common acknowledgement the most subtle and sophisticated discussion of pre-capitalist (one should really say "non-capitalist") social formations that Marx ever wrote' (Giddens 1981: 76). It is also, of course, a source for historical materialism of equal significance to the *Preface*. The most relevant element of Giddens's extensive argument concerns the relationship between the forces and the relations of production, i.e. the status of the 'base'. As Giddens (*ibid.*: 88) puts it:

> Production [Marx] says, is the first exigency of human life, the necessary basis upon which all other social institutions are built; hence we must infer that changes in the forces of production are the main medium of social transformation. But this argument, if taken at its face value, is clearly invalid. It certainly does not follow that, because material production is necessary to sustain human existence, the social organisation of production is more fundamental to explaining either the persistence of, or changes in, societies than any other institutional forms. Marx himself appears to recognise this explicitly at one point in the *Formen*, in the course of criticising Proudhon. The idea, Marx says, 'that human life has since time immemorial rested on production' is 'only a tautology' [Marx 1973: 489].

Giddens then develops the point that:

> There are major inconsistencies between Marx's evolutionary schemes [i.e. as set out in the *Preface*] and the views developed in the *Formen*. These views express quite a radical break with the forces/relations of production dialectic. Just as, Marx suggests, there is no 'economy' in non-capitalist societies — in the sense that this presupposes an institutional separation from other

sectors of society which only occurs in capitalism — so in these societies production is neither distinctly separate from communal organization nor is its expansion the focus of social change. '*The original conditions of production*,' Marx asserts vigorously, '*cannot themselves originally be products* — results of production' [Marx, *ibid*.] It is exactly this process, i.e. how production comes to be the motor of social transformation with the advent of capitalism, which we need to explain.

(Giddens 1981: 88—9)

Secondly, and one should note for a longer period, the whole suitability of the 'base—superstructure' model as commonly employed in historical materialism has been questioned. As long ago as 1957, for example, during the bitter debates over Stalinism within the British Left, E.P. Thompson argued that the model was simply inadequate: 'Production, distribution and consumption are not only digging, carrying and eating, but are also planning, organizing and enjoying. Imaginative and intellectual faculties are not confined to a 'superstructure' and erected upon a 'base' of things (including men-things); they are implicit to the creative act of labour which makes man man' (Thompson 1957: 131). In 1965 Thompson elaborated this point, maintaining that the base/superstructure model invites a process of reductionism, which 'is a lapse in historical logic by which political or cultural events are "explained" in terms of the class affiliations of the actors' (in Thompson 1978: 80). And he went on to note the fact depressingly familiar to archaeologists who listen to the criticisms of their discipline from anthropological colleagues: 'Anthropologists and sociologists have sufficiently demonstrated the inextricable interlacing of economic and non-economic relations in most societies, and the intersections of economic and cultural satisfactions' (*ibid*.). In addition, Thompson referred (1978: 82—3) to the Marxist argument pungently elaborated by Caudwell, for example in his essay on love in *Studies in a Dying Culture*, that the very category of economics developed at a certain stage in the growth of capitalism: 'In all the distinctive bourgeois relations, it is characteristic that tenderness is completely expelled, because tenderness can only exist between men. And in capitalism all relations appear to be between a man and a commodity' (Caudwell 1938: 50—1).

I have gone into these somewhat technical discussions on the utility of certain categories commonly employed in historical materialism for three reasons. Firstly, at a general level they are a useful reminder of the fragility of such category/metaphor thinking in a materialist context, for example, in the fields of cultural materialism, economic materialism and cultural ecology. At the risk of sounding banal, one can only plead caution concerning the utility of all categories, especially analytical ones, employed by archaeologists for whatever purpose. Categories are part of the sociology of knowledge, existing not above society but within it, and they take meaning as much from contemporary social attitudes as from their own history and existence. And, of course, it is precisely because of this fact that an uncritical use of categories can continue. Our own society is so obsessed with economics that it is almost bound to view itself through a base/superstructure metaphor and archaeologists tend to follow suit.

Secondly, one should ask in any case what remains of this now rather battered metaphor. It is fair to say that there exists today a more fluid way than formerly of perceiving its component categories, free of any absolute divide between them, with a recognition that they are only definable in terms of each other. Furthermore, in archaeological interpretation, it is unnecessary to accede to a strictly hierarchical sequence of categories, starting with technology and economics at the bottom, and proceeding via politics and social control to something vaguely called belief systems at the top. It may be readily accepted that base and superstructure interpenetrate both in historical reality and at various, and variable, levels in analysis — as countless ethnographic studies since Morgan have amply demonstrated. This attitude, however, is far from one of guesswork, agnosticism, or a determination to impose absolute bounds to the extent of archaeological knowledge in the name of 'the limitations of the evidence'. On the contrary, it is a recognition of the sociological limits of knowledge, and how these may be changed. As Childe once said with regard to scientific knowledge: 'Admittedly the science of any period is limited *by* the collective representation, the knowledge already accumulated and applied in practice by contemporary society. It is not limited *to* that. New data are observed; new productive forces are applied; and old categories are transformed' (Childe 1949a: 309).

Thirdly, it is unnecessary to leave the argument, as Childe himself does, at the level of scientific knowledge. If I might return for a moment to Leff's two kinds of knowledge, scientific and social; he maintains that, 'In contrast to the need to refine a scientific process we have in some measure to re-enact the original meaning in any work of human experience, whether it is a system of banking or a musical score' (Leff 1969: 212). Childe insisted, in opposition to Collingwood, that such a feat was impossible (Childe 1949b: 24; cf. Collingwood 1946: 215). But to so insist is surely to impede the recognition of 'new data' and so the transformation of 'old categories'.

While writing this essay I have had in mind a remark by Sheila Rowbotham: 'The pastime of fishing for a pure Marxism—Leninism with the last word on all subjects is still with us' (Rowbotham 1979: 63). Enough has been said, however, about the inadequacy of certain traditional concepts of historical materialism to question this apocalyptic tendency in Marxist thought, and to stress the dangers involved when it becomes bemused by its own, largely implicit, ideology. Archaeologists need not make the same mistake. They should surely relish, not bemoan, the ambiguities which society imposes on their subject.

Bibliography

Caudwell, C. 1938. *Studies in a Dying Culture.* London: John Lane, The Bodley Head.

Childe, V.G. 1949a. The sociology of knowledge. *Modern Quarterly* (n.s.) 4: 302–9.

1949b. *Social Worlds of Knowledge.* L.T. Hobhouse Memorial Trust Lecture No. 19. London: Oxford University Press.

1956. *Piecing Together the Past: The Interpretation of Archaeological Data.* London: Routledge and Kegan Paul.

Clark, G. 1947. *Archaeology and Society*, 2nd ed. London: Methuen.

1979. Archaeology and human diversity. *Annual Review of Anthropology* 8: 1–19.

Collingwood, R.G. 1946. *The Idea of History.* Oxford: Oxford University Press.

Giddens, A. 1981. *A Contemporary Critique of Historical Materialism*, Vol. 1. London and Basingstoke: Macmillan.

Leff, G. 1969. *History and Social Theory.* London: Merlin Press.

Marx, K. 1859. *A Contribution to the Critique of Political Economy.* Edited with an Introduction by Maurice Dobb. Moscow: Progress Publishers, 1970.

1973. *Grundrisse.* Harmondsworth: Penguin Books.

Mellor, D.H. 1973. On some methodological misconceptions. In C. Renfrew (ed.), *The Explanation of Culture Change: Models in Prehistory*, pp. 493–8. London: Duckworth.

Rowbotham, S. 1979. The women's movement and organising for socialism. In S. Rowbotham, L. Segal and H. Wainwright, *Beyond the Fragments: Feminism and the Making of Socialism*, pp. 21–155. London: Merlin Press.

Thompson, E.P. 1957. Socialist humanism: an epistle to the philistines. *The New Reasoner* 1: 105–43.

1978. *The Poverty of Theory and Other Essays.* London: Merlin Press.

Index